CASE STUDIES IN
SOCIAL WORK PRACTICE

CASE STUDIES IN SOCIAL WORK PRACTICE

Third Edition

Craig Winston LeCroy

WILEY

Cover Design: Wiley
Cover Illustration: © Lisa Stokes/Getty Images

This book is printed on acid-free paper.

Copyright © 2014 by John Wiley & Sons, Inc. All rights reserved.

Published by John Wiley & Sons, Inc., Hoboken, New Jersey.
Published simultaneously in Canada.

For general information about our other products and services, please contact our Customer Care Department within the United States at (800) 762-2974, outside the United States at (317) 572-3993 or fax (317) 572-4002.

Wiley publishes in a variety of print and electronic formats and by print-on-demand. Some material included with standard print versions of this book may not be included in e-books or in print-on-demand. If this book refers to media such as a CD or DVD that is not included in the version you purchased, you may download this material at http://booksupport.wiley.com. For more information about Wiley products, visit www.wiley.com.

Library of Congress Cataloging-in-Publication Data:

LeCroy, Craig W.
    Case studies in social work practice/Craig Winston LeCroy. — 3rd Edition.
        1 online resource.
    Includes bibliographical references and index.
    Description based on print version record and CIP data provided by publisher; resource not viewed.
    ISBN 978-1-118-41899-4 (ebk.) — ISBN 978-1-118-41622-8 (ebk.) —
ISBN 978-1-118-12834-3 (pbk.) 1. Social service—United States—Case studies. I. Title.
    HV91
    361.3'20973—dc23

                                                                  2013032295

Printed in the United States of America

SKY10033575_030222

To Kerry B. Milligan and the social workers of the world

Contents

Educational Policy and Accreditation Standards (EPAS) and Case Studies Crosswalk

The Council on Social Work Education's EPAS has set forth recommendations for students of social work to master 10 competencies. Within each competency are practice behaviors that further define the core competencies. *Case Studies in Social Work Practice* addresses the 10 competencies within the various case studies presented in the book. The following table lists the competencies and the case studies that reflect the competency most directly. This may be helpful to both instructor and student in relating the educational material in the book to the core competencies for effective social work practice.

Educational Policy 2.1.1: Identify as a professional social worker and conduct oneself accordingly.

Educational Policy 2.1.2: Apply social work ethical principles to guide professional practice.

Educational Policy 2.1.3: Apply critical thinking to inform and communicate professional judgments.

Educational Policy 2.1.4: Engage diversity and difference in practice.

Educational Policy 2.1.5: Advance human rights and social and economic justice.

Educational Policy 2.1.6: Engage in research-informed practice and practice-informed research.

Educational Policy 2.1.7: Apply knowledge of human behavior and the social environment.

Educational Policy 2.1.8: Engage in policy practice to advance social and economic well-being and to deliver effective social work services.

Educational Policy 2.1.9: Respond to contexts that shape practice.

Educational Policy 2.1.10: Engage, assess, intervene, and evaluate with individuals, families, groups, organizations, and communities.

	Professional Identity	Ethical Practice	Critical Thinking	Energy Diversity	Human Rights & Justice	Research-Informed Practice	Human Behavior	Policy Practice	Practice Context	Engage, Assess, Intervene, & Evaluate
1.1							✓			
1.2	✓						✓	✓		
1.3	✓				✓		✓	✓		✓
2.1	✓	✓			✓		✓	✓		✓
2.2						✓				
2.3									✓	
2.4							✓	✓	✓	✓
3.1		✓								✓
3.2							✓			
3.3	✓	✓								
3.4										
4.1	✓	✓	✓		✓			✓	✓	✓
4.2				✓	✓				✓	✓
4.3										
5.1		✓							✓	✓
5.2										✓
5.3	✓									✓
5.4									✓	
5.5						✓				

6.1

6.2

6.3

6.4

6.5

7.1

7.2

7.3

7.4

8.1

8.2

8.3

8.4

9.1

9.2

9.3

9.4

Case Study Topic Areas Matrix

Case Study	Treatment of Adults or Individuals	Advanced Treatment Methods	Advocacy	Brief Treatment and Managed Care	Case Management	Child Welfare	Children and Adolescents	Community Practice	Diversity	Ecological Model/ Generalist Practice
1.1			✓		✓					✓
1.2			✓		✓	✓				
1.3			✓					✓		✓
2.1	✓	✓	✓		✓			✓		✓
2.2	✓	✓		✓						
2.3		✓			✓					
2.4		✓	✓		✓					✓
3.1				✓	✓	✓	✓			
3.2		✓			✓					
3.3						✓	✓			
3.4				✓		✓	✓			
4.1		✓	✓	✓	✓	✓	✓			✓
4.2				✓		✓	✓	✓	✓	✓
4.3		✓		✓	✓		✓			
5.1	✓			✓	✓					
5.2		✓		✓						

Preface

This book provides a different format to learn about social work practice than is currently available in traditional social work textbooks. My intent is to provide students with an accordingly different educational experience, which results from reading and thinking about case studies.

Case studies are an action-oriented educational tool because they provide students with an opportunity to vicariously participate in the process of doing social work practice. It is critical to provide an interesting educational atmosphere for effective adult education.

In order to achieve this goal, I have asked many different people, primarily teachers and social workers, to write case studies that reflect their experiences. More than 45 people helped contribute to this book. The people chosen to write case studies reflect the diversity of social work practice. As a result, each case study is unique in approach, content, and writing style.

I have always told my students that doing social work is much more exciting and gratifying than reading about social work practice. Because the case study method of teaching allows students to participate in social work, there is a corresponding increase in interest and motivation for learning.

The objective of *Case Studies in Social Work Practice* is teaching students about the process of doing social work. The book is appropriate to many classes at the undergraduate and graduate levels. At the undergraduate level, it may be used to teach students about the range and diversity of the social work profession. In this context, the emphasis is on the various fields of practice, the organizational setting, and the variety of roles that social workers embrace. At the graduate level, it may be used as the primary text or as a supplement to a more theoretical textbook, with the emphasis on understanding the complex variables involved in delivering social work services.

Case Studies in Social Work Practice is also designed to be useful as a textbook for field seminars. Here the focus is to help students learn to discuss cases within a social work frame of reference. The instructor can use the case material and emphasize the practice principles relevant for the particular class and level of the student.

FOR STUDENTS

This book was designed to make learning about social work interesting and exciting. In it you will find fascinating experiences that social work practitioners have shared about their work. The focus is on what social workers actually *do* as professionals—a picture of their day-to-day lives. As you read these case studies, think about being confronted with each situation yourself. How would you feel? What do you notice? What would you do? By doing this, you can vicariously participate in social work practice. This will give you important clues about whether this is the profession for you and where your interests are in the various fields of practice.

The purpose of this book is to help you learn to integrate theory and practice by studying how practitioners have applied general social work principles to real-world case situations. In order to facilitate learning, each case study begins with a series of questions. These questions are designed to stimulate critical thinking and promote class discussion.

Classroom discussions about the case studies will investigate judgments made by the practitioners, answer questions you have about social work practice, and reveal the limitations of textbook generalizations. In many instances, information in the case studies may be incomplete, and students' opinions may be divided about the manner in which to intervene.

FOR INSTRUCTORS—HOW TO USE THIS BOOK

This book can be used in a variety of ways to teach students about social work practice. The book is designed to be used in a flexible manner, depending on your needs and the objectives of the particular course. Some suggestions for how this book might be used include:

- Having students think about what they might have done differently and why
- Having students write out treatment plans based on the information presented
- Using the case studies to discuss the range of roles and skills needed by social workers in a variety of settings
- Having students describe and analyze policies, organizational factors, and community implications inherent in the case studies
- Having students gather theoretical and empirical studies that could have been useful to the social worker in the different case situations

With this kind of book, it is important for you to decide how you can best use the case material. In my experience, I have found some of the following ways of using case studies helpful:

- *The case studies can be used to get students to think like social workers.* By reading the cases, students learn about the different environments that social workers must perform in, the decisions that social workers must make, and the importance of complex and competing factors in making those decisions. By vicariously participating in the practice of social work, students develop an understanding of how social work is performed, the social work environment, and human behavior in the social environment.

- *Use the case studies to help students develop a social work frame of reference.* Each chapter is an opportunity for students to explore the various aspects and roles of social work: advocacy, case management, community organization, clinical counseling, referral, resource development, mediation, evaluation, and so on. As a result of reading the case studies, students will develop skills in approaching various social work problems and an understanding of the function social workers perform.

- *In order to stimulate student thinking and class discussions, each case study is preceded with a series of questions.* The questions are designed to promote critical thinking and act as a catalyst for class discussion.

- *The case studies can be used for class discussion with many positive benefits.* With a group of students, many perspectives about the case will develop. Within this context, the instructor can examine with students their underlying theories and assumptions about human behavior and social work practice. The natural interaction and exchange of ideas and information will promote an atmosphere for critical discussion. Too often, students accept any approach to a case without critique and analysis. Group discussion of the cases can be a safe environment to teach students more critical problem-solving skills.

- *Teach students to examine the facts and opinions in a case.* Encourage students to take on the case situation and decide what they would do in some of the practice situations. Stimulate students to develop alternatives and choose the most effective course of action. Although each case contains its own particular approach to resolving a practice problem, each case also contains new problems to be addressed and new decision points that can be brought out in a class discussion.

- *You may also wish to use the case material to conduct role-plays with the students.* Students can be selected to act out the characters involved in the case study. As they take turns playing the social work practitioner, they will grapple with the real situations that social workers face in a variety of circumstances. You can provide students with feedback on skills and alternative courses of action. With experimentation you will find *Case Studies in Social Work Practice* to be an effective format for teaching social work practice.

- *The case studies will stimulate students to think critically, analytically, and objectively about social work practice.* Clear thinking skills are a necessity in social work, and the cases should be used to promote such skills. As students move from one case to the next, they will begin to develop an accumulation of experience in thinking and reasoning as applied to the very different problem configurations presented.

THE THIRD EDITION

It is very exciting to have a third edition of the *Case Studies in Social Work Practice* book! The overall organization of the text remains consistent with the first edition. The major changes include updating the case material and adding new cases. In particular, new material has been added that reflects newer changes in the field. For example, case studies have been added in areas such as mindfulness treatment, family systems approach, family drug courts, the use of supervision, multisensory interventions, geriatric depression, and the use of evidence-based practice. These changes, in addition to changes from the second edition, should have a broader appeal to social work students: undergraduates, foundation MSW students, and advanced MSW students. The book still maintains case material that represents both generalist practice and more specialized practice, both of which are needed in social work education. The goal of *Case Studies in Social Work Practice* continues to be the provision of case study material that is interesting and enlightening about the day-to-day practice of social work—material that is too often ignored in social work textbooks.

Acknowledgments

This book is the result of the many authors who agreed to graciously contribute a case study. Without them there would be no book, and I sincerely appreciate their efforts. Many people helped to make this a successful project. Emily Furrier and Molly Madeline Gebler were my research assistants, and they provided critical support in organizing and managing this project. Arizona State University, School of Social Work, provided the needed institutional support. The staff and editors at Wiley are to be thanked for their persistence in helping me get this material into the format of a publishable book. My longtime association with Peggy Alexander provided the impetus for this project, Rachel Livsey worked with me as the acquisition editor for this book, and Amanda Orenstein made sure the project was brought to completion. Lisa Gebo, now deceased, was responsible for making the second edition become a reality. Her vision and confidence in the case study approach to teaching social work is greatly appreciated.

Acknowledgments

About the Editor

CRAIG WINSTON LECROY is a professor in the School of Social Work at Arizona State University. He also holds appointments at the University of Arizona in the John & Doris Norton School of Family and Consumer Sciences, Family Studies and Human Development division, and the University of Arizona College of Medicine, Department of Pediatrics. He has been a visiting professor at the University of Canterbury, New Zealand; the Zellerbach Visiting Professor at the University of California at Berkeley; and a senior Fulbright specialist.

Professor LeCroy has published 10 books previously, including *Parenting Mentally Ill Children: Faith, Hope, Support, and Surviving the System*; *First Person Accounts of Mental Illness and Recovery*; *Handbook of Evidence-Based Treatment Manuals for Children and Adolescents*; *Handbook of Prevention and Intervention Program for Adolescent Girls*; *The Call to Social Work: Life Stories*, *Case Studies in Child, Adolescent, and Family Treatment*; *Case Studies in Social Work Practice*; *Empowering Adolescent Girls: Examining the Present and Building Skills for the Future with the "Go Grrrls" Program*; *Go Grrrls Workbook*; *Human Behavior and the Social Environment*; and *Social Skills Training for Children and Adolescents*.

Professor LeCroy has published more than 100 articles and book chapters on a wide range of topics, including mental health, the social work profession, home visitation, and research methodology. He is the recipient of numerous grants, including (as principal investigator or co-principal investigator) interventions for risk reduction and avoidance in youth (NIH), Go Grrrls Teen Pregnancy Prevention Program, evaluation of Healthy Families (a child abuse prevention program), a mental health training grant for improving service delivery to severely emotionally disturbed children and adolescents (NIMH), and Youth Plus: Positive Socialization for Youth (CSAP).

Contributors

Danie Beaulieu, PhD
Author of *Impact Techniques
for Psychotherapists* (Routledge)
and *Eye Movement Integration
Therapy (EMI)* (Crown House
Publishing)

Jennifer L. Bellamy, PhD
Assistant Professor
School of Social Service Administration
University of Chicago
Chicago, IL

Larry Bennett, PhD, LCSW
Professor
Jane Addams College of Social Work
University of Illinois at Chicago
Chicago, IL

Kia J. Bentley, PhD
Professor
School of Social Work
Virginia Commonwealth University
Richmond, VA

Betty Blythe, PhD
Professor
Graduate School of Social Work
Boston College
Chestnut Hill, MA

Charlotte Booth, MSW
Executive Director
Institute for Family Development Federal Way, WA

Yesenia Campos
Recovery Support Specialist
Pima County Family Drug Court
Tucson, AZ

Jeannine K. Chapelle, MAA
Associate Director of Community Initiatives
La Frontera Arizona, Inc.
Tucson, AZ

Kevin Corcoran, PhD
Professor
School of Social Work
Portland State University
Portland, OR

Martha Morrison Dore, PhD
Director of Research and Evaluation
Division of Child and Family Services
The Guidance Center/Riverside Community Care
and
Research Associate
Cambridge Health Alliance
Department of Psychiatry
Harvard University School of Medicine
Cambridge, MA

David R. Eddy, PhD
Clinical Director
Family Therapy Associates
Rockville, MD

Eric Garland, PhD, LCSW
Assistant Professor, College of Social Work
Assistant Director, Trinity Institute for the Addictions
Florida State University
Tallahassee, FL

Brent B. Geary, PhD
Director of Training
The Milton H. Erickson Foundation
Private Practice
Phoenix, AZ

Alex Gitterman, EdD, MSW
Zachs Professor of Social Work
Director of Doctoral Program
School of Social Work
University of Connecticut
Storrs, CT

Nancy Gladow, MA
Social Worker
Public Health
Seattle & King County
Seattle, WA

Kristen A. Gustavson, LCSW, PhD
Assistant Professor
School of Social Work
College of Public Programs, Arizona State University
Phoenix, AZ

Jan Jess, MSW
University of Kansas
School of Social Welfare
Lawrence, KS

Amber Kelly, LCSW
Private Practice
Gainesville, FL

Steven Krugman, PhD
Psychotherapy, Consultation,
and Coaching
Boston and Newton, MA

Jay Lappin, MSW, LCSW
Family Therapy Director
Centra PC
Marlton, NJ

Craig W. LeCroy, PhD, LCSW
Professor
School of Social Work
Arizona State University
Tucson, AZ

Cynthia A. Lietz, PhD, LCSW
Associate Professor
School of Social Work
Arizona State University
Tucson, AZ

Kathie Lortie, MSW
School Social Worker
Tucson Unified School District
Tucson, AZ

Randy H. Magen, PhD
Associate Dean, College of Health
Professor, School of Social Work
University of Alaska
Anchorage, AK

Deana F. Morrow, PhD, LPC, LCSW, LISW-CP, ACSW
Department Chair and Professor
Department of Social Work
Winthrop University
Rock Hill, SC

Paula S. Nurius, PhD
Grace Beals-Ferguson Scholar and Professor
Director, Prevention Research Training Program
School of Social Work
University of Washington
Seattle, WA

Carl Oekerman, MS
Instructor, Psychology/Communications
Bellingham Technical College
Bellingham, WA

Myrtle Parnell, MSW
Warwick, NY

Susan K. Parnell, LCSW
Court Mediator
Pima County Juvenile Court Center
Tucson, AZ

Shirley L. Patterson, PhD
Emeritus Professor
School of Social Work
Arizona State University
Tempe, AZ

Peter J. Pecora, PhD
Managing Director of Research Services,
Casey Family Programs
Professor, School of Social Work
University of Washington
Seattle, WA

Catherine Sammons, LCSW, PhD
Private Practice
Los Angeles, CA

Lawrence Shulman, MSW, EdD
Emeritus Professor and Dean
School of Social Work
University at Buffalo
Buffalo, NY

Christine Swenson-Smith, MSW
Division Director
Pima County Juvenile Court
Tucson, AZ

Frances E. Tack, MS, LPC, LCAS, CCS
Program Chair
Substance Abuse Program
Central Piedmont Community College
Charlotte, NC

Barbra Teater, PhD
Senior Lecturer in Social Work
University of Bristol, UK

Bruce A. Thyer, PhD, LCSW
Professor of Social Work
Florida State University
Tallahassee, FL

Richard M. Tolman, PhD
Professor
School of Social Work
University of Michigan
Ann Arbor, MI

Jo Vanderkloot, LCSW
Private Practice
Warwick, NY

Joseph Walsh, PhD, LCSW
Professor of Social Work
School of Social Work
Virginia Commonwealth University
Richmond, VA

PART I

Case Studies in Generalist Practice

The idea of generalist practice is an old one. The origins of the generalist concept are as deep as the social work profession itself. Social work pioneers such as Mary Richmond and Jane Addams have stressed the importance of understanding people in relation to their environment. The social workers' long-standing commitment of a dual focus on the individual and on the society supports the fundamental notions of generalist practice.

Although the notions of generalist practice are old, the emphasis of a generalist perspective in social work reemerged as social work programs began to offer Baccalaureate of Social Work (BSW) degrees. The BSW programs, as stipulated by the Council on Social Work Education, required education from a generalist perspective. Currently, most BSW programs focus their curricula on generalist practice, and MSW programs use the first year, or foundation year, for education on the generalist approach to practice. As Landon (1995, p. 1102) concludes, "in the quest for a theory for this broad practice base, social work education adopted notions from general and social systems theories and ecological thinking to undergird the foundation for all practice."

Generalist practice has reemerged as central to social work education. But what exactly is generalist practice? How is it defined? Not surprisingly, there is no one definition of generalist practice. However, important themes emerge in the various definitions.

Several generalist social work practice books describe generalist practice as beginning with a decision as to what the unit of attention should be—an individual, a family, a small group, an agency or organization, or a community (Johnson & Yanca, 2009; Krist-Ashman & Hull, 2008). The generalist model promotes a multimethod and multilevel approach, an eclectic theory base, and the dual perspective of social work. Schatz, Jenkins, and Sheafor (1990) generated a three-level model of generalist practice:

1. The generic or foundation level of knowledge necessary for all social workers, regardless of later specialization, includes the purposes, values, focus, and knowledge base of the profession.
2. The initial generalist level includes competency in direct and indirect practice based on multilevel assessment and the capacity to intervene on multiple levels, perform various practice roles, and evaluate practice ability.
3. Generalist practice at the advanced level delineates knowledge needed for practice in greater depth and in relation to more complex and technical issues.

Lastly, any discussion of the generalist perspective would be remiss to omit a discussion of the ecological perspective. The underlying theory of social work is rooted in social systems theory, particularly ecological-systems theory. Gitterman and Germain (2008, p. 20) describe the theoretical underpinnings of an ecological perspective, or what they refer to as the life model:

Ecology is a science concerned with the relations between living organisms—in this case, human beings and all the elements of their environments. It is concerned with how organisms and environments achieve a goodness-of-fit or adaptive balance and equally important, how and why they sometimes fail to do so.

Ecological-systems theory provides an understanding of the person-in-environment perspective, stressing how critical interactions occur between individuals and their environments. This model directs social work practice at the interface of these systems and helps social work practice maintain a dual emphasis. Social workers assess an individual in relation to the opportunities and obstacles that exist in one's environment.

In this chapter you will read three case studies that explicitly address a generalist perspective in social work practice. The first case study by Patterson, Jess, and LeCroy describes an ecological perspective and shows why it is considered the cornerstone of good generalist practice. It takes the fundamental concepts from ecological theory and illustrates how they can be used in direct social work practice. The case study demonstrates how the notions of ecological theory are tantamount to generalist social work practice.

The case study by Lortie presents a complex situation for a social worker in a hospital setting. It elucidates how generalist practice with a person-in-environment perspective must consider the resources available to a person. It is an excellent example of how critical good case management can be and shows that case management services represent social work at the interface of the person and the environment. A lot of social work practice revolves around helping individuals cope with a difficult environment.

In addition to helping them cope on an individual basis, we must help bring services to bear on their problems.

The last case by Chapelle extends the generalist model to community-based work. Too often, social work is focused narrowly on the individual. As this case demonstrates, good social work practice can take place at the community level. Using basic concepts of community practice, this case shows how a social worker can approach large-scale change in a community.

Together these cases represent a sample of how direct-line practitioners view generalist practice. It should give you a good, practical feeling for what it means to do generalist practice. Also, it should alert you to the difficulties and complexities of doing good social work. When our attention is focused on personal problems and social concerns, multilevel methods, and ecological understandings, we are faced with drawing on a broad range of skills and abilities. Social work practice offers a challenge for those who want to tackle social problems but need a large toolkit.

REFERENCES

Gitterman, A., & Germain, C. B. (2008). *The life model of social work practice: Advances in theory and practice* (3rd ed.). New York, NY: Columbia University Press.

Johnson, L. C., & Yanca, S. J. (2009). *Social work practice: A generalist approach* (10th ed.). New York, NY: Pearson.

Krist-Ashman, K. K., & Hull, G. H. (2008). *Understanding generalist practice.* Pacific Grove, CA: Brooks Cole.

Landon, P. S. (1995). Generalist and advanced generalist practice. In R. L. Edwards (Ed.), *Encyclopedia of social work* (19th ed., pp. 1101–1108). Washington, DC: National Association of Social Workers.

Schatz, M., Jenkins, L., & Sheafor, B. (1990). Milford redefined: A model of initial and advanced generalist social work. *Journal of Social Work Education, 26,* 217–231.

Case Study 1-1

Using the Ecological Model in Generalist Practice: Life Transitions in Late Adulthood

SHIRLEY PATTERSON, JAN JESS, AND CRAIG WINSTON LeCROY

This case uses the ecological perspective as a guide to generalist practice. This perspective offers a framework for how the social worker organizes her work and helps the client cope with a serious life transition.

Questions
1. Why is the ecological perspective considered a good framework for generalist practice?
2. What were the essential skills and abilities the social worker used in this approach?
3. How were ecological concepts used to help the social worker?
4. How was the concept of person and environmental fit used in this case?

I met Mrs. Lilly Goodman at the medical center in Kansas City on the long-term care unit where I work. She is a 77-year-old woman who is thin, small in stature, with straggly gray hair, who peers at you above her glasses, which keep slipping down her nose. When I met her for the first time, I was struck by her sad demeanor. However, as I got to know her, I came to love her wry sense of humor that is often masked to those who do not know her well.

Mrs. Lilly Goodman has been a hard-working laborer all of her life. She grew up in poverty—living in apartments and moving frequently as her father sought new work opportunities. She was not encouraged to go to school and, in fact, quit school after completing a fifth-grade education. Despite this, she is a well-spoken woman who is articulate, well-read, and has seized new learning opportunities all of her life.

Mrs. Lilly Goodman began work as a "cleaning lady" at 12 years old and has been doing it ever since, until she became too frail to continue. She recounts the very day she could not work anymore: "It was about half past noon when I bent over to put fresh sheets on the bed. As I tried to straighten up, my back experienced sharp shooting pains and I knew that I could not work any longer." As she tells me about her life, I can sense the confident, proud woman that she is. As she talks, you quickly get to know that one of her greatest achievements and joys is her home. She bought and paid for her own home, and she is very proud of having accomplished this goal. Also, her home is a central source of comfort: "I have lived in my home now for 30 years. I have one of the neighborhood's best gardens. My neighbors stop by to see me on a regular basis."

I try to think back to what life must have been like for her prior to landing in the hospital. I can see her getting up early in the morning to tend to her flowers, sitting and reading in an old overstuffed chair, and having a few old friends over for afternoon tea. Everything is different now. Her independence has come to an end, and she has not had much time to prepare for it. After suffering two strokes, one right after the other, and developing crippling and painful arthritis, I know that her life must have changed dramatically.

She, however, has not accepted these changes. Mrs. Goodman has consistently told the hospital staff that she plans to return home to live as soon as she gets out of the hospital. Because staff were unsure about the possibility of her returning to home, I was brought in as the long-term care social worker. Mrs. Lilly Goodman did not directly ask for help, but she willingly accepted my offer for help, proffered help—I was reaching out to her.

An ecological perspective was used in thinking about and guiding my approach to practice (Gitterman, 2009; Gitterman & Germain, 2008). From an ecological perspective, Mrs. Lilly Goodman is best understood as someone who is in a *life transition*. She is at a place in her life where she is facing a major transition—from an independent person who took care of herself to a person who is dependent and needs some assistance. There are three aspects of her life transition that help in thinking about how to offer her help:

Her developmental stage

Her change in status and roles

The crises she faces

Mrs. Lilly Goodman is in the final stages of growth. The *developmental stage* that confronts her has a biological base, and the associated tasks of this stage of development arise out of biological pressures and the social and physical environment. In other words, her residency in long-term care is not of her own choosing; rather, it is a result of illness, limited resources, and lack of family support.

Mrs. Lilly Goodman is also being thrust into some very new *statuses*, none of which she is particularly happy about. These include being:

A resident of a nursing home

A displaced homeowner

A dependent person

An older adult with fairly limiting health problems, which are difficult for her to accept

In addition to new statuses, Mrs. Lilly Goodman has new *roles* that she must adapt to, including being:

A lucid, ambulatory resident among many residents who are neither

A protected mother (and mother-in-law) in a sheltered environment

A welfare recipient, who receives Medicaid to supplement her social security that pays for her care in the long-term care unit

These roles are a striking contrast to the Mrs. Lilly Goodman of only a few months ago—someone who lived independently, tended her garden, cared for her home, and shared tea in the afternoon with friends.

As the team of workers at the hospital staffed this case, they recognized that Mrs. Lilly Goodman faces several *life stressors*. They are considered critical life stressors because they are situations that exceed the personal and environmental resources she has for managing them. The critical life stressors she faces include:

Loss of health

Denial of the limitations her strokes have caused

The threat of losing her home

Her daughter's poor health, which prevents her from providing her mother with support

Client strengths are an important part of the ecological model (Gitterman & Germain, 2008). As I thought about Mrs. Lilly Goodman, I needed to be aware that there is an innate strength in her—toward health, continued growth, and the development of new potentials. Although many of the people on the team exclusively discussed her limitations and what she could *not* do, I was always quick to point out her strengths—what she *could* do. As a social worker focused on helping Mrs. Lilly Goodman obtain self-determination, I empathized with her desire for discharge in order to live in her own house. Out of respect for her, I wanted to honor her wishes. Also, I knew that health could not be easily separated from obtaining satisfaction and meaning in life.

USING THE ECOLOGICAL MODEL TO GUIDE
PRACTICE: A TEAM APPROACH

As the team members began to get to know Mrs. Lilly Goodman, they could see a determined woman who really did deserve an opportunity to try to return home. The team agreed that this was a reasonable goal that everyone could help her achieve. We set about a specific set of actions to make this happen.

Being in the long-term care unit had taken an emotional toll on Mrs. Goodman. Over time she had become increasingly despondent. The first goal was to rejuvenate her passion to seek a more meaningful life. To do this, we agreed to provide her with *our* support to supplement the limited support she received from her daughter in her wish to return home. We spent time talking with Mrs. Goodman about her home—getting her to tell us what it was like and to describe what her priorities would be when she returned. One team member who is an amateur artist sat down with Mrs. Goodman and drew a picture of her house—the outside and inside. You could observe an instant impact from this intervention. This helped shift her focus away from being a "patient" and helped her focus on what she wanted to achieve.

The team knew that to release Mrs. Lilly Goodman back to her home, they would have to be confident that she could function independently. This called for an assessment of the feasibility of discharge. To conduct this assessment, different team members took on separate tasks.

The occupational therapist conducted a cooking evaluation with Mrs. Goodman. This was done in the hospital occupational therapy kitchen. The assessment did not focus on her skills of cooking but on her stamina in cooking for herself. Mrs. Goodman rather enjoyed this challenge. Trying these tasks gave her an opportunity to show others what she could do. Each team member was instructed to help emphasize the positive competencies that she was able to demonstrate. Indeed, Mrs. Goodman did have the necessary stamina for cooking.

The nurse set out to help Mrs. Goodman plan daily activities while she was still on the long-term care unit. This was done to help her develop the stamina to live alone and care for herself. Mrs. Goodman was encouraged to take on increasing amounts of daily living activities. Also, to improve her physical stamina, the nurse worked with her to increase the amount of walking she could do.

As the social worker on the unit, I helped Mrs. Goodman assess what resources and support she would need when she returned home. I talked with her about the kinds of resources other older persons I had helped found useful, such as homemakers, visiting nurses, meals-on-wheels, transportation, telephone reassurance, neighborly support, and the kinds of supplemental income she might be eligible for when she returns home. I also helped Mrs. Goodman realize that she was facing new changes in her life and that she had a lot of adaptations to make. I wanted her to become more accepting of her new challenges. I tried to help her see that she could face these new challenges with new solutions. Although adaptations had to be made, some resources could help make those adaptations easier.

Our work culminated when we decided to take Mrs. Lilly Goodman to her home for a visit. This allowed the team to make further assessments to bolster our confidence that she would be able to go home. In particular, we wanted to assess her *physical environment*. How easy was it for her to manage her home environment? Was her cooking stove easy to operate? Would she be able to run a bath for herself? How would she get the laundry done? We also examined the outside environment. How easy would it be for her to take the trash out? What kind of neighbors did she have? Would they be able and interested in helping her occasionally? We wanted to know what kind of support was available to her in her *social environment*. As we assessed the daily skills needed to operate a home, we could see how difficult it was for someone like her—with two strokes and painful arthritis.

Lastly, the team brought Mrs. Goodman and her daughter together for discussion of the home assessment and to provide specific information about finances, the daughter and son-in-law's support, and how the daughter felt about her mother's wish to go home. The team wanted to assess the quality of Mrs. Goodman's *interpersonal interactions*.

These assessments were focused on *action*, which takes place in physical, social, and interpersonal environments. The team approach operationalized the notion of treating Mrs. Lilly Goodman *as a whole person*. We were attempting to deal with all aspects of her life in order to facilitate a smooth life transition. From an ecological perspective, when habitats are rich in resources required for growth and development, then human beings thrive. However, when habitats are deficient in vital resources, then physical, social, and emotional functioning are adversely affected.

The primary function of the social worker in addressing life transitions is to help people move through stressful life transitions—to help them adapt and cope. The social worker acts simultaneously as an enabler, facilitator, and teacher. Our work with Mrs. Lilly Goodman certainly sought to enable her by embracing her desire to return home as an important way to help her cope with her life transitions. We helped her develop a plan to return home and helped her assess that plan realistically. We sought to empower her as an individual.

Overall, the team acted as facilitators by serving several different functions. The team supported Mrs. Lilly Goodman's competence through building her skills. We set realistic and measurable goals. For example, we made a contract with her to take more walks in the long-term care unit and assume responsibility for her medication. This aided her stamina and gave her renewed confidence in her own abilities.

We mobilized environmental supports by encouraging Mrs. Lilly Goodman's participation in an organized group in the hospital that was discussing discharge planning. We helped shift her focus from "patient" to consumer. In so doing, we helped her recognize that resources are available to her and that they can be used to help her meet her goals. She became more active and involved in working with us.

We also actively sought to help her develop a sense of self-direction. We knew that to empower her, she would have to take some degree of control over her life and accept increasing responsibility for her decisions and actions. Making age- and health-appropriate decisions and taking purposeful action was key to helping her fulfill her wish to return home. Team members facilitated this by setting up problems that she had to solve. For example, when it was decided that we should visit her home, she had to make the arrangements with her daughter to secure the house key. Although these actions were small, together they combined to create a new sense of self-direction.

Teaching was an important function in helping Mrs. Lilly Goodman. I took a major role in teaching her several critical skills. For example, I provided pertinent information about how she could manage following discharge from the hospital. This included not only talking about community resources but also teaching her exactly how to use these resources: where to find them, how to contact them, what to say to them, and how to follow up on contacts made. I knew from past experience that too often social workers only talk about resources rather than *teach* clients how to use resources.

Although ultimately Mrs. Goodman decided that she did want to return home, I provided a great deal of education concerning other alternatives that would be available to her. I helped her learn about the range of available options, such as assisted living, boarding homes, and the like. Although none of these alternatives were what she wanted, it helped her see that when you are facing difficult life decisions, resources are available to help you find the best fit for your circumstances.

My teaching also included helping her restructure her perceptions about certain issues. In particular, her reliance on her daughter's moral support and her own continued insistence that she could still care for herself as she had always done in the past. Lastly, the team members taught her the importance of systematic problem solving, which takes into consideration the individual abilities of the person and the resources available to the person. The problem-solving process was highlighted when we asked Mrs. Goodman and her daughter to meet with us to discuss what needed to be considered for a feasible and safe discharge.

CONCLUSIONS

This case study described the elements of the ecological perspective in recognizing and dealing with an older adult's life transition. The approach included understanding the developmental stage, the changes in status and roles, and the life stressors present in Mrs. Goodman's final stage of growth and development. The social worker—in conjunction with a team of professionals—worked to enable, teach, and facilitate discharge planning for the client. Of course, the unanswered question is: Did Mrs. Lilly Goodman go home?

She did not. After all the planning and work, *she* decided that the obstacles were too many and the support insufficient. In effect, there was not a good enough fit between her individual abilities and the resources and support in the environment. In the end, it was her decision, which made her subsequent adaptation much easier. Mrs. Lilly Goodman benefitted tremendously from the work the team had done. She made progress toward adaptation and learning to cope with her nursing home "home." She still is not completely satisfied, but now when she talks about going home, she adds, "I'd like to, but I'm not sure I can. I'm not the same person I used to be."

Further adaptation occurred for Mrs. Goodman a year later when she assumed a resident leadership role by assisting the long-term care professional team in designing an outdoor space for the residents to enjoy, spring through fall. Materials and labor for this project were donated by a local construction company, a concrete company, and a landscape nursery. The outdoor living space consisted of lovely tree and shrub plants, picnic tables and benches, comfortable seating areas, and a raised garden bed that accommodated wheelchairs. The latter, of course, was Mrs. Goodman's idea. As I look from my office window, I often see her tending her own flowers and helping other residents tend theirs.

REFERENCES

Gitterman, A. (2009). The life model. In A. Roberts (Ed.), *The social workers' desk reference* (2nd ed., pp. 231–234). New York, NY: Oxford University Press.

Gitterman, A., & Germain, C. B. (2008). *The life model of social work practice: Advances in theory and practice* (3rd ed.). New York, NY: Columbia University Press.

Case Study 1-2

Finding Resources: Case Management With Childhood Chronic Illness

KATHY L. LORTIE

Finding resources for families is one of the most important functions for social workers. This case study describes the social worker's effort to find resources for a family with a very sick child.

Questions

1. What were the social worker's goals in this case?
2. What resources were identified for this family?
3. How could the family have been helped to better use the resources that were available?
4. Why were resources critical to the success of this case?

Today, Jeffrey asked me to have lunch with him. It's been so long since a guy asked me to lunch that I was startled for a moment, but then I accepted, especially since I was kind of down and Jeffrey is a bright 12-year-old with cystic fibrosis who has spent the past week in the hospital where I am a pediatric social worker. Every day he has been stopping by my office to borrow the Game Boy or ask for candy, and today he said, "So, do you eat lunch?"

"Yes, I do."
"Do you like to eat here in the hospital cafeteria?"

"Usually that's all I have time for."

"I have a cafeteria pass. I've been eating in the cafeteria."

"I saw you there yesterday with your grandmother."

"When are you going to eat lunch today?"

"When I finish these phone calls."

"Would you like to eat with me, in the cafeteria?"

How could I say no? So we went to lunch, and he forgot to bring his medicines that he has to take before every meal to help with his digestion. I had to call his nurse, who said she would give the medicines to me if I came back to the floor for them. So I climbed the stairs, got the medicines, and rushed back to the cafeteria, collected Jeffrey from a table he had chosen that had no seats left for me, and we sat down to lunch.

During our conversation, he asked, "So what do you do?" And I tried to explain to a 12-year-old my job of hospital social worker, which coincidentally had earlier that week involved having a letter sent to his school asking that he be encouraged to remember to take his medicines every day before lunch. I briefly explained how, in addition to working with upset families, dealing with crisis situations, and contracting with children to take their medicines, I help people get things they need, solve problems, and find resources. And Jeffrey looked at me seriously and said, "That's easy. You have an easy job. You just help people get stuff."

I didn't mention the long hours of overtime for which I do not get paid, or the doctors who ask me to do the impossible for their patients and then fail to call me back when I page them, or seeing the sad eyes of parents whose babies die. And I didn't mention how the long hours are worth it when the doctors tell me I'm awesome, or when a child who was near death in our pediatric intensive care unit walks back into the hospital for a visit and gives me a hug. So just for you, Jeffrey—though you may not understand it all—because you asked and because the job sounds so easy, here's a story about what I do to help people "get stuff."

Late in the work day, I usually check with the inpatient units to see if there are any last-minute problems before I leave for the day. On this particular day about eight months ago, I went to the infant and toddler unit about 4:30 p.m. One of the pediatric doctors approached me and said, "Sometimes you seem to be able to work miracles with patients, and we have a family coming in that sure could use one. They are, to put it mildly, a social disaster. The patient is a 7-month-old baby boy who needs a liver transplant. The family has just moved to town to place the baby on the transplant list and wait for a liver. We think Child Protective Services (CPS) is involved with the family for noncompliance with medical care. The baby is very sick, the father is unsupportive, and the mother is not with it. If they can't get their act together, the baby will have to be taken away from them in order to qualify for the transplant. We were hoping you could help us out."

The next morning, I met the family. One of my colleagues, the social worker for the liver transplant team, had completed a psychosocial assessment, and she gave me a copy. Her job was to assess the family and recommend whether they met the criteria to be placed on the transplant list. In this case, the family was intact and consisted of the parents, Joe and Rosa, and their four children. In addition to the baby, Nathan, they had three girls aged 5, 7, and 9. Joe worked construction and Rosa took care of the children. Joe's family lived in a city about two hours away. Joe and Rosa had recently left that city to be closer to the hospital for the liver transplant. They had a small two-bedroom apartment and one old car. One of baby Nathan's problems was "failure to thrive," meaning that his height and weight were below the fifth percentile for his age. The transplant team's assessment was that Nathan needed to improve his nutritional status and gain weight before he would be eligible for the transplant. I decided my job was to do what I could to help the family meet those criteria.

I spent a lot of time that morning talking to Rosa about her problems in caring for Nathan. She explained, "This is so hard. I have to do it all myself. Joe doesn't help. Nathan cries all day to be held. I have three other children to take care of. I have to cook, clean, wash clothes, shop, and carry Nathan around all day. Joe comes home at night and wants to know what I did all day. Why is the apartment so dirty? Why isn't dinner ready? Joe's family lives 2 hours away, but no one will come and help. They didn't even help when we lived there. Everyone thinks I should be able to do this on my own. But I am just so tired."

Then I talked to Joe, who said, "I have to work in order to make money to provide a home and food for my family. If I don't work, I don't get paid. Then where do we live, what do we eat? I work hard all day, sometimes 10 to 12 hours. I come home, the apartment is dirty, there's nothing to eat, the baby is crying. My wife should be able to take care of the home while I work. I'm so tired when I get home."

After talking to them, I realized this was a story I hear all the time from families of chronically ill children. Caring for a child with complicated medical needs takes so much time and energy that there can be little left for the basic necessities of life. Caring for a sick child places added stress on a family, especially when that family is already stressed from inadequate resources, poor finances, and isolation. The problem is even worse for a single parent. How does a single parent work and meet the health needs of the child? How does a single parent find a childcare worker who can administer medication, perform treatments, recognize emergency situations, and not cost more than the parent earns at work?

In talking with parents of chronically ill children, I have often brought up the subject of counseling. Rosa gave the common response to this suggestion: "I've had counseling. The counselor says, 'Tell me all your problems.' So I do. Then the counselor says, 'Now don't you feel better?' Well, I don't. I don't need to talk about my problems, I need to do something about them. I don't need someone to talk to, I need someone to hold this baby so I can cook dinner." Rosa's experience with her chronically ill child is similar to that of parents with other disabled children (King & Meyer, 2006). Moersch (1978) observes:

> Parents need the understanding of professionals, but they also need concrete services to help them in managing and living with the . . . child. Some parents . . . have reported that they always had plenty of people to talk with them about their feelings . . . but it was very hard to find someone who could tell them what to do with feeding, toileting, or behavior problems.

It is even harder to find someone to help do those things with the child.

A social worker is in a unique position to help the family find whatever resources are available to help the family cope. In working with chronically ill children and their families, the use of social work does not change the course of the disease, but it does help families address the cumulative impact of the challenges they face. A central role for the social worker is in linking services to the needs of the child and family—with a focus on not just the child but the entire family facing the crisis.

My first task was to assess the family's current resources. They had a place to live, the baby had the state's healthcare insurance, the father had a job, and the baby was receiving Supplemental Security Income ($484 per month), which is available to families caring for a chronically ill, disabled child. In their hometown, the state's health insurance plan had assigned a case manager to the family to help with resources. After meeting this overwhelmed family, however, that case manager had called Child Protective Services (CPS). The CPS worker concluded that the family was doing the best they could under the circumstances. CPS offered the mother a parent aide, but then the family moved to our city and CPS closed the case. The family was very angry at the insurance case worker. I usually try not to get CPS involved when a family is apparently doing their best with what they have. In these situations, I involve CPS only as a last resort when all else has failed. Calling CPS, as this case illustrates, risks alienating the family from the healthcare team. Joe asked for a new case worker from the insurance company.

After investigating all of the above, I assessed that the following services might be available to this family:

- A local children's shelter provides volunteer parent aides to visit families who are at risk once a week. I called this service, and they were willing to move Nathan's family to the top of the waiting list and assign a parent aide immediately.
- Being diagnosed as "failure to thrive" placed the baby at risk of developmental delay and made him eligible for Department of Developmental Disabilities (DDD) services. These services include home visits by a developmental specialist, case management, and respite care in the home. I made a referral and asked them to expedite the intake procedure.
- The state provides long-term care benefits to patients with chronic illness and disability. These benefits include home nursing, physical therapy, occupational therapy, and respite services. I started the application process.
- When parents are in the hospital with a sick child and spend most of their day with that child, they often have to eat in our hospital cafeteria. This expense can add up over time. I give families a meal ticket to eat in our cafeteria when they have no money, are from out of town, and sometimes when I just can't think of anything else I can do for them. I gave Nathan's parents a meal ticket for lunch in the cafeteria about once a week.

The baby was discharged home. I thought the family now had some concrete resources to help them meet their child's healthcare needs. However, things did not turn out as I had planned. Rosa contacted the parent aide program and decided that because the aide would only come out and talk to her and not hold the baby while she cooked, she did not need this service. Rosa failed to return the calls of the DDD intake worker and never set up an appointment. Rosa tried to keep her appointment with the long-term care office but got lost on the way and never found the office. Joe lost his job and had to go on unemployment. Nathan missed two doctor appointments because Rosa forgot one and didn't have transportation for the other.

The baby was then readmitted to the hospital, still losing weight, and started on tube feedings through his nose into his stomach. The doctors were now very concerned about the family's ability to cope with these tube feedings at home. I began to worry about the family's ability to properly care for the baby. Families can be overwhelmed, but they still must find a way to meet the needs of the child, or that child may be in danger.

The medical team wanted to consider other placement options for Nathan outside of his home. There was discussion of a CPS referral. The team agreed that the baby needed a placement where he could receive the appropriate medical care and gain weight. However, in this situation, as in many, the child was so bonded to his parents that removing him from his home would possibly do more harm than good. As well as medical care, Nathan needed his family's love to get him through a major transplant surgery. In addition, we had a good relationship with this family, and I did not want to jeopardize that relationship by making a CPS referral. As sometimes happens when I am faced with the decision of whether to call CPS or not, I began to think I should have become a nurse instead of a social worker, but then I consoled myself with the idea that as a social worker I get to work with families and patients, but I don't have to deal with bodily fluids.

We decided to hold a meeting with the family and the involved physicians and social agencies. We drew up a contract with the family. We set weekly doctor appointments for the same day and time each week, alternating one week with the pediatrician, the next with the specialist. We set down in the contract exactly what was expected of the parents in caring for their son. I listed the set doctor appointments and phone numbers to call in case of emergency. I listed instructions on how to get transportation to appointments by calling the insurance plan 24 hours in advance. I gave Rosa a calendar with her appointments written on it. I gave her a notebook with paper and pencil to list her questions for the doctors. I included all instructions in this notebook, along with the contract and the calendar. I also included food logs to list exactly what she fed Nathan each day.

I set up Home Health to come out daily to check the tube feedings, weigh the baby, and look at the food logs. I convinced the insurance company to use our hospital's home health agency, even though the insurance did not contract with them, so that Nathan would be seen by one of our pediatric nurses instead of an agency nurse who might not have the appropriate pediatric experience. I had DDD do their intake at the hospital with Rosa. I had the long-term care worker do a home intake so Rosa did not have to drive to their office. I gave Rosa a copy of Nathan's medical records to give to the long-term care worker and expedite the process.

The baby was again discharged. Rosa lost the medical records and could not master tube feedings. She could not reinsert the tube herself when it came out. Instead of calling for help when the tube came out, she would wait for the nurse to show up the next day to reinsert the tube. As a result, Nathan missed valuable feeding time. The baby was readmitted, still not gaining weight.

This time, with the parents' permission, I gave the medical records to the DDD intake worker. Then, since Joe was still out of work, we encouraged him to become more active in his son's care. So Joe slowly became Nathan's primary caregiver. Because he was out of work and spending so much time at the hospital, Joe began to ask for a meal ticket every day. And to encourage Joe to continue to participate in Nathan's care, I gave him one. I began to see Joe and Nathan on a daily basis then, as Joe would wheel his baby down to my office in a wagon to get his lunch ticket and while Joe sang he would move Nathan's arms to make the baby do the Macarena. Rosa visited too. Because Joe was now caring for Nathan, Rosa began to talk about going to work to support the family. Together we explored her options for employment. We discussed her providing respite care for disabled children in her own home. We discussed her becoming a patient care technician at the hospital. We discussed her returning to school to improve her secretarial skills. Then one day Rosa asked about how to become a court interpreter. She was bilingual in English and Spanish and thought this was a job she could do. I made several phone calls, found a training program that offered financial aid, and gave her this information with my encouragement.

It was time for Nathan to go home again, but now he was being fed through a tube directly into his bloodstream instead of through his nose into his stomach as before. I talked to Joe about an out-of-home placement for Nathan. There is a house in our town that provides care for children with complicated medical needs. I encouraged Joe to consider this option so Nathan would gain weight and get his liver transplant. Joe was furious that I would suggest a "nursing home" for his son. Joe insisted that, with proper training, he and Rosa could learn to adequately care for their son. So the doctor and I decided to try to place Nathan at a special care unit at another hospital. The unit could provide intensive discharge training for the family and assess the family's ability to care for the baby themselves. But Nathan's insurance did not have a contract with that hospital. We had to call the insurance plan and try to convince them that Nathan needed to be transferred to the other facility. They said no. We called again. We wrote a letter. The doctor called the medical director of the insurance plan and finally the insurance agreed. Nathan and Joe went to the special care unit, and Nathan was discharged to his home within a month.

Two weeks after this discharge from the special care unit, the home health agency called to say that Rosa had been discussing future plans with her home health nurse. Rosa planned to enroll in the court interpreter program, get a job, and then divorce Joe. The agency also reported that Nathan's sisters were not attending school. Everyone was in a panic over this information. If Joe and Rosa were having marital problems and getting a divorce, it would jeopardize Nathan's chances for getting a transplant. Someone had to talk to the family about getting counseling and sending the girls back to school. I thought about trying to get the hospital to authorize a social work visit at Nathan's home, since I do not usually provide this service, but then the baby developed an infection and was readmitted to the hospital. Rosa assured me she would send her daughters back to school. Joe began to approach me about meal tickets again. However, I had used so many that we were running out of funds, and all I had to offer him were $1 discount coupons. He scoffed at them: "What can I get with this? Soup? I need more than that. Look, I'm down to my last $20. Oh well, it's better than nothing. Want to see Nathan do the Macarena?"

Shortly after this, Joe found a job and went back to work with a better understanding of how difficult and time-consuming Nathan's care could be. The family asked me to help them find a bigger apartment. They had contacted a local agency that helped families of Mexican heritage with housing. I wrote a letter about how Joe and Rosa were working together to care for their child and needed a bigger place to live. The agency gave them a subsidized, three-bedroom apartment. Joe and Rosa moved into their new place and stopped talking about divorce.

Then a DDD case manager called me and said she had been assigned to the family but could not find them. I asked her to come by the hospital to see the family and get their new address and phone number. This case manager helped with the long-term care application, and Rosa finally got DDD services, long-term care services, and someone to provide respite and hold Nathan while she cooked. Nathan was discharged, and we did not see them again for a long time.

One day their doctor, the same one who initially approached me about the family, stopped me in the hall and said, "You know, Nathan is a real success story. His family really turned around and is taking great care of him. He's gaining weight, he's on the transplant list, and now all he needs is a liver. You really are a miracle worker."

I think to myself, "Sure, I am a miracle worker and this job is great when a child gets well and walks back in to give me a hug, but sometimes it is not so great." Remember, all the psychosocial intervention that I can offer cannot change the course of a chronic disease.

Nathan was readmitted to the hospital for the last time about a month ago. He was so jaundiced from his liver disease that he looked as if he could glow in the dark. The doctors decided to keep him in the hospital until a liver became available for him so that he would be at the top of the list. Then Nathan got an infection and began to decline and was transferred into intensive care.

At this point, everyone realized that Nathan was dying—everyone except his mother. I went to see her after the transplant doctor talked to her about the baby being taken off the transplant list.

Rosa said to me, "The doctor told me that Nathan is going to die, but I don't believe him. I know God will save my baby. He will get over this infection and then get stronger and then get his transplant."

I couldn't argue with her. I remember hearing a mother of a seriously ill child telling another mother one day, "You have to be strong for your child. You have to believe that he will be okay. It's the only way you can get through it. You have to believe he will get better or you simply can't deal with it."

So I said to Rosa, "You understand that your son is very sick and that what he needs now is a miracle?" She nodded, and I said, "Well, we all hope you get it."

Sometimes facing a child's death is just too hard for parents, and they need to have hope until the very end to get through it. Because I was at a loss this time for what to do, I gave them a meal ticket. Joe said to me, "So my son has to get this sick in order for me to get a decent meal around here."

Soon afterward, Nathan developed another infection. The doctors talked to the family again about the lack of hope in this situation. They explained to the family that the baby was being kept alive now by machines and drugs that were only postponing his death. Faced with this information, the parents decided to disconnect the machines and stop the drugs. When I went in to see Rosa, she said to me, "How will I get through this? I've never felt love like this for anyone. How can I let him go? What will I do with his new shoes?"

So I called Nathan's doctor, and he came and knelt down beside Rosa and gently explained exactly how the staff would disconnect life support and what would happen. We encouraged her and Joe to hold their baby and sing to him. When the staff was ready to disconnect Nathan from the machines, Rosa looked to me and said, "Am I going to be okay?"

I don't usually give advice, but I nodded and said, "Yes, you are going to be okay. I know you can get through this for your baby."

So the staff turned off the monitors and the machines and the medications, and we left Rosa and Joe holding Nathan and singing to him as he died peacefully in his parents' arms.

Afterward, I went back in. The nurse was taking the baby from Rosa to place him back on the bed, but he was still hooked up to tubes and wires and difficult for the nurse to manage. She looked to me and said, "I need help, take him." So I held out my arms and took the body of the baby from the nurse and felt something cold and wet on my hands and realized that as a nurse she was wearing gloves that protected her from bodily fluids, but as a social worker I was not. We put Nathan back on the bed, and his mother washed him and dressed him in an outfit from home and put on his new shoes. We gave her a quilt to wrap him in. We took pictures for the family. We made a set of Nathan's handprints. While Rosa stayed with Nathan, I spent some time with Joe and discussed funeral options and grief counseling for the family. Then at the family's request, I told Nathan's sisters that their brother had died.

Finally, the family packed up Nathan's belongings and came by my office to say goodbye. Nathan's youngest sister was holding a bear. "Watch," she said, and she pressed the bear's paw and the bear sang "Hey, Macarena." That's when I cried.

So, Jeffrey, as you can see, I can help people get stuff. In fact, sometimes it seems that I can do miracles. But you are right, that is the easy part. I can get an insurance company to buy a $20,000 piece of equipment for a patient; I can get a pilot to fly a child to doctor appointments monthly for free; I can get a stressed, single mother 8 hours a day of attendant care for her child so the mother can work. But I can't do the hard part, as Joe reminded me one day when I asked what he needed, if he wanted to talk. He said, "I need for my child to not be sick anymore. I need for him to live. Talking about it won't make him better. But I could use one of those lunch tickets."

REFERENCES

King, G., & Meyer, K. (2006). Service integration and co-ordination: A framework of approaches for the delivery of co-ordinated care to children with disabilities and their families. *Child: Care, Health and Development, 32,* 477–492.

Moersch, M. S. (1978). History and rationale for parent involvement. In S. L. Brown & M. S. Moersch (Eds.), *Parents on the team* (pp. 1–10). Ann Arbor: University of Michigan Press.

Case Study 1-3

A Strengths-Focused Approach to Community Development

Jeannine K. Chapelle

Community development is a social work strategy to improve people's lives by enhancing certain aspects of the life that they have in common. This case study describes an effective approach to community development that leads to obtaining specific goals for the community as well as the development of the community's capabilities—in particular, the leadership capabilities of the community members.

Questions

1. How is a strengths-based perspective used in this case study?
2. What made the community development project successful in this case?
3. How did the social worker get the community involved in community development?
4. What role do you think community development can play in the social service agencies you are familiar with?

Community development is at once an art and a science. Its medium is the quality and character of human cooperative action. Its methods of investigation, intervention, and evaluation conform to rigorous standards. The success or failure of a community development project is as much influenced by the rapport and mutual respect the change agent establishes with the community as by the theoretical framework within which the agent operates. Practitioner beliefs about the competence of community members to participate in the change process determine the approach they take and the outcomes they expect.

This case study examines how a strengths-focused approach to community development produced positive results in an urban area in the Southwest, which I shall call Sandstone City. The reader will walk the journey with one of the participating families and observe their growth and development through the community change process.

WHEN WE ONLY LOOK AT THE PROBLEMS

Historically, most community work has taken a problem-focused approach, which Griffen-Wisener calls Needs Mapping (Griffen-Wiesner, 2005). The change agent trained in this approach enters the community and conducts an assessment to determine the presence and degree of dysfunction and maladaptation (which may be reflected in high crime rates, drug use and trafficking, domestic violence, or many other indicators). The key questions asked are, "What is wrong? How do we fix it?" The change agent analyzes the data from the needs assessment, perhaps presenting the results to the community at a public meeting, and suggests a course of action in which the community is encouraged to participate. The change agent is often in a position to acquire grant monies and other resources to support justifiable interventions, monies that will likely be granted to service providers rather than community residents. A neighborhood with a high degree of dysfunction will capture more resources, thus its members are encouraged to uncover and publicize their problems (Griffen-Wiesner, 2005). Evaluation strategies are designed to measure changes in frequency and intensity of problem behaviors. Approaching community development from this perspective, the focus is on the relative presence or absence of dysfunction. Behaviors that support health and well-being often go quietly unnoticed.

When I entered the high-risk neighborhood in Sandstone City, the residents were already weary of research and community development. In the words of Jasmine, a 35-year-old single mother of two young sons living on Aid to Families with Dependent Children (AFDC):

> I've lived in this neighborhood all my life. I don't know why they're sending someone else in here. We've had enough of that already. Nothing ever happens. Oh, yeah, they ask us what we want, get folks all fired up. Sometimes things are better for a while. But then the money runs out, they leave, and we're just where we were before. Nothing ever changes. I don't guess it'll be any different this time.

On the continuum of human services, the process of Needs Mapping described previously has value. It gives the change agent baseline data, identifies service needs, and provides a point of departure for appropriate intervention. But Jasmine has pointed out the dark side of a project that is expert-driven and problem-focused, where neighborhood residents are the recipients of services rather than active participants in planned change. Kretzmann and McKnight (1993) describe it this way:

Many lower income urban neighborhoods are now environments of service where . . . residents come to believe that their well-being depends upon being a client. They begin to see themselves as people with special needs that can only be met by outsiders. They become consumers of services, with no incentive to be producers.

WE MISS SEEING THE STRENGTHS

The missing element is the vast resource of the community itself. Residents know their community's history and are well aware of the needs that exist. They have witnessed the development of problems over time, know what has been tried before, what has failed, and most likely why it did. Each community resident has strengths: a lifetime of experiences, knowledge, and acquired skills. Locating and mobilizing these strengths for community development is what Griffen-Wiesner calls Assets Mapping. Here the role of the change agent shifts from expert to partner: One who helps create a supportive environment that encourages participation, facilitates the expression and implementation of ideas, and promotes beneficial alliances with people, agencies, and organizations that can provide resources to the change process. Within this perspective, people are viewed as competent contributors (Benard, 2012; Griffen-Wiesner, 2005; Henderson, 2007; Saleeby, 2012).

The goal of community development should be to engage community members and their organizational partners in an active, ongoing process of creating conditions and fostering personal attributes that promote the well-being of people (Hardcastle, 2011). The key question to be answered is, "Under what conditions do people in communities experience well-being?" This is very different from asking the question, "What problems need to be fixed?" It represents a search for strengths rather than deficiencies, successes rather than failures, competence rather than inability, and pushes development toward self-sufficiency rather than dependency. The question urges us to identify and do more of what works.

More than four decades of research on resiliency has given us reliable information about the characteristics of conditions that support human well-being. They include the following (Benard, 2012):

- The community is organized to provide networks of social support for its members.
- Needed resources are available (healthcare, housing, education, recreation, etc.).
- All members (youth and adults) are valued as resources and contributors to community well-being and have meaningful opportunities to use their knowledge and talents for the community's benefit.
- Families, community, schools, and other social institutions share power and collaborate for positive change.

With the essential elements of a strengths-focused approach to community development in place, let us turn our attention to Sandstone City and the neighborhood development project undertaken there.

THE COMMUNITY CONTEXT

Sandstone is a city in the Southwest desert with a population of about 300,000 people. It is located in a drug-trafficking corridor, with easy access from Mexico by interstate highway. The city's population is becoming increasingly diverse; however, the majority of that diversity occupies only a few neighborhoods in Sandstone City. Those neighborhoods define a high-risk corridor that bisects the city, according to numerous police, city, and university studies.

The neighborhood chosen for development is home to about 1,000 families. Only 20% of the residents in this census tract define themselves as Caucasian. The remainder make up a rainbow of ethnic diversity. This neighborhood's unemployment rate is twice that of Sandstone City, with a median income less than half that of the city as a whole. Its children are half as likely to graduate from high school and twice as likely to drop out. By all measures, the neighborhood is considered to be at high risk.

Residents have seen many intervention programs come and go. A social service agency, which I shall call the Mountain Center, is located adjacent to the neighborhood and offers a large menu of services, including GED classes, home repair, emergency food boxes, assistance with utility payments, and subsidized childcare. Long before the doors to the Mountain Center open, neighborhood residents who need services line up in front of the building. If you happen to be waiting with them, you will see children running and yelling exuberantly in the cool morning air, women clutching electric bills, pink slips, landlords' letters—telling their troubles to those standing near them as if rehearsing for the intake and assessment clerk inside. It was there I first saw Jasmine. She caught my attention because of the contrast she provided to the chattering crowd. Her children were under her affectionate but strict control. Together they seemed to form a bubble of family space that outsiders were not invited to penetrate. I waited quietly with the others for the doors to open, to begin my first day employed by the Mountain Center as a neighborhood program developer.

SANDSTONE NEIGHBORHOOD PROJECT— FIRST CONTACT

Based on my knowledge of anthropology and community development, I chose to enter the neighborhood as a learner and participant in community life. My first task, to discover the families with children in this neighborhood, was accomplished by hosting a neighborhood party for kindergartners and their families. Crafts, face painting, clowns, games, and food produced an impressive turnout, and many names with telephone numbers on a sign-in sheet. A videotape of the party was the first documentation of the project.

My second task was to contact those families after the party to arrange interviews to learn about the neighborhood and the issues about which people were most concerned. This would also give me the chance to explain my role.

Jasmine's name was in the middle of the list. Her youthful voice on the other end of the telephone line sounded suspicious. I explained who I was and why I was calling. The long pause and slow, deliberate monosyllabic response did not bode well for successfully scheduling a meeting. When I mentioned that I got her name from the kindergarten party list, she became excited. She asked, "Do you have the videotape? Can I see it?" My positive response clinched the interview.

As we watched the videotape together, I realized that one of Jasmine's great strengths was her passion for her children and her burning desire to give them opportunities to learn new things. I wondered if this commitment might extend to other neighborhood children. As the tape rewound, Jasmine cast her eyes downward and seemed embarrassed. "I don't know why I came. I don't usually do things like this. I don't know what made me say yes to this interview."

I asked a series of open-ended questions designed to elicit her views about the most important issues in the neighborhood. I included questions that set the stage for community development: "What can families do to start to solve the problems you face in this community?" and "What people or organizations can help families?" By encouraging people to tell their stories in a reflective manner, they are likely to produce narratives that move them to consider the possibility of action (Seidman, 2005). Jasmine didn't know what families could do about the community's problems, but she thought that getting together to talk about it might be a good idea. I thought that was a good idea, too.

THE FIRST 6 MONTHS

After collecting information through neighborhood interviews, we held our first meeting in the recreation facility at the Mountain Center. By unspoken agreement, this was a dress-up occasion. Jasmine appeared self-conscious in her pretty skirt and blouse, and her feet seemed unaccustomed to walking in her midsized heels. Many of these women had lived in the neighborhood all of their lives, yet few knew even one other person in the room. I kept the atmosphere informal, imposing no structure. Although we sat in a circle, Jasmine was able to isolate herself from the others by keeping empty chairs on either side of her.

We talked about our families, one thing we all had in common, while the children played outside. Then one of the elders who had been quiet spoke, "It's hard being a mother," she said. "Take Mrs. Johnson's 17-year-old granddaughter. She just had a baby, and her mother was so mad that she threw her out of the house. Mrs. Johnson, bless her, took her and the baby in, but that young girl doesn't know the first thing about raising a baby, and doesn't have anything for it." She concluded, "It just breaks your heart."

I watched with fascination how the group changed following this story. The guarded politeness that had characterized the beginning of the meeting was dropped. Women leaned forward, listening intently. They began to talk about what they could do to help this young girl. One offered baby clothes that her son had outgrown. Another knew a place that might donate diapers. Yet another said she would crochet a nice blanket. When the "virtual" box of baby items was complete, the room grew quiet again. I took this as my cue to ask, "I wonder if it might be helpful for this new mom to be able to talk to some experienced mothers?" After a pause, the excitement returned:

> "We could go see her and let her know we're there to help her learn to take care of that baby."
> "I know I was scared when I had my first one! I was sure glad my momma was there to tell me what to do."

Soon the plans were made for the whole group to call on the young mother and welcome her baby to the neighborhood. The Baby Box project was born.

After that first Baby Box delivery, the community grapevine was abuzz. Calls began to come into the Mountain Center informing us of recent or impending births and asking if boxes could be made. One of the volunteer mothers took responsibility for gathering and storing the needed items. Although she could have assembled and decorated the boxes in her home, she chose instead to bring all of the materials to the Center. Other mothers, including Jasmine, began to drop by to see if a Baby Box was under construction and to offer their help. With quiet efficiency, each person offered her talents to the project: Thelma was renowned for her pretty rainbow blankets made from the leftovers of many skeins of yarn; Sherry made a weekly visit to used clothing stores to collect the baby clothes that didn't sell; Connie made sure the local merchants saved their cardboard boxes for her; and Tina just had a knack for decorating them.

I asked once if they wanted to have requesters fill out a card with their names, addresses, and telephone numbers so we could keep track of them. Their reaction was immediate and unequivocal: No forms! "We have to fill out enough forms at welfare and every other place. No one who comes to us will ever have to fill out a form!" Although such a procedure would have given them useful information, they clearly did not want to replicate a system that many felt robbed them of their dignity. I respected that; this was their project, and they could make the rules. In the first 6 months, 10 boxes were delivered by this grassroots social support network. No funds were allocated to the Baby Box project—the volunteers managed it through their relentless quest for donations.

The group continued to meet on Friday mornings. Although Jasmine didn't often initiate conversation with the others, she responded pleasantly to inquiries about how her family was doing. Her children became fast friends with the sons of another woman who came regularly. Jasmine smiled more and seemed to be more comfortable with the group—but her chair was always the closest to the door.

THE SECOND 6 MONTHS

When Jasmine arrived at the Mountain Center recreation facility one Friday, about 6 months after we had begun meeting, a lively discussion was well underway:

> "Do you remember that box we delivered to Mrs. Scott last week? She asked me how could she get help to get her mother's house fixed. There was water all over the floor in that last rain we had."

Tina joined in, "I know what you mean. I'm always getting asked for advice. My neighbor always comes and talks to me about her sister and those devil drugs. She wants her to get help so bad. I wish I knew better what to tell her."

Connie spoke emphatically, "We need to know how to be better resources to our neighbors."

"What would need to happen to improve your ability to be neighborhood resources?" I asked.

"I guess we would need training," said Connie.

That simple conversation launched an impromptu planning session about how this could be accomplished. My questions to the group included: What kind of training would you need? How many topics should be covered? What agencies do you know in town that have this expertise? Where would the training take place? Who should come? By the end of the morning, a plan was in place. They identified six social service agencies that might be potential resources, and Tina volunteered to set up meetings. The group wanted to hold classes in their homes, "like a Tupperware party," rotating the responsibility for hosting among them. To my surprise, Jasmine asked if the first class could be at her house.

As they completed their plan, I reflected on the changes I had seen in my 6 months working in this neighborhood. That first experience of success with the Baby Boxes gave this group of volunteer mothers the confidence to tackle even bigger issues. They had formed the habit of thinking in terms of community conditions and had learned a simple planning process that they could use to take action on any issue of interest to them. I did not have to organize them; they organized themselves when they perceived that they were in an environment where people valued them and believed they had something important to contribute. Their unfailing attendance at the Friday morning meetings and their participation in the projects they designed convinced me that such an environment is addictive. With sufficient dosage of this supportive milieu, they began to discover strengths they didn't know they had and to take some risks they would not otherwise have attempted. Jasmine had predicted 6 months earlier, "Nothing ever changes. I don't guess it'll be any different this time." But this time the focus had shifted from deficiencies to individual and community strengths. The community was being supported in taking responsibility for its own well-being. And that was making *all* the difference.

A SELF-ACTUALIZING COMMUNITY

The Sandstone neighborhood development project continued to innovate and grow in its second year. The Baby Box project had welcomed more than 65 new babies to the neighborhood and proudly displayed their pictures on a special bulletin board in the Center. Women called to sign up as soon as they discovered they were pregnant. Many of the recipient mothers volunteered to visit other new babies and their families because they wanted to give back some of the support they had received. A local nonprofit family resource center was so enthusiastic about the project that they provided scholarships to the Baby Box families so they could attend infant massage workshops. The donations of baby clothes grew to include children and adult sizes, so a neighborhood clothing bank was opened and staffed by neighborhood volunteers.

The group completed the training they had designed, which included sessions on locating resources and making referrals, effective communication, the early warning signs of drug abuse, and effective parenting. A local foundation, impressed by the neighborhood's proactive projects, awarded scholarships to three volunteer mothers to attend a 2-day facilitator training given by a renowned international organization. Soon afterward, the leadership for Friday morning meetings began to rotate among the members. Coordinator position descriptions were written for the volunteer work that occupied most of their energy, including Baby Boxes, donations, and youth and family recreation.

In the summer of the second year, the issue that emerged in the circle's discussion was a concern about how to keep elementary and middle school–aged children occupied and out of trouble during summer vacation. The Sandstone neighborhood group collaborated with Junior Achievement to bring their youth entrepreneurship program to the neighborhood. New faces blended with familiar ones as parents were recruited to mentor the eager young officers of Kids' Business Opportunities (KBO), a neighborhood babysitting business. Mentors and young entrepreneurs celebrated together at the end of the summer, when the business paid a 20% dividend to its stockholders.

The core group made outreach a priority. Proud of their achievements, they wanted to invite more people to add their skills and wisdom to the group. They were eager to share with others the joy of transforming ideas into reality, making this Sandstone neighborhood a better place to live.

LOOKING BACK: JASMINE'S STORY

The most visible consequences of development occur at the community level, but before those changes are discernible, transformation is happening at the individual level. This was particularly true in Jasmine's case. When I met Jasmine, she was a guarded, private, young single mother on AFDC. Although she grew up in the neighborhood, she knew very few people who lived there. Most of her friends had long ago moved away. She didn't seriously entertain the thought of working, partly because she felt she had no marketable skills. It didn't really occur to her that her future would hold anything very different. And then, as she describes it, a "miracle" happened: She agreed to do an interview about her neighborhood.

She found herself among women who made no judgments. "They just accepted me for who I was," she said. Over time, she laid aside the protection of her aloof, inaccessible exterior and added her talents to the work being done. Her leadership skills blossomed with each training workshop she attended. "I can't believe I'm up here in front of these people. I never would have done that. You can ask anybody—that's just not me."

Jasmine had always had a way with children. "I play with them and they like me. They know I respect them and won't put up with no stuff." But instead of seeing this as a unique skill, she was afraid it was a sign of immaturity. At the Mountain Center, Jasmine was asked to help plan family recreation activities. She basked in the appreciation she received for planning the games, setting up basketball and other sports, and involving the young people in planning special events. When KBO started its business, Jasmine volunteered as a mentor and helped the young people decide how to market their services.

It has been 4 years since I met Jasmine. She moved away from the neighborhood after 2 years with the community development project, but we stay in touch. She wants to be a basketball coach and started taking classes at the local community college to get her AA degree. She had a great deal of trouble with her classes in high school, so she's surprised to find how much she enjoys her college courses. "I never thought I would be able to get up in front of the class and talk, but it is just like being at the Center." She and her children sit down to do their homework together, and she tells me she is proud that they see her getting her education. "I want them to know that learning is fun, and you can do it your whole life." I smile as I remember that my first insight about her was her commitment to her children's education.

Jasmine is working two jobs, each of which she loves. During the school day she is a teaching assistant at her youngest son's school. She also works for the city's Parks and Recreation Department as a recreation assistant in their after-school program. She credits the community development project with helping her recognize her gift for working with children. "I feel good when I'm at work. I look forward to getting up and going to work each morning. I feel like I'm really making a difference." Even with two paychecks it is hard to make ends meet, and her family has allowed her and her children to move back in with them until she can save up enough to get her own place.

Although Jasmine no longer lives in the neighborhood, she continues to include the volunteer mothers as part of her social network. They touch base by telephone once a month and reunite to share each one's significant life events: birthdays, weddings, funerals, or the birth of a new baby. "These women, they're part of my family now," she says. "We went through good times and bad together. We're part of one another and you can't take that away." Indeed, you can't.

SUMMARY

In a strengths-focused approach to community development, the change agent proceeds from the premise that people have the skills, knowledge, and abilities necessary to create the conditions that promote well-being in their communities. The change agent's role is to consciously build a supportive environment that encourages people to express their strengths and participate in the development process (Baker, 2003). The art and the science of effective community development blends the formation of supportive social relationships with the focused, intentional planning necessary to bring about sustained change.

REFERENCES

Baker, R. (2003). *The social work dictionary*. Baltimore, MD: Port City Press.

Benard, B. (2012). *Fostering resiliency in kids: Protective factors in family, school and community*. Portland, OR: Western Center for Drug-Free Schools and Communities, Ulan Press.

Griffen-Wiesner, J. (2005). *The journey of community change: A how to guide for healthy communities—healthy youth initiatives*. Minneapolis, MN: Search Institutes Press.

Hardcastle, D. A. (2011). *Community practice*. New York, NY: Oxford University Press.

Henderson, N. (2007). *Resiliency in action: Practical ideas for overcoming risks and building strengths in youth, families, and communities* (2nd ed.). Ojai, CA: Resiliency in Action.

Kretzmann, J., & McKnight, J. (1993). *Building communities from the inside out: A path toward finding and mobilizing a community's assets*. Evanston, IL: Northwestern University.

Saleebey, D. (2012). *The strengths perspective in social worker practice* (6th ed.). New York, NY: Pearson Education.

Seidman, I. (2005). *Interviewing as qualitative research: A guide for researchers in education and the social science*. Amsterdam, NY: Teachers College Press, Columbia University.

PART II

Case Studies in Integrating Theory and Practice

The profession of social work is built on the assumption that social workers will use theory to guide their practice. A well-known hallmark of being recognized as a profession is that a body of knowledge is organized into a consistent framework of theory. Thus, an important professional skill is the application of theory to practice.

In what ways does the application of theory enhance the practice of social work? Theory provides a lens through which a practitioner can obtain a better perspective and understanding of a practice situation. If we can understand a situation better, then we are more likely to find the best solution to that situation. In fact, practice theory should suggest the effects of a social worker's intervention. A school social worker might decide that if she can identify children who are at risk, then she can prevent the likelihood of them developing more serious problems later in life. Because of this theory, she begins the process of developing such a program.

All of the case studies presented in this chapter represent a different theory that guides practice. The approach to each case is quite different depending on the theory being used. Of course, the obvious question becomes, how do I know which theory to use? There are two general guidelines for the answer to this question: (a) the extent to which the theory is considered valid and (b) the degree of fit or appropriateness given the particular case.

A theory is considered valid if enough consistent scientific findings support its propositions. A well-supported theory in social work is the proposition that an empathic relationship will provide a basis to begin to help someone change. Without an empathic relationship, the prospect for individual change is less likely. This theory has undergone much scientific study. Most social work scientists consider it valid.

Although a theory may be valid or true, it may not necessarily fit the case situation. For example, good eye contact has been shown to enhance a person's ability to be perceived as empathic; however, this may not be the case with certain clients, such as Native Americans. Here a valid theory does not have a good fit with the particular client. Too often, social workers attempt to extend theories with which they are familiar to case situations that do not have a good fit.

Because fit is often a problem in applying theories to social work practice, the social worker must become familiar with several theories of practice. It is difficult for any one theory to be adequate for all situations. Most social work educators agree that practitioners need to select the theory and interventions that have the best fit with the client situation. Furthermore, the theories used should be valid (i.e., demonstrated empirically to be effective). A common term for this understanding is *systematic eclecticism* (Hepworth, Rooney, Rooney, Strom-Gottfried, & Larsen, 2009). This means knowing several different theories and interventions and being able to use them systematically, depending on the needed fit. For example, according to the latest literature, the most valid theory and intervention for treating depression is cognitive therapy. The social worker practicing systematic eclecticism would be familiar with cognitive therapy and recognize the fit between depression and cognitive distortions.

In this chapter, you will read about four different theories and their application to a case example. The first case study presents an application of ecological theory. Ecological theory is important for social work because it is considered to be a unifying framework (Gitterman & Germain, 2008). It is a unifying framework because it provides a theory to answer the question, What do social workers do? Although this theory is broad without much specification about practice guidelines, Teater's case study shows how this theory can be translated into social work practice principles.

The case studies by Thyer and Walsh represent two major theoretical perspectives in clinical social work: behavior modification and ego psychology. Although these two perspectives are major theories for many social workers, they rely on very different assumptions about human behavior. Social learning theory examines such variables as antecedents and consequences to discover their contribution in maintaining dysfunctional behavior. Ego psychology examines mastery of ego functions within the context of developmental stages and life tasks. Both theories offer useful guidelines in working with clients.

The last case study, by Dore, demonstrates the use of family systems theory. This approach is often used in social work because it encapsulates many fundamental principles of social work. Theories may not necessarily be incompatible with one another. By integrating different theories, you have a variety of vantage points from which to understand your client's behavior, and this can offer you different perspectives on how to help this person.

The challenge of learning social work is before you. You must grapple with many different choices and assimilate a large body of knowledge. Use this challenge to make social work exciting. Don't oversimplify what it takes to provide good social work services. Accept that this is a complex profession and that you must continue to learn everything you can in order to serve it well.

REFERENCES

Gitterman, A., & Germain, C. B. (2008). *The life model of social work practice: Advances in theory and practice* (3rd ed.). New York, NY: Columbia University Press.

Hepworth, D., Rooney, R. H., Rooney, G. W., Strom-Gottfried, K., & Larsen, J. (2009). *Direct social work practice.* Pacific Grove, CA: Cengage.

Case Study 2-1

Social Work Practice From an Ecological Perspective

BARBRA TEATER

T his section presents an overview of the ecological perspective by covering the ecological theory and the application of the theory through the life model of
practice. A theme throughout is the interaction of people with their environment and
the impact this relationship has on growth and development.

Questions
1. What was the social worker's focus at the beginning of the work together?
2. Who identified the life stressors and goals for the work together?
3. How was the environment considered in the work with the client?
4. What other theories and methods might be appropriate to use with this client alongside
   the ecological perspective?

Ecological theory is fundamentally concerned with the interaction and interdependence of organisms and their environment. Likewise, the profession of social work
was built on an acknowledgement that individuals, families, groups, and communities
interact with their environments and are shaped by them. Individuals do not operate in
isolation but are influenced by their physical and social environments in which they live

and interact. Taking an ecological perspective toward social work practice involves taking into consideration a person and the environment around that person and is referred to as the "person-and-environment concept" (Gitterman & Germain, 2008, p. 51). This chapter explores the ecological perspective by describing the ecological theory and the life model of social work practice. The chapter then turns to an illustration of how to apply the ecological perspective to social work practice through a case example.

THEORETICAL PERSPECTIVE

The ecological perspective was developed based on the biological science of ecology, which views all living organisms within their social and physical environments and examines the exchanges of people with their environments (Gitterman, 2009). Applying ecology to human beings in social work practice settings involves holding a perspective that humans interact with their physical, social, and cultural environments. Physical environments include the natural world as well as the built world, which includes buildings and structures designed and made by man. Social environments include the interactions with friends and family, social and community networks, such as colleagues or through membership or involvement with organizations or the community, and the societal structures that shape the way in which the environment operates and orders itself, such as through political, legal, and economic structures. The cultural aspect of the environment involves those values, norms, beliefs, and language that shape the individual's views, perspectives, and expectations. Taking an ecological perspective would involve seeing the relationships and connections among the individual, family, group, and/or community and the physical, social, and cultural environments and how each influences and shapes one another (Gitterman, 2009).

The influence and connection among the different parts of the environment is not static but, rather, evolves over time, taking into consideration the historical and cultural influences. Gitterman and Germain (2008) describe how the ecological perspective goes away from simple cause-and-effect linear thinking, where A causes B and, therefore, honing in on A as the target for intervention. Rather, taking an ecological perspective would involve focusing on the interactions and relationships between A and B, while also considering the environmental factors that could influence A and B's interaction and the ways in which they are responding. A social worker might find that the target for intervention is neither A nor B, but rather the family in which A and B belong (social environment) or the physical environment in which they live, which could be the source of stress and strain.

The ecological perspective to social work practice requires a specific "ecological" vocabulary, which includes such words as *adaptedness*, *stress*, and *person:environment fit* (Gitterman & Germain, 2008). The ecological perspective assumes that individuals try to maintain a good level of fit between themselves and their environment as they move through the life course. *Adaptedness* refers to a positive and healthy fit between the person and her or his environment. This is where individuals feel that their environment is providing the necessary and useful resources to meet their needs and that they, personally, have the strengths, resources, and capability to grow, develop, and be satisfied. When individuals feel that their environment is *not* providing the necessary resources, due to being unavailable, inaccessible, or nonexistent, and they believe and feel as if they do not have the strengths, resources, or capability to grow and develop, then they experience *stress*. Experiencing stress leads to a poor level of adaptive fit and often leads to individuals seeking help from social workers. The social worker is tasked with collaborating with the individual to improve the level of *person:environment fit*, which might involve changing the individual's perceptions and behaviors, changing the response from the environment, or trying to improve the quality of exchange between the individual and her or his environment (Gitterman, 2009).

PRACTICE PRINCIPLES AND GUIDELINES

When implementing the ecological perspective in practice, a social worker may use the life model approach, which aims to improve the level of fit between people and their environments. The level of fit can be improved by either: "(1) mobilizing and drawing on personal and environmental resources to eliminate or at least alleviate stressors and the associates stress; or (2) influencing social and physical environmental forces to be responsive to people's needs" (Gitterman, 2009, p. 232).

The ecological perspective assumes that individuals are striving to move through the life course while maintaining a good person:environment fit, which will positively contribute to their growth and development. The life model approach assumes that stress can arise during this process, particularly when individuals encounter difficult life transitions (e.g., puberty and adolescence, leaving home, having a baby, getting married or divorced) and traumatic life events (e.g., death of a loved one, natural disasters), environmental pressures (e.g., lack of resources and social provisions, such as money, housing, schooling, healthcare), and dysfunctional transactions in family, group, and community life (e.g., conflicted relationships; Gitterman, 2009). This stress can occur during these times when the individual believes that she or he does not have the strengths, resources, or capabilities to overcome the transition or pressure or deal with the event, and available resources are lacking in the environment to overcome the obstacle.

In using the life model approach, social workers need to holistically assess the client for life stressors, as well as how the client's environment is helping or hindering in alleviating the stress and returning to an adaptive person:environment fit. Interventions may then involve working with clients to change the ways in which they view themselves and the world, intervening in the environment to improve relationships and interactions, and/or intervening in the environment to challenge blocked resources or mobilize the environment to create new resources.

The life model approach can be implemented through four phases, which are described as follows (Gitterman, 2009; Gitterman & Germain, 2008). Each phase requires the social worker and client to work collaboratively in partnership.

Preparatory

This phase consists of the social worker preparing to enter the clients' lives, which will involve gathering information about clients, their environments, and their cultural influences. Expressing empathy is a critical component in this phase, which will enable the social worker to hear and read verbal and nonverbal communication as well as encourage clients to share their stories.

Initial: Getting Started

This phase involves an identification and definition of the life stressor(s) present in clients' lives. Clients should be encouraged to identify all life stressor(s) that they are experiencing and then select the ones on which they would most like to focus. In some situations, clients may be mandated to the service, and the social worker will need to address this situation with clients while also addressing any feelings of discomfort. Social workers should also discuss and identify clients' strengths, resources, and existing or previous coping skills. Once the life stressor(s) are selected to be the focus of work, the social worker and clients should establish an initial agreement that identifies goals, next steps, roles and responsibilities, and any other arrangements for the specific work together. It is important to note that addressing one life stressor often leads to an automatic alleviation of another life stressor.

Ongoing: Working Toward Goals

This phase involves working with clients and/or the environment to strengthen the person:environment fit by working through and resolving life transitional, environmental, and interpersonal stressors. A variety of interventions can be utilized at this stage depending on the identified life stressor(s). Interventions to address difficult transitions and traumatic events could include individual work, such as cognitive-behavioral therapy, solution-focused brief therapy, or motivational interviewing. Interventions to address environmental issues could include community social work, community development, or advocacy. Interventions to address dysfunctional interpersonal processes could include couples and/or family systems therapy, mediation, or advocacy.

Ending: Bringing the Shared Work and the Relationship to a Close

This phase involves a formal closure to the work together, where social workers and clients deal with feelings of ending the work, evaluate the work that was undertaken, recognize accomplishments, and develop a plan for the future.

Case Example

Michael Brown was a 17-year-old African American male who was referred to outpatient counseling services by his foster care worker at Child Protective Services (CPS). I was a social worker who provided outpatient counseling and therapeutic services to children and families who were involved with CPS. The agency in which I was employed worked from an ecological perspective and acknowledged that children and families cannot be viewed in isolation from the political, social, and cultural environments that continually shape and influence their situations and growth and development. I had this ecological perspective in mind when I received the referral for Michael and began to review his case history and the presenting problem that lead to his referral to the agency. The work with Michael followed the four phases of the life model approach from the preparation to ending phase.

Preparation

I began applying the ecological perspective in my work with Michael from the moment I received the referral. The referral stated that Michael was experiencing signs of depression, including not attending to his personal hygiene, sleeping throughout the day, not attending school, and remaining in his room when at his foster home. CPS was working with Michael to prepare him for independent living, but he was not engaging.

I quickly acknowledged that Michael was a 17-year-old African American male who was in foster care. I reflected on how our differences of age, ethnicity, and upbringing might impact on our work together and how I, as a 33-year-old White female who was single with no children, would need to take a position of curiosity with Michael in order to attempt to understand his reality and perspective (Lee & Greene, 2009). Although our differences should not have prevented us from working together effectively, I acknowledged that I would need to ensure that I did not assume I understood Michael's experiences, feelings, or reality, and I would need to consider how his life experiences, environment, and culture would influence him in a different way than how they influenced me as an adolescent. Based on this, I believed that the initial meeting with Michael should focus on building a relationship, gaining his trust, attempting to understand his reality, and assessing for life stressors when Michael was ready to talk.

Our initial meeting together took place at the agency office. Michael showed up on time, having arrived by taking the bus from his foster home to the agency by himself, which gave me an indication that Michael was willing to engage. Michael and I spent the first 15 minutes of our meeting having a general chit-chat. I asked Michael about himself, how he arrived to the agency, where he lived, and what he did during the day. Michael looked at the bookcase in my office where I kept board games and pointed out that he was very good at chess; he had won the chess tournament in middle school. During this brief 15 minutes, Michael's body began to relax, and he unfolded his arms. Although he visually appeared apprehensive of talking with me, he continued in the conversation, and I felt as if we could move into the initial phase of assessment of life stressors.

Initial Phase: Getting Started

As Michael and I continued to talk, we moved the conversation to the reason for his visit. I acknowledged that his foster care worker from CPS had referred him for counseling and asked if he could tell me why he showed up. I began to assess for life stressors, what might have contributed to the stress, and where the stress was coming from.

Michael told me that he went into foster care when he was 15 years old. He had lived with his mother, who struggled with substance misuse for many years, and he was the primary caregiver of his three brothers and two sisters; he did not know his father. He explained that the family never had any money and that any money they would receive would predominantly go to his mother's addiction. Although Michael hated his mother's drug misuse, he told me that he resorted to selling drugs in the neighborhood to make some money to buy food for his brothers and sisters. He talked about getting little sleep to make sure his brothers and sisters were fed and went to school. He described his own attendance at school as "a break."

When he was 15 years old, CPS came to his house. His mother had been gone for the past three days, and he was there alone with the five other children. The police along with CPS immediately removed him and his siblings, and he went into a foster care home on his own. Some of his siblings were placed together, but no foster care home would take all six siblings. Since being in foster care, Michael described that he only visited his siblings once a week and never saw his mother. Michael was soon to be 18 years old, and he had been told by CPS that he should start to consider independent living.

Michael began to express a genuine concern for living independently. He stated that although he pretty much "ran the house" when living with his mother, he did not know how to run a house on his own. Since being in foster care, Michael reported failing to attend school regularly because he "didn't have the energy." He described staying up late at night to play video games because that helped to keep his mind off of the anxiety of living alone and of worrying about his siblings; he stated he felt "very low." He slept well into the afternoon, missing school. He wasn't sure why he should go to school anyway because he was "so far behind." He also told me that he had no way of making money. He didn't have a job, and if he could get a job, he wasn't sure what he would be able to do.

I aimed to establish a good working relationship with Michael and to build his trust. I expressed empathy by acknowledging the difficult situations he experienced, the stress and strain of taking care of his family, and the work required to prepare for independent living. I had unconditional positive regard and remained nonjudgmental as he discussed his mother's addiction, his selling of illegal drugs, and his fears of living independently. I maintained nonverbal language that indicated a willingness to learn about Michael and asked open-ended questions and used reflections to illustrate my genuineness in hearing his story (Teater, 2010).

As Michael talked, I began to assess his current level of person:environment fit. It appeared that Michael was experiencing stress that was coming from several factors and led to a poor person:environment fit. Michael was experiencing a *difficult life transition* of moving from foster care into independent living, which was a source of stress. Michael identified that he had not been attending school, did not see that he had skills to gain a job, and did not have a place of his own. The stress from this difficult life transition appeared to be playing out through depressive symptoms, including Michael's feelings of anxiety, feeling low, not having the energy to attend school, and sleeping most of the day. Michael also appeared to not have the energy to attend to his hygiene. Michael was also experiencing *environmental stressors*. Michael was a part of the foster care system, through which he was removed from his siblings and was being "forced" (as he feels) to move into independent living. He did not believe that his school had anything to offer him because he was "too far behind" and did not have access to money or the skills to live independently.

Finally, Michael appeared to be experiencing stress from his *dysfunctional transactions* between him and his natural family. In particular, Michael explained that he was angry with his mother for putting him and his siblings in this situation. He stated he did not want to see his mother, and if he did, he'd "tell her where to go." Michael also explained that he missed his siblings and wished he could see them more. His relationship with his foster family was "fine." Michael stated that they are nice and friendly, and he knew he would stay in contact with them after he leaves.

I began to discuss with Michael how he felt his physical, social, and cultural environments were helping or hindering him in overcoming the stress he was experiencing. We discussed his physical living environment with his foster family. Michael stated that he had the attic bedroom, where he was removed from the rest of the family. Although Michael stated he liked his privacy, we discussed how this separation could also lead him to spend more time on his own. As Michael stated he enjoyed being around his foster family, I began to think that our work together might involve Michael spending more social time with his foster family, such as watching TV in the family room versus in his bedroom. Michael's social environment was both helping and hindering Michael. He felt that he had a good level of support from his foster family and his CPS social worker, but he felt that the school was not beneficial to him, he became angry when thinking about his relationship with his mother and siblings, and he felt that the legal and economic systems were pushing him to live independently without having access to income and resources to live. Finally, Michael's cultural environment had set certain expectations on him. He was the head of his family, and he felt as if he had failed his siblings by having to go into the foster care system. Michael's foster family are African Americans and were engaged in the African American community and in the local Baptist church, which Michael explained made him feel "more comfortable."

It was clear from our initial discussion that Michael was feeling a lack of strength and capability in achieving independent living and that he felt as if his environment was not providing the necessary resources to achieve this goal. Michael was feeling pressure to move into independent living and was feeling anxious and low, and he had a lack of motivation to attend school or to take care of himself. Michael stated that he was always in charge and the leader of the family, and now he needed to care for himself. This was scary for Michael; he was not sure how to do this.

Michael and I ended the initial session by identifying the main life stressors that he would like to work on in our time together. We discussed how I, within the agency, could provide counseling and support, but that we may need to pull from other sources of support, such as his foster care worker, school, and foster family, to best meet his needs. Michael identified the following three areas as the focus of work:

1. Moving into independent living (difficult life transition)
2. Going to school to gain skills for a job (environment)
3. Seeing his siblings and dealing with his feelings about his mother (dysfunctional transaction)

Based on these three areas of work, Michael and I established an agreement on goals and determined the next steps in working together. Michael identified the following four goals:

1. Attend a school that I like.
2. Get a job.
3. Find an apartment to live in.
4. Have more contact with my brothers and sisters.

Michael and I agreed to meet one hour per week for the next eight weeks, at which time we would review our work together. We identified that the work together would involve exploring and talking about his feelings of living independently, his relationship with his mother and siblings, and exploring schools, jobs, and housing to move toward independence. I hypothesized that gaining confidence and skills to live independently and dealing with feelings about Michael's mother and siblings would alleviate the depressive symptoms that he was experiencing.

Ongoing: Working Toward Goals

I met Michael over the following weeks to focus on achieving the goals that he had established in the initial session. Our initial focus was to explore new schools that Michael might find more useful to him. Before our next session, I contacted his foster care worker at CPS to discuss schooling options. She had identified a new school within the area that educated and trained students to gain skills necessary to enter the workforce within the geographic area. In particular, the school focused on computer technology, cosmetology, and housing construction. I wondered if Michael might be interested in the approach this school was taking, and I made sure to discuss it with him when we first met. I also discussed with the foster care worker Michael's concerns about his lack of contact with his siblings. I asked that the worker explore ways in which to increase their contact.

Michael arrived for our next session and, after a brief catch-up of the week, I informed him of what I had found out about his new school. Michael seemed very interested, particularly in housing construction, and commented about how he used to fix any problems in his old house. The school would teach Michael about housing construction and then allow Michael school credits for working on actual building sites, where he would make $10 per hour. Michael looked at the information and agreed that he would go to visit the school with his foster father the next week. Michael seemed pleased that a school could possibly provide him with useful skills while also allow him to make some money. I saw this as the first step in improving Michael's relationship and interaction with his environment and in achieving Michael's first three goals.

Michael and I began to discuss his ideal living space. Although he stated that he wasn't ready to move out on his own yet, he was interested in beginning to explore the options of apartments and locations. Michael described having a place that was small enough to maintain, but large enough to have his siblings come and visit. Michael expressed an interest in staying near his foster family and agreed to look through the availability of rentals near his foster home and bring some examples of potential apartments to our next meeting together. Michael stated that he would ask his foster parents to help him in his search.

Michael and I also began to discuss his feelings toward his mother and his siblings. It appeared that his dysfunctional relationship was greatly prohibiting Michael's growth and development and his ability to engage with his environment. Michael did not want to meet or see his mother, but he stated that there were many things he would "like to say to her." I asked Michael if he would be willing to write a letter to his mother expressing his feelings and to bring it to our next session together versus mailing it to his mother. Michael agreed to the task.

Over the following weeks, Michael began to move toward accomplishing his four goals and enhancing his person:environment fit. Michael was able to keep to tasks, particularly with the support from his social environment. His foster parents had become very concerned about Michael prior to our initial meeting and, therefore, they supported Michael in the tasks and decisions he had to make. Michael had visited the vocational school and subsequently enrolled in the construction course. He was undertaking the necessary classes before starting on his first construction job. Michael had also identified an apartment complex near his foster family that he hoped to move into once he had "some money saved." The foster care worker at CPS had enrolled Michael in an independent living course and was supporting him through this process.

The main work in our sessions involved his relationships and feelings with his mother. Each week Michael was able to express more about his anger toward his mother and how this was impacting his ability to "move on in life." Michael stated he would never have a relationship with his mother, but over the weeks he was able to accept his feelings and to put them aside so they did not keep him from moving forward. Although Michael acknowledged that he might have to revisit the feelings on occasion, he was not going to allow his mother to limit him any further. Finally, the foster care worker at CPS was able to increase Michael's visits with his siblings from once to twice per week, and she also indicated that Michael may be able to have visits and overnight stays when he moves into his new apartment.

Ending: Bringing the Shared Work and the Relationship to a Close

At the end of the eight weeks, Michael and I met to review the four goals that he had set, to evaluate our work together, and to acknowledge Michael's accomplishments. Michael reported he was attending a school that he liked and that the school was giving him the skills necessary in order to gain employment. Michael had just started his first construction assignment, and he reported that he felt comfortable in the environment and was "learning new things every day." Michael felt challenged by this type of work, which seemed to be contributing to his growth and development and was creating a more adaptive person:environment fit. I acknowledged Michael's regular attendance at the school and the start of his first construction job. Michael was earning $10 per hour for his work, and he was able to save most of his money, which was going toward his new apartment. This source of employment seemed to fit Michael's needs because he was doing something he enjoyed and was challenged by, but it also met the need of providing income.

Michael's goal of finding an apartment was an ongoing process. Michael had identified an apartment complex near his foster family where he would like to live. Michael was still apprehensive about moving out on his own, and because of this, Michael had negotiated that he would apply for an apartment at the complex in three months' time. His foster care worker would continue to work with Michael on independent living skills and work with Michael and his foster family to ensure that he had all the material resources in place before he made the move. The foster family also reassured Michael that they would be a source of support when he moved out. Michael reported feeling confident that his social environment was supporting him in a strong way that would lead to a physical environment that fully meets his needs. I acknowledged that moving out independently was a big step, but Michael was making great progress toward achieving his goal.

Finally, Michael and I had spent a lot of time talking through his feelings toward his mother. Although Michael acknowledged he would continue to struggle with his feelings of anger, he felt more capable of addressing his feelings when they arose. He felt more at peace with himself, and since learning that he would see his siblings more often, he felt less angry, less anxious, and less depressed. Michael reported that he had more energy and as if he could "see a future."

The work together involved not only talking with Michael to change his perceptions and behaviors in regard to attending school, looking for a job and an apartment, and dealing with his feelings regarding his mother, but also involved an intervention into Michael's environment, where an appropriate school had to be identified that could best meet Michael's needs and provide the necessary resources to allow him to grow and develop. The interventions took place while also considering Michael's immediate social environment of his foster family and foster care worker—those individuals whom Michael trusted the most and who could best assist in ensuring that Michael and his environment had the most productive and supportive exchange. Michael and I both reflected on how the work together had been successful, but we also acknowledged that there are difficult challenges along life's path. Together, we identified Michael's personal strengths and environmental resources he could draw upon when things began to appear too stressful.

REFERENCES

Gitterman, A. (2009). The life model. In A. Roberts (Ed.), *The social workers' desk reference* (2nd ed., pp. 231–234). New York, NY: Oxford University Press.

Gitterman, A., & Germain, C. B. (2008). *The life model of social work practice: Advances in theory and practice* (3rd ed.). New York, NY: Columbia University Press.

Lee, M. Y., & Greene, G. J. (2009). Using social constructivism in social work practice. In A. R. Roberts (Ed.), *The social workers' desk reference* (2nd ed., pp. 143–149). New York, NY: Oxford University Press.

Teater, B. (2010). *An introduction to applying social work theories and methods*. Maidenhead, UK: Open University Press.

Case Study 2-2

Social Learning Theory in the Treatment of Phobic Disorders

Bruce A. Thyer

T his case study uses various components of social learning theory in successfully helping a client with a phobic disorder. The client left treatment with a sense of accomplishment and a set of new strategies and behaviors that could be used in future situations with similar circumstances.

Questions
1. How does social learning theory explain the development of phobic disorders?
2. What treatment strategies are used to help the client change his phobic behaviors?
3. What factors do you believe led to the successful outcome in this case?
4. How was the client involved in the treatment planning?

SOCIAL LEARNING THEORY IN THE TREATMENT OF PHOBIC DISORDERS

I closed the file and sat back in my chair, reflecting on the materials I had just finished reviewing: client's name, Mr. Donald Scott, age 54, married for 30 years to his present wife, and employed for more than 25 years at an automobile manufacturing plant outside of Detroit, Michigan. All potential clients of our busy Anxiety Disorders Program completed and mailed in an extensive questionnaire packet for review prior to their first appointment. In these materials, Mr. Scott indicated that his presenting problem was being "terrified of people," and my quick review of his Fear Survey Schedule and Symptom Checklist 90-R responses certainly supported that view.

The phone buzzed, and my secretary told me that Mr. Scott was in the waiting room. As I entered the room, Mr. Scott and his wife looked up. They were sitting close together listlessly flipping through the tattered magazines on the table in front of them. I introduced myself, asked Mr. Scott to accompany me to my office, and suggested to his wife that she might find it more comfortable to wait in the hospital cafeteria down the hall. She agreed and said that she would go have a cup of coffee, promising Mr. Scott to be back in an hour, the time I estimated that he and I would be together.

Mr. Scott sat in the indicated chair alongside my desk, and I went into my routine spiel about who I was, my background, and the operation of the Anxiety Disorders Program, an interdisciplinary outpatient treatment clinic affiliated with the Department of Psychiatry at the University of Michigan Hospitals in Ann Arbor. I asked him to tell me why he had come to our clinic, and his story went as follows.

He had always been a somewhat nervous fellow, and for almost his whole life he had felt extremely uncomfortable around other people. His fears were so extreme that, in the presence of others, unless he had some secure object to sit on or lean against, he would develop very obvious tremors in his arms and legs. This made people stare at him, leading to a vicious cycle of anxiety feeding on itself. He had adapted to these fears by restricting his social life to a very great extent. He never went out to parties, had discontinued receiving communion at church (since this involved standing in line), and would not go to fast-food restaurants or to bank tellers or attend popular movies, all situations involving standing in lines with others present. His wife was distressed, not only for him but because her own social life was correspondingly curtailed. He was viewed by his coworkers and acquaintances as somewhat of a curmudgeon.

His story took more than 20 minutes to tell. He was articulate, earnest, and clearly at his wit's end. He knew he wasn't crazy, he said, but he felt like he acted that way sometimes. I asked him if he had anything else to add to his description of his difficulty. He did not, so I proceeded to inquire about some other possibly important features. I learned that if no one else was nearby—for example, if Mr. Scott was in the woods—he could walk alone or with his wife without discomfort or support. If approached at work by his supervisor, Mr. Scott could lean against his workbench and remain free from distress, but if the same person approached him in the middle of the room, after a few moments of conversation Mr. Scott could feel "the shakes" coming on and would invent some excuse to sit down or scuttle over to the wall and lean against it.

Apparently this problem had been present for years, with no sign of its lessening. He was moderately depressed over these circumstances but was unequivocal that the social fears came first. He was convinced that if he could overcome them he would no longer be depressed.

By now I was reasonably sure that Mr. Scott met the DSM-III criteria for social phobia (at the time I treated Mr. Scott, the DSM-III was the most current version available). I took down the worn green book from the shelf over my desk and read the relevant passage aloud to him: "A persistent, irrational fear of, and compelling desire to avoid, a situation in which the individual is exposed to possible scrutiny by others and fears that he or she may act in a way that will be humiliating or embarrassing" (American Psychiatric Association, 1980, p. 228). "Does any of that sound familiar?" I asked. Mr. Scott's face lit up. "Do you mean that there are other people like me?" I assured him that such was indeed the case and proceeded with further inquiries.

"As best as you can recollect, when or how did this problem with shaking develop?" Well, he knew all right; it was 35 years ago, when he was in the Army. During a morning roll call, all of the troops in his unit were assembled at attention when, suddenly, Mr. Scott's commanding officer stomped up and planted himself in front of Mr. Scott, verbally abusing him in a stentorian voice for all to hear, ostensibly because of some infraction Mr. Scott had committed. The abuse was both obscene and prolonged and was listened to avidly by the other soldiers. Dictates of military discipline prevented Mr. Scott from replying, even though, as it subsequently emerged, the commanding officer had picked the wrong man! It was not Mr. Scott who had committed the infraction but some other G.I. Finally the officer stormed off, leaving a quivering Private Scott feeling horribly humiliated and enraged at the unjustness of it all.

Ever since then, according to my client, face-to-face contact with others made him feel extremely upset and tremulous. Further questions revealed that the shaking was not evoked by small children, only by adults. Otherwise, it reliably occurred every time he stood face-to-face and unsupported with someone present (except for his wife and children). Apart from these social circumstances, the shaking never appeared. "What do you think would happen, Mr. Scott, if you found yourself forced to stand in front of someone without the opportunity to escape? Have you ever tried that?" "No!" he replied. "I think that would drive me out of my mind!"

Our time was about up, so I informed Mr. Scott that he had been most helpful and that I thought it was likely we could assist him to overcome his problem of shaking. We arranged a second appointment for the following week. I also gave him a copy of *Living with Fear*, a self-help book by Marks (1978), which describes in easy-to-understand language the various kinds of phobias and their behavioral treatments based on social learning theory.

In writing up my notes, it seemed to me unlikely that Mr. Scott's tremulousness could be attributable to an organic problem, such as vestibular dysfunction, or to some form of movement disorder, such as Parkinson's disease. The specificity of the controlling stimuli argued against that possibility. Although there were some symptomatic features superficially similar to agoraphobia, the absence of spontaneous panic attacks excluded both panic disorder or agoraphobia as differential diagnoses. He was not taking any medications with tremulous side effects, and he was in good physical health.

I had not conducted a formal so-called mental status examination with Mr. Scott, because it was obvious from his written materials and our interview that he was well oriented and was not psychotic or cognitively impaired. I knew from the literature on the etiology of phobic disorders that his case was fairly typical: Most individuals who meet the criteria for simple or social phobia report that the onset of their fears was associated with a traumatic experience with the objects or situations they had come to fear (Ost & Hugdahl, 1981). This seemed likely in Mr. Scott's case. He could recall the precipitating event clearly, and the problem had never occurred prior to the episode in the Army. He was a high-functioning person in virtually all areas of his life, excluding those related to his fears. There was no evidence of marital or family distress, apart from that engendered by his phobia.

CONCEPTUAL FRAMEWORK

I believed that it was reasonable to hypothesize that Mr. Scott's social fears were generated through respondent (i.e., Pavlovian) conditioning processes. An initially neutral stimulus (having someone stand in front of him) was paired with an extremely aversive event (humiliation, embarrassment, lack of opportunity to respond). This association resulted in the formerly neutral stimulus coming to elicit reactions similar to those he experienced during the initial aversive event. In more technical terminology, the event of face-to-face confrontation changed from an unconditioned stimulus to a conditioned one and came to elicit a conditioned response (anxiousness, tremors, and so on) similar to his unconditioned response following his being verbally attacked (see Thyer, 2012, for a review of the principles of respondent learning).

Such powerful and enduring effects following one-trial learning have been well demonstrated in laboratory conditioning research with human beings (Malloy & Levis, 1988) and are extensively supported by both formal studies on the etiologies of clinical phobics and at the level of anecdotal reports (Marks, 1987; Ost & Hugdahl, 1981). Once a conditioned fear reaction of this nature is set up, then operant conditioning processes come into play. Every time Mr. Scott successfully *avoided or escaped* from a face-to-face interaction during which he felt anxious, it is possible that the relief he felt accompanying such escape or avoidance *negatively reinforced* such behaviors. Negative reinforcement (which is not the same thing as punishment) is the process whereby behaviors are strengthened by the removal of aversive states or events. Everyday examples include turning down the volume of excessively loud or obnoxious music, putting on sunglasses in bright light, removing a chafing shoe, and so forth. Such acts are likely to be strengthened by their effectiveness in providing some form of relief. Similarly, Mr. Scott's escape and avoidance behavior, including holding onto secure objects or leaning on tables, chairs, or walls, provided him with relief from the noxious state of severe anxiety/agitation. Such behaviors would be correspondingly perpetuated, perhaps for very long periods. Wong (2012) provides an excellent recent review of operant theory for use in social work practice, as a means of conceptualizing client problems, and for construing how treatments may work.

The practice-research literature has clearly shown that the treatment of choice for phobic disorders is a clinical procedure known as real-life exposure therapy (Hoffman, 2010; McEvoy, Nathan, Rapee, & Campbell, 2012; Thyer & Pignotti, 2009). Exposure therapy is effective in producing substantial therapeutic gains for between 80 and 90% of clinical phobics, improving not only behavioral avoidance but subjective fears and physiological arousal as well. Such gains are well maintained, with controlled follow-up studies often lasting for years. Relapse following exposure therapy is low, and there is no evidence of the development of symptom substitution (Marks, 1987; Mortberg, Clark, & Bejerot, 2011). I also knew that exposure therapy is usually quite well tolerated, poses few side effects, and is highly acceptable to most clients if it is properly explained and conducted.

It seemed to me that exposure therapy was the first treatment option I should explore with Mr. Scott. In the event it would prove unacceptable to him, I was prepared to offer a program of exposure conducted in fantasy or of more traditional (and labor-intensive) systematic desensitization. The patient self-help book I had asked Mr. Scott to read, *Living with Fear*, describes the theory and conduct of real-life exposure therapy, so I knew he would have some background in what I was proposing when he returned for his next visit. More recently, exposure therapy has been shown to be equivalently effective when delivered with a live therapist, or via the Internet. Internet-based treatment offers great promise in making effective psychosocial treatments more widely available to clients such as Mr. Scott (Andrews, Davies, & Titov, 2011).

THE TREATMENT PROCESS

Mr. Scott arrived on time for his next appointment; he had read the book and was full of questions. I first dealt with his questions and then described in easy-to-understand language how I viewed the nature of his problem. I outlined my rationale for beginning with a course of exposure therapy, if he was agreeable. I also explained treatment alternatives but noted that they were liable to take much longer and be somewhat less effective. I assured him that there would be no tricks or surprises, that everything would be explained to him in advance, and that his permission would be obtained prior to introduction of new levels of exposure. Furthermore, he could terminate a session any time he felt it necessary.

With these reassurances, he was ready to proceed. After explaining the procedures, we began as follows: I pushed all of the office furniture against the walls, leaving an open area about 8-by-8-feet square. I described to Mr. Scott the use of the subjective anxiety scale, whereby he could roughly quantify his feelings on a 0 (feeling completely relaxed) to 100 (absolutely panic-stricken, as frightened as he had ever been in his life) scale. Such scales are commonly used in social work practice (Hudson & Thyer, 1987), and this particular one has reasonably good convergent validity, correlating well with physiological measures of arousal (Thyer, Papsdorf, Davis, & Vallecorsa, 1984).

As I sat in my chair, I had Mr. Scott stand in the center of the room, unsupported. He was comfortable. I then obtained his permission to stand directly in front of him about 1 foot away. Mr. Scott was about 5 feet 8 inches tall, whereas I am a little over 6 feet tall, so I more or less loomed over him. Within a few moments a remarkable transformation came over my client. He developed obvious tremors in his hands, arms, and knees and became quite agitated. "See," he said. "It's always like this; I have to sit down!" I was appropriately supportive and encouraged him to remain standing there, which he did with a great deal of difficulty. Profuse perspiration broke out on his forehead, and he made several abortive movements toward the wall. I kept up a running chatter about how well he was doing, and explained that the reaction would soon subside if he would only give it time. I asked him to reflect on and tell me about his internal sensations, and every two minutes I had him rate his level of anxiety using the 0 to 100 scale.

As social learning theory predicted, Mr. Scott's anxiety reaction soon began to subside. After about 12 minutes, the tremors began to diminish, the sweating stopped, and he began to feel better. I encouraged him to note these reactions, and he was quite astounded when, after 20 minutes, he found himself relatively calm and relaxed yet had not had to resort to any external means of support to lean on or to sit down. "I can't believe it! I haven't done this in over 30 years, to stand in front of someone and not shake!"

I terminated the exposure procedure after some 20 minutes had passed, and we sat down over a cup of tea to process what had happened. I once again explained to him how respondent (i.e., Pavlovian) theory would predict how a conditioned response (his shaking and other upsetting reactions) would slowly undergo extinction if the conditioned stimulus (someone standing in front of him) were constantly repeated or continued. The difference, I noted, between the experience he had just undergone with me and the routine episodes of exposure he encountered in everyday life was that the exposure was prolonged until he was calm and that operant avoidance behaviors (leaning on a wall, fleeing the situation, sitting on a chair, and so on) were not permitted to occur. By repeating such experiences in progressively more difficult and realistic life situations, I thought he would be able to overcome his social fears, irrespective of their severity or duration.

His skepticism had vanished, because he could see that substantial therapeutic changes had literally occurred before his very eyes. He was almost euphoric as we made our third appointment (second treatment session) for the following week. In this second treatment session, I basically repeated the procedure employed the previous week, and then did so again during our third session. I recorded Mr. Scott's subjective anxiety rating during each of these therapeutic trials, and the data are depicted in Figure 2.1. As can be seen, the severity of Mr. Scott's peak anxiety reactions declined over the course of the sessions until this exposure technique elicited very little response by the third trial.

Over the next few weeks, I moved Mr. Scott from the confines of the consulting room to more real-world contexts. I reserved the private use of a large instructional auditorium and repeated the exposure process of me standing in front of him, this time with Mr. Scott being dozens of feet from any means of support. I went with him to nearby movies on dollar night, when the lines stretched around the block. I had us take our place at the end of the slowly moving line and engaged my client in conversation. "Could you tell me what your worst fears would be in this situation?" "Sure, I am afraid I would start to shake and that people would notice and laugh at me." "OK, let's see what would actually happen. I will begin to shake like you used to as we stand here, and you carefully watch the reactions of others. Will you do that?" With his consent I began to display a palsylike reaction in my crooked right arm as we shuffled up the line. After we got to the ticket window several minutes later I pulled Mr. Scott out of line and we rejoined it at its end, repeating the exposure cycle. "Well," I asked, "what did

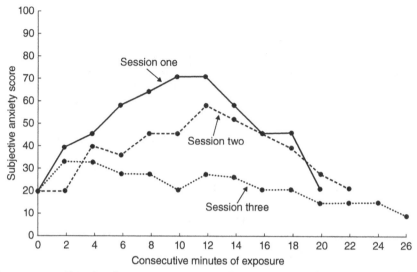

Figure 2.1 Client's subjective responses to three consecutive sessions of exposure therapy for a social phobia. (From *Treating anxiety disorders: A guide for human service professionals*, by B. A. Thyer, 1987, Newbury Park, CA: Sage.)

they do?" "Most people ignored you, or if they noticed they looked away." "Yes, that was my impression also. Now let's try something else. I would like you to deliberately shake like you used to, to try and bring attention to yourself, so you can gain a more realistic idea of how people would respond." With a little coaxing he complied, and of course nothing untoward happened.

After our success at the movies, I asked Mr. Scott to undertake some carefully structured homework assignments relating to his self-exposure to situations he formerly avoided. For example, I asked him to go to church and to sit in the back and join the communion line just before the communion service was over, when the line was at its shortest, then to begin joining the line when it was a little longer at subsequent services.

He came back for a few more scheduled exposure sessions with me. For example, we went to McDonald's during the lunch rush and stood in the lines. After one trial with me, I had Mr. Scott go through the line alone and buy a drink, fries, and a burger. All progressed relatively smoothly. At his own initiative, he attended a wedding and stood in the receiving line. He sought out coworkers and engaged them in conversation while carefully refraining from any avoidance behaviors. I gradually faded my involvement in Mr. Scott's treatment: He came to see me a few more times, wherein I basically served as a consultant to his own self-exposure homework tasks; then we had a few appointments by telephone; and finally I was simply available as necessary.

Three years later, I tried to call Mr. Scott at home one evening, but he was not there. I spoke with his wife instead, who informed me, after I identified myself, that he was out with his bowling league! She remarked that he seemed like a changed man, for the better; that they now had an active social life; and that he was no longer troubled by "the shakes."

CONCLUSIONS

I believe that as a case example Mr. Scott's story reasonably illustrates the integration of social learning theory into social work practice. The etiology and maintenance of the client's problem was conceptualized in terms of the principles of both respondent and operant learning processes. Similarly, the treatment program was developed with these processes in view, and the success of social work intervention corroborated (but could not confirm) the validity of these etiological hypotheses. Treatment involved elements of respondent conditioning (prolonged exposure of a conditioned stimulus resulted in the extinction of the conditioned response) and operant conditioning (refraining from negatively reinforced avoidance behaviors, such as seeking support or sitting down, that resulted in the operant extinction of these actions as well). Throughout treatment I modeled reactions I wished Mr. Scott to develop and used his realistic observations of how people reacted to his and my deliberate shaking in a therapeutic manner.

The client was thoroughly involved in treatment. He was given appropriate reading materials describing the nature and treatment of problems similar to his. These were discussed in our sessions, and I was open and aboveboard in all respects with regard to how I thought we should proceed. I obtained his consent for all the procedures used prior to their employment and facilitated the generalization and maintenance of treatment gains by taking the therapeutic process out of the confines of the consulting room and into the real-world contexts of Mr. Scott's own life. I gradually faded my own involvement in the active management of the case as Mr. Scott undertook more of the therapeutic tasks on his own.

In keeping with the tenets of contemporary clinical social work practice, I based my treatment program on the empirically based practice-research literature and employed rudimentary single-case evaluation procedures to help ascertain that Mr. Scott had benefited from treatment. In retrospect, I judge the approach I used with Mr. Scott to be very congruent with the five-step process of evidence-based practice (EBP):

1. I crafted an answerable question ("What are effective treatments for social phobia?")
2. I consulted the highest available research evidence pertaining to effective treatments for clients with social phobias.
3. I critically reviewed this literature to judge its potential applicability to Mr. Scott's situation.
4. In conjunction with Mr. Scott, we agreed to and completed a treatment program, drawing on this practice-research literature, his own preferences, my own clinical skills, relevant ethical standards, and available resources.
5. And I used a simple form of single-subject research design to help evaluate the initial effectiveness of treatment.

Although it was not a formal component of the EBP process model, my etiological conceptualization of the client's problem and of the possible mechanism for how the treatment may work was thoroughly grounded in contemporary social learning theory. Although the case seems relatively straightforward, it is a mistake to conclude that behavioral social work practice requires any lesser degree of clinical skill and acumen or complexity of conceptualization than other approaches to practice. Conventional therapeutic relationship variables are cultivated, but their role is seen more as adjunctive to treatment than as a central therapeutic mechanism.

REFERENCES

American Psychiatric Association. (1980). *Diagnostic and statistical manual of mental disorders* (3rd ed.). Washington, DC: American Psychiatric Press.

Andrews, G., Davies, M., & Titov, N. (2011). Effectiveness randomized controlled trial of face to face versus Internet cognitive behavior therapy for social phobia. *Australian and New Zealand Journal of Psychiatry, 45,* 337–340.

Hoffman, S. G. (2010). Recent advances in the psychosocial treatment of Social Anxiety Disorder. *Depression and Anxiety, 27,* 1073–1076.

Hudson, W. W., & Thyer, B. A. (1987). Research measures and indices in direct practice. In A. Minahan (Ed.), *Encyclopedia of social work* (pp. 487–498). Washington, DC: National Association of Social Workers.

Malloy, P., & Levis, D. J. (1988). A laboratory demonstration of persistent human avoidance. *Behavior Therapy, 19,* 229–241.

Marks, I. M. (1978). *Living with fear.* New York, NY: McGraw-Hill.

Marks, I. M. (1987). *Fears, phobias and rituals.* New York, NY: Oxford University Press.

McEvoy, P. M., Nathan, P., Rapee, R. M., & Campbell, B. N. (2012). Cognitive behavioural group therapy for social phobia: Evidence of transportability to community clinics. *Behaviour Research and Therapy, 50,* 258–265.

Mortberg, E., Clark, D. M., & Bejerot, S. (2011). Intensive group cognitive therapy and individual cognitive therapy for social phobia: Sustained improvement at 5-year follow-up. *Journal of Anxiety Disorders, 25,* 994–1000.

Ost, L., & Hugdahl, K. (1981). Acquisition of phobias and anxiety response patterns in clinical patients. *Behaviour Research and Therapy, 19,* 439–447.

Thyer, B. A. (2012). Respondent learning theory. In B. A. Thyer, C. N. Dulmus, & K. M. Sowers (Eds.), *Human behavior in the social environment: Theories for social work practice* (pp. 47–81). Hoboken, NJ: Wiley.

Thyer, B. A., Papsdorf, J. D., Davis, R., & Vallecorsa, S. (1984). Autonomic correlates of the subjective anxiety scale. *Journal of Behavior Therapy and Experimental Psychiatry, 15,* 3–7.

Thyer, B. A., & Pignotti, M. (2009). Treatment plans for clients with Social Phobia. In A. R. Roberts (Ed.), *Social workers' desk reference* (2nd ed., pp. 1115–1120). New York, NY: Oxford University Press.

Wong, S. E. (2012). Operant theory. In B. A. Thyer, C. N. Dulmus, & K. M. Sowers (Eds.), *Human behavior in the social environment: Theories for social work practice* (pp. 83–123). Hoboken, NJ: Wiley.

Case Study 2-3

Relational Theory With a Young Adult Experiencing Interpersonal Problems

JOSEPH WALSH

This case uses relational theory in the approach to practice and demonstrates how this model uses the relational context as part of the therapy.

Questions

1. What are the underlying assumptions of relational theory?
2. How is relational theory different from or similar to other theories?
3. How was the relational context used to help this client?
4. How does this case study demonstrate the role of theory in social work practice?

Ever since I worked as a psychiatric hospital ward technician, my supervisors have told me I'm "good at establishing relationships" with challenging clients. I got along well with our inpatients who had serious psychotic, mood, and personality disorders. When I got my Master's degree in social work, I learned a variety of intervention strategies but was always most comfortable providing what I came to know as "ego reflective" interventions (Goldstein, 1995). From this I eventually developed an interest in relational theory. I don't think these are better ways to practice than any other approach, but they are what I am drawn to. What follows is an illustration of how I utilized relational theory while working with a young female who was experiencing chronic depression and interpersonal problems. (I also incorporated cognitive and behavioral interventions into our work.) Before I introduce the client, however, I will describe the theory behind my intervention.

RELATIONAL THEORY

Relational theory incorporates elements of the psychodynamic, object relations, and interpersonal perspectives (Borden, 2009). It asserts that the basic human tendency (or drive) is toward relationships with others, and our personalities are structured through interactions with significant others. Relational theory incorporates a strong value of supporting diversity in human experience and avoiding the pathologizing of differences. The social worker continuously evaluates the relational context with regard to diversity issues such as age, race, and gender.

Relational theory assumes that all patterns of behavior are learned in the give-and-take of relational life and are adaptive ways of negotiating experience in the context of our need to elicit care from, and provide care for, others. Consistent with object relations concepts, serious relationship problems are seen as self-perpetuating because people have a tendency to preserve continuity in their interpersonal worlds. What is new is threatening because it lays beyond the bounds of their experience, in which they recognize themselves as cohesive beings.

The relational perspective enriches the concept of empathy by adding the notion of mutuality. The ability to participate in a mutual relationship through empathic communication contributes to the client's growth. Contrary to traditional analytic notions, the relational social worker expresses a range of thoughts and feelings "in the moment" with the client to facilitate their mutual connection (Freedberg, 2007). Intervention focuses on here-and-now situations in the client's life, including those involving the social worker and client. Current social work literature reflects diverse views regarding the degree to which practitioners should self-disclose with their clients, but the general consensus calls for the worker to maintain a neutral, objective persona (Walsh, 2000). In relational theory, however, the more the worker expends energy on keeping parts of herself or himself out of the process, the more rigid and less genuine he or she will be with the client. Relational theorists encourage the social worker's natural, authentic manner of engagement with the client, the strategic use of self-disclosure, and the encouragement of the client to regularly comment on the intervention process. The social worker also tries to avoid relegating the two parties into dominant and subordinate roles.

To expand on these points, relational theory incorporates a major focus on the intersubjective basis of self-development (Perlman & Brandell, 2011). There is a mutual recognition of the self and the other as people with unique experiences and differences, and each person influences the other in conscious and unconscious ways. This does not imply a neglect of appropriate boundaries, however, as the social worker must maintain a clear sense of self while engaged in the emotional and cognitive integration necessary for empathy to be effective. The intervention process features many *enactments*, or discussions about the ways in which the social worker and client are relating to one another. Through this process, the client gradually becomes able to recognize other people's uniqueness, developing capacities for sensitivity and a tolerance of difference. The client is freed from the pull of problematic relationship patterns.

From the relational perspective, the limitations of manualized treatment becomes clear. Still, despite its limitations with regard to generalizable validation, the assumptions of relational theory are consistent with the findings of the American Psychological Association (APA) on the significance of the worker/client relationship. The APA has systematically evaluated the significance of the practitioner/client relationship in determining intervention effectiveness and concluded through a series of meta-analyses that several relationship variables are *demonstrably* and *probably* effective. (Norcross & Wampold, 2011). Another review concluded that the quality of the worker/client relationship, in combination with the resources of the client (extratherapeutic variables), accounts for a majority of the variance in intervention outcomes (Miller, Duncan, & Hubble, 2005).

With this overview I will now introduce Chloe, whom I saw over a period of 18 months at a community mental health center.

The Client

Chloe was a 25-year-old Caucasian female seeking therapy for depression and anxiety. She lived with her same-age boyfriend in a small apartment and described the one-year relationship as "steady and good." Chloe had an undergraduate degree in art and worked two part-time jobs as an animator. She was nicely but casually groomed with good eye contact.

The Presenting Problems

Chloe struggled with depression, feelings of self-hatred, and high social anxiety. She became tearful when describing how she felt paralyzed "all the time," unable to make decisions in her personal and work lives, and fearing rejection when "putting herself out there," or taking chances. She wanted to feel "competent, successful, and worth something." Chloe always compared herself negatively to others and worried obsessively about what they thought of her. Her anxiety was so great that when speaking with someone new, she became overwhelmed to the point that she didn't hear what they were saying. She struggled with remembering names, people, and conversations. Chloe also doubted her competence as an artist, although she did well in school and got regular compliments about her work. She had a poor work history, mostly because of interpersonal problems with coworkers and employers. She said they "didn't like" her, and she always wound up having arguments with them.

Chloe felt guilty for seeking help, saying "others have experienced worse." She felt badly about wanting others to feel sympathy for what she has gone through. She was not suicidal but explained that she was "self-destructive"—picking at her skin (arms, chest, and legs) and leaving bruises in the process. At times she bit her nails short and then stuck pins beneath them to pull out the skin. She explained that these behaviors made her "feel better."

Chloe had a group of casual friends, but she said they were "messed-up people" who drank excessively and behaved irresponsibly, and "I don't want to be like that anymore." For most of the past two years, Chloe had been sporadically unemployed and homeless, "couch surfing" with friends and acquaintances. When she was not working, she slept 13 to 14 hours per day and spent most of her time "just trying to get the basics done." She reported drinking heavily as well, approximately 20 drinks per week of beer and wine. She had had several boyfriends before the current one, but she said "they were bad relationships; I always felt neglected and demeaned." At this time Chloe reported so much anxiety that she was having trouble leaving the house.

Chloe's goals were to improve her confidence and self-esteem, plan a future, and move forward. She also wanted to work on resolving her past negative experiences but worried that doing so would be painful. She stated: "My life would be so much better if I could just forget the past." Chloe reported that her primary conflicted relationship was with her mother, with whom she has always had a tumultuous relationship.

The Client's Personal History

Chloe was born in an urban area two hours away. Her parents had never married; she was the product of a brief affair. Chloe and her mother lived with her maternal grandparents until she was 11 years old. She said her mother was preoccupied with her own social life and did not take care of her. She described her mother and home life as "awful." Chloe remembers her mother as attending only to her own interests (getting a college degree and becoming a realtor). She recalled her mother as always berating her, implying that having Chloe had almost ruined her life. ("I could have been so much more if it wasn't for you.") She never saw her biological father but expressed great fondness for her grandparents, especially her grandfather who cared very much for her. Chloe's mother married when Chloe was 11 and had a son, who was now 14 years old and living with their mother. They moved to a house in a small town an hour away from the grandparents. She had a good relationship with her brother, and said her stepdad had been "okay" but not always a responsible influence, as he often bought Chloe and her friends alcohol and tobacco when they were in high school. The step-father died of a heart attack when Chloe was 19. She was sad but "not overwhelmed" by the loss.

Chloe was always awkward and insecure around others. She hated school and felt out of place there. She was once hospitalized for depression at age 14 after a suicide attempt. Chloe had a series of boyfriends beginning in mid-adolescence, but "they were always thoughtless and critical" of her. She never trusted her boyfriends and expected the worst of them, which is what she got. Chloe believed she had "wised up" in the past year, however, recognizing that she wants a more stable lifestyle. However, she stated, "I'm only attracted to men who are bad for me, and I'm not attracted to men who might be good to me." Her current boyfriend fell into the latter category. "I'm not attracted to him, and I'm always looking for someone else, but maybe I just have to settle for a dull life."

My Diagnostic Impressions

From a relational theory perspective, it seemed that Chloe had never formed a healthy attachment to her mother, the primary significant other throughout her childhood and adolescence, and never had a stable father figure (despite her relationship with her grandfather). This set in motion a pattern of Chloe's feeling badly about herself, unworthy of care, and finding herself in relationships with others, both friends and romantic partners, who played out the role of her mother, being neglectful and verbally abusive. She could never allow herself to risk emotional intimacy with others for fear of being rejected, even though she desperately desired being loved and cared for. Chloe's pattern included looking to sexual activity as her only reliable means of feeling connected to others. Unlike some persons with interpersonal problems, Chloe never developed a "surface competence" and was thus always uncomfortable around others. Her situation was hindered in some ways by her physical attractiveness. That is, she was regularly pursued by young men and found opportunities for romantic relationships, but these men were ultimately rejecting of her.

Relational theory does not place great importance on the DSM diagnostic process (Bachant, Lynch, & Richards, 1995). All people are truly unique and defined in terms of their relationships, and the process of labeling reduces each person to a type. Nevertheless, this practice was required at our agency, and I diagnosed Chloe as having chronic major depression and generalized anxiety disorder. She met the criteria for a personality disorder, but I didn't have the heart to include it (evidence of my transference) and instead listed "borderline personality traits" on Axis II. I discussed all of these diagnoses with Chloe, showing her the DSM criteria to get her opinions and emphasizing that they only represented general behavior summaries and did not capture her individuality. She actually was relieved to "qualify" for receiving help.

As a relational practitioner, I needed to monitor my own interpersonal patterns as they played out with Chloe. I have always enjoyed working with clients who experience interpersonal problems because it seems that the dilemma of seeking intimacy while preserving autonomy is universal in this culture. I quickly came to like Chloe for her personal qualities as well. She was an artist, which always impresses me, was eager to receive help (always coming on time), and I perceived a basic goodness in her. That is, despite her traumas, conflicts, and mistrust of others, she continually expressed a sincere desire to experience mutually caring relationships. Still, I was unsure of my suitability to work with Chloe because I was a Caucasian male (although 20 years older than she was), and I wondered if she would be able to confide in and trust me. I asked her about this at our first session and, while agreeing that this was a concern, Chloe said she would "give it a try." I thought that if she could learn to connect with a male on a nonsexual basis, perhaps in my case as a father figure, then she might experience interpersonal growth. I should add that while I did perceive Chloe as being physically attractive, I had no concerns about this fact interfering with my ability to work with her because of the age difference and my own life situation. I was aware, though, that I am sometimes inclined to "rescue" clients with whom I feel connected, so I would need to be careful about letting my positive feelings cloud my judgment as we worked together.

Intervention

My 18-month intervention with Chloe focused on four themes. I will summarize them separately, although they overlapped considerably.

Managing Her Anxiety

Chloe wanted to begin our work by addressing her incapacitating social anxiety. I readily agreed to this task focus, partly because clients with avoidant interpersonal styles sometimes feel threatened by a practitioner's analyzing their relationship patterns right away. Chloe's small household had become a safe haven from which she rarely ventured alone. She was terrified of encountering any strangers on the street who would look at her and "realize (she was) a loser." It was even difficult for Chloe to sit in her car at a stoplight because she assumed the driver in the next lane was gazing at her critically. Together we worked out a series of cognitive-behavioral tasks (all of which I initiated, but she approved) for her to practice during our sessions and on her own, including exposure (gradually becoming able to go outdoors, walk down the street, and sit in the presence of others), relaxation and mindfulness strategies (for which I made copies of resources from a book), self-talk (writing down scripts of what she could tell herself when encountering others to minimize the influence of her distortions), and thought substitution (the triple-column technique).

We worked extensively on her written and verbal communication skills. Chloe often damaged relationships with her employers by not being able to speak effectively with them about her work concerns. She left a generally negative impression on her employers, who wrongly perceived her as being unenthusiastic about her work. I encouraged Chloe, and helped her, to write scripts of what she wanted to say to others in advance of important meetings. The two of us engaged in much role-play in these areas. I also helped Chloe with her job search skills, reviewing her applications and making suggestions about how she presented herself in cover letters and on her resume.

Chloe enjoyed this action focus, although she often became frustrated with her perceived slow progress. She required my prompting to work consistently on her assigned tasks, as she tended to get caught up in her "distresses of the moment" and lose her focus. Still, these activities quickly advanced our relationship. I was verbally active with her, and while not all of my feedback was positive, it was always constructive and delivered with empathy. I regularly pointed out her strengths and exceptions to her assumptions of ineffectiveness, and Chloe developed the ability to (sometimes) laugh at her mistakes. I asked her at the end of every other session how she felt about our working together, if she felt we were moving on the right track, and how it felt to be working with me. Her responses were always affirmative.

The Relationship With Mom

Chloe knew that her mother was the primary source of her low self-esteem and was angry about this. Their ongoing contacts, which Chloe always shared with me, featured themes of Chloe's feeling demeaned and manipulated. One event that occurred during our work together was her mother's attempt to withdraw money from their once-shared bank account, an episode that Chloe only interrupted by threatening legal action. Chloe had hoped for most of her life that they might develop a more positive relationship, but she finally decided it would be best to separate herself entirely from her mother.

It was painful for me to see Chloe being hurt during her failed efforts at reconciliation with her mother. I did not know her mother, but I listened empathically to Chloe's stories and her distress and affirmed the validity of her feelings. I reviewed with her the characteristics most people would ascribe to a caring mother so she could compare these with her own experiences. I had to be careful not to take sides against a woman I had never met, and I shared this dilemma with Chloe even as I empathized with her desire to feel worthy of care from others. I supported Chloe's desire to differentiate from her mother but advised her to be cautious in the process, knowing that the pull of the nuclear family can be strong.

Chloe eventually decided that her mother was a narcissist (she looked up information about this personality type online), and while neither agreeing nor disagreeing with this characterization, I supported Chloe's conclusion that her mother was likely incapable of the kind of acceptance and love she needed. Chloe became able to recognize that her mother tended to be dismissive of everyone in her life, not only her. Chloe thought this insight represented progress for her, but she worried that she, too, might be a narcissist, having been raised by one. I pointed out the many ways in which she was not like her mother. I was aware at these times that I might be trying too hard to rescue Chloe from her distress, and I told her this, but she concluded that my perspective was more balanced than her own.

Chloe was not entirely successful in keeping distance from her mother, but their interactions became fewer and Chloe felt "much better, and relieved of the burden" of being her mother's daughter. For her mother's part, she sent texts to Chloe on occasion complaining that she was ungrateful. I conveyed to Chloe my sincere belief that she didn't need to apologize for any of her needs. When I asked Chloe how it sounded for me to say that, she responded, "I wish I could believe that."

Leaving Her Boyfriend

Rather early in therapy, Chloe stated that she wanted to resolve her ambivalence about her boyfriend. She repeatedly stated, "I'm not attracted to Eric at all, but he's my best friend." Chloe was largely unhappy with the relationship and had a hard time engaging in sex with Eric, never enjoying it and fantasizing about being with other "attractive men." To her credit, Chloe shared these concerns openly with Eric. He was deeply hurt by them, which made her feel guilty. She told Eric that she didn't want to end the relationship, but she wanted to get her own apartment and learn to live on her own. She believed she had always been too dependent on others. Eric worried that this was her first step in ending their relationship—as it turned out to be.

I was concerned about Chloe's readiness to live independently, because she seemed to know little about making such arrangements and had always "hated" being alone. I reviewed the pros and cons with her of getting her own place, and admitted that part of my concern came from my own first experience of living on my own (at about her same age), which resulted in a difficult year of adjustment. I wanted her to understand that if I was overreacting, my feelings came out of concern for her. I encouraged her to be careful with Eric's feelings, too, because in many ways it was a good relationship. I felt that a healthy part of her was valuing their friendship as a basis for staying together. As always Chloe listened carefully to what I said. Still, she was determined.

Chloe surprised me by working out the logistics and finances involved in moving over a period of two months and finding a comfortable apartment. I was reminded during this process of the self-care strengths she possessed. I told her she had done much better than I had in that regard, which she appreciated. Not surprisingly, however, her actual transition was difficult. Chloe felt "panicky" when she was by herself for even one full day, and Eric stayed with her most of the first three weeks. Eventually Chloe relaxed and began to meet other men through an online dating service. Eric felt betrayed for his faithfulness, although (as I reminded her) Chloe had been honest with him about her desire to meet other people. Living alone was emotionally stressful for Chloe without Eric's steady support, but she was determined to stay where she was. We spent many sessions dealing with crises related to Chloe's feeling alone and self-destructive. She never acted on those feelings, but her drinking increased for a period of time.

Other Relationships

After breaking up with Eric, Chloe began seeing other men (she was never out of a relationship for long), and she wanted to work on changing her relationship patterns. She said, "I always try to take care of the guys I'm with, to prove that I have worth, but I want someone to take care of me, too." In addition to addressing the topic of her attraction to men who were ultimately neglectful of her, Chloe wanted to address her tendency to "recklessly" jump into relationships, seek affirmation in sex, and then pull back emotionally when a man was becoming close to her. She knew the reasons for these behaviors but wasn't sure how (or if) she could change them. Because of our gender difference, I made a point to ask Chloe during these conversations if I could talk with her about sex, and gave her "permission" to do so herself, as I thought the subject might become a point of tension. We became able to address the issue openly.

Each time Chloe entered into a new relationship with a potential romantic partner, I helped her think about the nature of her attraction. I talked with her about the potential benefits of moving slowly, giving herself time to know the other person, and to be known as a whole person. We worked together on strategies to achieve this goal. These included her setting out to not engage in sex with a new male companion for a period of time, learning to more clearly communicate her needs, and learning to engage in conversations that might help her assess the character of a new friend. Chloe tried to implement these ideas as best she could, but as is the case with anyone trying to break long-standing patterns, change came slowly. I reminded Chloe during her struggles that at her core was a strong desire to experience shared intimacy, although she hadn't yet figured out what that meant for her.

I always felt sad, and sometimes helpless, when Chloe shared a disappointing or hurtful experience with me, or had a tearful breakdown in my office when she despaired about ever having close friends. I continually reminded her that she was a good person, not "crazy" (as she sometimes said), who could attract good people. I was sensitive to her moods and actively processed her relationship dilemmas. I did fall partly into a caretaker role with her, which is something she wanted from others. She occasionally mentioned that it was odd to be with someone who cared about her.

Chloe's problematic interpersonal patterns also played themselves out in her relationships with friends and employers, most of whom were women, whom she tended to see as threats (like her mother). Her poor communication skills and chronically high anxiety states prevented her from being able to work through conflicts (real or perceived), especially with supervisors, so she ended up believing the worst and either fled or was asked to leave. We addressed Chloe's trust issues by encouraging her to "experiment" with risking certain personal disclosure with people, perhaps beginning with friends, to learn if they might be empathic to her feelings and even trustworthy.

Intervention Summary

Chloe and I stopped working together when she accepted a professional job offer in a large city four hours away. She had not achieved all of her goals, and would have continued working with me otherwise, but she recognized that she had made significant progress. She was less anxious in general, tolerated better what anxiety she did experience, and no longer "hated" herself. She had higher self-esteem, recognizing her artistic talent and formulating clearer career goals (as evidenced by the new job). She had a better idea of her needs and what she wanted in relationships (love, respect, trust, being cared for). She realized she could trust at least some other people and how she could test them in that regard. Chloe developed an array of positive coping, self-care, and interpersonal skills. She was more flexible with her assessments of herself and others. She could hear positive aspects of herself without disputing them.

Chloe and I had engaged in many tasks to help her view herself and others differently, but the continuous give-and-take of our active relationship was the catalyst for her changes. We talked about our relationship during our final few sessions. I knew Chloe had been deeply troubled, but I always perceived her as strong, competent, personable, and talented, and I believe she eventually internalized these qualities. She perceived me as genuine, caring, and "wise" (her word, not mine), and she trusted me.

I was always aware that I wanted to protect Chloe from being hurt, taken advantage of, or demeaned. It was often painful for me to bear witness to her disappointments, but she told me how much she appreciated this. Regarding our relational enactments, these came to light most often when we shared concerns and agreed or disagreed about problem-solving strategies. We seemed to connect well, and through that process Chloe experienced a nurturing relationship for one of the few times in her life.

REFERENCES

Bachant, J. L., Lynch, A. A., & Richards, A. D. (1995). Relational models in psychoanalytic theory. *Psychoanalyic Psychology, 12*(1), 71–87.

Borden, W. (2009). *Contemporary psychodynamic theory and practice.* Chicago, IL: Lyceum.

Freedberg, S. (2007). Re-examining empathy: A relational-feminist point of view. *Social Work, 52*(3), 251–259.

Goldstein, E. G. (1995). *Ego psychology and social work practice* (2nd ed.). New York, NY: Free Press.

Miller, S. D., Duncan, B. L., & Hubble, M. A. (2005). Outcome-informed clinical work. In J. C. Norcross & M. R. Goldfried (Eds.), *Handbook of psychotherapy integration* (2nd ed., pp. 84–102). New York, NY: Oxford University Press.

Norcross, J. C., & Wampold, B. E. (2011). Evidence-based therapy relationships: Research conclusions and clinical practices. *Psychotherapy, 48*(1), 98–102.

Perlman, F. T., & Brandell, J. R. (2011). Psychoanalytic theory. In J. R. Brandell (Ed.), *Theory and practice in clinical social work* (2nd ed., pp. 41–80). Thousand Oaks, CA: Sage.

Walsh, J. (2000). Recognizing and managing boundary issues in case management. *Journal of Case Management, 9*(2), 79–85.

Case Study 2-4

Using a Family Systems Approach With the Adoptive Family of a Child With Special Needs

MARTHA MORRISON DORE

This case study illustrates the use of a family systems approach to working with a new family constellation that has been created out of tragedy. This therapeutic intervention, informed by family systems theory and practice, incorporates elements of attachment theory and the dynamics of kinship adoption, an understanding of the effects of complex trauma on individual and family functioning, recognition of the impact of culture, class, and immigration status, as well as contextual social factors such as racism and sexism, on the functioning of the family system in relation to its individual members, as well as on the functioning of the family in a larger context of community and the dominant culture.

Questions
1. How can family systems therapy help a family newly formed through adoption learn how to meet the emotional and social needs of each of its members?
2. Can a family system that has been formed as a result of grievous loss create a new, more positive identity for the future?

3. What is the best way to help adoptive parents of a child with serious emotional and behavioral challenges manage their child's needs while still attending to their own?
4. What are the special concerns, if any, when working with a family from a different culture than one's own?

Even though I have been a social worker for nearly 40 years and a family systems therapist for almost that long, every time I explore a case using a family systems lens, I feel a kinship with the very first professional social workers—like Mary Richmond—who understood well the importance of the family system in interpreting the psychosocial dynamics of the individual. Although in the 21st century we know a great deal more than our professional foremothers and forefathers did about the biological basis of human behavior, these early professionals recognized the importance of observing family members together "acting and reacting upon one another" (Richmond, 1944/1917, p. 137). The family in all of its dimensions has historically been the purview of social workers (Carr, 2009; Dore, 2012; Walsh, 2011). Whether working in child protection, adoption, child guidance, family services, eldercare, or in a specific setting like a hospital, school, or community mental health clinic, social workers have recognized that the individual could only be truly understood in interaction with his or her environment, the most essential element of which is the family.

THE FAMILY

The particular case I have chosen to use to illustrate family systems therapy is that of the Laurent family. The family consists of the father, André, age 36; mother, Marie Clothilde, age 32; and their adopted son, Michel, age 10, who is also Marie Clothilde's nephew. André Laurent immigrated to the United States as a young teenager when his parents fled Haiti after the first overthrow of President Jean-Bertrand Aristide in the early 1990s. They settled in the greater Boston area, where André attended school and learned to speak English fluently. He graduated from a technical high school, where he studied information technology, and since graduation he has been consistently employed in IT services in the pharmaceutical industry. Marie Clothilde immigrated more recently, coming to the United States in 2005 to stay with an older sister in the hopes of finding work to help support her family back in Haiti. Because Marie Clothilde spoke very little English, her employment options here were limited. She worked primarily on a cleaning crew that maintains office buildings at night. Shortly after she arrived in this country, she met André through a cousin. They married in 2007. Even though André had a good-paying job, Marie Clothilde continued to work after their marriage so that she could send money back to her poverty-stricken family in Port-au-Prince.

THE PRESENTING SITUATION

Everything changed for André and Marie Clothilde on January 12, 2010, the date of the devastating earthquake in Haiti. Marie Clothilde spent frantic days after the disaster trying to find out what had happened to her family. Eventually, through a family friend, she learned that her entire family in Port-au-Prince had been killed, with the exception of her sister's son, Michel, who was dug out of the rubble of the extended family home still alive two days after the earthquake. With the aid of her priest, who is also Haitian, she was able to locate Michel in a makeshift orphanage in Port-au-Prince and arrange for him to come to this country. Michel, who lost his only parent and grandparents in the earthquake, along with his uncle, aunt, and two young cousins, was still in shock when he arrived at Logan Airport in Boston in April 2010, to begin a new life in a strange country with adoptive parents he hardly knew.

Marie Clothilde was struggling emotionally as well. Her family had been decimated in the earthquake, and she barely had time to process the loss when she was confronted with an emotionally distraught child to care for. She assumed the role of mother, a new one for her, and relinquished the role of wage earner because Michel required all of her time and attention at home. André, feeling he needed to make up financially for Marie Clothilde's lost income and not a little displaced in his wife's attentions by his new son, began to spend more time at work. Marie Clothilde enrolled Michel in the neighborhood elementary school, but her inability to speak much English prevented her from fully communicating what had happened to Michel with school personnel. Thus, school personnel, who placed Michel in a mixed class of children who were non-English speaking, were totally unprepared for the problems he began to manifest. For one thing, Michel was unable to sit quietly at a desk for any length of time. He would begin to pace the classroom and, if requested to return to his seat, would begin scream-ing and thrashing about, pulling at his hair and babbling in Haitian Creole. If a teacher attempted to touch him to guide him back to his seat, Michel would shrink away, sob-bing and crying, flailing his arms and shouting about *petro loas* (evil spirits) who were possessing him. At these times, Marie Clothilde would be summoned to the school and told to calm Michel down or take him home until he gained better control of himself.

One day Michel became so out-of-control, alternatively cowering under his desk, crying and shaking uncontrollably, and striking out aggressively, cursing at anyone who tried to come near him, that the school contacted the mobile crisis team from the child and adolescent inpatient psychiatric unit at the local hospital. In consulta-tion with André, who had rushed to the school from his job, and Marie Clothilde, the mobile crisis team recommended that Michel should be hospitalized briefly for further evaluation.

Although many Haitian people believe that the kind of serious emotional and behavioral disturbances that Michel was exhibiting are caused by a curse from a *loa* (sometimes spelled *lwa*) or evil spirit who is upset at being disobeyed, André and Marie Clothilde recognized that Michel's problems were likely related to the severe trauma and multiple losses he had experienced back in Haiti. Fortunately, because the greater Boston area has the fourth largest Haitian population of any city, including those in the country of Haiti, the community hospital where Michel was admitted belongs to a behavioral health network that supports a mental health team of Haitian Creole–speaking professionals. The child psychiatrist on this team, Dr. Odette Jean-Baptist, evaluated Michel in the hospital and diagnosed posttraumatic stress disorder suffered as a result of the complex trauma he experienced during and after the earthquake in Haiti exacerbated by the process of immigrating to the United States and adjusting to a radically different life in a strange new family, school, and community.

Dr. Jean-Baptist prescribed a short course of a mood stabilizer to help Michel manage his explosive outbursts and scheduled regular follow-ups to monitor his response to the medication. She also made a referral to the local children's mental health agency, where I am employed, for ongoing family treatment to help Michel integrate into his new family and to help his adoptive parents learn ways to support their son as he mourns his former life and embraces his new one.

JOINING THE FAMILY SYSTEM

Through contracts with the state Department of Mental Health designed to prevent long-term out-of-home placement of children and adolescents with serious emotional disturbances, my agency offers family-based services to children and their parents in their own homes, in community settings, or in our offices, depending on the family's preference. If a child is already in a psychiatric placement, as was Michel, then we meet with the family in the placement setting and include in our first session the mental health professionals working with the child there. In this case, Dr. Jean-Baptist joined us to offer her insights regarding Michel's diagnosis, his current psychosocial functioning, and her team's recommendations for his further treatment. As if sensing my unspoken concerns about the Haitian culture's belief regarding disability, especially mental disability, as something the individual has brought on himself, a punishment for offending the spirits or God in the case of Haitian Christians, and how this belief might affect Michel's parents' response to his illness, Dr. Jean-Baptist explained to them in lay terms in both Haitian-Creole and English how experiencing profound trauma can alter the functioning of a person's brain, particularly in children whose brains are still developing and thus are uniquely vulnerable to the physiologic changes that take place in response to high levels of traumatic stress. This explanation helped alleviate André and Marie Clothilde's expressed concerns about their ability to parent Michel, particularly when I explained how I would be working closely with them to figure out the best ways to help Michel manage his own emotions and behavior. I added that I would also be connecting them with community resources that could offer them support with Michel into the future.

Assessing Family System Dynamics

As a therapist working from a family systems perspective, it was important at this point to join with the parents to support their capacity to adequately meet their new son's needs by becoming part of the family caregiving system so that they did not feel so alone and overburdened. Although Marie Clothilde had extended family ties to Michel that would help sustain her commitment to him during the challenging work ahead, André had no such ties, and I was concerned that his emotional investment in Michel might be more limited, particularly if he experiences Michel as coming between him and his wife. This dynamic is frequently seen in family systems when one parent, usually the mother, becomes so invested in caring for a child with special needs that other family members, often the father and the child's other siblings, feel shunted aside with their emotional needs going unmet. This dynamic could be complicated by the patriarchal tradition in Haitian culture that lays the burden of caring for a child with a disability solely at the feet of the mother. There is a great deal of shame and stigma associated with having a disabled child in Haiti. If a child is born with a visible disability, the father may leave the home and take up with another woman, who will become pregnant and bear a child without a disability, thus proving that the father is not the cause of the child's impairment. As a result, disabled children in Haiti are often raised by single mothers. Knowing this, it will be important for me to assess the degree to which André and Marie Clothilde ascribe to these beliefs and determine how to keep André engaged with his new son so that Michel's care is not left entirely to his wife.

Strengthening the Adult Partner Subsystem

I knew I must also find ways to help André and Marie Clothilde communicate openly about their own needs and feelings so that Marie Clothilde does not begin to feel over-burdened by Michel's care and André doesn't feel closed out of the mother-child subsystem in the family. A common strategy in practice informed by family systems theory is working to strengthen and develop what is called the *marital subsystem* in the traditional family therapy literature, but what could more accurately be termed the *adult partner relationship*, as it can also refer to unmarried same-sex or opposite-sex partners. This strategy is also important in a single-parent household, especially when the parent has formed a co-parenting alliance with one of the children, usually the oldest girl. The idea here is to establish and support a family hierarchy in which the adults are in charge, and to ensure that the adults have a relationship with one another that is separate from their roles as parents. Developing such a relationship requires open, clear communication of needs and feelings, as well as mutual understanding and support. Family systems therapists believe that a solid adult partner relationship is the key to a family system that responds adequately to the needs of all of its members.

The Impact of Adoption on the Family System

In addition to cultural and adult relationship considerations, there are issues around adoption, particularly the adoption of an older child with special needs, which I must be aware of in working with the Laurent family. At the point that I met with the family in the hospital, I knew nothing about the couple's desire to have children of their own, whether this was something that they had wished for but had been unable to conceive, or whether they had decided not to have children, which I thought was rather unlikely given the high value placed on children in Haitian culture. In family systems practice in adoption, it is essential to understand a couple's intentions regarding childbearing and what their efforts have been to have a child of their own. For some people, the inability to conceive and/or carry a child to term is viewed as a personal failing with accompanying self-blame and depression, making the emotional investment in an adopted child more challenging. When a kinship adoption is thrust on a couple unexpectedly, as was the case with André and Marie Clothilde, there is little or no time for them to consider what the addition of a new member will mean to their family system and to prepare for likely changes.

If one partner is more eager to adopt a child than the other, particularly if the less-invested partner is simply going along with the adoption to please the other person or to salvage their relationship, then the addition of a child to the family system through adoption can result in a significant shift in the partner relationship. Adoption of an older child also brings its own challenges to the family system. Although Michel is a member of Marie Clothilde's extended family, she has not seen him since he was a toddler and can only surmise about his prior upbringing in an extended family household that included not only her sister, Michel's mother and a single parent, but also her mother and her father who was an alcoholic, as well as her older brother, the only wage earner in the family, his wife, and their two young children. Like approximately 80% of Haitians, the family was very poor and lived in the section of Port-au-Prince known as Cité Soliel, an infamous urban slum.

Marie Clothilde knows from her own experience that the primary school that served Cité Soliel children before the earthquake was a ramshackle building lacking in basic resources such as electricity and running water. The cost of uniforms and textbooks made sending any but the eldest male child prohibitive for families like hers. She isn't sure just how much schooling Michel actually had back home but, like many Haitian immigrant parents, she is anxious that he should be placed in a classroom based on his age rather than his prior educational experience or ability. She is unfamiliar with the special resources available to children with Michel's challenges in the Boston-area community in which the Laurent family lives and, again like many immigrant parents, relies on school personnel to make the best decisions for Michel.

Helping the Family System Incorporate a New Member

Marie Clothilde's unfamiliarity with the local education system provided me with the opening I needed to engage André, who, as a result of having gone to high school in the area, was more familiar with the system and at ease with school personnel. Appealing to André's authority on the local education system not only increased his involvement with Michel and his special learning challenges but also brought him back into an alliance with Marie Clothilde on behalf of their child, as together, with my coaching and support, they worked with the special education staff at Michel's school to obtain a full educational evaluation and design an Individualized Education Program (IEP) to meet his learning needs. Under the Individuals with Disabilities Education Act (IDEA), parents are entitled to be considered full partners with special education personnel in contributing to planning the IEP.

Strategies to Strengthen the Parental Subsystem

My experience in working with immigrant parents, many of whom come from cultures that place educators on a pedestal, is that they are often hesitant to question the decisions of school staff or to advocate for their child if they feel his or her learning needs are not being met. This seems to happen more often when the child's learning is impacted by serious emotional and behavior disorders. As is true in most states across the country, we are fortunate to have a very effective educational advocacy group in Massachusetts, the Professional/Parent Advocacy League (P/PAL), for families whose children have mental health challenges. P/PAL can arrange for a legal advocate who is thoroughly familiar with education law to accompany parents to an IEP planning meeting if they are at all concerned that their child will not receive appropriate or adequate educational services from the school. If I am working with a family with a child with a serious emotional and/or behavior disorder, I routinely put them in touch with a P/PAL representative, who is usually an experienced parent of a child with similar challenges who offers support and information about local resources. P/PAL also sponsors psychoeducation groups that meet weekly in specific locations throughout the state for parents whose children are struggling with mental health concerns. In addition, the organization holds picnics and other fun events for families who may feel more comfortable socializing with other families with similar childrearing challenges.

One of the most significant changes in family systems practice in recent years is the recognition that the families we work with are embedded in networks of community supports and services that can be tapped to strengthen the family system in myriad ways. Family systems work used to focus almost completely on the nuclear family system, the constellation of dad, mom, and kids. As this constellation changed markedly over the past several decades to encompass a variety of family forms, family therapists recognized the need to broaden their purview, first to include extended family members and close friends in their therapeutic interventions, then to add to the family's network in more creative ways. Nowadays, rather than expecting the family to meet one another's emotional and social needs exclusively, family therapists assess a family's life cycle stage and locate resources that can support the family in their current developmental process.

For example, in working with the Laurent family, which has suddenly moved from the couple stage, with its focus on the adjustment of the marital subsystem, to the addition of a new family member, a child with special needs, I looked for community resources that could support them in this process. In addition to introducing them to P/PAL to help them navigate the education system, I also put them in touch with Adoptive Families Together (AFT), which, as the name suggests, is a grassroots organization of adoptive families, many of whom have adopted children with special needs and challenges. AFT not only offers parent support groups throughout the greater Boston area, but also sponsors an online discussion group, which adoptive parents can access for information, advice, and general support. Families who join AFT receive a free copy of *In Their Own Words . . . Reflections on Parenting Children With Mental Health Issues: The Effect on Families*, a book written and published by members of this organization. Because this book is available only in English, which Marie Clothilde is unable to read comfortably, we agreed that André would read a chapter to her each evening after Michel had gone to bed, and they would discuss issues the material raised, noting any concerns they wanted to bring to our by-then weekly meetings together.

Addressing Individual Member Concerns
From a Family Systems Perspective

As I noted previously, there is a large Haitian population in the greater Boston area, which luckily means that many resources are aimed specifically at the Haitian community in the area where the Laurents live. Because I had concerns about Marie Clothilde's response to the deaths of nearly her entire family in the earthquake, which I felt she had delayed facing because of her need to attend to Michel's mental health issues, I hoped to locate a support group for Haitian women who had experienced similar losses in that tragedy. The Association of Haitian Women in Boston, an advocacy organization for Haitian women, was able to refer Marie Clothilde to a women's group that met locally through the auspices of the Cambridge Haitian Services Collaborative. I also learned of an extensive women's literacy program offered by this organization, which could help Marie Clothilde become more fluent in English, enabling her to better negotiate the various service systems on behalf of her son.

In making these inquiries and referrals, it was essential that I actively engage André in the process in order to maintain balance in the family system and to honor the role of the husband and father in Haitian culture. My agency runs an ongoing father-son group in our community for fathers of boys, ages 10 to 15, who are struggling with emotional and behavior challenges. Most, though not all, of the dads in the group live apart from their sons and are seeking ways to strengthen the attachment with their boys. It is primarily an activities-recreation-adventure group that draws heavily on the many arts, education, and sports-related resources in the greater Boston area. I thought since parent-child attachment is one of the ever-present themes in this group, it might also be appropriate for André as an adoptive father seeking to build a relationship with his new son. One of the two male leaders of this group is a Haitian American social worker, Emile Richard; the other is an African American psychologist, Ed Gaines. André was hesitant about joining the group with Michel given the boy's emotional and behavior challenges, but he agreed to meet with Emile and Ed to see if the group was a fit for him and his son. As it turned out, André and Emile were distantly related through their mothers, which cemented André's willingness to try the group.

From the group leaders' modeling, André learned some effective strategies for managing his son's behavior in public situations, as well as attunement skills to help Michel build capacity for self-regulation. André connected with several of the other fathers in the group, and a small group of them with their sons, all around Michel's age, began meeting in a local park on Saturday mornings to play pickup soccer. Through the fathers' group, which occasionally met at a local sound recording studio, André and Michel discovered a mutual love of Kompa (in English called *compas*), the traditional music of Haiti. They often listen together to old LPs made by Kompa artists like

Nemours Jean-Baptist and Rene Saint-Andre that were given to André by his father. Michel wistfully remembers his grandfather playing the same records back in Haiti.

Finally, as the theme of trauma runs through this family system, I used the strategy of storytelling to aid healing among its members (Kiser et al., 2012). Storytelling is also an important technique in adoptive families to help members co-construct a narrative that binds their lives together. The goal of this strategy is for each member to move from owning an individual story to collaborating on a shared narrative of their evolving family system. This technique was particularly useful in working with this family because Michel was initially unable to talk about his experiences during and after the earthquake in Haiti, expressing his feelings and fears through night terrors and overwhelming anxiety attacks during the day. As he listened intently to his adoptive parents tell the stories of their own childhood experiences, particularly their individual immigration stories, each of which involved emotionally painful loss and renewal, Michel gradually became able to put his own experiences into words, which described an ordeal so terrifying that it was difficult for the adults in his life to hear. My role was to help André and Marie Clothilde manage their own affective responses to this difficult material and to learn how to use reflective listening skills to accurately and empathically respond to Michel's efforts to communicate his needs and feelings to them.

In one of our most significant family sessions, Marie Clothilde sat with tears streaming down her face as Michel described being able to hear his grandfather's weakening voice in the rubble, urging Michel to be strong until searchers could find him. By the time rescuers came, no one except Michel was left alive in the debris. Marie Clothilde opened her arms and Michel, who had been sitting by himself on a small chair somewhat outside of the family circle, hesitated only momentarily before flinging himself into her arms, sobbing noisily. André got up from the couch where he had been sitting and, pulling another chair close to his wife's, embraced his wife and son as they cried together, mourning their mutual losses. It was shortly after this that the family, with my guidance and support, began to co-construct a narrative of their emerging life together as a new family system. This story included the routines, rituals, and traditions they were developing, as well as some of the obstacles they had faced and overcome as a family.

CONCLUSION

I recognize in presenting this somewhat complex case of family systems work that the contemporary approach to this type of practice is heavily dependent on viewing the family in the context of larger systems and on using available resources outside of the family to strengthen the functioning of both individuals and family subsystems. The kinds of resources I was able to draw on in working with the Laurent family as Haitian-born immigrants are not available in many parts of the country, particularly in poorer and more rural communities. Clinicians are often surprised, however, at what is actually available when they are seriously committed to connecting family members to resources that can enhance resilience in the family system. Mentors can be found almost everywhere with a little effort, as can activity groups. Support groups for parents who have adopted special needs children or whose own children have serious emotional or behavior challenges are as close as the Internet, although the clinician must be vigilant in ensuring that the client's online privacy is protected and that the website is sponsored by a recognized legitimate entity before recommending this resource.

In summary, my work with the Laurent family, although informed throughout by a family systems perspective, was also dependent on my knowledge of adoption dynamics (Reitz & Watson, 1992), particularly the unplanned adoption of an older child and its impact on an existing family system; of complex trauma and its biopsychosocial impact on a latency age child as well as an adult; and of the public education system and how to manage its response to a child with serious emotional and behavior challenges, all with an overlay of Haitian culture and the immigrant experience. Although the specific issues in each family that presents for treatment are different, or as Leo Tolstoy put it so well, "Every unhappy family is unhappy in its own way," a family systems approach easily accommodates these unique factors, giving structure and overall direction to the work.

REFERENCES

Carr, A. (2009). The effectiveness of family therapy and systemic interventions for child-focused problems. *Journal of Family Therapy, 31*, 3–45.

Dore, M. M. (2012). Family systems theory. In B. A. Thyer, C. N. Dulmus, & K. M. Sowers (Eds.), *Human behavior in the social environment: Theories for social work practice* (pp. 369–410). Hoboken, NJ: Wiley.

Kiser, L. J., Baumgardner, B., & Dorado, J., Lacher, D. B., Nichols, T., & Nichols, M. (2012). Connecting with kids through stories: Using narratives to facilitate attachment in adopted children (2nd ed.). London, UK: Jessica Kingsley.

Reitz, M., & Watson, K. W. (1992). *Adoption and the family system: Strategies for treatment.* New York, NY: Guilford Press.

Richmond, M. E. (1944, reprint). *Social diagnosis.* New York, NY: Free Press. (Original work published in 1917)

Walsh, F. (Ed.). (2011). *Normal family processes* (4th ed.). New York, NY: Guilford Press.

PART III

Case Studies in Child and Family Welfare

Child and family welfare represents social work's concern with the well-being and protection of children and the support and rights of families. Child and family services are typically needed when parents are unable to properly care for their children, when children have special needs, or when certain resources are needed. The National Association of Social Workers (NASW; 2013) reports that about 16% of social workers are employed in child services and about 12% work in family services. Although child and family welfare has historically been considered the heart of social work, in recent years interest in traditional child welfare has declined. This is unfortunate because there are great opportunities to use a range of social work skills in this setting.

There are many roles for social workers to play in the field of child and family welfare. Social workers are child protective service workers, adoption workers, foster-care specialists, residential care workers, and sex abuse therapists. The settings for child and family welfare are equally broad: residential care centers, state departments of welfare, state departments of health (pregnancy prevention), and family counseling centers. The case studies in this chapter represent some of these settings. In each of the cases, the social worker uses two fundamental skills: relationship building and contracting.

Since the beginning of the profession, the social work relationship has been seen as a principle of effective practice. The skill of developing effective social work relationships is capitalized in one essential skill: empathy. The development of empathy, which is the ability to perceive and communicate the feelings and experiences of the client, is widely recognized as a necessary, although not always sufficient, condition of effective practice. Almost every approach to treatment recognizes the importance of building a good worker-client relationship in creating change for the client. A good rapport enhances the client's interest in being open and honest with the worker, encourages the client to explore his or her issues completely, and motivates the client toward change. An effective worker-client relationship builds the relationship components of liking, respect, and trust, which result in the relationship consequences of communication, openness, and persuasiveness (Goldstein, 1980; Hepworth, Rooney, Rooney, Strom-Gottfried, & Larsen, 2009).

Each of these case studies represents an example of the contracting process. Contracting is considered one of the essential components of effective social work practice (Hepworth et al., 2009). A contract is an agreement between a social worker and a client about the work they agree to do together to accomplish their goals. It involves three essential aspects: (1) clarifying the purpose, (2) clarifying the roles and responsibilities of each person, and (3) reaching an agreement about the work to be done together.

Clarifying clients' expectations will enhance your ability to work effectively. Clients, as you might imagine, have many expectations regarding how a social worker can help them. They might question, for example, how is this person going to help me? Have I made the right decision to seek help? What is the likelihood that I will be helped? What are the fees? How long is this likely to take? and so on. Therefore, a critical part of the helping process is clarifying the client's expectations and determining how they match with your ability and the available resources.

This chapter presents several different cases that all revolve around child abuse. Child abuse is a complex problem in our society, and each case study approaches the problem from a different context, agency position, and treatment perspective.

The case by Sammons describes practice in a specific context, the inpatient hospital. She describes a multidisciplinary team approach to dealing with a complex case of childhood schizophrenia and sexual abuse. Here the social worker is involved in many aspects of the treatment and planning for her client. Swenson-Smith and Campos address another context—the family drug court—and demonstrate a therapeutic jurisprudence approach, where social work and the legal system work together to resolve complex social problems. It is an inspiring success story of how family drug courts can be effective in addressing significant problems. Lietz presents a case study of supervision in child welfare. Many social workers advance rapidly into supervision roles, and her case helps students understand the role supervision plays in social work practice. Also, her case study reveals how workers can maximize their experience when receiving supervision. The last case study by Krugman demonstrates the exemplary relationship he establishes with his clients. Engaging the violent couple into a long-term relationship of therapy is a respectable accomplishment. His work demonstrates the skill of "starting where the client is at." Krugman also establishes a clear contract with his clients, which is necessary in case situations where you are responsible for protecting your client.

In all of these case studies, important relationship dynamics are taking place. In some of the cases this included an abusive relationship. The social worker had to clearly establish that he or she would not allow such an abusive relationship to exist and would protect the best interests of his or her client. As you read the case studies, think about the contracts that were developed between the social workers and others involved in each case. Also, think about how the worker-client relationship was critical in the success of these cases.

REFERENCES

Goldstein, A. P. (1980). Relationship enhancement methods. In F. H. Kanfer & A. P. Goldstein (Eds.), *Helping people change* (2nd ed., pp. 18–57). New York, NY: Pergamon Press.

Hepworth, D., Rooney, R. H., Rooney, G. W., Strom-Gottfried, K., & Larsen, J. (2009). *Direct social work practice.* Pacific Grove, CA: Cengage.

National Association of Social Workers. (2013, April). *Children and families.* Retrieved from www.socialworkers.org/pressroom/features/issue/children.asp

Case Study 3-1

Clinical Social Work in an Interdisciplinary Team: An Adolescent Inpatient Psychiatry Case

CATHERINE SAMMONS

Interdisciplinary teamwork in a hospital setting calls for a variety of social work functions and roles. This case study illustrates the multifaceted nature of team-based psychiatric care and several essential contributions of the psychiatric social worker.

Questions
1. What is the social worker's role on an interdisciplinary team?
2. When sexual abuse is first identified, what are the high-priority interventions?
3. How does the social worker provide service coordination for the team?
4. How does the social worker's role shift in response to the changing needs of this case?

In several practice settings, the social worker is at the hub of a network of interacting professional disciplines and social agencies. A classic example is hospital and other healthcare agencies, in which the effective social work practitioner must master the role of coordinator of various parties concurrently interacting with the client. Although social work education is primarily oriented toward direct clinical interventions with the primary client (known as the identified patient in a medical setting), the psychiatric social worker in a hospital setting draws on skills in group facilitation and interagency advocacy to provide comprehensive care that bridges hospital with community.

This case is presented to highlight the complexities and special issues in clinical social work as practiced in an interdisciplinary team. In a secured (locked) inpatient hospital unit for adolescents with severe psychiatric disorders, including psychotic, affective, and conduct disorders, many of the patients have co-occurring developmental disabilities. The average length of stay is now typically 1 to 3 weeks, although it was considerably longer at the time this case was originally written. Teens at this university medical center receive a comprehensive evaluation, initial treatment, and recommendations for ongoing treatment in the community. Frequently, the postdischarge disposition plan (also known as the aftercare plan) involves placement in a residential treatment center.

CRISIS OF DISCLOSURE

About 12 team members and clinical trainees from the adolescent service assembled for their weekly case conference in the large dining room of the inpatient unit serving about 15 youths. The trainee for this day's case presentation, a child psychiatry fellow, provided a brief history of the patient, Kamila, who was beginning her third week of hospitalization and was thus well known to the team.

The senior child psychiatry professor, a jovial and kind-spirited older Asian American man, smiled as Kamila, a petite, waiflike African American 14-year-old girl, was escorted into the room and seated next to him at the front of the group. She appeared calm and cooperative as the clinician asked her a few general questions about events leading up to the admission. At one point he asked, "Have you ever had any unusual experiences?" His intent was to explore for bizarre thoughts and perceptual experiences. However, Kamila's calm answer was like a quiet bomb in the room: "Yes, my father's been screwing me." "What do you mean by that?" asked the professor. Like everyone else in the room, he'd been caught off guard, but he quickly mobilized to continue the conversational interview flow. Kamila went on to define in basic but clear terms her sexual molestation for the past 2 years by her adoptive father.

Aware of and experienced in this all-too-common problem among children and adolescents,[1] the team was not surprised by the content so much as the timing of this disclosure. The presenting complaint at admission, the first days of evaluation and treatment, had yielded a long problem list for young Kamila, but no incest indicators had been detected. The social worker once again appreciated the advantages of inpatient

---

1   There is evidence that children with special needs (in either developmental disability or mental illness) are at higher risk of intrafamilial abuse: Goldman, J., Salus, M. K., Wolcott, D., & Kennedy, K. (2003). *A coordinated response to child abuse and neglect: The foundation for practice.* Washington, DC: Office on Child Abuse and Neglect, The Children's Bureau, U.S. Department of Health and Human Services. Also, presence of a stepfather increases the risk of sexual abuse: Finkelhor, D., & Associates. (1986). *A sourcebook on child sexual abuse.* Thousand Oaks, CA: Sage.

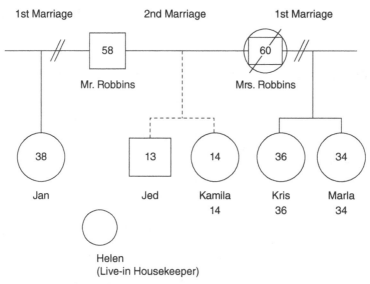

Figure 3.1 Blended Family Structure

treatment: the intensity of the setting and the distance from home and family often provide the safety needed for youths to risk high-stakes disclosures.

BACKGROUND

Kamila had been brought to the hospital by her adoptive father, Mr. Robbins, a Caucasian 58-year-old small business owner whose wife of 24 years, an African American woman, had died 6 months before, after a short struggle with cancer. He described himself as a recovering alcoholic. He appeared depressed and actively still grieving the loss of his wife, and yet he portrayed himself as devoted to the care of his two adoptive children, Kamila and her adoptive brother, Jed, a Caucasian 13-year-old.

Mr. Robbins had sought help because of Kamila's recent behavioral changes, which he described as "a total personality change," from an easygoing, happy young teen with mild developmental delays (primarily cognitive) into an irritable, oppositional youth. Especially troubling were her auditory hallucinations (commanding her to jump off a building, to "die and be with my mother"), somatic and religious delusions, and thought broadcasting and insertion. The family reported withdrawal, confusion, and illogicality ("not making sense when she talked"), but it was difficult for them to precisely date the onset, since the maternal illness and death had so consumed their attention for the past 2 years. They were also concerned with her disturbed sleep with nighttime wakefulness and pacing, as well as her significantly diminished appetite.

The family configuration was fairly complex and is perhaps best conveyed by a genogram (see Figure 3.1). Kamila's household at the time of hospitalization included her adoptive brother Jed, her adoptive father, and a longtime family friend and housekeeper,

Helen (Filipina in her mid-60s). Kamila's two adoptive sisters (biological offspring of Mrs. Robbins and her first husband) also resided locally but not in the home.

TEAM TREATMENT GOALS AND INTERVENTIONS

The adolescent unit team generated the following treatment goals for Kamila:

1. Improved self-care and resumed participation in activities of daily living, including increased food intake and increased periods of nightly uninterrupted sleep
2. Verbalizing feelings of safety and protection from further abuse
3. Increased contact with supportive family members
4. Access to a safe and supportive home environment upon discharge

Although each discipline addressed more fine-grained treatment objectives, such as grief processing in her individual therapy and attention span lengthening in her classroom program, these four goals were seen as core indicators of discharge readiness and therefore a higher priority for contribution by all disciplines.

In order to most effectively plan and enact interventions, people from various professional disciplines evaluated Kamila:

The *care coordinator*, a medical doctor (MD) in advanced psychiatry training (post-residency fellowship) was the primary therapist for Kamila, meeting with her one-on-one at least three times per week. She also prescribed and monitored medications. The fellow's role also included integrating the team's assessments into a comprehensive diagnostic formulation and coordinated treatment plan.[2] She also assisted in family sessions in collaboration with the unit's *clinical social worker* (LCSW). The MD and LCSW functioned as cotherapists in family meetings, obtaining clinical history, managing the family's adaptation to the inpatient program, providing updates on their child's progress, and guiding the family toward more adaptive communication and symptom management. The focus was typically strengths-based and psychoeducational, incorporating social learning and behavior management principles.

The *psychologist* (PhD) evaluated Kamila's intellectual and emotional status using standardized tests. Even when she was not manifesting psychotic thinking, Kamila appeared emotionally immature, with a minimal vocabulary and academic achievement well below her chronological age. A complex diagnostic task was administered to differentiate between temporary impairment in cognitive skills secondary to psychosis and mild mental retardation and/or learning disabilities as a preexisting condition.

The *occupational and recreational therapists* (MS, OT/L, and RTC) assessed Kamila's leisure time skills, her ability to interact appropriately with peers in both task and social groups, and her fine and gross motor functioning. The inpatient *educators* (MA consultant and licensed teachers) conducted academic assessment and provided a daily classroom program.

---

2   In many psychiatric units, especially private ones, the social worker also serves as care coordinator, but in university hospitals, where training of psychiatrists is the central mission, the student psychiatrist (medical resident or fellow) assumes this role, with the social worker providing coaching in nonmedical aspects of that role.

A *psychiatric nurse* (RN) designated as Kamila's primary nurse formulated a nursing care plan that addressed all areas of daily living: meals, sleep, personal hygiene and grooming, general health habits, and peer relationships in the unit milieu. The primary nurse helped Kamila adjust to the unit's behavioral system and understand the rules and rewards. She also provided emotional support and coaching at numerous times throughout the day. A counterpart to the primary nurse served the same functions on the evening shift.

The *speech and language therapist* (MACCC) clarified and described language deviances versus delays and also guided the team in techniques for enhancing Kamila's verbal expressiveness.

Following the sexual abuse disclosure, an extensive physical examination was performed by a *pediatrician* (MD consult) with specialized training and experience in this area. She noted key physical signs of abuse, described these in a report documented on county-issued forms, and she later testified in court. Because of her expertise and experience, she accomplished these interventions with sensitivity and minimized Kamila's sense of further physical and emotional intrusion.

ROLE OF THE SOCIAL WORKER

In addition to the basic social work functions of family assessment, support, and therapy, in the case of Kamila (as with most inpatients), the LCSW provided a variety of therapeutic interventions. Kamila's disclosure of sexual abuse necessitated (in accordance with state law) immediate telephone and written reports to the local department of children's services as well as to law enforcement in the city in which the abuse had occurred. The social worker also maintained telephone contact with these agencies in subsequent days to facilitate their investigations, as well as to advocate for the teen and her special needs. These activities had significant clinical relevance (e.g., communicating directly with the patient about these agencies' activities; the emotional impact of this information) as well as disposition relevance (e.g., aftercare plans could not be finalized without these agencies' cooperation; consent for Kamila's care was now shared with the family court).

As treatment progressed, placement in an adolescent residential program appeared to be the best option for maintaining Kamila's safety as well as longer-term treatment. The LCSW explored various residential treatment centers, managed the application process together with the children's services social worker, and eventually facilitated a smooth transition from the acute care hospital to a 6- to 12-month care program. This process required the LCSW to communicate closely with the team educator, psychologist, and speech therapist, in order to fine-tune her understanding of the ideal (or, at least, satisfactory) therapeutic environment.

Another community agency with an active role in Kamila's aftercare plan was the local service center for persons with developmental disabilities. The LCSW initiated and monitored the eligibility process so that Kamila would benefit from entitlements she would likely need as an older teen, such as supported living and supported employment. A notable challenge in this interagency work involved educating each agency about aspects of Kamila with which they were not already familiar. For example, the disabilities centers tend to be poorly informed about major mental illness, whereas children's services is less familiar with cognitive disabilities. The LCSW's expertise regarding eligibility and entitlement laws, as well as her diplomatic coaching of colleagues in these agencies, helped Kamila receive an appropriate individualized plan of care (see Figure 3.2).

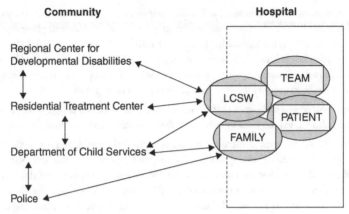

Figure 3.2 Community patterns

FAMILY INTERVENTIONS

Following the sexual abuse disclosure, Kamila adamantly refused to see or talk with her father. This was adaptive in two ways: (1) it protected her from further abuse or intimidation about having reported; and (2) it also reduced her guilt feelings by not exposing her to her father's vivid hurt affect and protestations of innocence. At this point, he was vehemently denying the allegations. The disclosure created a crisis for every family member, and alliances shifted in the process. Figure 3.3 illustrates how the therapists' initial perception of family members' relationships changed after disclosure.

Clearly, a major breach in the father-daughter relationship had occurred, or more accurately, a longstanding but secretive breach had been exposed. Also, Kamila's contacts with her brother became brief, superficial in content, and limited to phone conversations, because Mr. Robbins refused to bring Jed to the hospital for visits or sibling therapeutic sessions.

Two of Kamila's three adult sisters became very involved and intensified their contacts with Kamila. One sister, Marla, coped well with her understandably "mixed-up feelings" of shock, anger, sadness, and guilt over not having detected the problem herself and "rescued" Kamila. She also found it difficult to accept Kamila's psychiatric problems, since she hadn't spent much time in the home in the past year. The second sister, Kris, could not accept Kamila's report as truthful; she insisted that psychiatric illness had distorted the teen's sense of reality and past events so that Kamila was *mistakenly* blaming their father instead of a "real perpetrator" whose identity was simply not yet revealed. Although Kris was flooded with sadness and concern when visiting Kamila, she often expressed more sympathy toward Mr. Robbins and described him as "the second victim." The team hypothesized that perhaps Kris had also been molested by Mr. Robbins at an earlier age, and that her younger adopted sister's disclosure had reignited some of her own traumatic memories. Although we could never confirm or refute this theory, we did learn that both Marla and Kris had as young adults fended off inappropriate sexually themed verbal advances by their stepfather while he was intoxicated. The third sister, Jan, had little ongoing contact with the other sisters and had declined to speak with hospital staff.

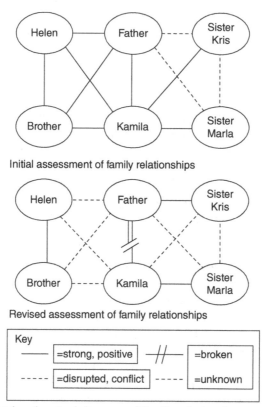

Figure 3.3   Initial and revised diagram of family relationships

The LCSW and care coordinator, in the one postdisclosure session with Mr. Robbins before his arrest, described his reactions to the disclosure as partial willingness to accept that abuse had occurred, but complete denial that he was the perpetrator. He attributed Kamila's "false report" to her "confused mental state." At this point, the team was reluctant to process the disclosure in great detail because of their protective stance toward the patient and their sense that he was mobilizing his legal defense. Before he could be referred to an independent therapist, he was arrested and incarcerated, and the team ceased contact with him.

The care coordinator, as a psychiatry trainee, is typically at a beginning level in skills of family evaluation and therapy. The team LCSW mentored this care coordinator and advised that the family focus shift to the elder sisters Marla and Kris, with the LCSW taking the lead in coaching them through visits with the patient, helping them express their support for Kamila, and educating them about her various impairments and issues. The LCSW shared this role with the primary nurse, the team member with the most intensive daily contact with Kamila. The sisters were assisted in adjusting their expectations of Kamila and appreciating her strengths, such as persistence, sense of humor, and affectionate warmth.

Kamila's loss of her father compounded the abandonment issues she had already experienced when her mother died; these exacerbated any preexisting identity, belongingness, and attachment issues typically experienced by adoptees. Her mother, described as very nurturing and supportive, also had been unaware of or unable to address Kamila's victimization, and direct communication with the mother was no longer an option to address and repair that breach of parental protection. A potential family strength in this regard was their housekeeper, Helen, who had served as another consistent nurturer to Kamila over the years. However, in the course of disclosure, Kamila told her therapist/care coordinator that she had tried to enlist Helen's help in dealing with her father, but Helen had not taken any action. At this time, Helen denied any prior knowledge, so Kamila thus felt ambivalent and confused about this formerly supportive "second mother." Helen visited and appeared to "wall off" this topic and instead engaged in pleasant here-and-now chatting and expressions of affection toward Kamila.

Although various family members provided "emotional parenting," authority in decision making and planning fell to the children's services social worker (with court authority) regarding Kamila's postdischarge disposition.

The LCSW's role vis-à-vis these adult familial relationships was to coordinate and facilitate interactions that were conducive to Kamila's functioning and recovery. Not all parties would accept direct support or join in a therapeutic alliance with the LCSW. Frequent communication with all parties was required to gather essential history, keep them informed about treatment, and manage their interactions with the unit staff. Each adult voiced a unique point of view, level of understanding, and type and strength of emotional reactions, as well as desire and availability to assume an active role in Kamila's life going forward. The psychoeducation function was intense, with content ranging from IQ interpretation to symptoms of psychosis, combined with grief reactions and sexual abuse dynamics. The LCSW was acutely aware that as adults process this information about a child close to them, they are also perhaps revisiting their own childhood experiences, which may include sexual molestation. The needs of this family system were tremendous and not atypical of the adolescent inpatient population; the LCSW's greatest challenge was not so much the quality of care she provided to this family, but instead, how she could maintain high standards across a whole caseload of similarly complex patients and families.

CONCLUSIONS

The rich detail and depth of a case such as Kamila's is difficult to convey in a brief written summary. However, her case does illustrate three key points about social work practice in the child/adolescent inpatient psychiatry setting:

1. The clinical complexity and multiproblem nature of hospitalized clients.
2. The social worker's activity is embedded within a team of other disciplines, and she serves as the boundary spanner between the hospital professional system and the community agency system.
3. The critical importance of social work functions that occur *outside* of the therapy session.

Case Study 3-2

Family Drug Court

CHRIS SWENSON-SMITH
AND YESENIA CAMPOS

In 1997, the Adoption and Safe Families Act (ASFA) significantly changed child welfare practices in the United States (ASFA, 1997). Recognizing the profound negative effects on children that resulted from "foster care drift," state child protection and foster care agencies, as well as the courts, were obligated to identify a permanent placement for every child in out-of-home care within 12 months of the child's removal from home. The effect was immediate, and the number of children in foster care, group homes, and shelters across the United States declined rapidly.

Unfortunately, there was an unintended consequence to this system change that ironically contradicted a basic tenet of child welfare: that children fare better growing up in their own homes, assuming the home is safe and healthy. While child protection agencies and the courts continued to make the "reasonable efforts" to reunify children with their parents that the laws demanded, those reasonable efforts could not speed up the recovery process for parents who struggled with drug and alcohol problems.

In jurisdictions with high rates of parental substance abuse allegations in their child welfare cases, the rate of severance cases—or cases in which there is a termination of parental rights—skyrocketed, while the number of children being reunified with their families declined. The availability of adoptive homes for these foster children—especially sibling groups, older children, and children of color—dwindled. Once again, the number of children in out-of-home care increased.

A juvenile court judge in Reno, Nevada, had observed the success of drug courts in criminal cases, and suspected that a similar "therapeutic jurisprudence" approach would work in court dependency cases where there were parental substance abuse allegations. The first Family Drug Court was established in Reno in 1994, and it implemented some of the same key factors that had improved outcomes in criminal cases: frequent judicial oversight, an emphasis on treatment, and a collaborative team approach on each case (N. G. Young, 1998).

There are now more than 400 Family Drug Courts (sometimes called Dependency Treatment Courts) in the United States, and the Substance Abuse and Mental Health Services Administration and Office of Juvenile Justice and Delinquency Prevention provide significant funding to U.S. jurisdictions to implement, expand, and enhance Family Drug Courts. Multisite evaluations have demonstrated that this approach to dependency cases significantly improves treatment completion rates, family reunification rates, and recidivism in child welfare cases that involve parental substance abuse (Cohen, Deblinger, Mannarino, & Steer, 2004; Marlowe & Carey, 2012; Powell, Stevens, Lo Dolce, Sinclair, & Swenson-Smith, 2012; Wheeler, 2006; N. W. Young, 2003).

Pima County Juvenile Court in Tucson, Arizona, launched a Family Drug Court in 2001, and it was designated one of five U.S. Peer Learning Courts in 2012, based on its use of evidence-based, trauma-informed, and gender-specific approaches, and its excellent outcomes. This case study describes the experience of Kim, a 23-year-old woman whose infant daughter was removed by Child Protective Services 2 days after the child was born.

Kim: The day my daughter was removed from my care at the hospital was at the time the worst day ever. Here I was an active crack cocaine user really believing that I was going to be taking my baby home. Knowing my history and the fact that I had been warned by the department that they would take my baby, I was still in denial and in complete shock when the CPS investigator came to my door and told me that my baby was no longer in the hospital and asked me to sign a paper stating I understood that I no longer had custody of my baby. I thought: how horrible ... who can just walk into a hospital room and just tell someone, "Sign here; your child is now in CPS custody"? I got that I messed up and caused the situation that was in front of me but believed I should have been treated like a human. I was not a monster! I was completely broken; I don't remember the hospital social worker speaking to me about what had just happened.

Once I left the hospital, I did what most drug addicts would do. To numb the pain that I was feeling, I went to what I knew best: crack. Most people who don't understand what addicts go through would wonder why the removal of my daughter wasn't an eye opener and caused me to give up my drug lifestyle. The best way I can explain it is that I had been irresponsible and selfish for the last 4 years, where my world revolved on getting, finding, and using drugs. No matter how painful the situation, that was not going to change in one day. I had also realized that I wasn't going to stop for anybody if it wasn't for me. Today, as I think back to that day, it was the best thing that could have happened; had it not I honestly don't know where my baby or I would be.

Kim's behavior immediately after her baby's removal was, unfortunately, not uncommon. Adult substance abuse is often correlated with underlying depression, anxiety disorders, or posttraumatic stress disorder. Individuals may use drugs and alcohol to mitigate the symptoms of these mental health problems. In Kim's case, the trauma of having her child removed, the resulting grief and loss, and the anxiety about what would happen next most certainly exacerbated her anxiety symptoms, and she responded by doing something that made her feel better: She used.

Within a week of the baby's removal, Kim and the baby's father appeared in Juvenile Court at their first dependency court hearing. Child Protective Services developed— and the judge ordered—a case plan for the parents, with a goal of family reunification. In addition to taking random drug screens, a substance abuse assessment and treatment, and a psychological evaluation, Kim was strongly encouraged by the judge and her attorney to take advantage of this program. Kim did not do so for the first 4 months of her case plan, and she continued to test positive for cocaine and/or marijuana.

> **Kim**: After my baby was taken from me at the hospital, I stayed out using until January. I was so overwhelmed with grief, guilt, and shame that I continued to use. I've learned two meanings for the acronym "FEAR": Face Everything And Recover or Forget Everything And Run. I chose the second one. I was terrified of facing my demons and not having much success with my first dependency. I thought, "What's the use?" My addiction had progressed this second time around, and I had little support from my family.

Kim's CPS case manager convinced her to participate in Family Drug Court, and a Family Drug Court Case Specialist met with her and completed an initial assessment. Kim told the FDC Case Specialist that she began using marijuana at age 14 and crack cocaine at age 21. She had also used crystal methamphetamine, "shrooms," and Ecstasy. She was now enrolled in an intensive outpatient treatment program for pregnant and postpartum women through a community behavioral health provider, and reported she had stayed clean for 3 weeks before relapsing on crack cocaine and marijuana 2 weeks prior to the intake.

Kim reported that she also had two older children who were in the sole custody of their father. She had little contact with them. Her current boyfriend, the father of the new baby, was actively abusing cocaine and often pressured Kim to use with him, she reported. Kim also reported a prior arrest for driving on a suspended license, failure to appear in court, and possession of drug paraphernalia.

The staffing protocol tool developed internally by the FDC project evaluator was a free-flowing document that did not include a long list of questions, emphasized the client's strengths and supports, and gave the client the opportunity to tell his or her story in a way that felt comfortable. The FDC Case Specialist asked Kim about her support system, and she listed a good friend with 2 years of recovery, her mother, her church, her CPS Case Manager, and Family Drug Court as her supports. The Case Specialist noted that this was "overall a strong support system, but Kim is struggling to break away from some of her current friends and associates who are users." The Case Specialist asked Kim to consider moving into a residential treatment center, which would mitigate the pressure from these associates and allow her to focus solely on her recovery. Additionally, the residential treatment facility would allow the baby to be placed with Kim, increasing bonding and attachment opportunities.

Residential treatment can be especially effective for clients who are influenced by a negative or dysfunctional environment, or who have failed to benefit from outpatient treatment. And infants and toddlers have better developmental and mental health outcomes when they have one consistent, nurturing caregiver (Ashley, 2003).

Despite these potential benefits, Kim declined residential treatment. She was accepted into Family Drug Court and began appearing before the Family Drug Court judge weekly. Pima County Family Drug Court uses the "parallel model" as opposed to the "integrated model" of family drug treatment courts: That is, one Juvenile Court judge makes findings and orders regarding the dependency (regarding placement of the child, the case plan, and parenting time, as well as "reasonable efforts" by the child welfare agency, and the permanent plan for the child), while the Family Drug Court judge makes findings based solely on the parent's compliance with substance abuse treatment and any other services specifically offered through the drug court (Marlowe & Carey, 2012).

> **Kim**: I remember when I first observed Family Drug Court I thought it was weird at first because I had never experienced a court hearing where everyone was so positive and excited. I thought to myself, "This is interesting but not for me." Then I had a craving to use and had nobody to call except for my FDC Case Specialist. I remember calling him but hoping he wouldn't answer. What was I going to say and how was he going to help me? What if he didn't want to help me? I am so grateful that he did answer, because that day I found someone who really truly cared and wanted to help me. This was huge for me because I had lost all support from my family; I had burned all my bridges. I felt alone and as if nobody understood me or cared to get to know me and help me. With my Case Specialist it was different; he saw me as a person, not as a crackhead like everyone else. For the first time in a long time, I didn't feel alone.

A few days after Kim's first appearance in Family Drug Court, a FDC Case Aide made an outreach home visit. The Case Aide reported in her case notes that Kim seemed only superficially interested in discussing her treatment and recovery; her focus, instead, was on having her baby returned to her. She requested that the Case Aide take photos of her apartment, in order to demonstrate that she was ready to parent her baby.

Motivational Interviewing theory asserts that a person's "readiness for change" is strongly correlated with the effectiveness of drug and alcohol treatment (Miller, 1991). In Kim's case, she was in the Precontemplative phase, often referred to as denial, for many months after the removal of her baby. Although she was currently enrolled in treatment, she seemed to be exhibiting a false sense of confidence that her struggles with substance abuse were over. One of the key elements of family drug courts is that there is immediate response and acknowledgment of both successes and setbacks. When the FDC Case Aide met with Kim's assigned Case Specialist after the initial home visit, they both suspected that this client was setting herself up for a fall by minimizing the seriousness of her addiction and focusing so much energy on her baby and her apartment.

Still, it was important to allow Kim to follow the often-rocky path that is substance abuse recovery, because every failure is an opportunity for the client to develop additional tools and knowledge.

In fact, at her next weekly appearance in Family Drug Court, Kim was found to be in noncompliance for missing a random drug screen and missing her treatment group the previous Friday, stating she had to travel to Phoenix that day for a family matter. The FDC Judge and staff suspected this was a lie, but the relationship between the client and the FDC Case Specialist and Case Aide was very new and would not be strengthened by a demonstration of mistrust or confrontation. Potential clients who observe Family Drug Court sessions often list the nonjudgmental atmosphere as a deciding factor in their decision to join.

New clients are given clear expectations and specific information about the sanctions that may be ordered by the judge for missing drug screens, testing positive on a drug screen, missing treatment, missing a Family Drug Court session, and for violating another client's confidentiality. So long as these sanctions are used consistently and fairly—and this is demonstrated easily because all FDC clients are present when the judge addresses each client—they are not likely to undermine the client/social worker relationship.

Kim called her FDC Case Specialist a few days after the hearing and admitted that she had relapsed the previous Friday. She had provided a urinalysis sample at the lab that morning, as ordered by CPS, and told the Case Specialist it would be positive. Kim sounded discouraged, and the Case Specialist reflected this back to her, but he also thanked her for being honest with him and emphasized this honesty as a positive step toward recovery. They discussed the next steps, and the Case Specialist asked Kim what was working for her and what wasn't. She admitted she did not like her outpatient groups. The Case Specialist reminded her of the residential treatment option, and Kim agreed to attend an intake appointment at a women's facility. The judge ordered her to attend this intake as her sanction for missing a drug screen, for having a positive drug screen, and for missing outpatient treatment.

> *Kim*: When I first joined FDC it was difficult for me to stop using and to reach out for help. I knew that my Case Specialist was there for me. I just wasn't ready to stop, but at the same time I didn't want to lose the support. The one thing that I was able to do was to stay in communication with him and be honest about what I was doing. One of the first things that I learned in drug court was how to trust another person, even though I didn't trust myself or anyone I knew. I had no hope or belief that I would be able to recover and regain custody of my children, but I was able to believe that he believed, and clung to the hope that he had in me until I was able to believe in myself.

The residential facility required Kim to enter a medically supervised detox facility for a few days before starting the residential program. Although detox from marijuana and cocaine—Kim's drugs of choice—does not require medically supervised detoxification (like opiates and alcohol; Tintinalli, 2004), Kim's cravings were so strong that the treatment team believed supervised detoxification would be more likely to result in Kim following through with the next step in her treatment.

Kim was scheduled to remain in detox for 5 days, but she left after 3. She asked the Case Specialist to talk with the residential treatment staff and confirm her bed there, stating she would meet the Case Specialist at 8:30 a.m. on the day she was to start. She did not appear, but again called the Case Specialist and stated she had overslept. Although extreme fatigue is to be expected during drug detoxification, the Case Specialist was losing patience with this client and expressed this to the FDC Supervisor during their clinical supervision appointment. The Supervisor observed that the Case Specialist had many previous clients who missed appointments and relapsed, and did so for a far longer period of time; the Case Specialist had not been ready to request suspension or termination of services so early in these other cases. Was there something different about this particular client? The Case Specialist, when asked this question, admitted that Kim was perhaps the brightest client he had worked with, and that she had many other strengths, including an engaging personality, a sense of humor, and compassion for others. "I *know* she can be successful," he stated. He admitted that he may have set a higher bar for her, one she was no more likely to reach than any client in a similar situation. The Supervisor listed all of the things the Case Specialist had done right in this case:

- He established a trusting relationship with the client by responding promptly to phone calls, making frequent home visits, and listening to what she wanted.
- He carefully reviewed her history and researched her eligibility for treatment options, advocated for the appropriate treatment, and assisted in the enrollment process (including accompanying her to her appointments if warranted).
- He worked closely with the assigned Case Aide.
- He participated as a team member with Kim's treatment providers and CPS case manager.
- He recommended appropriate and fair sanctions.

Why not trust his instincts and experience, and give this client more time, so that she could demonstrate what he already knew she was capable of? He agreed that he would back off, not pushing the client but continuing to be available and monitoring her drug screens. Kim surprised the Case Specialist by asking him to schedule another intake appointment for residential treatment and then following through. Without saying so, she appeared to have recognized that she needed to work at least as hard as her Case Specialist.

> *Kim*: When I kept using and not showing up for court, I thought for sure this program will end up terminating me and, like everyone else, leave me when I need help. This was not the case. He kept answering my calls, kept encouraging me, and kept believing in me. I remember when he first mentioned the idea of me going to a residential treatment facility, I fought it tooth and nail and pleaded with him not to make me go, and him responding that getting help was my choice and he was just giving me options. After a month of trying things on my own, I decided to surrender and again trust that his suggestions were sincere and were really in my best interest. I remember asking him to get me into RTC and not following through on my part, which was just to show up. Again, I thought for sure he was going to give up on me like everyone else, but he did not. He allowed me to make my own choices, and when I made bad ones, he was there to help me see how my choices were impacting my case and my child.

On my last binge use I had been up for 7 days and had been using crack and meth. I was hallucinating and it was on that night that I had my "spiritual awakening." I had walked into a hotel room to get high and saw two kids who I thought looked exactly like my kids, and I knew that I needed help. I got on my knees on the bathroom floor and asked God to take my life if this was how it was going to be. I took that last hit and instantly felt the symptoms of overdosing. I called my friend to pick me up and take me to detox. This time I stayed for 10 days, and on the day that I was released from detox, my Case Specialist and Case Aide picked me up. I remember being embarrassed for them to see me. I was expecting a lecture and them looking at me with judgment. This was not the case, ever. Not once did they condemn me or belittle me or make me feel shameful in any way.

Kim engaged quickly in the residential treatment process, participating in education groups, parenting classes, relapse prevention, and trust-building activities. She had 3 stable weeks, and her baby was transported from her foster care placement to the residential treatment facility once or twice per week for visits. She did not see any of her children on Mother's Day, but observed other clients with their children that day. The Case Specialist visited Kim the next day, suspecting that this would have been difficult for her. He acknowledged her feelings, adding "and you didn't use," a technique used to both foreshadow the many struggles that lie ahead for every client and to acknowledge their ability to manage these struggles without drugs and alcohol.

Another struggle for Kim was her relationship with the father of her baby. He had accomplished little of his court-ordered case plan and was still testing positive for drugs. The FDC Case Specialist was concerned that Kim seemed to minimize these behaviors and expressed disappointment that the baby's father could not attend a FDC-sponsored family event. In the court dependency process, each parent receives an individual case plan and is considered separately in the judge's decision-making around visits and placement. However, when one parent is in compliance and another is not, the judge must also be sure that the compliant parent will put the child's safety above the romantic relationship if the child is returned to the custody of just one parent.

Kim demonstrated a few weeks later that she was not yet ready to do this, by sneaking out of a Family Drug Court hearing to rendezvous with her boyfriend in the court parking lot. She was confronted at a case staffing meeting at the residential treatment facility by her CPS Case Manager, who warned Kim that this type of behavior could decrease her chances of being reunified with her infant daughter. The FDC Case Specialist was present for this staffing, and was careful to stay in his role, acknowledging Kim's progress in treatment, her period of sobriety, and advocating for her to continue in her current treatment. At the same time, he knew that this situation could very well undermine Kim's progress. She was allowed to stay in treatment, was given a sanction in FDC the following week to write an essay on honesty and how it relates to recovery, and apologized openly in court for disappointing the judge and the FDC team. It was clear that Kim was gaining humility and maturity, and that she now had an internal locus of control, rather than believing that CPS, the Court, the treatment providers, or even her boyfriend controlled her behavior. The Case Specialist was encouraged by these developments, which his experience told him boded well for Kim.

He had worked with clients who were always compliant and knew that the problem with this was that he never got to observe how the client handled relapse or other setbacks; any future relapse would be without the safety net of Family Drug Court.

Now that Kim was established in her residential treatment routine, and was free from drugs and alcohol, she began meeting with an individual therapist. Early in the therapeutic relationship, the in-house therapist educated Kim about the correlation between childhood trauma and adult dysfunction, including drug and alcohol addiction. She did not question Kim about her own childhood, but at the following session, Kim disclosed childhood abuse that she had not discussed with any other professional. She told the therapist that she sometimes had flashbacks of this abuse and then panic attacks. She remembered many occasions when she used drugs or alcohol to control these panic symptoms.

This was a breakthrough for Kim, and it was vital that the therapist address the underlying traumatic stress that could lead to Kim's relapse into drug addiction. The therapist used an adaptation of the Trauma-Focused Cognitive Behavioral Therapy approach to help Kim control her stress, modulate her affect, recognize the triggers for panic, and create a "trauma narrative" to replace the previous cognitive process that usually led to panic (Stevens, 2003). Kim also received a prescription for an antidepressant with an antianxiety component.

> *Kim*: While in treatment I was able to address some issues that I had been trying to avoid for so many years. I was able to process the pain and trauma that I went through during my previous relationship. I established a relationship with my higher power and began to see what my Case Specialist had been trying to point out to me for so long, that I was valuable and that I deserved to have a better life. Knowing that I deserved a better way of life was just half of it; learning how to make the right decisions in order to achieve it was another. Although I was not using drugs or alcohol, the addict behavior was still present: I wanted what I wanted when I wanted, and most of the time I wanted everything now! Getting clean is only half the battle; changing mindsets and respecting and following rules was a challenge for me. It was only through experiencing consequences that I was able to finally make the change and truly realize that my actions were causing my problems and that I couldn't go on blaming people, places, and things. I had to be accountable.

After 4 months of stability, Kim reached another turning point in her journey. She learned that she was pregnant by her daughter's father, who had at last engaged in treatment, was working, and hoped to co-parent both children with Kim. She began to break some of the residential treatment house rules in order to be with her boyfriend, and she was consequently discharged. Although she remained clean and sober, Kim's FDC judge and dependency court judge had no choice but to find her in noncompliance for failing to complete her recommended substance abuse treatment. Before another treatment plan could be made, however, there was the problem of stable housing.

The FDC Case Specialist took advantage of the stabilization housing contract FDC had established with a local agency and requested a bed for Kim. Because of his relationship with this agency, and Kim's history of treatment compliance, they suspended their rule that did not allow for pregnant clients, and Kim moved into a group home setting with seven other women. Many of these women were transitioning out of prison, and the rules required that all residents work with an employment agency to complete a job readiness course and begin a job search in order to pay a portion of their rent. The FDC Case Specialist increased his frequency of contact with Kim during this high-risk period: She had lost her therapist, her housing, her friends in residential treatment, and was instantly thrown back into the real world, where she was expected to find and hold a job while she continued to comply with a CPS case plan.

> *Kim*: In the beginning, when people mentioned transitional housing, I was not willing to look into it. But I was serious about my recovery, and my boyfriend and I decided it would be the best thing for us both, especially since it was the first time in our relationship that we were clean. The stability and support the halfway house offered was ideal, and we needed all the support we could get.

Next, back into treatment. The FDC Case Specialist had seen a lot of success with a local intensive outpatient treatment program for pregnant and postpartum women. Although the program used a harm-reduction model of substance abuse treatment (Bigg, 2001), the FDC Case Specialist met with Kim and the program staff and emphasized that Kim was still expected to remain completely drug and alcohol-free. The interruption of treatment and the change in living situations delayed the progress of Kim's dependency court case. The case was approaching the 12-month Permanency Hearing mandated by the Adoption and Safe Families Act of 1997. At that hearing, the FDC Case Specialist was sworn in and testified about the length of Kim's sobriety, her engagement in services, and the progress she had made since the baby was first removed. Kim's judge ordered that Kim and her boyfriend should have an additional 3 months to achieve reunification with their daughter, and all parties in the case agreed.

For the last few months of Kim's case, she and the FDC Case Specialist worked as partners, keeping each other informed, searching for treatment and housing options together, and planning for Kim's future after Family Drug Court. The Case Specialist was no longer Kim's advocate; she had learned to be her own.

Kim and her boyfriend found a subsidized apartment in a safe neighborhood. She gave birth to a second daughter, and both mother and baby tested negative for drugs and alcohol. CPS chose not to file a dependency petition on the new baby, and Kim and her boyfriend took her home with them. Kim graduated from Family Drug Court to rousing applause. Her toddler was returned to her custody, and her dependency case was closed.

> *Kim*: We had our baby girl and were very happy to bring her home with us. The road was long and hard and I took many detours, but in the end it was all worth it. When I graduated FDC I committed to share with whoever would be willing to listen about how FDC helped me change my life and find recovery.

Over the course of the next 7 years, Kim:

Married her daughters' father

Worked as a licensed insurance agent

Gained shared custody of her older son and daughter

Began attending a 4-year university

And ended up back in Family Drug Court, but this time, as a professional Recovery Support Specialist, working alongside an FDC Case Specialist to provide the same intensive case management support and advocacy that was provided for her. She remains solidly in recovery. She is the coauthor of this case study. She is "Kim."

Yesenia: Today, it is an honor to serve alongside this wonderful team at FDC. I share my experience, strength, and hope with all clients. I also do my best to be to others what my Case Specialist was to me: a guiding light in a dark and lonely tunnel. I honestly don't believe that I would be here today had it not been for the unconditional, nonjudgmental support that I received from my Case Specialist, Case Aide, and the entire FDC staff.

REFERENCES

Adoption and Safe Families Act (ASFA), Pub. L. No. 105–89 (1997).

Ashley, O. M. (2003). Effectiveness of substance abuse treatment programming for women: A review. *American Journal of Drug and Alcohol Abuse, 29*(1), 19–53.

Bigg, D. (2001). Substance use management: A harm reduction-principled approach to assisting the relief of drug-related problems. *Journal of Psychoactive Drugs, 33*(1), 33–38.

Cohen, J., Deblinger, E., Mannarino, A., & Steer, R. (2004). A multi-site, randomized controlled trial for children with sexual abuse–related PTSD symptoms. *Journal of the American Academy of Child and Adolescent Psychiatry, 43*(4), 393–402.

Marlowe, D. B., & Carey, S. M. (2012). Research update on family drug courts. Retrieved from www.NADCP.org

Miller, W. A. (1991). *Motivational Interviewing: Preparing people to change addictive behavior.* New York, NY: Guilford Press.

Powell, C., Stevens, S., Lo Dolce, B., Sinclair, K., & Swenson-Smith, C. (2012). Outcomes of a trauma-informed Arizona family drug court. *Journal of Social Work Practice in the Addictions, 12*(3), 219–241.

Stevens, S. M. (2003). Traumatic stress and gender differences in relationship to substance abuse, mental health, physical health, and HIV risk behavior in a sample of adolescents enrolled in drug treatment. *Child Maltreatment, 8*(1), 46–57.

Tintinalli, J. K. (2004). *Emergency medicine: A comprehensive study guide.* New York, NY: McGraw-Hill.

Wheeler, M. (2006). *Family dependency treatment court: Applying the drug court model in child maltreatment cases.* Baltimore, MD: National Drug Court Institute Drug Court Practitioner Fact Sheet, 5(1).

Young, N. G. (1998). *Responding to alcohol and other drug problems in child welfare: Weaving together practice and policy.* Washington, DC: Child Welfare League of America.

Young, N. W. (2003). *Family drug treatment courts: Process documentation and retrospective outcome evaluation.* Irvine, CA: Children and Family Futures.

Case Study 3-3

Child Welfare Supervision Case Study

Cynthia A. Lietz

Questions:

1. In what ways might Maria's age, race, and gender impact her supervision?
2. What values do you have that might interfere with objective decision making in social work practice?
3. How were Family-Centered Practice principles modeled by Maria in her supervision?
4. A supervisor is in a position of authority. How do you feel supervisors should handle this authority when supervising child welfare workers?

As social workers advance in their level of knowledge and experience within a particular field of study, it is not uncommon for them to be promoted to the position of supervisor. Social work supervisors serve a very important function by ensuring the quality of social work practice. Social work supervision is different from disciplines outside of our field in which a boss is there to manage employees. Instead, social work supervisors serve multiple functions that go beyond just management. They typically meet regularly with their staff to process cases in one-on-one supervisory conferences or in-group supervision meetings to monitor practice and work with supervisees to develop new skills. The purpose of this case study is to describe how one model of supervision can be applied to a child welfare setting. In this chapter, the case study is not referring to a client, but instead references a supervisee with whom a supervisor is working.

THE THREE FUNCTIONS OF SOCIAL WORK SUPERVISION

Social service supervisors are responsible for monitoring and mentoring the practice of social workers. Kadushin and Harkness (2002) suggest supervisors typically serve three functions: administrative, educational, and supportive. The administrative function involves assigning cases, reviewing and signing off on paperwork, and monitoring the quality of practice. The administrative function represents the aspect of supervision that involves ensuring the quality of practice. Administrative supervisors are responsible for observing the work of their supervisees to make sure practice is consistent with agency policy and procedures. Supervisors must also ensure that practice adheres to professional standards as defined in the NASW Code of Ethics and by state licensure boards.

The educational function of social service supervision involves mentoring professionals with less experience for the purpose of professional development. When supervisors help their supervisees to apply content learned in the classroom, they serve the educational function by helping new professionals understand how theoretical material can be applied in the context of specific practice settings. Supervisors also serve an educational role when they provide training and teach supervisees about policies and procedures at their setting. Finally, clinical supervision involves initiating the learning process by having in-depth case discussions that allow a supervisee to develop critical thinking skills. Therefore, the educational function may involve a didactic process where the supervisor teaches a skill, or the process of education may be accomplished through a more discussion-oriented process that uses reflective questions to prompt critical thinking.

The third function of supervision involves providing support. Just as practitioners must form a therapeutic alliance with clients to foster the change process, supervisors develop professional supervisory relationships grounded in give-and-take respectful communication. This function involves providing both practical and emotional support. Practical support can include being available to supervisees, providing clinical direction, and connecting supervisees with resources clients may need. Emotional support involves listening, demonstrating genuine care and concern for the supervisee, and helping supervisees to develop self-care strategies. Although emotional support is an essential part of managing vicarious trauma and burnout, it is important that supervisors avoid becoming the personal counselor of their supervisees. Just as in social work practice, supervisory support occurs in the context of professional boundaries that are appropriate for a supervisor–supervisee interaction.

CHILD WELFARE SUPERVISION

Child welfare (CW) involves a system of policies, programs, and services that were created to provide for the well-being of children. The public child welfare system is tasked with the responsibility of implementing national and statewide policies that respond to reports of child maltreatment. CW supervisors may monitor the practice of hotline workers who take calls from professionals and community members regarding potential incidents of abuse or neglect. These supervisors may supervise investigators who conduct assessments to determine whether maltreatment occurred, to identify ongoing threats to safety, and to evaluate the level of risk of future maltreatment. CW supervisors may manage ongoing workers who establish and monitor parents' progress on a case plan, or they may collaborate with social workers in the area of adoption. Regardless of the roles within the system, CW supervisors are expected to ensure that their workers are engaging in practices that are consistent with agency policy and procedures.

The nature of child welfare work has caused CW supervision to remain administrative in focus (Dill & Bogo, 2009; Ferguson, 2009). Because of the increasing number of policies and procedures and mandates regarding reporting, these demands can cause a supervisor to remain focused on administrative tasks, spending less time on the educational and support function. Strengths-Based Supervision (SBS; Lietz & Rounds, 2009) is a model of supervision developed for child welfare that seeks to increase intentionality regarding the full range of supervisory tasks. Specifically, SBS integrates four elements:

1. To fulfill the administrative, educational, and support functions
2. To utilize both individual and group supervision modalities
3. To integrate task and reflective processes in supervision
4. To parallel or model principles of Family-Centered Practice (FCP)

The first element of SBS involves being more deliberate about fulfilling all three functions of supervision. As mentioned earlier, CW supervision has historically remained more administrative. There is a growing interest in enhancing clinical supervision within child welfare, which would involve more fully engaging with the educational role (Dill & Bogo, 2009; Ferguson, 2009; Salus, 2004; Strand & Badger, 2005). CW workers make decisions in the context of complex situations. The ability to process cases with a supervisor and develop critical thinking skills is now recognized as essential to quality CW practice. In addition, research suggests that CW workers are in great need of increased support. Supervisor support has been linked to increased retention and job satisfaction for a workforce that faces a high level of stress. Therefore, increasing support is also an important initiative across CW settings.

Second, SBS uses both one-on-one and group supervision modalities. Both modalities are recommended because each offers different benefits. Individual supervision allows supervisors to get to know their supervisees and their cases in greater depth. It provides a safe place when constructive feedback needs to be given. Group supervision fosters a sense of belonging at the workplace by building a team atmosphere. In addition, group supervision can prompt critical thinking, as unique experiences and the perspective of a diverse group of professionals can foster creative problem solving (Lietz, 2008).

The third element of SBS involves using task and reflective processes in supervision. Task-centered supervision represents a more directive approach. It provides answers and a clear direction to supervisees regarding questions they bring to supervision. Reflective supervision is an approach characterized by fewer answers and more questions. It seeks problem solving through discussion. Developmental supervision suggests that newer supervisees require more direction and answers from their supervisors, whereas more-experienced workers may benefit from increased level of reflection. CW supervisors should assess the needs of their supervisees and foster a supervisory process that is consistent with their professional development.

The final element of SBS suggests that CW supervisors increase intentionality around paralleling or modeling Family-Centered Practice (FCP) principles in supervision. FCP is a model of CW practice that is strengths-based, collaborative, and seeks to incorporate the voice of children and parents in decision making (U.S. Department of Health and Human Services, 2007). Parallel process suggests that practitioners often replicate the supervisory process in their own interactions with their clients (Cohen, 1999; Shulman, 2005). In other words, if a supervisor values the perspective of the supervisee in supervision, then the worker is more likely to value the perspectives of children, youth, and families in their work. Because public CW agencies seek to remain family-centered, supervisors can support implementation of FCP by modeling the practice principles in supervision.

CASE STUDY

The purpose of this case study is to describe how a supervisor, Maria Salazar, implemented SBS as she worked as a public child welfare supervisor in a rural area in the Southwest. Maria is a 34-year-old Latina woman who was recently promoted to supervisor of a unit in a rural area. Maria graduated with her MSW and was hired on at CPS about three years ago. Maria had been working as an ongoing worker within an office at a different location, but she will now be supervising a unit that includes two investigators and three ongoing workers. As part of her supervisor training, she attended a class on SBS and will be using this framework to guide her work.

Maria decided to start her supervisory approach by implementing both individual and group supervision. First, she scheduled individual meetings with each person during her first week. This allowed her to get to know each person, to listen to their concerns, to identify things that are working, and to discuss her own style. Essentially, these early meetings represent the early phases of supervision. During this time, a relationship is being formed, trust is being established, and patterns of communication are developing.

Supervisors face many complicating issues as they take on a new unit. First, they are coming to a unit with its own past, culture, procedures, and at times loyalty to previous supervisors. SBS honors culture and the expertise of the group, so Maria is respectful of the unit's history. Therefore, she decided to be intentional about not changing many aspects of the team's functioning and schedule before getting to know the group and its history. She also wants to model FCP by incorporating the voice of her supervisees in discussing any changes she plans to implement as the new supervisor.

Another complication is the fact that Maria is supervising two workers, Bob and Yvette, who have more experience than she does. Bob has been with CPS for almost 10 years. He has never desired to become a supervisor and has worked contentedly first as an investigator and now currently he is an ongoing worker. Maria recognizes Bob as a natural leader of the team. The unit has been without a supervisor for several months. The group has often turned to Bob for advice and support during this transition. It is essential in a situation like this that Maria not feel threatened by Bob's leadership, knowledge, or experience. FCP is a strengths-based approach that seeks to work with the assets of a family when fostering change and addressing problems. In the same way, the respect Bob has earned has been an important part of this team surviving without a supervisor for a relatively lengthy time, making him an important resource of this team.

When Maria met with Bob, she was able to honor his position within this group by acknowledging the respect he has earned and commenting positively about the influence he exerts within the team. She was also able to thank him for his service and for going above and beyond during this transition. Bob smiled and laughed, and said he was just glad they now have a supervisor to take over. He acknowledged he was willing to help out, but stated he does not aspire to be a supervisor and was pleased that he could let go of this extra workload now that Maria is here.

During this conversation, Maria was able to convey her respect of Bob, leading him to feel comfortable relinquishing some of his power, along with some of the responsibility he took on but did not necessarily want. This approach also allowed Maria to avoid potential power struggles that could have arisen in a situation where someone like Bob was given unwritten authority that could be threatened as a new person takes over. By joining with Bob and the common mission Bob and Maria share around enhancing the well-being of children, Maria was able to avoid a common pitfall of overexerting authority with a supervisee who has established his own influence within the team. In fact, after their one-on-one supervisory conference, the other four members of the team went straight to Bob to ask him what he thought of Maria, a further illustration of Bob's respect among his peers. Bob was able to respond that he had a good meeting with Maria and felt optimistic about her, something that helped to establish her authority with the group.

The second supervisee with more experience than Maria is Yvette. Yvette has been with the department for just over 5 years. Different from Bob, Yvette is interested in a promotion to supervisor. In fact, Yvette applied for the position of supervisor, but Maria was chosen over Yvette for the position. Supervising workers with more years of experience can create some distrust because workers are concerned that their experience will not be valued. This is particularly challenging when one person competed with the current supervisor for the position. Although Maria should not assume there are bad feelings toward her for getting the position, it is important that she understand the position of her new supervisee and address these issues.

Similar to Bob and the other supervisees on her team, Maria scheduled an initial one-on-one supervisory conference with Yvette. When the meeting began, Maria sensed some tension, so shortly after getting started, Maria acknowledged that Yvette might have feelings about not getting the position and encouraged her to process this with Maria. Initially, Yvette was taken aback by the question and became somewhat agitated when speaking about the fact that Maria got the position over Yvette. She was particularly frustrated by the decision considering Yvette has more years of experience with the department.

It would not be uncommon in a moment like this for a supervisor to feel uncomfortable with Yvette's feelings. Supervisors might even feel tempted to defend their own qualifications and their worthiness of receiving the position. Supervisors should remain mindful of their own reactions, because a defensive posture could shut down the supervisee from sharing more, which could limit the ability to come to a resolution. This can be especially true of new supervisors like Maria, who may have some self-doubt and insecurity with taking on this position of authority.

If tough questions such as these are to be discussed in supervision, the supervisor must remain emotionally grounded and willing to truly listen to the concerns of the supervisee. It does not mean a supervisor is submitting supervisory authority to demonstrate interest and concern for a supervisee. In fact, in some ways, being willing to face highly charged issues may in fact help supervisors to establish respect. In addition, this type of supervisory interaction remains consistent with a family-centered approach, something Maria would like to model for her supervisees.

Understanding this meeting could be tough, Maria prepared herself emotionally prior to meeting with Yvette. She also sought to remain self-reflective during their meeting by managing self-talk that could increase her reactivity and instead remaining focused on Yvette and her experiences. Therefore, in response to Yvette's initial agitation, rather than becoming defensive and bringing the focus of the conversation back to herself, Maria chose to validate Yvette's concerns and ask more questions to draw out Yvette's story. Through their conversation, Yvette explained she felt Maria got the position over her because Maria has her MSW and Yvette has a Bachelor's degree in an unrelated field. Yvette's frustration then shifted away from Maria onto their larger organization, which she feels continually fails to value her input because she does not have a degree in a related field. Underlying Yvette's agitation was a fear that she would never be promoted because of not having the right degree.

This further conversation allowed Maria the opportunity to validate Yvette's frustrations and concerns and to discuss professional development opportunities. Maria was aware of a tuition reimbursement program that could cover the costs of Yvette's MSW if she decided to go back to school. The women then spoke about options regarding how Maria could work with Yvette's work schedule to help her to negotiate her class schedule if she was interested. Yvette left the meeting reporting that she felt heard and valued. She was also very excited that someone was paying attention not just to her work, but also to her own professional development and career goals.

During the individual supervision meetings with Bob and Yvette, Maria was careful to acknowledge their experience as a strength. In this way, she was modeling principles of FCP in that starting with one's strengths can set the tone for growth and development. She also demonstrated ideas associated with developmental supervision in that she was more task-centered with her newer workers but took more of a reflective approach with Bob and Yvette, her more experienced staff. For example, Maria had three additional meetings that first week with Christa, Alice, and Andre. Christa and Alice have been with the unit for less than 6 months, and Andre just completed core training, meaning he is just entering the field for the first time. During these meetings, Maria still listened and focused on building an alliance with these newer workers. But in these cases, they had more questions for her. Being newer, they wanted to understand more about how she viewed certain policies and what would be expected of them, leading to a more directive approach consistent with task-centered supervision as compared to Maria's style with Bob and Yvette.

After meeting with all of the team members for individual supervision, Maria scheduled their first group supervision meeting. Group supervision is a meeting led by a supervisor with his or her supervisees. It is less structured than a traditional meeting with an agenda and instead focuses on discussion-oriented problem solving. Group supervision often involves one person presenting a complicated case to the group to solicit feedback. The supervisor is there to facilitate the process and to ensure that group think—when a group convinces one another that a bad idea is a good idea—does not happen.

Group supervision represents a place where the team can come together to solve problems related to cases. The varied experiences of the group members prompt creative problem solving that is less possible in the individual supervision modality. Individual supervision is useful for getting to know supervisees in greater depth, and some conversations, such as the one Maria had with Yvette, are more personal and better handled in a one-on-one supervisory conference. However, talking about procedures and the history and culture of the teams and lending support to one another regarding tough cases are all discussions that fit well with group supervision.

Maria decided to again model a family-centered approach in her group supervision by starting the first meeting asking the team members to discuss the strengths of the team. Maria had a whiteboard and wrote words on the board that team members used to discuss positive aspects of their team. By the end of this discussion, the board was filled with phrases such as "committed to protecting children," "care about families," "willing to go the extra mile," and "there for each other." Being able to hear each other speak about the team in these ways fostered a sense of belonging for the team. Seeing the words listed on the board offered further acknowledgment of what connects members of this team.

This conversation also allowed Maria to get to know her supervisees as a team, and this activity indicated her commitment to knowing them rather than changing them. She then acknowledged the potential discomfort of the team as they take on a new supervisor, so she opened up the meeting for their questions, and she responded to their concerns. By the end of the meeting, Maria asked everyone about the process, and the team members agreed that they really enjoyed being able to take 1 hour and get together not for a "meeting" where someone talks "at them," but to instead talk together about common concerns.

Maria then suggested they meet for group supervision two times per month. She explained the process would look similar in that it was not one more meeting, but that instead this time was carved out for them to support one another through shared problem solving. This team had not participated in group supervision before, so this initial meeting served as an important orientation to what the process could look like. The team agreed and set an ongoing schedule for case presentations, where each person took turns bringing a case to the group to seek feedback. Some teams prefer to meet weekly for group supervision. Although there are advantages to that structure, being a supervisor in a rural area means supervisees have to travel for any meeting. Maria felt that two times per month was reasonable, whereas increased scheduling might put undue pressure on her team. In addition, Maria worked hard to schedule her group supervision on days when her workers often had to come to the main office for another reason, thereby increasing both the efficiency of the task and communicating respect for the complications that arise when working with a team consisting of members who are located at different offices with extended travel required.

As time moved forward, Maria advanced beyond the beginning stages of supervision, which are focused on relationship building, establishing trust, and setting expectations through contracting, to the middle phase of supervision, which involves monitoring and mentoring practice. To accomplish this goal, Maria continued to meet with her supervisees for regular individual and group supervision.

The frequency of individual supervision was dependent on a developmental assessment of her supervisees. For Yvette and Bob, Maria was able to meet with them twice per month. Their process was more reflective in nature and often involved Yvette and Bob talking more, with Maria asking a few questions as a way to monitor practice. For Andre, Christa, and Alice, Maria met with them for a consistent appointment each week. In addition, Maria found that she had to be much more available for crisis-oriented supervision with them than was necessary for her more-experienced workers. With these newer workers, Maria found herself talking more, because she needed to make sure all three workers were aware of the agency's policies and procedures. She also worked on skills development and asked questions that would help her understand how these newer workers interacted with children and families. Finally, Maria also conducted live supervision by shadowing her workers on home visits and by attending court hearings to watch their practice live. When workers are new, it is critical for a supervisor to see the worker's practice firsthand to monitor the quality of practice and to see areas of mentoring that can be brought back to supervision meetings, thereby serving the educational function.

An example of the middle phases of supervision involved a recent meeting with Andre. As mentioned earlier, Andre is a brand-new worker. Andre recently graduated with a degree in business, but he was unable to find a job in his field. When he saw an advertisement for a job as a child welfare investigator, he was interested because his family fostered children for many years. He is clearly committed to protecting children and youth and understands from his experience living with foster youth the detrimental effects that child abuse and neglect have for children. Andre's commitment to children and his focus on safety is a great strength. However, at times, Andre seems quick to remove children from their families when alternative safety plans might be possible. He also discusses in supervision his hesitancy to place children with relatives for fear they have the same problems as the parents. Although these concerns are understandable, the child welfare system is overloaded, and there are not enough foster homes to meet the needs of children without using relative foster placements. In addition, a family-centered approach is grounded in the idea of preserving family whenever possible, and when this is not possible, maintaining connections with extended family is highly valued.

To remain consistent with the agency's practice model and with generally accepted best practices within child welfare, Maria recognizes that she must challenge some of Andre's perspectives in supervision. Because this issue is personal and value-driven, this topic is probably better addressed with Andre in individual supervision. A general conversation about what it means to be family-centered could be raised with the team in group supervision. However, the more-involved conversation with Andre about his own values, his history, and how this impacts his decision making is a better fit for individual supervision. In addition, this is an ongoing conversation, not something that Maria would raise just one time.

Issues such as these are complicated and require ongoing reflection and dialogue. Consider the complexity: If Andre chooses to not engage extended family to serve as relative foster placements because of his own history and corresponding values, he is making decisions based on values and not based on an objective assessment of that case. However, if Maria were to reprimand Andre and he decides that he always places with relatives, that could also be a problem. In some respect, it is another example of value-laden decision making. The first decision was based on what he heard from foster youth in his own home, but the second decision is based on a desire to please his supervisor, which is not a bad thing, but in fact is another value. Maria needs to impress on Andre that decision making should not be based on his past or based on pressure he feels from her, but instead, his clinical decisions should be based on the available evidence he has about each particular child and family.

To address this issue, Maria chose to ask Andre to talk in his supervision meeting a bit about what interested him in child welfare work. Embedded in our good intentions are often values that can support good practice or can hinder solid decision making. As Andre talked about growing up in a home that fostered, he was able to share some stories that informed his work. Maria let him talk for a while and then asked Andre in what ways his experiences helped and in what ways his experiences could hinder best practice. As they deconstructed his experiences and how they inform his work today, he was able to see that his experiences were his experiences, but they are not necessarily that informative when working with *all* cases in his current position. They talked about how he could recognize his own bias and when to seek supervision about decisions, such as placing with extended family, that may be hindered by his own values. They agreed that working on self-awareness through his own reflection and challenging him to make decisions grounded in objective evidence would be a theme of ongoing supervisory meetings. Maria's ability to have these open conversations was grounded first in their ability to develop a supervisory relationship grounded in trust. Clearly, Andre respected Maria, which allowed a difficult topic to be accessible.

As child welfare supervisors seek to implement SBS, many other issues come up that are beyond the scope of this chapter. Issues of power must be managed. Supervisors are in a position of authority, and appropriate use of authority is an issue with which many supervisors must contend. Supervisors are also in a hierarchical position related to the children and families with whom they interact, which is another important consideration. Related to power, supervisors must address differences in race and ethnicity that can help and hinder the supervisor process. Cross-cultural supervision involves the ability to supervise effectively across culture, something social work supervisors seek to achieve. Organizational factors also impact a supervisor's ability to supervise effectively. Particularly in large organizations such as Child Protective Services, budget cuts that eliminate positions and lead to increased caseloads can pull supervisors away from supervision, leaving cases of their workers unsupervised. In addition, local, state, and federal policies determine in many ways what child welfare workers can and cannot do, which therefore impacts the supervisory process. What supervisors can suggest to their workers is driven by policy, and supervisors are responsible for monitoring adherence to these policies; therefore, much of the content of supervision is policy related.

In summary, CW supervisors serve an important function in that they monitor the quality of child welfare practice. Their jobs are important and complicated. Being intentional about building the kind of relationships, processes, and procedures that can support quality practice is essential to accomplishing this objective.

REFERENCES

Cohen, B. (1999). Intervention and supervision in strengths-based social work practice. *Families in Society, 80*(5), 460–466.

Dill, K., & Bogo, M. (2009). Moving beyond the administrative: Supervisors' perspectives on clinical supervision in child welfare. *Journal of Public Child Welfare, 3*(1), 87–105.

Ferguson, S. (2009). Clinical supervision in child welfare. In C. Potter & C. Brittain (Eds.), *Child welfare supervision* (pp. 296–329). New York, NY: Oxford University Press.

Kadushin, A., & Harkness, D. (2002). *Supervision in social work*. New York, NY: Columbia Press.

Lietz, C. (2008). Implementation of group supervision in child welfare. *Child Welfare, 87*(6), 1–48.

Lietz, C. A., & Rounds, T. (2009). Strengths-based supervision: A child welfare supervision training project. *The Clinical Supervisor, 28*(2), 124–140.

Salus, M. (2004). *Supervising child protective caseworkers*. Washington, DC: U.S. Department of Health and Human Services.

Shulman, L. (2005). The clinical supervisor-practitioner working alliance: A parallel process. *The Clinical Supervisor, 24*(1/2), 23–47.

Strand, V., & Badger, L. (2005). Professionalizing child welfare: An evaluation of a clinical consultation model for supervisors. *Children and Youth Services Review, 27*, 865–880.

U.S. Department of Health and Human Services, Administration for Children and Families, Children's Bureau. (2007). *Children's Bureau Child and Family Services Reviews Practice Principles*. Retrieved from www.acf.hhs.gov/programs/cb/cwmonitoring/tools_guide/hand-2.htm

Case Study 3-4

Challenging the Tradition: In Some Families, Violence Is a Way of Life

STEVEN KRUGMAN[3]

The couple in this case developed a relationship that incorporated significant incidences of violence. Breaking this pattern of violence became the goal for successful resolution of the problem.

Questions

1. How does the social worker challenge the family's values in this case?
2. What factors could be attributed to maintaining the violence in this family?
3. How was the couple kept involved in the treatment?
4. What personal attributes or family experiences do you have that could affect your ability to work with similar cases?

A dog barked at me while I waited on the porch of the ramshackle house for someone to open the door. A young woman in her mid-twenties wordlessly let me into the kitchen. There, five or six adults were sitting around the table, smoking cigarettes and

---

[3] "Challenging the Tradition: In Some Families, Violence Is a Way of Life," by Steven Krugman, 1986, *Family Therapy Networker, 10*(3), pp. 41–43. Reprinted with permission.

drinking coffee. A baby slept in a port-a-crib, while two older boys played with used auto parts in the living room.

The baby and the two boys were the ostensible reason I was there. A social worker at the hospital where the baby had just been born had learned that the infant's mother, "Kathy"—the young woman who had let me in—had a long history of drug abuse and that both she and her two young sons had been beaten by her first husband. The worker, concerned about Kathy's ability to take care of her new baby, had filed a child abuse and neglect report. I was there following up on that report as the representative of a family intervention team of the State Department of Mental Health.

I had already gotten some background information on Kathy. She was a tough Irish girl from Boston who had grown older and a little wiser over the years. At 17 she had married a man who worked sporadically, sold drugs, and regularly abused her and their two boys. After one especially vicious beating, Kathy's brothers helped her escape and return to her parents' home. That ended the marriage. Back home she quickly resumed her long-standing job of taking care of everyone else and keeping the lid on the ever-stewing pot of family conflict. She was the fourth of 10 children. She had kept out of trouble by staying close to her volatile, sometimes alcoholic, mother; running errands; and hauling in stray family members. Then she met 40-year-old "Tony," whose maturity seemed to offer the possibility of a more stable, less violent family life. They had been married for 2 years at the time of this first visit.

The relationship with Kathy was Tony's third try at a family. His first marriage had broken up because his wife wouldn't take his abuse and left with their daughter. According to him, the second marriage "just ended," that's all. Tony carried himself like a coiled spring and let everyone know he was not someone to mess with. But evidently someone had ignored those signals along the way, because Tony had once done 10 months in prison for assault.

As I entered the kitchen, Tony offered me a seat and went on talking with his buddies. I just sat there wondering if either Tony or Kathy would acknowledge that we had set up a meeting a few days before. Neither one of them did. Finally I said we needed to get started. With drudging ceremony, Tony ushered his friends from the kitchen, shrugging his shoulders and asking one of them to wait in the living room.

I explained about the report I had received from the hospital's protective worker. Tony immediately let me know that he wanted to be no part of whatever I was selling. Everything was fine except for the "goddamned Department of Social Services." He stated that neither he nor Kathy needed any help, and I should leave. I felt like an intruder and was more than a little intimidated by Tony and his friends. Kathy hardly said a word. There was no room for discussion. As I left, I told Kathy and Tony to call if they felt I could be of use.

A SURPRISE CALL

The following Sunday night, I answered a crisis call. It was Tony. Kathy was in the hospital. She'd "hurt herself" while high on Valium and alcohol. Could I see the two of them? The next morning, I learned that Kathy had been stuporous and badly bruised when she was admitted to the hospital. The emergency room sent her to a shelter for battered women. The kids seemed to be all right.

Later that day, Kathy came to the session with an advocate from the shelter. She and Tony cried together while the shelter worker and I sat by uncomfortably. They were both tremendously apologetic and remorseful. Kathy was angry at herself for breaking a promise she had made to Tony about using pills. She was, however, confused about how she had gotten so bruised. Tony swore he had only "slapped her around a little" to revive her. He said that he had been scared to death when he saw her looking all doped up.

I asked Kathy if she knew what Tony wanted her to do. She said, "Sure. Stop using pills. Be home when the boys get home from school. Stay in at night because it's too dangerous. Not see anyone, just wait for him." As she spoke, she got angrier and more sarcastic. "Yeah, I know what he wants. He wants to control me."

Still smarting from my first encounter and puzzled by Tony's call to me, I wanted to shift the responsibility for choosing therapy to the clients. "It seems to me that you've both apologized and forgiven each other. The last time I spoke with you, Tony told me that everything was okay. I wonder if there's any need for us to meet? Maybe Kathy should go for counseling at the shelter." This time they both said that they wanted to go to therapy; they didn't want this relationship to go down the tubes like the others had.

CHALLENGING THE FAMILY'S VALUES

Once I began meeting with Tony and Kathy, it was clear that they were much more experienced than I with violence of all kinds. Both had grown up witnessing violence at home and in the street. They jokingly called their neighborhood "Dodge City." During the 2 years they had been married, Tony had threatened Kathy numerous times; shoved her on two occasions (prior to the current incident); pushed around Kathy's 9-year-old son, Kevin, several times; and had a fight with her ex-husband. Yet these acts had barely registered on their scale of life events.

With Kathy and Tony, as with other violent couples I see, the first phase of treatment was governed by three principles:

1. *Safety first.* I help the victim and the family establish as much safety as they can. To do this I negotiate an explicit contingency plan in which both partners agree on how they will deal with a violent crisis. The plan then becomes a technique for creating alternative choices, like timeout periods and physical separation, to counter abuse and victimization. My emphasis on the plan challenges the family's belief that now that treatment has begun, the danger is over. I insist that it lies ahead.

2. *Responsibility and control.* With violent couples it is essential to give a clear message that the hitter is responsible for his hitting and that rationalizations like "she provoked me" or "I couldn't help it" are not acceptable. Tony insisted that when he hurt Kathy he was "out of control." I told him that I had a hard time believing that an experienced streetfighter like him had so little control over his hands. He repeated my observation, enjoying the irony. There was something about this way of looking at his relationship with Kathy that struck home with him. Invoking the image of the battle-scarred streetfighter who was unable to control himself with his wife provided tremendous leverage throughout the course of therapy.

3. *The rights of the victim.* Along with the emphasis on the responsibility of the abuser comes a concern with the rights of the victim—namely, the right not to be hit. In many families, this challenges the accepted value system regarding the use of physical force. While emphasizing that Tony was also hurting and needed help, I strongly supported Kathy's right not to be hit or coerced. "I've never had a safe place," she told me. "I want my home to be safe."

After 4 months of weekly meetings with Tony and Kathy, there had been no further physical battles, and I confronted a familiar problem in working with violent couples. If you succeed in putting a check on the violence, then the family's motivation to change is likely to diminish dramatically. Going from the crisis and initial engagement to a longer-term working alliance is difficult. Many cases get lost at this point. Making the transition to ongoing treatment requires either a high degree of motivation within the family (often the wife says "Unless you change, I'm leaving") or consistent external pressure coming from the courts or the Department of Social Services (DSS). At times, family and church networks can provide it as well.

Violent families rely heavily on denial and minimization as a way of warding off their feelings of being out of control and vulnerable. Dropping out of therapy at the first sign that things are better is a predictable response. After all, going on in treatment means dealing with upsetting memories and experiences. So, when Christmas arrived, Tony and Kathy decided to break for the holidays and call me if they wished to see me again.

PHASE TWO

What happened next makes the case of Tony and Kathy unusual in my experience. Typically, either one or both of the partners in a violent relationship are reluctant to be in treatment. The investment of the mental health system with such couples is more in the way of crisis intervention than ongoing treatment. If therapy is to continue past the initial crisis, then the therapist must ally with both partners while insisting that the violence must stop. This can be a difficult balancing act to pull off. Somehow, in this case, both Kathy and Tony had come to see me as someone who had something to offer, and 4 months later, I heard from them again.

Tony, working long hours and under a lot of financial pressure, "lost his cool" one night, pushed Kathy around, and slapped her. In a similar incident some days before, Tony slapped Kevin after the boy told him "not to yell at his mother." Kathy was furious. She told Tony, "I did what you asked. I haven't used Valium. But I married you to spend time with you, and you're never home. I need my own life. You can't control me. I won't put up with your hitting and shoving me and the boys. I don't want those kids hit by anyone ever again."

Tony seemed to get the message and reaffirmed his commitment to no more hittings. I agreed with Kathy that Tony was trying to control her life, but I reframed it as "too much caring." Tony agreed to see me individually to find some better way of handling Kathy's wish for more autonomy.

Meanwhile, Kathy's son Kevin told his guidance counselor about the violence at home. Another DSS worker got involved and raised the question of whether Kathy's three boys should be removed from the home. Although no specific action resulted, Kathy became very anxious at the possibility of losing custody. She even talked about leaving Tony if staying with him jeopardized her custody of her sons. For the first time, Kathy and Tony were faced squarely with the possibility of losing either their children or their marriage.

OTHER SYSTEMS

A basic ground rule in working with violent family situations is to make use of all available community resources. Yet anyone who has ever dealt with the courts and DSS knows that their interventions are often ineffective and poorly coordinated. In this case, though I had worked closely with the protective agency, the threat to remove Kathy's children was never discussed with me. I suggested a meeting to develop a plan including the school and DSS, but before the meeting could be held, the caseworker left the agency. The case, evaluated now as "low risk," went unassigned for months. A relieved Kathy and Tony left therapy once again.

About six months later, Tony and one of Kathy's brothers had a terrible fight over some money that had disappeared from the house. The police, arresting no one, filed a child abuse report. A new worker was assigned, and the family was once again encouraged to resume treatment. By this time the pattern of ebb and flow of tension was becoming clear, and together we focused on understanding how the episodes of violence fit into Tony and Kathy's life with each other. Tony had long ago cut himself off from all familial ties. As is true for many men, abusive and nonabusive, his wife had become his sole source of emotional attachment. Yet her wish that he be home more left him feeling "hemmed in" and anxious about making enough money.

The later and harder Tony worked, the more entitled he felt and the more alone and vulnerable to her family Kathy found herself to be. Furious at Tony for not fulfilling the role of protecting her from her family, which he had assumed earlier in their relationship, she distanced herself by using drugs and going out with friends. Tony experienced this withdrawal as deeply threatening. His fear and anxiety would generate a crisis of violence that, like a powerful summer storm, would clear the air and reestablish their connection.

As they came to recognize that violence was their way of regulating closeness when no other means seemed available, Kathy and Tony began to feel more connected. He began to come home for dinner several nights a week. They agreed to set limits with Kathy's intrusive family and become more involved with the boys. By this time, the pattern in Tony and Kathy's relationship with me was also becoming clearer. Some crisis or external push (e.g., from a new DSS worker) would trigger a new round of therapy. We'd meet regularly for several months, and then the demands of daily life would override our scheduled meetings. I framed the waning energy as Tony and Kathy's taking control of the therapy. We ended this phase with me saying, "Call me when you'd like to meet again. Remember, you don't have to wait for a crisis."

TRANSGENERATIONAL ISSUES

Tony called 6 months later to report another crisis: Kathy had moved out with the boys. They had had a fight, but—he emphasized—he hadn't hit her. When I saw Tony and Kathy together, I learned that her mother had died, her father had moved in, and in his wake the brothers and sisters followed through the open door. "I've lost control of my house," she said.

Tony said, "This is how it started. I thought that when her mother died, we should take care of her dad. Kathy blew up. She said, 'If you like my family so much, you can have them.' I was hurt. But when she said she was leaving I saw red."

The death of Kathy's mother brought all of the transgenerational themes underlying their conflicts into focus. Kathy had been ambivalent about her mother all along. Her covert function as surrogate mother became overt when "Mom" died, as did her lifelong resentment about being put in that role. For Tony, having Kathy's father around was a little like having his own deceased father around again.

Creating boundaries around the nuclear family with Kathy's father living there was next to impossible. Finally, pursuing the issue of how Kathy and Tony could be available to each other in the midst of all this conflict generated the idea of a vacation. "Pops" could either go with them to Florida or go stay with one of her older sisters. With great difficulty, Kathy allowed her father to live elsewhere. A year later he was still living with her older brother, and Kathy and Tony were together and doing well.

CONCLUSION

Physically violent families tend to be closed systems. They are organized around secrets and a fearful view of the world. Obtaining the trust of such families is a trick in itself. Engaging the abusive members, along with others in the family, means going from being seen as a nosy intruder to a valued resource who can help the family to change what hurts.

Engaging any closed or rigid family system is a challenge, but with violent families the challenge goes deeper. The therapist takes a clear moral position on the unacceptability of violence in the family, a position that typically challenges the family's subcultural values. By supporting the vulnerable members—both those being hit and victimized and those who feel emotionally one-down and disempowered—the therapy begins to help the individuals and the family reorganize around their needs for physical and emotional safety.

Although they hardly matched the stereotype of the ideal therapy consumers, Kathy and Tony went much further in exploring the roots of the violence in their relationship than most couples I have treated. In each installment of their treatment, we were able to focus more on the larger familial context maintaining their problem. Recently, I spoke with Kathy to sound out how things were going for her and Tony. "Good and bad," she told me. "Things between Tony and me are fine. He hasn't been violent in years. When things get 'tight' we talk it out—like you taught us. I'm not afraid anymore that he's going to hurt me. That's the good news. The bad news is that my dad's back with us, and he's driving me nuts!"

PART IV
Case Studies in Family Therapy

T he early foundations of social work practice were firmly rooted within a family perspective. Mary Richmond, one of the great leaders in social work, wrote in 1930 about the importance of the family. Richmond believed that the family was a pivotal institution about which human lives revolved. Although the history between social work and the family has not always been strong, today much, if not most, of social work is practiced from a family perspective.

The strong family emphasis is largely a result of the family therapy movement, which began in the 1950s. That movement continues as social workers and other professionals specialize in family treatment. Social workers work with families in numerous capacities, such as offering assistance to families who are grieving over loved ones, providing divorce mediation, performing family therapy, working with families who have abused their children, doing case management with families confronting developmental disabilities and chronic mental illness, and working with foster families who provide a family substitute. Clearly, families are an important part of social work practice.

The family therapy, or family systems, perspective perceives individual dysfunction as largely related to the dynamics of the family (Corcoran, 2003). Family practitioners typically see symptoms of family members as a systemic function in the family. The treatment focuses not on a client with symptoms but on a family with certain dynamics influencing the symptoms. The assessment of a family examines the functional relationship between the individual problem and the dynamics of the family. Although a family perspective is a powerful way to understand families, it is equally important to understand the relationship between individual and family dynamics and environmental factors. A family perspective has often led practitioners to neglect the importance of individual and environmental factors.

All family therapy approaches address some aspect of the family, but there are important differences in the way different models conceptualize, operationalize, and intervene to help families. Family therapy is often described using two major categories: (1) growth-oriented approaches, which include psychodynamic, Bowen family systems, and experiential models; and (2) problem-solving approaches, which include structural, strategic, and behavioral models of practice (Walsh, 2011). In recent years, the problem-solving approaches to family therapy have grown because of the current focus on evidence-based treatments.

These family therapy approaches attempt to understand how families function and use a variety of different concepts to understand families. Some of the more familiar concepts include family structure and power; family boundaries; communication and interactional patterns; family rules, myths, and rituals; family decision-making processes; and family roles (Walsh, 2011). In general, the family therapy practitioner gathers information about the sequences and patterns of behavior, the emotional and cognitive reactions of family members, and the specific actions of family members.

Whatever the approach in working with family members, it is critical to successfully engage them in the treatment. This requires good clinical skills, such as providing reassurance and normalizing problems (helping clients understand that when they are in stressful circumstances, it is understandable that problems exist), communicating empathy to family members, establishing positive expectations for change, and encouraging positive motivation.

The case studies in this chapter demonstrate many of these clinical skills and present some different models of family treatment. The chapter begins with a case study by Gladow, Pecora, and Booth that presents a detailed account of how the Homebuilders program works toward family preservation. This case study incorporates an evidence-based approach and presents a clearly specified treatment model with lots of concrete examples. The case study by Lappin and VanDeusen describes a complex case that demonstrates the need to look beyond family factors to the ecological context. Their family therapy approach shows the importance of obtaining coordination from large public agencies in order to help multiproblem families. The last case study is by Eddy, who helps family members resolve their grief over the suicidal death of a family member. It demonstrates the use of a particular family therapy procedure—ritual—and shows the adept clinical skills necessary to work with families successfully.

REFERENCES

Corcoran, J. (2003). *Clinical applications of evidence-based family interventions*. New York, NY: Oxford University Press.

Walsh, F. (2011). *Strengthening family resilience* (2nd ed.). New York, NY: Guilford Press.

Case Study 4-1

Homebuilders: Helping Families Stay Together

Nancy Wells Gladow, Peter J. Pecora, and Charlotte Booth

I ntensive in-home services are a powerful social work tool for helping families. This case study illustrates the use of goal setting and relationship building, which are critical in the Homebuilders model of home-based treatment.

Questions
1. What are some examples of relationship building used in this case?
2. How did the social worker intervene to reduce conflicts between the father and son?
3. What is a "teachable moment," and how was this incorporated into the treatment?
4. What are some of the advantages and disadvantages of a home-based treatment model?

The following case involves conflict between a single-parent father and his 13-year-old son. The treatment agency is the Homebuilders® Program of the Institute for Family Development (IFD), headquartered in Federal Way, Washington. Homebuilders is an intensive, home-based family preservation services program. Through child welfare and children's mental health system contracts, IFD provides Homebuilders to families who have one or more children at imminent risk of being placed outside the home in foster, group, or institutional care.

Home-based family preservation programs now exist in many states and other countries. Although theoretical approaches, clinical techniques, caseloads, and length of treatment vary from program to program, the goal of these programs is the same: to prevent unnecessary removal of children from their homes and to help multi-problem families cope with their situations more effectively (Allen & Tracy, 2009; Nelson, Walters, Schweitzer, Blythe, & Pecora, 2008; Walton, Sandau-Beckler, & Mannes, 2001). Although some models of family preservation have not been tested, some research evidence suggests that programs with high fidelity to the Homebuilders model can result in a cost savings to the state (Miller, 2006).

Homebuilders is an intensive model, with a time frame of 4 to 6 weeks per family and a caseload of two families per therapist. Therapists provide an average of 38 hours of face-to-face and phone contact to each family. The program is a skills-oriented model that is grounded in Rogerian, ecological, and social learning theories. The intervention involves defusing the immediate crisis that led to the referral, building a relationship with the family, assessing the situation and developing treatment goals in partnership with the family, and teaching specific skills to help family members function more effectively and achieve these goals. Evaluations of Homebuilders indicate that the program is highly effective in reducing out-of-home placements and increasing the coping abilities of family members (Fraser, Pecora, & Haapala, 1988; Haapala & Kinney, 1988; Kinney, Madsen, Fleming, & Haapala, 1977). There is also evidence that the model can decrease racial disproportionality in the child welfare system (Kirk & Griffith, 2008).

In Washington, referrals are made to Homebuilders primarily through Child Protective Services (CPS) and Family Reconciliation Services (FRS), which are two subunits of the public child welfare agency. In CPS cases, the state worker determines that placement of one or more of the children outside the home will occur if the family does not make immediate changes to ensure the safety of their children. In FRS cases, either parents or children have themselves requested out-of-home placement for the child because of severe family conflict or child behavior problems. In one region of the state, referrals are also made through the mental health system, with the goal of preventing psychiatric hospitalization.

CASE OVERVIEW

The following case study highlights some of the Homebuilders treatment philosophy and techniques with an atypical, but increasing, type of case situation: a single-parent father and his son. However, this case was similar to most cases in that the family had a history of family problems and conflict. In this case, the child had no previous out-of-home placements: 49% of Homebuilders clients have already experienced previous placement. Selected client sessions are described for each of the 4 weeks of service. All of the names and identifying information have been changed to protect the family's privacy.

Because of space considerations, the three contacts and work with the boy's mother are omitted, along with the contacts made with the school psychologist and other school personnel. In addition, a considerable amount of time was spent working with the father regarding his use of marijuana, which was not interfering with his job performance but was a concern to his son. Interventions such as working with a local church and Narcotics Anonymous were attempted (with some success) but will not be discussed in order to focus on the therapist interventions regarding client relationship building, chore completion, school behavior, and anger management.

INTERVENTION

Week One: Gathering Information, Relationship Building, and Setting Treatment Goals

It was 7:30 p.m. as I drove up for the first time to the Barretts' small three-bedroom house located in a working-class neighborhood. The referral sheet from the FRS caseworker said Dick Barrett had been a technician for a large manufacturer in Seattle for 10 years and that his 13-year-old son, Mike, was in seventh grade. FRS became involved after Mike had told his school counselor that his father had been smoking marijuana for 15 years. (This was the first time that the state had come into contact with his family.) Mike said he hated drugs, was tired of his father's constant yelling, and wanted to be placed outside the home. He also said he was afraid of his uncle, who had been living with the family for 2 months. The school counselor had already been concerned about Mike, a seventh grader for the second year, who frequently neglected to turn in his homework and disrupted class by swearing at both students and teachers. Mike had already been suspended twice that semester. The referral sheet said that Dick voluntarily agreed to have the uncle move out and to quit using drugs, although he was unwilling to begin a drug treatment program. It also said the family had tried counseling several months ago through a local agency, but Mike had disliked the counselor and refused to continue.

Dick, a tall man of around 50, opened the door soon after I rang the bell. Dick invited me to sit at the kitchen table and called for Mike to join us. The family cat jumped on my lap. Dick and I began chatting about cats as Mike slowly walked into the kitchen, looking at the ground and making grumbling sounds. Mike smiled when he saw Tiger sitting on my lap and being scratched under the chin. Mike began to tell me stories about Tiger, and I responded with interest and a funny story about my own cat. I felt no pressure to hurry the counseling session along, as taking time for small talk and showing interest in what was important to family members was a key element of relationship building that would be the foundation of any later success in confronting clients and teaching new behaviors.

Dick began to discuss the difficulties his family had been experiencing. He said he was upset about Mike's behavior problems and lack of motivation in school. Dick said he had tried everything he knew to get Mike to improve but with no success. As Dick talked, I listened reflectively—paraphrasing parts of the content and feelings that Dick was expressing. For example, when Dick said, "Mike does not even try to improve his behavior in school," I responded with, "It is frustrating for you that Mike does not seem to want to improve." After Dick spoke about Mike's abilities being much higher than his actual achievement, I said, "So it seems pretty clear that Mike has a lot more potential than he is using."

Reflective or active listening serves several purposes. First, it helps family members deescalate their emotions. As they tell their stories and begin to feel that someone understands, they calm down and are more likely to be able to take constructive steps to improve their situation. Second, by conveying understanding, active listening helps build up a positive client-therapist relationship. Third, active listening helps the therapist gain more information about the family without having to ask a lot of questions. People frequently expand on their stories when the therapist is listening reflectively. Asking many questions seems to limit what people say, and it creates the impression that the counselor is the expert who will "do something to" the family. With Homebuilders clients, it works better to recognize and treat clients as partners in the counseling process. Clients have more information about their lives than does the therapist, and their active participation in the change process is crucial. However, sometimes asking a few key questions at the right time is the most efficient way to gain behaviorally specific information. For example, in this situation, I wanted to know just what Mike's grades were. (He was in three special education classes and was earning one B and two Cs in those. In his other classes he was earning two Fs and a D.)

As Dick talked, Mike remained silent, although his facial expressions and body movements frequently suggested anger toward his father. "You do not look too pleased, Mike," I said. "What do you think about all this?" Again I listened reflectively as Mike began to talk about how he hated school and his father's frequent yelling. Mike told stories about several arguments he and his father had that resulted in both of them swearing and saying things calculated to hurt each other. Dick agreed that this was true. I summarized, "So learning how to fight less and deal with your anger constructively is something both of you might like?" They both nodded. Dick went on to say, "Mike makes me so angry. If he would not say some of the things he does, I would not get so mad." (I thought to myself that Dick could benefit from learning a basic principle about anger: No one can *make* you angry—you are responsible for your own anger. I did not mention my thought at this point, however, because pointing out errors in thinking and teaching too soon before there has been time for sufficient information gathering and relationship building is often ineffective.)

"You have mentioned that you argue a lot more than either of you would like. Tell me what kinds of things you argue about," I requested. Dick described frustration about trying to get Mike to do chores around the house, saying if Mike was not willing to help, he would prefer Mike find somewhere else to live. Mike complained that his Dad was always ordering him around. Dick had been working especially hard lately to fix up the house so that it could be sold in a few months and finances between him and Mike's mother could be resolved. Dick and his ex-wife had gone through a difficult divorce 3 years ago after 28 years of marriage and four children, the older three being over 18 years of age and currently living on their own. Through mutual agreement, Dick had received custody of Mike.

"I get the picture from the caseworker that drugs have been a big issue in your family," I commented. Dick described how he had been smoking marijuana for about 15 years. He said he had also gotten into "some other things" during the time his brother-in-law, Mike's uncle, had been living there. Dick said once the school and the caseworker became involved, he realized it was important to have his brother-in-law move out, which he had done. Dick said he had stopped using other drugs and had also voluntarily stopped using marijuana a few days earlier. Dick stated that he respected Mike's right to live in a drug-free home and that he thought it would benefit himself as well to stop his drug use. "I can't afford to get fired if my work finds out about this," Dick commented.

"What do you think about this, Mike?" I asked. Mike remained silent. "If I were you, I might be a little worried that my Dad was not really going to quit using drugs," I said. "Is that anything like you are feeling, or am I way off base?" Mike opened up a little to say that his Dad had said he would quit before and had never stuck with it. Mike talked about how his siblings all use drugs and how he had been scared when, 3 years ago, some "bikers" had come to the house to get his oldest sister to "pay up" on some drugs. Mike said he also worried about having his father's health go downhill from drug use. I could tell from Dick's expression that this was probably the first time he had heard Mike express these concerns openly.

Soon it appeared that Mike was getting tired, and it was time to end this 2½-hour initial session (about the average amount of time for a first-session Homebuilders program). I explained more of the specifics of the Homebuilders program and gave them my home phone number as well as the backup phone numbers of my supervisor and our beeper. All of this is an effort to be available to clients 24 hours a day, 7 days a week. I then summarized the session in terms of treatment goals. "It sounds like what you two most want help on is (1) working out a way to build in more cooperation on household chores; (2) learning how to fight less and to deal with anger more constructively; (3) Dick, your receiving support in your efforts to be drug-free; and (4) improving your school performance, Mike. Is that how you see it?" They both nodded. Summarizing in this way checks my perception of the family's priorities for change and also gives direction for future counseling sessions. In this intake session with the Barretts it was easier to establish goals than it is with many families. There is really no rush to determine all four treatment goals (a typical number for a 4-week intervention) at the intake session, although Homebuilders therapists generally try to have one or two goals established by the end of the first week.

The last thing I did during the first visit was to set up individual appointments with Dick and Mike. Unless family members are opposed to them, individual meetings can be helpful initially to gather additional information and continue building relationships. Later, one-on-one sessions can facilitate work on each person's goals. I gave Mike a sentence-completion sheet to fill out for our next session and checked to make sure he understood how to do it.

When I came back 2 days later to pick up Mike for our individual session, he was listening to his stereo. I listened to a few songs with him. As we drove to McDonald's, we talked about various musical groups and our favorite TV shows. He seemed to be feeling much more comfortable with me by the time we sat down with our Cokes and french fries. I looked over the sentence completion sheet, which included sentences such as "My favorite subject in school is ___," "In my spare time I like to ___," and "I feel angry when ___." Instead of asking Mike a lot of questions, which teenagers frequently dislike, I read some of his answers in a tone of voice that encouraged him to expand on the topic. When he did, I listened reflectively to his responses, and he frequently elaborated even further. I learned that he was especially upset about his father yelling at him on a daily basis. When his father yelled, Mike found himself quickly feeling angry and sometimes yelling back. I reflected Mike's feelings of worry, embarrassment, fear, and anger about his father's use of drugs.

I also checked out with him what kind of system they used at home regarding who did what household chores and if Mike earned an allowance. (I was thinking that coming up with a mutually agreed upon chore system might be the first goal we would tackle, because it was so important to Dick and was a goal with which we were likely to make concrete progress.) Mike said there was no system; his dad just gave orders and Mike either complied or didn't. I suggested a system whereby he earn an allowance for doing certain agreed upon chores, and I asked what he thought a fair allowance would be, assuming his father would approve of this plan. He said the plan sounded agreeable and suggested $15 per week. I gave Mike an assignment to complete before the next meeting. He was to write down (1) two things he'd like to be different in his family; (2) two things he could do to help get along better with his dad; and (3) two things his dad could do to help them get along together better.

My appointment with Dick alone began with his showing me the work he had done around the house to get it ready to sell. This led him to talk about his past marriage with Rita, his feelings about the marriage ending, and how Mike had gone back and forth between their homes for almost two years up until about a year ago. Dick thought some of Mike's troubles were a result of his going from home to home, plus the pressure of Dick and Rita's continual fighting. After an hour of active listening to these subjects, I felt pleased that Dick was opening up, warming up to me, and appearing relieved to get some of these things off his chest. When he brought up his older children's drug involvement, I saw it as an opportunity to gently begin talking about his own drug use. (This is an example of a "teachable moment." A teachable moment is a time when clients may be particularly receptive to learning because they can see the relevancy of it in their lives.) We then spent some time discussing this issue and developing a plan of action.

Before ending the session, I introduced the idea of having Mike's chores be based on allowance. Dick's reaction was positive, saying he thought more structure would be helpful. I noted two benefits to such a system: (1) Mike would experience the consequences of his actions, and (2) it would reduce the number of times Dick would need to tell Mike what to do. Mike had developed a tendency to blame much of his behavior on others rather than taking responsibility for his actions. In addition, like most teenagers, Mike hated to be told what to do, yet their previous system was based completely on Dick giving daily instructions. We briefly discussed what he thought a reasonable allowance would be. We agreed to negotiate this new system with Mike at the next session. I also gave Dick the same homework assignment I had given Mike.

Week Two: Active Work on Goals

As Mike, Dick, and I sat down together in the living room, I asked how things were going. Meetings often start in this way, as events may have recently occurred that need to be discussed or worked out before clients will be able to concentrate on the current agenda.

When I asked if they had done their homework, Dick had and Mike hadn't. Dick agreed to do something else for a few minutes while I helped Mike complete the questions. Then both of them told what they would like to be different in their family. Dick said he would like anger to play less of a role and for the home to be drug free. Mike said he would like less arguing and to go places together more. In discussing what each person thought he could do differently, Dick said he could try not to get angry when frustrated, and he could also be more consistent with Mike. Mike said he could help more around the house and try not to get angry so much.

On the subject of what the other person could do, Dick said Mike could be more responsible with housework and schoolwork. Mike said his dad could stay off drugs and yell less. I took this opportunity to talk about how problems in a family are almost never one person's fault and how each family member can do things that can help the other family members. I also noted the similarities in the changes they wanted and stated that I had some ideas that might help them with some of these changes.

Next we began work on the new chore system. I explained that we would be deciding together what chores Mike would be responsible for, when they were to be done, how much allowance he would earn, and what he did and did not have to pay for with his allowance. We began by writing a list of all the chores possible and gave Mike a chance to pick some he would be willing to do. Dick added a few he would like Mike to be responsible for. After a little more negotiation, we came up with a list both of them felt they could live with. Mike said he really did not like doing chores. Rather than letting Dick jump in with a lecture, or responding with one myself, I opted for humor. I chuckled and told Mike I certainly could understand that, as Ajax and vacuum cleaners had never thrilled me either. I gave a couple of examples of how my husband and I split up chores so that neither one of us would have to do all of the work. Then Dick and Mike decided how often each chore needed to be done, to what standards, and by what time of the day. We discussed which chores involved the most and the least amount of work and determined point values for each.

In deciding on allowance, Mike thought $15 per week was fair, and Dick thought $10 per week was more appropriate. After discussing it further, we agreed on a system whereby Mike's basic allowance would be $10, and all he would have to pay for was his own entertainment. On the weeks when he earned 97 percent of the points or above, he would get a $5 bonus and earn $15. We put this all onto a chart and filled it out as though Mike had done a perfect job (see Figure 4.1). The crossed-out squares on the chart indicate days the chore need not be done.

On a blank chart, we wrote the possible points next to each chore and agreed on the time when Dick would check the jobs and fill in the points. We specified which day would be payday and where the chart would be placed. When Mike got a phone call, I took the opportunity to share with Dick some hints on making the chore system work most successfully. I suggested he use the chore checking as a chance to develop goodwill with Mike by praising him for work he does well. I gave Dick a handout on "97 Ways to Say 'Very Good.'" I also suggested that when Mike did not do a chore or when he did it poorly, Dick handle it matter-of-factly rather than with anger. Past experience indicated that Mike became less cooperative when Dick was angry.

The last session in week two was with Mike and Dick together. Mike was upset because his father had not filled in the chore chart the past 2 days. We got the chart off the cupboard and filled it in together. Dick agreed with Mike that Mike had done all of

Figure 4.1 Weekly chore chart

BEHAVIOR	DAYS AND NUMBER OF POINTS EARNED							
	Mon	Tues	Wed	Thurs	Fri	Sat	Sun	Total
Straighten bedroom (by 5 pm)	4	4	4	4	4	4	X	24
Bring in wood (by 5 pm)	3	3	3	3	3	3	3	21
Do dinner dishes (by 9 pm)	6	X	6	X	6	X	X	18
Take out garbage (by 9 pm)	3	3	3	3	3	3	3	21
Vacuum house (by 6 pm)	X	X	X	X	X	11	X	11
Change cat litter (by 6 pm)	X	X	X	X	X	5	X	5

Weekly Total 100 Pts

Every 10 pts. = $1.00
97-100 pts. = $10.00 + $5.00 bonus
Sunday evening payday
X = Chore not required on that day

his chores so far that week. I encouraged Dick to appreciate Mike's efforts and success, and we practiced this. Mike enjoyed the encouragement.

Because anger management was one of our main goals, I introduced the topic by showing a picture of an "anger thermometer" (see Figure 4.2). I talked about 0 as the point where a person was calm, relaxed, and feeling no anger at all. At 2 or 3 a person often felt irritated or frustrated. At 5 a person was definitely angry, at 6 or 7 quite angry, and by 9 or 10 so enraged that he or she was out of control. At these top points, people often say and do things that they would not otherwise say or do and that they often regret later.

I had both Mike and Dick identify times when they had been at various points on the thermometer. They both acknowledged that some of their most hurtful and useless fights had occurred when they were at a 9 or 10 on the scale. I asked them to identify physical symptoms they experienced at various points on the scale, especially at 7 or 8 before they were out of control (e.g., having a fast heartbeat, feeling hot, or having sweaty palms). I requested that they identify how they could tell that the other person was at these points. We then discussed the concept of removing oneself from the situation before losing self-control in an effort to avoid destructive fighting. I said that their symptoms at 7 or 8 should be seen as cues to temporarily leave the situation. We discussed where each person could go to calm down (e.g., Mike to his bedroom, Dick to the basement to work on a project). Mike and Dick agreed they would try to remove themselves from the situation to avoid fights.

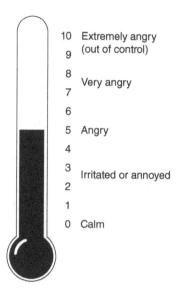

Figure 4.2 Anger thermometer

At some point when we were alone, Dick commented, "If Mike would just do what he is supposed to do and not talk back to me, I wouldn't have this problem of anger." I gently challenged him: "I see things a little differently. I agree that Mike doing his chores and schoolwork would help. And certainly the way Mike talks to you has an influence on how you respond. But I see your response back as your responsibility and not Mike's. Each one of us is responsible for our own behavior—Mike for his and you for yours. In fact, the only behavior any of us can truly control is our own." Dick thought a minute and agreed.

We got back together with Mike, and I talked with the two of them about using self-talk to decrease and control anger. To illustrate this point, I gave several examples. Then we read a short children's story together called *Maxwell's Magnificent Monster* (Waters, 1980b). This story illustrates the point that our self-talk causes us to become angry. Mike put the two concepts together and said that the monster was when a person was at a 9 or 10 on the anger thermometer. Dick was quiet and seemed reflective. He said he liked the story and asked to keep it for awhile.

Week Three: Teaching, Learning, and Some Application

The first session of the week was spent initially with Dick alone. Dick talked about the meeting he had gone to at school that morning with Mike and the school psychologist. It was the first day back after vacation, and Dick had been required to go because Mike had been suspended the 2 days before the break. I listened reflectively as Dick told of "Mike's rude behavior" toward him and the psychologist. Dick expressed his frustration at not being able to "make" Mike improve in school. I reiterated that a person has the greatest control over his own behavior and that Dick could only do so much to influ-ence Mike. I suggested that concentrating on staying drug free, decreasing his own angry responses, and being consistent with checking and praising Mike on chores are all areas he could control that could indirectly have an impact on Mike's functioning at school. We reexamined the ineffectiveness of yelling as a means to improve Mike's school performance. I suggested he not spend too much energy on this issue now, and let Mike have more responsibility or ownership for the school problems.

Mike then joined us, and we talked about the morning school appointment. When I brought up the issue of Mike's behavior with the school psychologist, Mike quickly mentioned some things his Dad had said to the psychologist that had embarrassed him. I said I could understand his embarrassment. However, his actions and words toward the school counselor were still his responsibility and could not be blamed on his father. I reinforced the idea that what he says and does is his responsibility, just as what his father says and does is his father's responsibility. Because I knew this was a message Mike would not like hearing, I said it in a concise and friendly way and then moved on to the next topic. Dick said Mike had been doing extremely well on chores and had earned the full $15 the past week. It was obvious from Mike's expression that he liked hearing his dad's praise.

The next day I picked Mike up at school, and we went to McDonald's again for our session. Mike had a long list of complaints about his father, especially that his dad got upset and yelled about such small things. Mike said he also worried about his dad drinking more beer. I simply listened, focusing largely on reflecting the feelings Mike was expressing. At one point I used a sheet with 20 feelings and accompanying faces showing those feelings. I had Mike pick out the feelings he felt frequently and explain when he felt them. My hope was that simply having the opportunity to vent his emo-tions would be helpful to Mike. However, I purposely avoided any statements blaming his father. I wanted to encourage Mike to take responsibility for his own actions rather than blaming someone else for everything. I talked with Mike about what he could and could not control. I mentioned that he could not control his father's substance abuse, that this was largely his father's choice. I suggested several phrases that he could use to share his feelings about it with his father, if he would like. (Example: "When I see you drinking beer, I feel scared and worried.")

We discussed the support group his school counselor had told me about—a group for teens whose parents have problems with substance abuse. Mike made an agreement with me that he would go once and evaluate it. I talked about how Mike does have con-trol over his own behavior, both at home and at school. I said I thought it was great he was doing his chores so regularly and how this had already improved things. I listened to Mike's feelings about school and then talked concretely about all the positive things his dad, counselor, and I saw in him. I encouraged him to try a little harder in school and talked about the potential of increased self-esteem and future employability. We also discussed a few career possibilities, and I told stories of some people I knew who had dropped out of school early and ended up in very low-paying jobs.

During the next session with Dick, I asked if he had read the article I had given him at our last meeting: "The Anger Trap and How to Spring It" (Waters, 1980a). Dick said yes, that it made an excellent point. He was able to summarize the main idea: Anger is a choice, and other choices are available. I emphasized that by opting to interpret a situation in a different way (changing one's self-talk), anger can be reduced, and more helpful responses can be chosen. I explained again the basic concept of rational-emotive therapy (RET). This time I drew the RET triangle as I illustrated that it is not situations or events (A) that cause feelings (C) but rather our self-talk or interpretation (B) about the situation (Ellis & Harper, 1975; see Figure 4.3). I gave some examples from my own life, and Dick was able to identify some situations in which using this technique could have helped him.

We discussed a handout on "The Six Steps to Anger" (Hauck, 1974), which identifies common self-talk leading to problematic anger, and then I provided him with a list of calming self-talk and challenges to angry self-talk. We discussed the need to catch oneself using anger-producing self-talk and to substitute that with calming self-statements. When a friend of Dick's dropped by, we had covered so much material—Dick had been very eager for help with anger—that I saw it as a good time to end. I quickly gave Dick a book I had bought for him, one of the Hazelden Daily Meditation Series based on the 12 steps of AA (Hazelden Foundation Staff, 1988). I knew that the book fit well with the concepts Dick admired in his church group, and it could be helpful to him in his struggle with substance abuse. Dick was surprisingly touched that I would buy him this book. He read the meditation for that day out loud. (Dick's readiness to accept and use written materials is definitely greater than in most Homebuilders cases. A large percentage of clients will not read materials, so therapists spend considerable time discussing and role-playing concepts with families.)

The third session of the week, held with both Mike and Dick, was very encouraging. They were in good moods when I arrived, having spent a fun afternoon riding dirt bikes together. They said they had forgotten how much fun each other could be. When Dick said he planned to do more things with Mike in the future, Mike was visibly pleased. When I saw that the chore chart was filled out and that Mike had done all his work for the second week in a row, I smiled and complimented Dick and Mike.

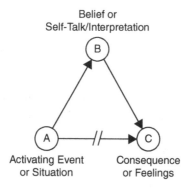

Figure 4.3 The rational-emotive therapy triangle

Dick said he had been working on the anger management techniques we had discussed and that they were helping. He gave an example of an incident that had occurred that morning in which Mike had approached him angrily. Rather than responding with anger as he previously would have done, Dick had been able to remain calm. Dick said it kept Mike from escalating and resolved the situation sooner. Mike confirmed that his dad was calming down and that this made it more relaxing to be at home.

The remaining time was spent learning the skill of I-messages. I explained the basic concept of I-messages as a way of communicating how another person's actions are affecting you in a manner that is most likely to be received well. The point of an I-message is to say how you feel without attacking the listener's self-esteem or saying things that are going to make the other person more defensive (Gordon, 1970). To illustrate, I told of a situation and then stated my feelings in an unhelpful, critical, and blaming way (a "You-message"). For example, "You were a thoughtless idiot to have left the gas tank empty when you came home last night. You never think of anyone but yourself." We discussed how they felt hearing that statement, how likely they were to want to cooperate with me, and what they felt like saying in return. Then I expressed my feelings in I-message form. "When you left the gas tank on empty, I felt irritated because I had to go to the gas station first thing and ended up being late for work." We discussed the difference. I pulled out the anger thermometer and pointed out how I-messages can be used when a person is at a low point on the scale. This increases the chances of resolution of the problem at an early stage and avoids the gunnysacking effect that can occur when a person lets a lot of irritations go unaddressed. Dick said he had a tendency to hold back his irritation and shared a few examples of this behavior.

I diagrammed the parts of an I-message on a large pad I had brought along. "When you (behavior), I feel (emotion), because (effect on you)." I gave Mike and Dick an assignment to write four I-messages for one another: two using positive emotions (proud, happy, relieved, and so on) and two using uncomfortable emotions (angry, hurt, discouraged, and so on). While Dick worked on these on his own, Mike and I moved to another room where I helped him write his statements. We then shared what they had written and discussed the experience.

Week Four: Progress Continues but Setbacks Occur

Dick said he was hungry and wanted to go to a nearby coffee shop when I arrived for our appointment alone. I drank coffee while he ate dinner. He said Mike had continued to do well on his chores. Dick said he thought the system was helping, and he had even noticed Mike looking for ways to improve the decorating in his bedroom. Dick said he was calming down quite a bit after realizing that he could choose responses other than anger. He said Mike also seemed calmer and that they were warming up to one another.

Mike and I had our last individual session at the same coffee shop to which Dick and I had been. Mike said he had seen his father using marijuana the previous evening. Mike expressed concerns that Dick would stop doing the chore chart, become more irritable, and use drugs more often after I was gone. We talked about some ways the likelihood of this could be minimized. I said I would have a follow-up session or two with them. I encouraged Mike to look at the behavior he could control and stressed that rather than giving up, he could put his main efforts into continuing to do his chores and his home-work and working on the anger-management skills we had learned. Briefly, I went over the RET triangle with him, as I had with Dick, and gave him a list of possible calming self-statements. I suggested he consider using an I-message to tell his dad how he felt about seeing him use marijuana again. We wrote out a couple of possible I-messages together.

The next evening I received a phone call from Mike. I asked if he had shared the I-messages. He said no, that he had gone right to bed. He went on to say that he had been suspended from 1 day of school for saying "Jesus Christ" to the teacher that day. I listened reflectively to his story and feelings. Knowing that saying "Jesus Christ" at his house was part of the norm, I was not surprised that he felt puzzled about how it led to suspension. I talked about why that might have been offensive to the teacher and how different types of talk were appropriate for different settings. We went on to discuss different teachers' expectations for quiet versus talking when students are finished with work. Mike said he was shocked that his dad had not yelled at him when he learned of the suspension. Dick had simply said, "School is your responsibility." Mike said the two of them had agreed Mike would be restricted to the house on the day of suspension. I was very pleased to see that Dick had been able to apply the concept of letting Mike take greater responsibility for school and avoid making it another area of major friction between them. It was clear from Mike's response that Mike was more able to look at his own behavior when the problem was not complicated by an enormous argument with his father.

The termination session was with Mike and Dick together. First we discussed school issues. Dick said he had talked to the school counselor, who said Mike had improved on getting his homework in, although his classroom behavior was still a problem. We discussed some ideas Mike could try: saying his angry words to himself rather than out loud, keeping an index card with the calming self-statements on it in his notebook to read over when getting angry, and picking a student whom he likes (but who also gets along with teachers) to model after. We also discussed the possibility of Mike being placed in a classroom for behaviorally disordered students, an idea the school counselor had suggested. Dick said he had consciously chosen not to get mad about Mike's school suspension, saying he had realized it would not help either of them. I praised Dick for this choice and asked Mike if he had noticed his father getting angry less often. Mike said, "No kidding. My dad's attitude has really changed." Dick and I could not help but chuckle at Mike's comment, but it was obvious it meant a lot to both Mike and Dick.

We looked at the chore chart. Dick said Mike had earned the full allowance for that week, too. I raised Mike's concerns that the chore chart would not be continued after I left. We agreed that Mike could remind his dad to check chores if he forgot. We role-played how Mike could phrase his request to maximize the chances of Dick responding favorably.

We discussed the progress they had made over the past 4 weeks: Mike was doing chores, and there were fewer arguments over this subject; the frequency and intensity of fights had decreased as they were able to express their feelings; Mike was making small improvements in school; and there had been progress in getting Mike into a more appropriate classroom setting. Mike and Dick both said they were getting along together better, despite Dick's less frequent but continued use of drugs. Dick said he no longer wanted Mike to live elsewhere, and Mike agreed. We set up a follow-up appointment for 2½ weeks later.

CONCLUSIONS

This case illustrates some of the treatment techniques used by Homebuilders' staff to help families change their behaviors. In the Barretts' case, these included using a mutual goal-setting process, chore charts, the anger thermometer, rational-emotive therapy, I-messages, and other anger-management techniques. It demonstrates how intensive home-based services can help families improve their functioning in a variety of areas. Part of the reason for the effectiveness of these interventions is because a flexible treatment model can address a wide variety of family problems, the therapist relationship with the family, and the emphasis placed on teaching clients techniques to resolve real-life problems.

REFERENCES

Allen, S., & Tracy, E. M. (Eds.). (2009). *Delivering home-based services: A social work perspective*. New York, NY: Columbia University Press.

Ellis, A., & Harper, R. A. (1975). *A guide to rational living*. North Hollywood, CA: Wilshire.

Fraser, M. W., Pecora, P. J., & Haapala, D. A. (1988). *Families in crisis: Findings from the family-based intensive treatment project* (Final Technical Report). Salt Lake City: University of Utah, Graduate School of Social Work, Social Research Institute; Washington, DC: Behavioral Sciences Institute.

Gordon, T. (1970). *Parent effectiveness training*. New York, NY: Peter H. Wyden.

Haapala, D. A., & Kinney, J. M. (1988). Avoiding out-of-home placement among high-risk status offenders through the use of home-based family preservation services. *Criminal Justice and Behavior, 15,* 334–348.

Hauck, P. A. (1974). *Overcoming frustration and anger*. Philadelphia, PA: Westminster Press.

Hazelden Foundation Staff. (1988). *Touchstones*. New York, NY: Harper/Hazelden.

Kinney, J. M., Madsen, B., Fleming, T., & Haapala, D. A. (1977). Homebuilders: Keeping families together. *Journal of Consulting and Clinical Psychology, 45,* 667–678.

Kirk, R. S., & Griffith, D. P. (2008). Impact of intensive family preservation services on disproportionality of out-of-home placement of children of color in one state's child welfare system. *Child Welfare, 87*(5), 87–105.

Miller, M. (2006). *Intensive family preservation programs: Program fidelity influences effectiveness—Revised* (Document No. 06-02-3901). Olympia: Washington State Institute for Public Policy. Retrieved from: www.wsipp.wa.gov/rptfiles/06-02-3901.pdf

Nelson, K., Walters, B., Schweitzer, D., Blythe, B. J., & Pecora, P. J. (2008). *A 10-year review of family preservation research: Building the evidence base*. Seattle, WA: Casey Family Programs, www.casey.org.

Walton, E., Sandau-Beckler, P., & Mannes, M. (Eds.). (2001). *Family-centered services*. New York, NY: Columbia University Press.

Waters, V. (1980a). *The anger trap and how to spring it*. New York, NY: Institute for Rational Living. (Mimeograph)

Waters, V. (1980b). *Maxwell's magnificent monster*. New York, NY: Institute for Rational Living. (Mimeograph)

Case Study 4-2

Humanizing the Impossible Case: Engaging the Power of a Family-Larger Systems Intervention

JAY LAPPIN AND JOHN VANDEUSEN[1]

W orking with multiproblem families is difficult because there are many needs and many agencies that must work together. As this case reveals, sometimes an organized effort at involving all of the agencies is necessary before any progress is made.

Questions

1. How would you assess this family's difficulties?
2. What strategy did the social worker use as part of the team in this case?
3. What factors made this case successful?
4. What are the lessons learned from this case in working with multiproblem families and large public systems?

---

[1]   "Humanizing the Impossible Case: Engaging the Power of a Family-Larger Systems Intervention" by Jay Lappin and John VanDeusen, 1993, *Family Therapy Networker*, November–December. Reprinted with permission.

Mr. and Mrs. Peters, who were in their seventies, lived in a crowded, rundown rowhouse along with their 12 sons and daughters and 21 grandchildren and great-grandchildren. To the dozen frustrated public agencies who had become involved with their case, the Peterses were simply and pessimistically know as "The Family."

The Peters's house was condemned 2 years ago by the city's fire, health, and building departments, but every time their case came to court, judges took pity on the elderly Peterses and either granted a delay or suspended the fine. The state office of Child Protective Services (CPS) also had investigated two of their daughters for child neglect, but no action had been taken. During a single month in the summer of 1992, police were called more than 50 times to investigate reports of assaults, gambling, drug dealing, noisy crowds, and a child in a wheelchair wandering the streets outside their house at 1 a.m. A drug raid netted 37 vials of crack and some heroin. Although police suspected one of the grandsons was the dealer, there were simply too many people living in the house to pin the charges on anyone, and no arrests were made.

At the Peters's house, there were no boundaries. Police found eight mattresses on the bedroom floors—the only sleeping accommodations for the 35 residents of the house. The furnace did not work; there were no smoke detectors; the refrigerator was turned off and filled with flies. Water taps were broken, and leaks dripped from one floor to the next, pooling in the basement. Human feces covered parts of the floor.

Although the Peters family did not have the funds necessary to make any repairs, they refused to leave their home and avoided all contact with city agencies. It was the sort of situation that often ends either in quiet tragedy or public disaster—police officers evicting crying children and frail, elderly people in front of angry neighbors, while the local news media looks on.

In July 1992, Sergeant Jim Nolan, a member of the city police department's community policing division, instituted a different approach to the Peters's case. Nolan, who has a Master's degree in social psychology but little experience with family therapy, decided to take a network approach to the case. Network interventions that bring together an extended family and the system of helpers connected with it seem to many clinicians like a quaint throwback to the 1960s. That's too bad, because larger systems interventions can be efficient, effective, and inspiring, especially with cases that would otherwise be considered hopeless. Nolan made sure that the heads of several departments were involved, creating an unprecedented level of interagency cooperation and administrative clout.

The interagency task force soon discovered that they had their work cut out for them: Different agencies had conflicting information about the family, and there were huge gaps in their collective knowledge. Their discussions tended to reinforce stereotypes of the Peterses as a poor, multiproblem, African American family. The quality of follow-through on recommendations made in the interagency meetings was difficult to assess: Some agencies were felt to be dropping the ball, while others were judged as being too tough on the family. It appeared that their efforts to join forces in dealing with the Peterses was only creating greater difficulty.

As the task force participants struggled with these issues, Sergeant Nolan met a member of our consultation team at the city's Police Department and told him about his "crazy case." The team member asked Nolan to draw an ecomap to help clarify who was involved with the family. The ecomap is a basic graphic tool developed by family therapist Ann Hartman to aid social workers in the task of identifying the quality of a prospective adoptive family's social network. Just as a blueprint illustrates the concept of a house, ecomapping reveals specific links between family members and persons and organizations in the larger environment. To appreciate the value of this method, just imagine trying to build a house solely from a written description!

Nolan's ecomap of the Peters family (Figure 4.4) indicated extensive contact with public sector agencies and few ties to other resources (e.g., friends, neighbors, employers). In reviewing the ecomap, task force members for the first time began to develop a shared picture of the family's complex involvement with multiple helping agencies.

By identifying the full array of social forces acting on the family, the ecomapping exercise was a giant step toward mastering the complexities of the Peters's case. But while the map provided us with a membership list for this social system, it did not reveal how the system actually performed, or how and where to effect useful changes. To get this missing piece of the puzzle, we advised Sergeant Nolan to "throw a party" and invite the Peters family to meet directly with the task force. One of the consultation team members volunteered to act as a facilitator for the meeting, in exchange for allowing our team and trainees to observe the process.

Sergeant Nolan was intrigued. Nothing like this had been tried before. He went to the Peters's house—out of uniform—and met several times with one of the sons, trying to get the family to agree to the meeting. At first, the family was dubious, but they finally consented. Meanwhile, the task force finally brought a coordinated hammer down on the family, forcing a crisis. The fire marshal and building inspectors issued new notices requiring the family to vacate, while CPS workers informed the family that unless living conditions were changed dramatically, all of the children would be removed from the home. The workers then started helping the family make plans to place the children. Two of the Peters's daughters, each with seven children, were bumped to the top of the public housing waiting list, and two vacant apartments were made available.

The Peters family responded preemptively: Within 24 hours they had placed all 21 children with family and friends. Determined that the state would not take their children, they had, in effect, matched the state's power. The stage was now set for a crucial network meeting to be held at a local community center. The meeting was held in October 1992. Even before the Peterses arrived, more than 40 people were present, including representatives from 10 agencies and the police department and a dozen members of our own training group.

The task force members had agreed to hold this meeting only if we all met first, without the family present. Sergeant Nolan had introduced one of our team members, John VanDeusen, as the meeting's facilitator, and we began to discuss the purpose and agenda for the meeting. VanDeusen had hoped to arrive at some level of consensus before the family arrived, but the newness of the network approach, the size of the group, and the uncertainty about outcomes created sufficient role ambiguity and anxiety to keep some people firmly entrenched in their most official roles.

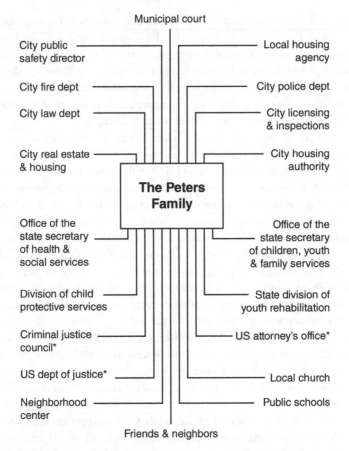

*Indirectly involved, via participation in the Weed & Seed grant.

An ecomap is a basic graphic tool first developed by Ann Hartman (1973) to aid in identifying the qualities of a prospective adoptive family's social environment. Depicting a family's social network visually enhances the ability to "see" relationships between members of the system. Like a huge familial jigsaw puzzle, both trouble spots and possible reconfigurations of the system become more apparent and available to all members of the group.

Figure 4.4 The ecomap

While one department head argued strenuously that the Peters's situation was intolerable and must be changed, another official came to the family's defense. Still another worried that the family would feel "ganged up on" in such a large meeting. VanDeusen challenged this last point, reminding us that only the family could judge its own comfort level, and he would ask them. This kind of polarization was unanticipated by us, even though it frequently occurs in the early stages of a network meeting.

The family arrived in the hallway, and the bickering stopped. Like a classroom of kids suddenly on their best behavior when the teacher steps into the room, the members of the task force put their differences aside and adopted an uneasy wait-and-see attitude. Then, in walked six African American women, led by Leslie, the oldest daughter and matriarch-elect, a teacher who lived in another part of the city. As she and her sisters entered the room, the tension gave way to cautious hellos and smiles. Everyone spoke softly as the group attempted to come to terms with itself and the pain reflected in the family members' eyes. Pride, shame, sadness, hope, and anger all seemed to coexist—waiting to see which would win out.

VanDeusen greeted the family by asking if they were comfortable with the seating arrangements. As Leslie shook her head, "No," he asked her what rearrangement they'd like to make. "In one big circle," said Leslie. "It's more hopeful and it's friendlier." The agency representatives moved their chairs, and the stage was set for the family to tell its own story, one that had long been recorded in case files but now would be given human voice and meaning.

Leslie, clutching reams of "official" papers, said the women were here to represent their parents. In order to set a positive, collaborative tone and deter negative finger-pointing, VanDeusen asked which agencies had been most helpful. Leslie and her sisters named Child Protective Services and Sergeant Nolan. "I was skeptical at first because I've never seen the police reach out to anyone like Sergeant Nolan has to us," Leslie said. She went on to say that one of the biggest problems was getting appropriate care for her parents, who were both quite ill. Mr. Peters had suffered a stroke a few years earlier and now had difficulty speaking.

"We tried to get my parents into a highrise apartment, but at this stage of their lives, they don't want it. That house is all they have. If they had to move now, it would just kill them." She began to cry. "I visit my mother and see her sitting around the house, wringing her hands because she's got so much on her mind—and that's not my Mom," she said. "My Mom was always so strong for us, she was a pillar."

Then another sister, who lived in the house with her seven children, spoke tearfully. "I just want to say the reason why the house was really overcrowded. My father was adopted when he was very little and he always had this thing that he would always have a home for his kids—no matter how many of them—and his grandkids and that if we were ever in need, there was always a home for us. And I guess . . ." pausing, she looked down and then to her sisters, ". . . that we took advantage of it, you know what I mean? We could have done better. We could have gone out there and got homes. I guess it just backfired on us." For the skeptics in the room, that moment changed everything. The Peterses shifted from being "the problem" to being real people in need, a family whose love and loyalty had created bonds they could not break.

One of the most pressing problems was that, even though apartments had been found for the two daughters, they had no kitchenware or furniture. All of the task force members reassured the family that they were there to help. To make this pledge real, VanDeusen circulated a signup sheet. Voluntary offers of furniture, clothes, kitchenware, and time filled the empty page. By the time the paper got back to the family, it was clear to them that people were there to help, professionally and personally.

Just as seeing the family made them real for the task force, seeing the members of the task force go beyond their official roles made the city's desire to help real for the Peterses.

The meeting ended with a plan for the children to remain with family and friends until their mothers could move into the public housing apartments that had been found for them. Other agencies promised to do everything possible to find funds to repair the family home. For their part, the family agreed to vacate the house for repairs as soon as it could be safely boarded up. After the meeting, several task force members accompanied the family on a tour of the vacant apartment that one of the daughters would be moving into. Our team gave a videotape of the meeting and this tour to the daughters, to take home to their parents and the rest of the family. This videotape and the experience of those who had attended the meeting was enough to finally convince the elder Peterses to move in temporarily with their daughter, Leslie. Their house was then boarded up while the city agencies applied for funds to renovate it.

One month later, the task force met again with the Peterses at a neighborhood church suggested by the family. This time, without mentioning names, some family members alluded to the fact that others had drug problems. At a third, smaller meeting 4 weeks later, the daughter with the drug problem was named, and arrangements were made for her to enter a drug treatment program—a sister agreed to accompany her to ensure she would get there. Connections were made between CPS and mental health agencies for counseling with various family groups, all coordinated with the schools. In all, five meetings were held with the family over a 5-month period. During this time, calls to the police declined from 50 in June to 0 in December.

By the next spring, the Peters family had received a $50,000 grant to repair their home. A furnace was donated, and plans were begun to return to the house. The daughter who entered drug treatment remained on methadone maintenance. Two other daughters and their children were living in public housing apartments, one successfully and the other precariously close to being evicted for overcrowding (some of "the problem" at the Peters's old house had been transferred to the new apartment!). A fourth daughter continued to work, and her children were doing well in school. A fifth—one of the most capable—died unexpectedly of a brain aneurysm, and one of her children died of pneumonia. Her other children went to live with an aunt. CPS soon closed its several cases involving the family. For the first time in generations, the Peters family was on its way to self-sufficiency.

Large public institutions set up systems of uniform rules and procedures in order to keep from sinking into the very chaos they are supposed to remedy. But to the families who are knit together through emotional ties of love and need, the narrow role definitions, rigid chains of command, and the floating, interchangeable faces of the bureaucracy's personnel too often seem inhuman. Furthermore, large, established organizations seem to be subject to the same laws of inertia as ancient planets; the weight of internal politics, hidden agendas, and implicit social prejudices keep them moving in the same orbit forever unless they are shaken out of it by a very strong, opposing force.

Paradoxically, however, both clients and agency personnel share certain similarities. Families like the Peterses are stuck in very much the same kind of inertia as big, public institutions; they too are somehow unable to transcend their own self-perpetuating system of implicit rules, roles, lifelong attitudes, and habits. Furthermore, both systems—family and institution—are equally determined to survive and recognize, however grudgingly, that they are necessary to each other. Needless to say, each system is often deeply ambivalent about the other, engaged in a kind of wrestling match alternating between anxious collaboration and mutual resentment.

And yet, the force that can knock each system *out* of its inertia also exists *within* each system. However impersonal and alien each side appears to the other as an abstraction—as evidenced in phrases such as "those people," "them," and "The System"—however different the languages spoken by each culture, individually, the members of each system bring whatever knowledge, understanding, and crude working tools he or she can muster to what everybody knows will be a difficult encounter. Banal as it sounds, what is required to interrupt the mutual inertia is not a cataclysm but a strategic and well-directed nudge that awakens the capacity for empathy and goodwill in those involved.

Leslie's demand that the task force and the family sit in one big circle was symbolically right on target. In a circle, there is no obvious authority, no stratified rows to hide behind, no clear-cut separation between public organization and private family, no beginning or ending. Everybody in a circle looks out into the faces of everybody else and discovers that they are not really so different from themselves after all—mutual recognition, appreciation, trust, and optimism become possible. At that point, the system is transcended and a human community emerges.

Although the networking meetings with the Peterses got off to a powerful start in the Fall, we did not realize how thoroughly progress would be set back by elections in November. A new mayor entered office, staffs were reshuffled, and, by January, nearly all of the members of the original task force had been replaced by people who were not present at the network meetings. While the original participants had gotten to know the Peterses, and had been deeply touched by their plight and attached to them as human beings, the newcomers did not know them at all. They were yet another anonymous, difficult, time-consuming case; an individual family had once again become part of an uncounted number of them. Inertia once more set in.

CONCLUSIONS

Communities can regenerate, and the strong, working coalition between the Peterses and the task force can be reestablished, but it will take time. Organizational development practitioners find that larger systems take longer to transform than do most families—2 to 4 years on average. Faces and roles change continually, and there is no inherent appeal to ties of love or blood. As before, it will take the consolidated and determined efforts of *individuals* from *within* the separate systems to make it work. And, as before, a real conversation has to be initiated, a uniquely human talent for personal encounter, not successfully undertaken by either machines or organizations—or even people en masse. Systems don't talk to systems—only people talk to one another.

We agree with the reviewers on the need for family therapists to move beyond only thinking of one family at a time. In this case, we made sure to include our own trainees as participants in the first two SPARC sessions as our way of seeding the notions of embracing diversity, collaboration, and searching for strengths as the core values in this kind of work.

REFERENCES

Hartman, A. (1995). Diagrammatic assessment of family relationships. *Families in Society: The Journal of Contemporary Human Services, 1,* 111–122.

Case Study 4-3

Completing Brad's Dreams

DAVID EDDY[2]

Suicide can dramatically crystallize a family into a pattern of sadness and grief. Social workers can use strategic therapy techniques to mobilize a family into positive action.

Questions

1. What responses might be expected from family members as they grieve the suicidal death of a member?
2. How can anniversaries and rituals used to mark sad occasions be helpful to families?
3. What are some ways a social worker joins with a family?
4. What family therapy techniques are used to help mobilize this family into problem-solving action?

A few months ago, a former trainee living in Iowa phoned for an emergency consultation with the warning, "I think I've got a challenging one for you this time." While working at a psychiatric hospital, she had been assigned the case of a 15-year-old boy, "Adam," who was hospitalized after telling an outreach worker that he planned to kill

---

[2]   "Completing Brad's Dreams" by David Eddy, 1986, *Family Therapy Networker, 10*(5), pp. 32–33. Reprinted with permission.

himself on the anniversary of his brother's death. Two years earlier, his only sibling, Brad, age 15, had committed suicide.

The therapist reported that the entire family—mother, father, and most of all Adam—was depressed. The previous year they had all had a very difficult time passing the anniversary of Brad's death. A shroud of guilt enveloped them. Contacts with friends or relatives who might have helped them through the loss were limited. Holidays were not celebrated, special occasions were avoided, and visitors were not welcome. Since Brad's suicide, time had stood still.

For Adam, Brad's death meant the loss of a best friend as well as a brother. They had played, shared secrets, and even planned future exploits together. The day that Brad shot himself, he had asked his brother to come to the basement with him. Adam, suspecting some sort of joke, had not gone. A short while later, Brad was dead and Adam's guilt and doubts began. Had Brad intended to take Adam with him on his journey?

The therapist said on the telephone, "I've never seen such a hopeless family. Where should I begin?" I realized that it was essential to talk about Brad, but in what context?

I remembered an idea being developed by Cloe Madanes about reducing a client's feelings of depression, worthlessness, or guilt by motivating him or her to perform anonymous good deeds. I suggested that the therapist ask the family if they would prefer to discuss Brad immediately or at some agreed-on time in the future. After discussion of Brad began, she was to say that she had noticed a valuable ability in this family to look to the future, and that that's what she wanted to talk about. She should say that Brad obviously had been a young man with dreams and a desire to make contributions. What accomplishments would he have made in life? She was to prompt the family's responses, if necessary, by asking about Brad's interests, likes, special projects, friends, and so on. Throughout, the emphasis was to be on the positive, and the family was to be given as much time as they needed to discuss Brad and his potential contributions. Then the therapist was to make a summary speech along the following lines:

> You are all very fortunate to have known Brad so well that you can clearly imagine all he would have accomplished. Knowing you, I have little doubt he would have done all you've mentioned and probably more. You've been left with much to be done on Brad's behalf, so I suggest we begin. Your love for Brad is great, and yet your thoughts of him are troubled. You have an opportunity to complete Brad's dreams and bring peace to your thoughts of him.
>
> To begin, you must each make a contribution on his behalf. At a time of your choosing and in a way known only to you, you are to do a special good deed for someone on Brad's behalf. You each knew Brad in a unique way, so your good deed should reflect all that he meant to you. This should be done on a date of your choosing. The date is to become a celebration of Brad and his life. It is very important, however, that it be done anonymously so that you've done it on Brad's behalf and receive no personal credit. Each year this date is to be celebrated through a special effort. Each of your efforts, however, is to be known only to you.
>
> In addition, you are to have a family meeting and together plan a special good deed project. Again, as with your personal effort, the project is to be an anonymous

contribution on Brad's behalf. The project should express your combined efforts. It should be on a date that becomes an annual occasion to celebrate Brad as a member of the family.

The therapist was delighted. A call to action was just her forte, hopefulness was her strength, and subtle persuasion was a special talent. She would begin immediately.

Two weeks later, the therapist reported that the family agreed immediately to discuss Brad. Each contributed to the discussion of what Brad would have accomplished. While at first there was a sense of hopelessness about all that was lost with his death, a marked change resulted when the therapist outlined the plan of action for each family member and the family as a unit.

Several sessions followed, each more positive than the last. A sense of purpose and well-being began to appear in the family, along with a reduction of guilt. Adam was released from the hospital, and, at an informal ceremony before discharge, he presented the staff with a baseball cap that was a special trademark of his. Only the therapist knew that the cap had originally belonged to Brad. The mother got a job that she enjoyed—her first employment in 20 years. The father became active in teaching a seminar on self-esteem.

The presenting drama in this family revolved around self-inflicted violence. Brad had killed himself, and Adam said he planned on doing the same. It might have been tempting to inquire into the circumstances of Brad's death, but I thought such an approach was unlikely to raise the family from the grimness of their loss and their feelings of hopelessness. It seemed to me that the therapist needed to project the family into the future, beyond their quiet depression. I wanted to help her prepare the family for a discussion that would lead to action. Families filled with regret and guilt frequently engage in "if only . . ." conversations about things they wish they had done. This plan addressed what each person and the family "could do."

As with most therapy, the question of how to begin was essential. In a directive therapy, there is a careful balance between joining people and telling them what to do. Courtesy is a powerful joining approach and was emphasized in asking permission to discuss Brad and in listening respectfully to each person. Milton Erickson was noted for a carefully planned balance between telling people what to do and remaining courteous. In this case, the balance was achieved by offering a choice—"Would you prefer to discuss Brad now or a while later?"—while giving the implicit message that Brad would be discussed.

The major challenge of this therapy was to rally the family to action. Before that could be done, the therapist needed to create a context that would overcome the finality of Brad's death. By inquiring about what Brad would have accomplished, the therapist enabled the family to project him into the present and future. The speech the therapist presented was intended to inspire, motivate, and persuade the family. Word selection, order, and pacing usually require a thoughtful delivery. Practicing such speeches may be helpful, though the risk of losing spontaneity is always a concern.

Persuading families is one aspect of a directive therapy. If, however, a useful plan of action is not developed to change the sequence within the family, the therapy is likely to fail. Performing anonymous good deeds that could be attributed to Brad offered this family the opportunity to forget their "if only . . ." wishes and engage in activities that were hopeful and helpful.

The therapist had said that no one would be asked or was to discuss what was done on Brad's behalf, and, therefore, she had no way of knowing what each person, or the family, did as their good deed. The community was small, however, and over time she was able to detect the contributions of each member of the family. In particular, it was impossible for her to miss a television program done by a family about the loss of a son and brother through suicide. The program was filled with hope and fond memories as Adam and his parents talked about Brad.

PART V

Case Studies in Treating Adult Problems

I t is estimated that 2 out of every 10 adults in the United States suffers from one or more mental disorders. Mental disorders include such problems as anxiety disorders, substance abuse, affective disorders (such as depression), and schizophrenia. The care and treatment of people who suffer from these disorders is provided by social workers, psychiatrists, psychologists, and mental health nurses. However, the social work profession provides the bulk of mental health services. These services are provided in a variety of settings, including community mental health centers, private psychiatric hospitals, child guidance clinics, psychiatric clubhouses, group homes, and state and county hospitals.

Much of social work concerns the management and treatment of adults who suffer from such mental disorders. Such problems present special challenges to social workers. The social worker may be involved in clinical treatment; case management—especially through aftercare treatment planning; development and coordination of community services (e.g., establishing clubhouses for persistently mentally ill clients); life skills training to help clients function in the community; court proceedings that involve commitment and guardianship; and family counseling.

The case studies in this chapter present examples of practice with adults who suffer from various mental disorders. In each case, the difficulty the person faces produces disability in his or her personal, social, or occupational life; the difficulties, therefore, qualify as mental disorders.

Social workers need to learn about different mental disorders, but it is important to point out that mental disorders, not individuals, are classified. Thus, clients diagnosed using the DSM-V as having a particular disorder are different in many ways. The only similarities are the symptoms that represent the disorder. As Maxmen and Ward (1995) point out,

> Some schizophrenics (and diabetics) are delightful, some obnoxious, some brilliant, and some stupid. When, for brevity's sake, a patient with schizophrenia is called a "schizophrenic," it should be done with the understanding that the disorder is an attribute of the person, and never his totality. (p. 5)

Because each of the mental disorders is quite different, social workers must obtain and master specialized knowledge in order to provide effective services and treatment. This knowledge includes what treatments are effective with different disorders, the effects of various medications on the disorders, how to best manage each case, and how to use community and social supports. The case studies presented in this chapter show the diversity of social work practice in treating adult dysfunction and demonstrate the need for this specialized knowledge. Oekerman presents a day in the life of an emergency mental health worker. Starting with the sound of his beeper going off in the middle of the night, readers travel with him as he confronts his first decision of the night: whether to commit a client to the hospital because of a suicide attempt. Geary presents a case study that focuses on depression, one of the more frequent adult disorders, showing how to use cognitive therapy with a depressed man. The study is a good example of treatment effectiveness, because cognitive therapy is recognized as the treatment of choice for depression. Bentley tells an engaging story about the use of psychiatric medications. She discusses the importance of developing a partnership with her client and working in collaboration with other professionals when psychiatric medications are used. Beaulieu presents a creative approach to her work including multisensory interventions. This innovative approach to therapy still needs empirical support but her clinical descriptions of working with the client are informative. Kelly and Garland are also on the cutting edge presenting a case study that describes the application of mindfulness-oriented recovery enhancement for chronic pain. This case presents a newer model of treatment and shows practitioners in detail how to apply mindfulness approaches.

REFERENCE

Maxmen, J. S., & Ward, N. (1995). *Essential psychopathology and its treatment.* New York, NY: Norton.

Case Study 5-1

Nightshift

CARL OEKERMAN[1]

Emergency mental health or crisis intervention is a primary social work intervention and will continue as such, particularly in light of limited resources in the human services. This case study presents a day in the life of an emergency mental health worker and demonstrates the difficult decisions such workers confront.

Questions
1. What are the primary responsibilities of the emergency mental health worker?
2. How did the workers respond to the client's needs and at the same time not get taken advantage of by the client?
3. How does the social worker assess the dangerousness of the client?
4. What are some of the difficulties imposed on the worker by the managed care system?

I'm just drifting off to sleep when my pager goes off. My first thought is that I hope it's not another call from that woman I spoke to earlier tonight. She'd intentionally burned her forearm last week. Then, since it had stopped hurting, she'd sprayed oven cleaner on the injury. She'd wanted to know what I was going to do about it. I check the phone number on my electronic adrenaline pump; it's the emergency room. I grope for

[1] "Nightshift" by Carl Oekerman. *Family Therapy Networker*, May–June 1997. Reprinted with permission.

the phone and my log sheet to note the time of the call. My brain's starting to refocus just as one of the ER doctors comes on the line.

"We've got a 29-year-old woman here. Talking about killing herself. Pretty depressed. Apparently tried to overdose about a year ago. Wants to be hospitalized," he says.

I ask, "Does she have any alcohol or drugs on board?" I want to know if a drug screen or a blood-alcohol level should be started before I get there.

"She doesn't seem toxic and denies drinking tonight. The police brought her in with bottles of Tylenol and Zoloft. I guess her boyfriend called 911 before she took them. Time for you to go to work. . . ."

I work as an emergency mental health professional in the northwest corner of Washington State. We're called County Designated Mental Health Professionals (CDMHPs). In addition to taking after-hours calls from folks like the Oven Cleaner Lady, we provide face-to-face mental health evaluations and decide whether a person needs to be involuntarily hospitalized. Most states have someone identified to do what I do—sometimes it's a doctor, sometimes it's a police officer.

In Washington State, lawmakers decided the best way to ensure a client's rights and to avoid any conflict of interest would be to designate an independent specialist to provide an assessment and make a recommendation. If a person meets the legal criteria of being in imminent danger of self-harm, of doing harm to others, or is gravely disabled because of a mental disorder, we have the legal authority to have someone placed in a mental health facility for up to 72 hours.

Although the criteria for involuntary commitment may vary from state to state, people in my business strive to detain only in the most acute cases. The chronically mentally ill are managed largely on an outpatient basis, a fact evident by a quick scan of any urban area. We see plenty of people for whom frequent visits to the emergency room are a part of their lifestyle, but our biggest dilemmas come with clients whose emotional crisis has escalated into a potentially life-threatening situation.

In a daze, I get dressed and drive the few miles to the hospital. Before a CDMHP is called, several things have already happened: The admitting staff has done their work; then the nurses and doctors, assuming there weren't more urgent cases to address first, have examined the patient, ruled out any medical problems, and assessed whether the primary issue seems to be mental health related. Then they page us. Given all the variables, a person can sit in an exam room for an hour or two before seeing a mental health professional. If the patient comes in with any feelings of powerlessness, victimization, or has trouble with authority, these issues will be good and stirred up by the time we arrive.

Entering the emergency room, I can see the wall board indicating the patients' names, locations, and presenting problems. My client is in Room 5, where most mental health patients are placed. Room 5 is a small, brightly lit, completely bare room, secured by a door with steel reinforcing beams and two deadbolt locks. It's more of a cell than anything else. A closed-circuit video camera is mounted high in one corner, so staff in the ER can monitor what's going on, if they're not busy with other emergencies.

I pull out the patient's chart and read it. The nurse has noted that this woman was brought in by local police after getting into an argument with her boyfriend over the phone. He called 911 after she threatened to overdose on her pills and then hung up on him. The demographic sheet lists her name as Mary Henson; 29 years old, she lives in town, is unemployed, and receives state disability.

I also see a file with older hospital records. I flip through them and learn that last year she had taken a pretty significant overdose of medication, was evaluated by one of my coworkers, and was involuntarily hospitalized on the mental health unit for 3 days. The discharge summary indicated she'd stabilized and had been set up with a local therapist. I check in with both the nurse and the doctor who have been assigned to this patient; their consensus is the woman is depressed and considering suicide. Now it's up to me to figure out what's going to happen next.

I glance at the small TV screen in the nurse's station. The image is a little blurry; it looks like someone spit on the camera lens again. I can make out a forlorn figure huddled in one of two white plastic lawn chairs. She's dressed in jeans and a sweatshirt. Her feet are bare because the hospital's policy is to remove shoes with laces as a suicide precaution. Her arms are crossed protectively, and her head is hung low over her chest. I walk down the long hallway and knock on the big door to Room 5 before I start undoing the locks.

I open the door just enough to stand in the entry. My senses are on alert. Even though I haven't had any indication that she might get violent or want to bolt out of the room, I'd rather not take any chances. The woman looks cautiously my way, but otherwise she remains put. She's got scraggly hair, is somewhat overweight, and has a rather withdrawn, guarded presence. It's as though she's trying hard not to be noticed.

"Miss Henson? Hi. I'd like to talk with you if I may."

Watching the floor, she asks quietly, "Is there any way I can get out of this room? It's awful in here."

"Not right away, I'm afraid," I say as I ease into the empty chair. "My name is Carl Oekerman. I'm a County Designated Mental Health Professional. The hospital called me in to speak with you. We help decide whether someone might be a danger to themselves, to others, or might be gravely disabled. If they are, we have the authority to have someone involuntarily hospitalized for a period of up to 72 hours. Because of that, you have the right not to speak with me. You also have the right to have an attorney present here while we talk."

Her eyes widen in alarm. "Am I under arrest? God, I just want to go home . . ."

"No. You're not under arrest," I try to reassure her. "That's the speech I need to give everyone before we start talking. But if you're willing, I'd like to ask you a few questions. First off, what happened tonight that you ended up here?"

I want to get right into the interview. I've already gotten the impression she's not going to attack me, and I think she recognized that I'm the guy she's going to need to talk to before much else is going to happen tonight. As long as she's willing to answer my questions, we can move through the process. We're both looking at a minimum of 2 hours' work ahead of us. For me, that means I'm not likely to see my bed again much before 2:30 a.m.

"I just can't handle it anymore," she says hopelessly. "I can't make anybody happy. They all just leave. Why bother?"

I ask, "Who leaves?"

"Everyone!" she says hopelessly. "My boyfriend, for starters. We don't get along." Her voice drops, "I don't trust him."

"How long have you been together?"

"Off and on about three years."

"Is there any violence in the relationship?" I ask.

She hangs her head down again and doesn't respond. Not a good sign. I probably need to be gentle here. If she were a private client in my therapy office, back in the good old days before managed care, I'd want to proceed slowly, to let her sense of trust and safety build. That could take several visits. But now I need to get enough information from this woman to make a recommendation about what to do with her. Tonight.

"It sounds as though you've been having a pretty rough time of it," I say, trying to be both supportive and to invite her to share more. She's crying quietly now, hugging herself. I ask, "Have you been thinking about hurting yourself?"

"I was going to take all my pills tonight. After my boyfriend said he wanted to split up again, I figured I just couldn't go through all the pain another time. . . ." Now she doubles over in the chair, crying harder.

Okay. She's got a reason, a plan, the means to do it, and at least one prior attempt that I know of. Not good signs. I want to see how truthful she'll be about her history; if she's not going to operate in good faith, that will factor into the decision I have to make. I ask her, "Have you ever tried to hurt yourself before?"

"About a year ago," she says without looking up. "I took all my pills then. They put me in the hospital for a week."

For my own benefit, I need to make a distinction: "Mary, do you want your life to be over or do you want to stop hurting?"

She stops and thinks about that one for a long while. "I just don't want to hurt anymore."

I go through the rest of my standard questions. Mary lives by herself; she's been on state support for 2 years now, "because I'm too depressed to work"; she's been in therapy or receiving various support services for at least 15 years. Her doctor has been prescribing an antidepressant. One brother, 3 years older, lives out of state; mom, who died 5 years ago, was alcoholic; dad was abusive of everyone, at least physically and possibly sexually; she hasn't seen dad in at least 10 years; "boyfriend" drinks a lot and gets abusive; no children; few friends. Spends her days watching TV and reading, and spends her nights being afraid. Lives alone in subsidized housing.

I don't want to put this woman in the hospital tonight, potentially fill up the unit, and then in 2 hours find myself in this same room with some wildly psychotic person who really needs immediate hospitalization. We get a little selfish in this business. I have no way of knowing what else I'll have to deal with on my shift. I need to guard my limited resources, some of which are external, like hospital beds, and some of which are internal, like my own energy and patience.

I try to consider what she needs therapeutically. Not knowing a thing about the work she's done so far in therapy, I hope I can reach her therapist tonight to discuss it. I just met this woman. How do I know whether she's being manipulative or if she's truly at the end of her rope? And I don't want to read about Mary's suicide in tomorrow's paper.

I go through my mental checklist as Mary's teary gaze drifts to the upper corners of the room. Is she actively psychotic? No. Is she in danger of serious self-harm? Maybe.

Is she in imminent danger of serious self-harm? No, I don't think so. Can she manage on her own? Well, she can generally manage her own affairs; she can obviously feed and clothe herself. But tonight? I'd rather not push it. I wouldn't feel good about sending her home by herself, even if we kept her pills here. She seems pretty resourceful and might find a way to hurt herself just to make a point. Even if she got through the night okay, she'd be without her antidepressants. Does she need someone to hold and monitor her meds for a while?

Okay. She doesn't absolutely have to be in the hospital from a legal or clinical standpoint. That rules out involuntary hospitalization and all the attendant legal hoops and hassles. Time to see what else I can find out before we make a decision on a voluntary admit.

I stand up and say, "Mary, I'm going to try to reach your therapist or your doctor on the phone. I'll be back in a little while."

"Can I at least get out of this room?" she asks hopefully.

"Not for the time being. But what I'll do is leave the door open. I don't think you need to be locked in."

She seems to appreciate this. I don't see her as a flight risk, and after a half hour in there with her, I'm starting to feel claustrophobic, too.

I walk through the nurses' station and into the doctors' dictating station to look up the phone number of Mary's therapist. When I dial her, I get her answering machine. I leave my name and number and a brief rundown of what's going on. I do the same when I also get her doctor's machine. When I reach her boyfriend's answering machine, I leave a message, hoping he might be screening the call, but no one picks up. I'm not impressed by this guy's compassion, given that he's apparently made no contact with the hospital to inquire if she's still alive. I wrestle with my own desire to prejudge this guy. As my last option, I have Mary's doctor paged. I need to talk with someone who's actually seen Mary and can give me a sense of whether she's currently worse, better, or the same.

"BEE DEEE! BEE DEEE! BEE DEEE! BEE DEEE!" My pager goes off again. Great. Just when I can expect a call back from Dr. Williams, Mary's doctor. I log the time and number. It looks kind of familiar. Maybe I should wait a few minutes to hear back from the doctor before I respond to the page. Maybe it will be a quick call, but in this business, especially when several things start happening at once, that's not likely.

Again the pager goes off. This time I recognize the number. It's our answering service. They're the folks who screen calls for the clinic and page us when someone needs immediate response. I call them back from the closest phone.

"Hi, it's Carl. What's up?" I ask.

"Sorry to bother you, Carl. It's the service," says a female voice I don't recognize. "That guy I paged you about a few minutes ago? He's called twice in the last minute. He says he's going to kill himself if he doesn't get to talk to you. He's really insistent."

"Okay, did you get a name?" I ask.

"Andy Lindeman," she says.

My tension drops as my irritation rises. Andy's one of our regulars. He's got a long list of issues, with hysteria right at the top. This is usually about the time he calls. The local hotline has refused to take any calls from him for the past month because he gets so verbally abusive. He has a case manager at our clinic and knows the CDMPHs are available 24 hours a day.

I dial the number. "Hello?" drones the familiar voice.

"Andy. It's Carl . . ."

Before I get any further, he interrupts, "I think you should know I've already cut my wrists with a knife and blood's running down my arm now. I think I should be in the hospital, or maybe I should just bleed to death and show all of you. On second thought, I don't want to give any of you the satisfaction. Those fuckers at the hotline won't talk to me, and my case manager hates me. Your fellow CDMHPs won't talk to me either . . ."

Because Andy's got a case manager and a psychiatrist who work with him at our clinic, we try to keep our after-hours contact to a minimum and redirect him to his primary treatment team. The plan we've worked out is to assess his safety, intervene only when absolutely necessary, and keep his case manager in the driver's seat. Unfortunately, he doesn't get along well with anybody. I overlook the mention of the cut wrist. He knows the system well enough to use suicidal gestures as a way to get through the answering service to us. I talk to him at least twice a month on my night shifts. He starts each call with a dramatic monologue.

"Andy. What's bugging you?" I feel a need to get to the point.

"I'll tell you what's bugging me! That asshole at the clinic!" he shouts into the phone.

I ask, "Which asshole? We have so many."

Andy chuckles, his tone suddenly changing. "You're so sweet. Couldn't you be my therapist?"

"Then who would you have to talk to in the middle of the night?" I ask. "So who's bugging you?"

"That idiot John Sanford. He won't let me change case managers." John is the case manager supervisor at the clinic. "I'm typing up a letter to the executive director and the entire board of directors telling everyone how incompetent and unprofessional everyone is. Except you, of course, and Sandy, and Mark." So there are three of us left he hasn't managed to alienate.

The overhead speaker announces, "Dr. Williams for CDMHP on line three. Dr. Williams for CDMHP on line three."

"Great, Andy. I'm glad to hear you're working on getting your needs met. Here's what I want you to do: Finish typing your letter and take it to the clinic tomorrow. When's your next appointment?"

"Next week, Tuesday."

"Okay. Tomorrow, I'll leave a note for your case manager that we spoke tonight. If you need to speak with him before your next appointment, you can leave a message with the receptionist." I'm watching the phone lines. I know the doctor I want to talk to is behind that flashing arrow on line three. "I suppose you want me to clean up my arm, too," he says sarcastically.

"Your choice," I reply.

"Well, most of it's dried already. I didn't do a very good job this time."

He's sounding a lot calmer than when we started.

"Listen, Andy, I'm kind of in the middle of something . . ." I'm trying to wrap it up and not keep the doctor waiting too long.

"Oh, all right," Andy says with a big sigh. "But I still want you to be my therapist. You have a good night now."

We say goodbye and I punch the flashing button on the phone.

"Dr. Williams?" I switch gears back to the first case. "I apologize for the hour, but I appreciate your quick response."

I introduce myself and give her the present situation regarding her patient. I ask, "When was the last time you saw Mary in your office?"

"Oh, about two months ago, I think. I'd have to check her chart to be certain."

"I understand you've been prescribing Zoloft for her."

"Yes," the doctor responds. "She's been depressed for quite some time. I know she tried to overdose about a year ago. She's been working with a therapist since that time. We've had a few brief conversations about Mary."

"What was Mary like the last time you saw her?" I ask.

"Well, pretty much the same as always," she says. "Unhappy, tearful at times. I know one of the reasons she was hospitalized last time was that she'd actually taken the pills. Once it was clear she was medically stable, I think they wanted to observe her until they were sure she was emotionally stable, too. That she wouldn't go right out and do it again."

I suggest, "It's interesting to me then that she didn't actually take her pills tonight. She gave the police time to show up. Maybe she remembers what it's like to have a tube stuck down her throat and have her stomach pumped. I don't really think she needs to be in the hospital, but I don't want her to go home and be alone, either. I'd like to suggest to her that she spend at least tonight in the Crisis Respite House operated by our clinic. That way, she can be with a staff person tonight, someone who could keep an eye on her. And tomorrow, we can get in contact with the therapist for an appointment and mobilize her other resources. What do you think?"

"Sounds like a plan to me," she responds. "I could also see her in my office the day after tomorrow, if she'd like."

I thank the doctor for her time and we say goodbye. Now I need to see whether we've got a bed available at the Respite House.

I glance at the clock. It's almost 1:30 a.m. It's been 45 minutes since I left Mary in Room 5. I stick my head out of the dictation room and glance at the tiny TV screen. Mary is still sitting where I left her, slouched in the plastic chair. Better give her an update.

I open the door to Room 5 and Mary looks up.

"I wasn't able to reach your therapist or your boyfriend, but I did get to talk with Dr. Williams," I say, sitting on the edge of the empty chair. "I'd like you to be somewhere tonight where you can be safe, but I'd prefer it not be the hospital. I'm checking into another program run by our clinic. It's a small house where you can stay with someone from our staff."

"Will I be locked up at this place?"

"No," I hope to allay her fears, "you'd be free to leave if you chose. It's purely voluntary. That's one of the reasons I'd prefer you not be on the hospital's Mental Health

Unit. It's kept locked, as you know. If you'd be willing to consider the respite program, I still need to make a couple of calls to be sure they have a bed available."

"Okay," she consents.

Back in the doctors' station, I look up the home number of Sharon Johnson, the on-call crisis-response specialist tonight.

I fill Sharon in on the information I've gotten. Sharon has her own checklist to run through to determine whether it would be appropriate for Mary to spend the night. The program has been set up to provide respite for people who might otherwise end up in a hospital bed. Sharon finishes her questions, satisfied that Mary meets the admissions criteria. She asks for a half hour to get dressed and over to the house, so she can be there before Mary arrives. I agree to call the cab company our clinic uses in situations like this. They'll provide transportation for Mary between the hospital and Respite House.

Back in Room 5, I explain our plan to Mary and that she'll need to wait another half hour before she can leave. She's looking tired and beaten. It's 2:00 a.m. She's been here almost 3 hours now. She's gotten to interact with someone for maybe 45 minutes. The rest of that time, she's had to sit alone in a bright, empty room with locks on the door.

Mary glances at me and says weakly, "Thank you."

I walk back to the doctors' station to let the doctor and nurse know of our plan. In other situations, I'll include the medical staff in the discussion of options. Sometimes, I need their input, but other times, they just want to be part of the process. The ER doctor is fine with my plan and seems happy to sign off the case; the nurse wants a diagnosis so she can print out discharge instructions. The unit clerk reminds me to complete a billing sheet.

I slide back into the corner desk in the doctors' station to begin my paperwork. I'm suddenly feeling exhausted. We've done about as much as we can for Mary, and from her standpoint, it may not be very much. She needed some help and got locked up for several hours. A guy asked her some basic questions and decided she wasn't crazy, just depressed. We didn't get to what was really bothering her—her deeper issues. Indeed, we may have succeeded only in pushing them deeper.

CONCLUSIONS

This is the nature of emergency mental health work. There may be moments when we can connect with a person in trouble, but they are as brief as they are rare. We gather what information we can and do a quick assessment. Often, we have to follow our instincts more than anything else. The person who's come in for help ends up face-to-face with a rather miserly system. Mary stays alive for another day. I turn her over to the next tier of crisis workers, who will monitor her and work to reintegrate her back into her daily routine.

Mary's cab is here. I say goodbye, and the nurse shows her the way to the exit. As I turn to finish my paperwork, the ambulance doors open, and a police officer is pulling in a barefoot young woman in shackles. She's bone thin, has short hair, dyed blond, and is dressed only in a torn T-shirt and shredded cutoffs. Her face and arms are covered with red scratches, and she's wailing, "I want to die . . . I want to die . . . I want to die!" I take a deep breath as one of the nurses glances my way and says, "Guess you better not go home yet."

Case Study 5-2

Individual Treatment of Depression Using Cognitive Therapy

Brent B. Geary

Depression is one of the most common problems among adults. This case presents the most widely used treatment for depression: cognitive therapy.

Questions

1. Why is cognitive therapy considered the treatment of choice for depression?
2. What are the central concepts of a cognitive approach to treating depression?
3. What is the function of task assignments in this approach to treatment?
4. What cognitive therapy techniques were most helpful in reducing the client's depression?

Jim was a 42-year-old, divorced, unemployed man who sought psychotherapy for depression, complaining that "every area of my life is a mess." His 14-year marriage had ended 8 years earlier, and he stated, "I just never have recovered from that." Jim had made several attempts to change from an unsatisfactory career in computer programming, but he had not found a vocational niche. When he entered therapy, Jim was living with his sister and her husband. Although they were well-to-do and supportive, it was apparent from Jim's description that their patience with his situation was wearing thin.

The client grew up in a secure but emotionally unexpressive home. He and his sister, who was 2 years younger, both did well in school. Jim progressed through college with a B average and married during his junior year. He obtained a job with a growing data-processing firm on graduation. Well-liked by his fellow employees, Jim was recognized several times for profit-generating innovations he devised. After he turned 30, however, he experienced increasing disenchantment with his work and distance from his wife and two sons. He discovered that his wife was having an affair with another man. Several sessions of marital therapy proved ineffective. Jim's wife filed for divorce and moved with the children to a neighboring state to live with her new lover. Jim had tremendous difficulty coping with the transition, and his job performance deteriorated significantly. Approximately six months after the divorce, Jim terminated employment with the company.

Jim attempted to establish several consultation and freelance business ventures, but all of them failed within a year. These entrepreneurial forays were generally impulsive and not well thought out. He eventually landed a job as a counselor at a residential facility for delinquent boys. He remained in this position for 3 years and found particular enjoyment and satisfaction in teaching the youths computer skills. Jim developed novel treatment programs incorporating computers, which proved to be quite successful. The lack of an advanced degree hampered his advancement, however, and Jim found himself "topped out" in the organization. His savings depleted from the failed business endeavors, Jim was unable to meet financial obligations (including child support) on his meager salary. This situation forced him to leave the treatment facility, to everyone's regret, and accept his sister's offer to live temporarily with her family. Here he had remained for 15 months, without employment, when he entered therapy.

Information gained from Jim during the intake interview signaled that cognitive treatment was appropriate. The client had undertaken psychotherapy intermittently over the past 6 years. He described these ventures as "focusing on my feelings" and as being highly expressive (i.e., cathartic) in nature. Though he was helped to feel better, he stated, "I still don't think very well of myself." Several other indications of cognitive dysfunction were present in his self-report: Jim said that he frequently found himself "brooding" and that, even when his mood lightened, "I'll talk myself back down into depression." When asked what he meant in describing himself as his worst enemy, Jim said that he believed the root of his problem lay in "these thoughts I carry around inside of me." The client denied suicidal ideation or intent but added "I don't want to live like this the rest of my life, and I'm beginning to wonder if things will ever change." Jim reported that his sleeping and eating patterns were only sporadically disrupted; social activities ("I rarely go out") and cognitive functions ("I can't seem to think clearly") evinced general and lasting disturbance. Cognitive therapy was indicated as the treatment that would best address the modalities (behavioral and cognitive) showing the most dysfunction.

OVERVIEW OF THE INTERVENTION

Succinctly, the aim of cognitive therapy is "to help depressed individuals to identify, evaluate, and modify their dysfunctional personal paradigm" (Covi, Roth, & Lipman, 1982, pp. 459–460). A. T. Beck (1976) hypothesized that the "personal paradigm" is a unique assumption framework that underlies psychogenic depression, containing an individual's negative beliefs regarding himself or herself, the world, and the future. Cognitive therapy defines three essential concepts as central in specifying and altering a depressogenic personal paradigm:

- *Cognitions* are ideas and images brought to consciousness in a given situation. Cognitions exert direct influence on affect and behavior, comprising what an individual thinks *in* (not about) a particular occasion (A. T. Beck, 2005; Rush, 1983).
- *Schemata* are assumptions or beliefs that are formed by early experience and that guide the content of cognitions. The manner in which experience is evaluated and distorted is determined by a person's schemata (A. T. Beck, Rush, Shaw, & Emery, 1979).
- *Cognitive distortions* are logical errors that result from negative cognitions. These inaccurate inferences and conclusions regarding events intensify depressive symptoms (Hollon & Beck, 1979).

Cognitive therapy is an active and directive approach that employs didactics extensively to supplement the ongoing supportive therapeutic relationship. A "collaborative empiricism" is fostered in which therapist and client together formulate treatment strategies (Beck et al., 1979; Kuyken, Padesky, & Dudley, 2009). Cognitive therapy is designed to be delivered in a negotiated, time-limited procedure, generally 15 to 25 sessions.

Jim was seen on 21 occasions over a period of 6 months. The framework of his sessions was tapered so that he received therapy twice per week for 4 weeks, once weekly for 8 weeks, four times biweekly, and in a follow-up session 1 month after the previous visit. Sessions were typically structured in the following format:

1. Reactions to the previous session
2. Events since the last session
3. Homework review
4. In-session agenda
5. Formulate homework
6. Feedback and process commentary

Jim completed the Beck Depression Inventory (BDI; A. T. Beck, 1978) before each session to provide a marker of progress. The Automatic Thoughts Questionnaire (ATQ; Hollon & Kendall, 1980) was filled out monthly to determine the nature and frequency of Jim's self-statements. The client purchased, read, and completed exercises in *Feeling Good* (J. Beck & Tompkins, 2007; Burns, 1980/1999), a self-help book about cognitive therapy that serves as a valuable adjunct to treatment, and the importance of homework assignments was explained to him.

THE COURSE OF THERAPY

The first four sessions with Jim, completed over a 2-week period, were devoted to establishing rapport and gaining a history, providing a rationale for treatment, and educating the client regarding the nature of depression and the cognitive model. Jim's BDI scores ranged from 28 to 32, indicating moderate to severe depression. Although the client indicated that he experienced nothing more than passing ideation regarding suicide, this was closely monitored. Jim stated that he was less likely to perform self-injurious acts "now that I'm finally doing something constructive for myself" (i.e., engaging in therapy).

Jim read the first two chapters of *Feeling Good*, remarking, "This book was written about me!" This provided an opportunity to normalize his depression, pointing to the frequency of dysphoria and depression in the general population and helping to alleviate the client's self-imposed onus of thinking himself different (i.e., inferior), isolated, and unique. Jim reported that a typical day consisted of "sleeping a lot, watching some tube, and talking to my sister's family until they get sick of me." He left the house very little and communicated only sporadically with friends and acquaintances ("Who wants to hear a depressive's tale of woe?"). When he did go out into public, Jim said that he felt like he was wearing a neon sign that read "I'M DEPRESSED" and that people were uninterested in him.

Behavioral measures were begun in this initial phase of therapy to counteract Jim's low activity level and social withdrawal. He started a Daily Activity Schedule (Burns, 1980, p. 88) with mastery and pleasure ratings. Jim also collaborated in devising graduated task assignments, keyed to ventures he had been meaning to undertake but had not achieved. These activities ranged from taking walks to going to the public library to shopping for cards and small gifts to send to his children. In addition to reactivating the client, these strategies served as tangible indications of Jim's motivation and compliance. They also opened the door to both in-session and experiential challenging of Jim's self-negating set.

When Jim reviewed accomplishments in his task assignments during sessions, it was commonplace for him to punctuate his reports with statements such as "But that's no big deal," "I feel stupid telling you these silly things," and "Anybody can do this stuff." The therapist acknowledged that the activities were small, perhaps even silly, but that the accumulation of small steps formed the pathway to change. Jim's alterations in volition were also highlighted; he was continually reinforced for choosing to help himself. To strike these points home, Jim was asked to twice daily (e.g., at noon and at bedtime) review his Daily Activity Schedule and then, on a separate paper, write what he would have done in that given time (e.g., a morning, afternoon, or evening) before he entered therapy.

The client was highly cooperative in completing his homework assignments. Although he continued to disparage the activities, he increasingly anticipated and vocalized the therapist's counter ("I know, I know. . . . It's a small thing but it shows progress"). His activity level increased, and it seemed appropriate to move into examination of Jim's cognition process.

The next six sessions were primarily devoted to illustrating the thought-affect-behavior sequence, identifying patterns of cognitive distortion, and specifying cognitions that gave rise to Jim's negative moods. The client's reading of Chapters 3 through 9 in *Feeling Good* supplemented the therapy. Jim's BDI values ranged from 22 to 29, and he reported for the first time seeing some hope in his situation, though he quickly tempered his proclamation with skepticism that results could be lasting.

Jim quickly became adept at isolating thoughts and images that contributed to his feelings of sadness, anger, frustration, anxiety, and the like. He began to recognize cognitive errors at every turn in his thinking. When asked which distortions seemed to be most frequent, he replied, "All of them." Questioned further, he listed "all-or-nothing thinking," "minimization," "should statements," and "labeling" (terms from

Feeling Good, pp. 40–41) as most prominent. Jim completed the Automatic Thoughts Questionnaire; his most frequent self-statements clustered in the negative self-concepts and negative expectations dimension (Hollon & Kendall, 1980). He remained relatively active, with periodic lapses. However, Jim remarked that he had become "trapped" because, during periods of inactivity, "all I think about now is my distorted thinking, and I'd rather be doing things."

A method for combating Jim's negative automatic thoughts was instituted in session. The client began to counter his harsh self-statements by use of the "triple column technique" (Burns, 1980, p. 60). In the first column, Jim entered automatic thoughts he noticed; in the second column, he identified the cognitive distortion(s) contained in the self-statements; and in the third column, he generated rational and reasonable responses to the automatic thoughts. For instance, Jim found that he frequently said to himself, "I should be doing better than this" (first column), which involved a should statement, minimization, and all-or-nothing thinking as cognitive distortions (column two). He was able to counter with "Although at times progress seems slow, I am doing better and better" and "What I'm doing now is better than before, and I can reasonably expect to continue improving" in the third column. Jim likened this process of offsetting negative automatic thoughts to "reprogramming the old computer."

The next several weeks (around sessions 12 to 15) contained events that proved to be vital in Jim's therapy. A relapse occurred, evinced in the client's BDI scores (which rose to 32 and 30 at sessions 12 and 13, respectively) and his report that his mood plunged despite his attempts to counter depressogenic self-statements. While exploring and working to identify what was different during this time (when his mood dived), the following interchange took place:

Client: Well, I was beginning to feel better and I was more active, so I began to think about getting back to work. But I got this wave of panic and despair.

Therapist: Panic and despair. Any particular thoughts or images as you felt that?

Client: Yeah, like "I can't cope," "I can't handle work." All of a sudden I felt as though life was sweeping me aside. I had this picture of myself swimming out into the ocean toward something but being pushed back to shore by the waves. It was like I was powerless, like I was at the mercy of the waves and the tide.

Therapist: So, it was like you were trying to "get back into the swim" vocationally, but there were these powerful forces working against you.

Client: Right . . . and I had a lot of other thoughts whenever I considered working.

Therapist: What thoughts?

Client: Like, "I'll never hold a good job," "They'll [employers] reject me," "I guess I'm unemployable."

Therapist: And that would indicate what about you?

Client: Well, that I'm powerless to earn my own way . . . that if I can't even handle a job . . .

Therapist: Then that would mean what about you as a person?

Client: That would mean I was pretty worthless. I mean, if I can't even hold a job, what good am I to anybody?

Therapist: If I can't demonstrate that I'm competent then I'm worthless.

Client: Yep.

Jim's rich imagery and his developed ability to recognize automatic thoughts yielded valuable clinical material. This exchange and further probing evoked memories for the client. In particular, Jim remembered numerous instances as a child when he felt powerless to elicit affection and emotional expression from his parents. His achievements at school, though, reliably drew their praise and attention. He remembered his father, a successful businessman, rewarding these accomplishments with money. But he was then sent out on his own to buy things for himself with the money. And he remembered continuously buying and paying for things with his childhood and adolescent friends. "I worked a lot as a kid—paper routes, lawn-mowing jobs, stuff like that—so that I'd have money to spend and be able to keep my friends," Jim reminisced. His descent into depression began when he couldn't "keep" his wife, even while he was succeeding at work. And the failed attempts to revive his career made him feel even more hopeless about proving his value as an individual.

This turning point in Jim's therapy marked a shift in the level of analysis of Jim's automatic thoughts. Specifically, it represented a transition from *horizontal exploration* to *vertical exploration* of the client's thoughts (Safran, Vallis, Segal, & Shaw, 1986). Horizontal exploration surveys automatic thoughts across a variety of contexts. This process demonstrates to the client the relationship between thinking and mood and provides a general indication of the client's thinking style. Vertical exploration pursues deeper meanings behind automatic thoughts, particularly those that reflect on the client's sense of self. This latter procedure uncovers core cognitive processes—central assumptions and beliefs that make up the schemata. In the present case, the event of considering work evoked numerous negative automatic thoughts for Jim. The collaborative investigation of these thoughts by the therapist and the client revealed that his sense of personal value was highly dependent on performance and material gain.

The focus of treatment turned to devising behavioral assignments that would disconfirm Jim's depressogenic assumptions. He talked to his sister and reestablished contact with friends and acquaintances. He discussed therapeutic insights with people and received valuable feedback that they cared about him, not his material products. Jim arranged an extended visit with his children, during which he concentrated on his relationship with them rather than activities and gifts. He began volunteer work 5 hours per week at a convalescent center. And, he obtained a dog at a local animal shelter, remarking, "She doesn't care what I have or what I make—she just loves me."

Jim's BDI scores progressively decreased, reading 14 (mild mood disturbance) by the 18th session. His visits with the therapist were spaced to once every 2 weeks. Jim reported that, although he at first had difficulty believing his worthiness independent from his performance, "It's hard to ignore the evidence" he accumulated in his experiences. In-session work concentrated on defining realistic expectations of himself and future planning. His gains were reinforced and consolidated.

When Jim presented for the follow-up session 1 month after his previous visit (BDI = 8; much less frequent negative self-statements on the ATQ), he listed several notable changes in his life. He had secured a part-time job and a small apartment for himself and his dog. He was still performing the volunteer work and was initiating a social life. Though he still had his "ups and downs," he had become adept at stopping himself and using cognitive strategies to reappraise situations. Jim reported greater confidence, enjoyment, and fulfillment and an enhanced sense of security. He promised to check in periodically with the therapist and to return promptly if he encountered difficulty.

In closing, Jim returned to symbolism of an earlier session. He stated that he had replaced his former neon sign with a new one that read "I'M WORTHWHILE." "You know," he said, "people respond to this one a lot better. So do I."

CONCLUSIONS

The foregoing account illustrates a straightforward use of cognitive therapy in the treatment of depression. This particular client was highly motivated and quite compliant. It is common for depressed individuals to require more protracted therapeutic efforts at various treatment junctures than did Jim. But the sequence of therapy remains essentially the same: stabilization of the client's mood, instillation of hope, behavioral activation, application of cognitive strategies, and establishment of an orientation to the future. Cognitive therapy is primarily indicated when clients' thought patterns constitute the modality of most dysfunction. Other treatment approaches may be more appropriate when affective reactions, interpersonal dynamics, or physiological functioning dominate presenting concerns. Careful initial assessment is essential to match intervention strategies to the client modality producing the most distress (J. Beck, 2011; Rachman, 1980).

When cognitive therapy is employed, *Feeling Good* frequently serves as a valuable adjunct to ongoing therapy. The book is written in a very readable style and helps to bridge in-session work to clients' everyday life. Extensive clinical material is generated from client reactions to the reading, the completion of (or failure to complete) activities recommended in the book, and pertinent issues contained in the topical chapters (e.g., anger or self-esteem).

Other adjunctive strategies are easily incorporated into the treatment with cognitive therapy. Social skills training, marital or family therapy, clinical hypnosis, group psychotherapy, and other treatment approaches can effectively supplement cognitive therapy. A strength of cognitive therapy lies in its structure, which encourages a comprehensive treatment package; practitioners can remain mindful of potentially beneficial points of departure and supplementary work.

Cases such as Jim's, in which long-standing depression patterns are counteracted, provide therapists with some of the most tangible and heartening products of their efforts. Cognitive therapy has significantly enhanced the therapeutic repertoire available to combat depression. It is nice to remember that this work translates into enhanced lives for thousands of people.

REFERENCES

Beck, A. T. (1976). *Cognitive therapy and the emotional disorders.* New York, NY: International University Press.

Beck, A. T. (1978). *Depression inventory.* Philadelphia, PA: Center for Cognitive Therapy.

Beck, A. T. (2005). The current state of cognitive therapy: A 40-year retrospective. *Archives of General Psychiatry, 62,* 953–959.

Beck, A. T., Rush, A. J., Shaw, B. F., & Emery, G. (1979). *Cognitive therapy of depression.* New York, NY: Guilford Press.

Beck, J. (2011). *Cognitive behavioral therapy: Basics and beyond* (2nd ed.). New York, NY: Guilford Press.

Beck, J., & Tompkins, M. (2007). Cognitive therapy. In N. Kazantzis & L. L'Abate (Eds.), *Handbook of homework assignments in psychotherapy* (pp. 51–63). New York, NY: Springer.

Burns, D. (1980). *Feeling good: The new mood therapy.* New York, NY: Morrow.

Burns, D. (1999). *Feeling good: The new mood therapy (Revised and updated).* New York, NY: Avon.

Covi, L., Roth, D., & Lipman, R. S. (1982). Cognitive group therapy of depression: The close-ended group. *American Journal of Psychotherapy, 36,* 459–469.

Hollon, S. D., & Beck, A. T. (1979). Cognitive therapy of depression. In P. C. Kendall & S. D. Hollon (Eds.), *Cognitive-behavioral interventions: Theory, research, and procedures.* New York, NY: Academic Press.

Hollon, S. D., & Kendall, P. C. (1980). Cognitive self-statements in depression: Development of an Automatic Thoughts Questionnaire. *Cognitive Therapy and Research, 4,* 383–395.

Kuyken, W., Padesky, C., & Dudley, R. (2009). *Collaborative case conceptualization.* New York, NY: Guilford Press.

Rachman, S. (1980). Emotional processing. *Behavior Research and Therapy, 18,* 51–60.

Rush, A. J. (1983). Cognitive therapy for depression. In M. R. Zales (Ed.), *Affective and schizophrenic disorders: New approaches to diagnosis and treatment.* New York, NY: Brunner/Mazel.

Safran, J. D., Vallis, T. M., Segal, Z. V., & Shaw, B. F. (1986). Assessment of core cognitive processes in cognitive therapy. *Cognitive Therapy and Research, 10,* 509–526.

Case Study 5-3

Jasmika, the Docs, and Me:
A Short Story With a Happy Ending About
Partnership, Collaboration, Social Work,
and Psychiatric Medication

Kia J. Bentley

The use of psychiatric medications by clients of social workers across settings has steadily risen over the past 20 years. Social workers can and do play key roles in ensuring that the medication-related questions, decisions, and dilemmas of clients are responded to in compassionate and competent ways, as this case demonstrates.

Questions

1. What specific roles does the social worker play in helping this client with a range of issues related to psychiatric medications? Who is the client in this case?
2. How does the social worker embrace the concept of partnership and client-centered care in this case? What other social work values and perspectives seem to be reflected?
3. What actions were likely the most beneficial in helping this client and why?
4. What is the relationship between psychiatric medication use and social work intervention in this case? What challenges can be anticipated in managing parallel care?

DEALING WITH A DIAGNOSIS

Jasmika originally came to me because of her boy, Derrick. He had just been diagnosed with attention deficit disorder (ADD), and Dr. Hawes had put him on a daily dose of 10 mg of Adderall, starting with 5 mg twice a day to see how he did. Jasmika wanted to know if this medication was the same as Ritalin and if the stuff about stunted growth was true. I noted that Adderall is a stimulant like Ritalin and acknowledged her fears and concerns about the overwhelming and sometimes confusing information that is out there on the Internet. I said that, to the best of my knowledge about the research, initial claims about slowed growth may have been exaggerated, but we could review and assess the information together, and if necessary, generate specific questions for Dr. Hawes. We would need to keep an eye on side effects, especially headaches, dizziness, insomnia, and loss of appetite, as well as note any therapeutic effects, such as improved impulse control and concentration. Jasmika seemed somewhat relieved and plopped down in my upholstered chair.

Derrick was a good kid, all in all, most of the time, she said, maybe a little self-centered and abrupt . . . and demanding . . . and sometimes uncontrollable. His daddy had left when he was 4 years old, 6 years previous, when it was becoming apparent that Derrick was not going to be a jock like himself, a small-town, high school football star running back. That wasn't the reason Dwight left, but it may be part of the reason why he never comes by and only calls on Christmas and Derrick's birthday, or at least the day after. Everyone agreed that Derrick had inherited Dwight's good looks. Derrick's photograph showed he has gorgeous deep brown skin, short thick black hair with a straight-line part down the left side, a high forehead, big hazel eyes, and a charming smile highlighted by a deep dimple on his left cheek. He was wearing a black-and-red-striped shirt in the school picture taken just 2 months earlier. Jasmika said he liked to wear striped shirts and had a closet full of them. She never really asked him why. She suspected it was because they had seen LeBron James in person at summer camp wearing a gold-and-crimson-striped Cleveland Cavaliers rugby shirt. This was before James moved to south Florida and the Miami Heat, obviously. Luckily, this meant Derrick needed no prompting to get up and dress himself. Putting his dirty clothes in the hamper, his Nike Hyperdunks in the closet, his Transformers in the big plastic bin at the foot of his bed—well, those were another story.

I told Jasmika (pronounced Jazz-MEE-ka)—who I *now* know was named for her mother Jasmine and father Michael—that I was very pleased Dr. Hawes had referred her to me for information about her son's diagnosis and medication. At this time, Dr. Hawes was a relatively new consultant to the James River Community Mental Health Center. I said he was a board-certified child psychiatrist and had been hired by the medical school as an assistant professor a year and a half ago. He consulted a half-day per week with us, did research, and supervised the psychiatry residents on rotation. Privately, I was also thankful that he was part of the new breed of psychiatrists—the kind that values social workers like myself and other nonmedical human service providers. He even tries to understand and honor our own notion of our roles and responsibilities, which data suggests tend to be broader and more complex than how other professionals view them.

I had first met Dr. Hawes at the welcome reception in his honor. I remember he lit up when he met me; he said he had heard my reputation preceded me for forming so-called partnerships with clients and working closely with the docs around medication issues. He wanted to set up an appointment right away and chat about our beginning collaboration. You could have blown me over with a feather at this warm reception. Deep inside, though, I wished I had thought of it first. That appointment, 3 weeks after the reception, was delightful, a most pleasant surprise. Because I had kicked myself for not suggesting the first meeting, I made up for it by suggesting we go out for a Starbucks coffee. On the way down the street, I puzzled over whether I should pick up the tab because he was new and I was the one who had invited him to go out. Or would that appear to be pandering to his stature? Maybe he would try to pick up the tab in an unintentionally condescending or even sexist kind of way, because his training practically forces him to think of me chiefly as a helper to *his* work. Maybe we should go Dutch and keep our boundaries intact. I rolled my eyes at myself, decided to abandon the unnecessary analysis, and, at the appropriate moment, I picked up the $6.37 tab with pleasure.

During that visit, Dr. Hawes told me about his training at the University of Virginia. His most heart-rending case was a 14-year-old male client who committed suicide after coming out to his parents. His most memorable case involved an 8-year-old boy with both epilepsy and autism who experienced a sort of breakthrough after a new experimental brain surgery. I told him about my MSW training at the University of Tennessee's Nashville branch and my previous work on a psychiatric unit of a small general hospital outside of Tallahassee, Florida. Let's just say the only psychiatrist for that 19-bed unit, Dr. Jenkins, was not of the "new breed." Dr. Hawes (he said to call him Darryl but it took me a year to be able to do it comfortably) said—with one exception—that he has worked with terrific social workers in his career. He appreciated them and relied on them heavily for psychosocial assessments and interventions, case management, education, consultation, and advice.

I remember describing my theoretical orientation as a mix of cognitive-behavioral, empowerment, and narrative, but I spent most of the time explaining the partnership model of practice I use—perhaps "strive for" is a more accurate way of putting it. I tried to articulate the rationale for decreasing the distance between myself and my clients, for sharing more power with them, and for demystifying the helping process in general. He too had been exposed to content in medical school around "shared decision making" and was genuinely intrigued by the notion of treating clients as if they are the experts on their experience, at putting what the client wants in the center of practice, and operating from a strengths perspective.

"But didn't clients also seek and pay for professional expertise?" he asked. "Didn't they also want someone who knew more than they did, someone who had a clue as to what was wrong and how to fix it?" Well, yes, absolutely; in fact, I thought helping happened in the mutual sharing of expertise and experience. Helping happens when we suspend disbelief, share knowledge and information, spend way more time affirming clients and validating their perspectives than we do judging them, telling them what they should be doing, or trying to get them to "act right." Even in the face of the complexities and demands of healthcare, we must first take the time to know who clients are as individuals and to empathize with their unique struggles, both past and present.

This basic foundation has to be built before we can start in with any specific change strategy or intervention plan.

He slowly nodded, perhaps with skepticism, noting the time constraints of practice today. I asked him about the sole exception to the terrific social workers he had known. He said she was an older social worker who was the director of social services at his old hospital. She was "too Freudian." It was the last straw, however, when she subtly implied to the parents of a 4-year-old kid he was treating that it was mostly their fault the child suffered from severe depression, and then apparently she offered to see the couple in the small private practice she kept on the side. Yes, Dr. Hawes and I would get along just fine.

Jasmika and Derrick were lucky to have Dr. Hawes as Derrick's psychiatrist. Bona fide specialists in children's mental health were hard to come by, especially one with the credentials of Dr. Hawes, not to mention his openness and approachability. We all hoped he'd continue to work at our rather humble public mental health center after he got tenure. Then again, public, private, for-profit, not-for-profit—we all look about the same anyway. I guess the most important thing about Dr. Hawes and me, then as now, is that I trusted him and he trusted me. I knew that if he referred Jasmika and Derrick to me that I could be confident that extreme care had been taken in the assessment and that he was using state-of-the-art research and algorithms to guide his pharmacotherapy decisions around dosage and administration, at least initially. I knew he'd probably already referred Jasmika to our center's Parent Training Series. He knew I would try to form a meaningful partnership with both Derrick and his mother, assess any additional needs for information, support, counseling, and such, and proceed accordingly. In this case, the referral was pretty simple; Jasmika wanted to know more about ADD and Adderall, and that was about all. I agreed that the individualized support and consultation would be a perfect complement to her Parent Training and Derrick's school intervention. Neither of us knew at the time how this case would develop and evolve, but I better not get ahead of myself.

I very much appreciated Dr. Hawes' e-mail telling me personally of the referral. I remember I retrieved Derrick's file from the confidential electronic drop box when my 10:00 a.m. appointment, a new case, didn't show up. The file was brief and unremarkable. A guidance counselor had originally sent a note home to Jasmika expressing concern about Derrick's behavior in the classroom and suggesting an evaluation. By the time I joined the case, the evaluation had already been done by Mr. Stevens, a school psychologist and specialist in ADD, who then referred Derrick to Dr. Hawes and the center. Although the chart did not contain the details of his school testing, a referral form noted a history of several months of classroom difficulty, including a general inability to sit still, distracting fidgeting of the hands, disengagement from the lessons, and a tendency to intrude on or interrupt others' conversations or activities. Dr. Hawes' progress note followed, noting his choice of medication and dose and his referral of Derrick's mother to me and the Parent Training Series, which coincidentally was starting a new cycle in a little over a week. It was also noted that Mr. Stevens would see the boy at school regularly, as was typical in these cases, thank goodness.

FORMING A PARTNERSHIP

That was all I knew when Jasmika came in that first day and asked about stimulants and stunted growth. We agreed to meet at least twice, including that first time. She thought that would be plenty of time for me to convey her requested information about Adderall (and perhaps other medication choices as well) and ADD and to answer any questions she might have before her training series started. I could always be available in the future if specific individual concerns arose, she thought. That sounded good to me, but I encouraged flexibility. As you can probably tell, we spent a lot of time at that first meeting talking about Derrick, but I also learned a lot about Jasmika.

As she shared part of her family's story with me, I reflected her seeming frustration and exhaustion in her role as a single parent, as well as her pride and pleasure in a job well done in the face of overwhelming responsibility. I unexpectedly learned a bit more of her failed marriage to Dwight and sensed tremendous loss and disappointment there. She teared up, and we sat in silence for a few minutes. I tried to "start where the client is" and pursue her feelings a bit more, but she reminded us both that we were here to talk about Derrick's medication. I proceeded to explain that it is estimated that 3% to 5% of children are thought to have ADD, and thus it is the most common psychiatric disorder in children. Males are at three times the risk. I explained that 70% to 80% of children responded positively to various forms of amphetamines and methylphenidate. These, plus a newer drug called Strattera, are by far the most researched and used psychostimulants for children with ADD. I did not go into a lot of detail about theories of neurotransmission at this point but gave a cursory overview of the rationale for pharmacological treatment. She asked why Derrick had to take it more than once a day instead of just one larger dose, so I explained about the half-life of medications and the fast metabolism rates for children. I explained that Derrick's initial dosage, which would be medically monitored by Dr. Hawes, was based in part on Derrick's weight and that adjustments were likely. If appropriate, the doctor might eventually switch to a time-release capsule.

I gave her a copy of a reading list our staff and members of the support group had compiled for parents. In addition, I got Jasmika to share moments where she was particularly confident and pleased with her behavioral management of Derrick and times where she wasn't. I praised her successes lavishly and empathized with her less successful efforts. At one point, we even found ourselves laughing out loud at the occasional craziness in her house. I made myself available for consultation around the behavioral management of Derrick's ADD if she was interested either during or after her parent training. "Did I have children?" she asked. "No," I said. Although I do sort of count my two male Abyssinian cats, Tyler and Zach, as "children," but I knew this was probably not what she meant.

I offered to meet the second time at Jasmika's apartment and expressed a desire to meet Derrick. She declined, but she said she could come in again during her lunch hour in 2 weeks. And she did. By then, Jasmika, who looked a little tired, had read everything I had given her and then some. She had already been to the first session of the Parent Training Series. It also turns out that a second cousin, her mother's cousin in Hopewell, has a 14-year-old child with ADD, and they had had lunch and talked. She had told her all about our meeting and even shared some of the stuff I had given her (I was flattered). I pointed out that many of the graduates of the Parent Training Series started attending the local parent and spouse support group, called Central Virginia CHADD (Children and Adults with Attention Deficit Disorder), which meets at St. Paul's Episcopal church, just two blocks away. I wondered if perhaps that group would be useful for one or both of them. She didn't think her cousin could afford the gas money. Unfortunately, a grant that at one time paid for transportation for some folks had dried up. She asked if any other black people went to the group. I said we had a black couple that came a few times about a year ago. She got real quiet, maybe even a little sad. I mistakenly let it go.

Actually, she thought she was doing okay with this ADD thing, and Derrick was already showing some improvement. He really likes Dr. Hawes and Mr. Stevens, who he is seeing at school on Mondays (individual) and Thursdays (group). Mr. Stevens teaches the kids a new behavioral technique for self-monitoring their own behavior that involves a beeper and a recording sheet with rewards for meeting certain goals. I told her that in the past 2 years, Mr. Stevens has also done some innovative teacher training programs as well. I saw a brochure on one just last week about how teachers can increase the predictability and structure in their classrooms, build in shorter work periods, and use positive reinforcement more effectively. She seemed pleased with his expertise. Dr. Hawes talks to Mr. Stevens every week, because they have several clients in common. I would have thought more about calling him myself before Jasmika's second meeting with me, but it hardly felt like Derrick was my client, and this case looked moments from closure. Actually, when she left that day, I thought it was over. I made a brief final comment in Derrick's chart about my meeting with his Mom and the information and support I had conveyed. I also e-mailed Dr. Hawes—Darryl, that is—a more personal and upbeat note about my contacts.

Jasmika called back a month to the day exactly. I remember because it was my birthday, the 17th of the month. She asked me to come over and said that she was home from work in bed, crying, and she had no one to turn to. My mind quickly flashed back to our two previous meetings. What could be going on? Did I miss something? Well, clearly I must have. Jasmika said she had called in sick and taken to her bed, depressed. She hadn't been eating or sleeping and was having thoughts of, well, scary thoughts. I gently commended her risk-taking and courage for calling. I went over to her apartment, and for just under 3 hours, I listened to Jasmika share much more of her story with me. I just wanted to be present for her. This very day was the 1-year anniversary of her mother's death. She and her mom had been extremely close, talking on the phone at least once a day and texting practically nonstop in between. She often took Derrick for a few hours or the whole day to give Jasmika time alone. Her mother had been her major support, a respected church leader who made a living out of her home as a seamstress for the community. Breast cancer had taken her relatively quickly. I told Jasmika I could sense the love and respect . . . and loss and loneliness that she seemed to express.

She also talked about the divorce. How Dwight, her ex, had made promises he couldn't keep, how he wouldn't work on their communication problems, how he wanted sex all the time but not the cuddling after. It wasn't all him, she said. She loved him once, but the passion faded quickly. She had experienced a few doubts before they married, but she went through with it anyway. She had become severely depressed in high school, after a bout with mononucleosis that had hospitalized her for 10 days during her junior year. She had even been put on antidepressant medication for 2 years, but she thought the marriage to Dwight would cure her of the hopelessness she felt. "Gosh, it sounds like you were really in a lot of pain," I reflected. She nodded and closed her eyes, and tears fell.

There was a long silence. There had been other bouts with depression too. "Had she gotten counseling or anything in addition to the medication?" I asked. "No." The pills the first time were oblong, light blue, with a word beginning with "P" with an "X" in it. "Could it have been Paxil?" I questioned. "Yes, that was it." Maybe she'd been depressed her whole life, she reflected. She'd miscarried twice, and the depression had worsened. Her mother had been there for her. In fact, despite all you hear about African Americans and their lack of formal help-seeking, her mom suggested she go to Dr. McGilicutty, her family's physician for 40 years, to get medication that she had read about in *Parade* magazine. But then she got pregnant with Derrick and again thought it was going to be her salvation from depression and her strained marriage. And perhaps Derrick *has* saved her life, after all, since she has never really actually attempted . . . anything stupid.

And so that's how the afternoon of my 51st birthday went. I felt humbled and honored to be allowed to come inside Jasmika's life, into the inner rooms. I was both moved and hopeful. I really thought I'd be able to help her. I looked forward to it, actually, because I saw so many strengths: her openness and caring, her intellect, her commitment to mothering, and her dependability and competence at work, which I haven't even detailed here. The flood of ideas about what we could do together was actually the major problem for me at that meeting in Jasmika's home. I'd have to be careful not to rush things, and instead hold fast to the principle of partnership (which I had so eloquently shared with Dr. Hawes over coffee a couple of years prior to this occasion).

As you can imagine, one of the first things we did when Jasmika came to my office the next day was to review her history a little more systematically. It was like reading the DSM section on major depression (which I actually got out and showed her a little later). I also flipped through the center's 2-year-old copy of the *Physician's Desk Reference*, and we cataloged the few medications she had been put on at different times, and her responses as best she could remember. We called it her Medication Log. Interestingly, even though she had never gotten counseling or psychotherapy, she did go talk to her pastor one time just before the marriage to Dwight. He had some rather provocative ideas about "cherishing" her depression as proof positive of her humanity and the depth of her feelings. He suggested she meditate on Psalm 116 and pray about it. She took his advice and says she felt a little better afterward. Here's what we came up with:

Dates	Medication	Response	Reason for Discontinuation
1993–1995 late high school	Paxil	Took "a while" to work; made her groggy	Didn't want to take it anymore; got married
1997 for a year in early marriage	Celexa	Helped but some side effects: dry mouth, not able to go to the bathroom	Worried about medication and trying to get pregnant
1999 Derrick's birth	Valium	Like drinking one beer	Didn't need it
2011 Mother's death	Xanax	It helped calm her down	Didn't want it any longer

Dr. McGilicutty had prescribed her antidepressant medications in those early years. Jasmika actually responded fairly well to them but continued to act as sole judge in their discontinuation, which, according to Jasmika, had little to do with symptom improvement and more with "other factors." Dr. McGilicutty had prescribed the Valium once without even asking her if she wanted it, saying she would probably need it to help her deal with new motherhood. Likewise, when she happened to see her dentist for their long-standing appointment and mentioned the stress of her mother's impending death from cancer, he gave her another unsolicited prescription for Xanax, a benzodiazepine and commonly prescribed antianxiety drug. She only took one pill before throwing them away during a cleaning frenzy one Saturday the previous spring.

Jasmika and I also explicitly discussed our changed relationship: mine from purveyor of knowledge about Derrick's Adderall and support to her parenting, to *her* clinical social worker and *partner* in the quest to improve her own mood and interpersonal well-being; hers, from a relatively passive recipient of brief support and education about her son's diagnosis and treatment to active participant and *partner* in mutual problem-solving and personal healing processes. Even though we talked extensively about her past medications, Jasmika was not interested in medication for herself at this time, despite this admitted improvement in the past. She was convinced that because she had never gotten counseling before, she should try that by itself first. I shared with her my understanding of the literature, which suggests that a combination of medication and psychosocial interventions usually have the most bang for the buck. But this is what she wanted, at least for now, so I supported the decision. There had been so many losses and challenges of late, that she wondered if those might really be the main problem, even if she did have some sort of "biological predisposition" to depression. I wondered out loud where she had heard about that since we had not yet even had a chance to talk about theories of etiology. She'd heard about it on the *Today* show this time.

HELPING WITH DEPRESSION

Jasmika's insurance company approved eight counseling sessions right off the bat. We proceeded with our mutual problem-solving process and, after the rest of the assessment, collaborated to develop some modest goals, clearly leaning on cognitive and behavioral theories to help us frame her depression and its treatment. Jasmika was comfortable with my explanation of the options and asked lots of questions about what we might do together. One of the things we chose was cognitive restructuring, a painstaking process, which is much more difficult than the textbooks would have us think. However, it has been shown to be very useful in getting folks to reframe or rewire their negative or unrealistic thoughts into more accurate or positive ones. We also used published workbooks, set up reinforcers for the homework assignments, and used a 25-item scale to quantify her level of depression so we could monitor her progress. The behavioral stuff was familiar to her from her Parent Training and Derrick.

Jasmika almost always did her homework and was improving, just not quite as fast as she or I hoped. In our sixth meeting, she surprisingly asked if we could revisit the topic of medication. I was careful not to suggest that because we were discussing medication again, it meant that she or I had failed in any way. I took a good 20 minutes to tell her about the three kinds of antidepressants and their very basic differences. I even explained what reuptake was and how the neurotransmitters serotonin and norepinephrine were thought to be implicated in the regulation of mood and drives. Despite these theories, I noted that the guidebooks still say "the exact mechanisms for action are not fully known." I warned about side effects, especially the ones that seem to be most associated with noncompliance, like changes in weight or sexual functioning.

We actually completed a "pros versus cons" discussion of the possibility of taking psychiatric medication. The key advantages were likelihood of further symptom improvement in light of the research, her strong desire for more rapid improvement, her previous success with the pharmacological treatment, and so on. The disadvantages centered on her fear of side effects and just not wanting to be a person on medication—psychiatric medication at that. The whole meaning of medication has been of particular interest to me and, in my view, a neglected aspect of pharmacotherapy. So we talked a lot more about how medication might change her view of herself, how she might feel when she goes to the drugstore to have her prescription filled, and what messages she has picked up from coworkers or even the media about these kind of drugs and how they made her feel. I shared a bit about my other experiences with clients and antidepressant medications, both the positive and the not-so-positive.

Although I have never taken any kind of psychotropic, except for a brief trial with Ambien, they seemed like a reasonable option for many folks. She asked if I *would* take antidepressants if I was as depressed as she was. Wow, great question. I'll admit it, there was a major pause on my part. I said I couldn't be sure unless I was actually in the situation, but I thought it was likely I'd want to take advantage of every reasonable option. I would, no doubt, have some reservations (hence, the pause), related to my intense (and perhaps distorted) sense of self-sufficiency. Yes, she understood. In the end, she decided she would like the referral to the center's psychiatrist. It seemed to really matter that her mother had been supportive of the idea in the past.

I told her about Dr. Tamara Daly, our medical director for the past 8 years, an older woman and a psychiatrist who knew more about psychopharmacology than anyone I've met. In fact, in several professional presentations, Dr. Daly had told her audiences about her own depressive episode in medical school. The way Dr. Daly and I usually worked was to meet as a team for the first time, all three of us, if that was okay with Jasmika. This way there would be open sharing of information, clear communication, and an understanding of roles. I agreed to set up the appointment. We walked through some scenarios of what to expect in that first joint meeting, and Jasmika even wrote down a few key questions she wanted to ask. I always enjoyed these meetings with Dr. Daly, a brilliant but reserved doctor who listened to every word you said but waited a long time before speaking. In that meeting, just a few days later thankfully, Dr. Daly asked Jasmika to summarize our work together. I really didn't add too much other than to point out some important strengths Jasmika had brought to the partnership and to highlight a few things from the Medication Log. Dr. Daly started her on 75 mg of Effexor once a day in the morning. It's a popular new-generation antidepressant that came out around 2007, known for its effect on anxiety as well. Dr. Daly prescribes it a lot.

MAKING PROGRESS

It took several weeks for Jasmika to "tell any difference," although she was certainly prepared for that reality. A few bothersome side effects kicked in early, specifically diarrhea, which improved over the first few weeks. As the weeks passed, Jasmika reported feeling much better "inside," although she knew that everyone might not see it. I told her I sensed more energy available for our other work. I asked how she was feeling about herself as a person on antidepressants and reminded her of some of the things she had said right before our meeting with Dr. Daly. She was reflective and said she wasn't sure if she could explain it. I pushed a piece of blank printer paper over to her and some markers and said, "Could you draw it?" I think she thought I was kidding. I said, "Why don't you draw a picture that represents yourself before and then after the medication?"

I got up to get us some decaf, light and sweet for me, just cream for Jasmika. I fiddled with some paperwork for about five minutes and sipped my coffee as she put the finishing touches on her quickly crafted artwork. She smiled as she turned it around to show me. The first drawing was of a three-dimensional cube with a tiny stick figure in it. She said, "This is me before my treatment, small, in a glass box without windows or doors." She explained that she could see everyone else outside, but she couldn't get out. I asked her what she'd title the piece. "Suffocation," she said, because the walls were moving in on her like that galactic garbage compactor scene in *Star Wars*. The second picture was a simple jigsaw puzzle with all of the pieces fitting together. She had drawn an arrow to a piece that represented her medications, another that represented her counseling with me, another to her job (the center piece), and one to her new relationship with a man named Rutherford. She called this picture "Almost There."

Because of the addition of medication to her treatment, the insurance company actually ended up giving us four more sessions in addition to several simple medication checks. Dr. Daly, Jasmika, and I all agreed to use them as "booster sessions" and scheduled them as far apart as the insurance rules would let us without losing them. The only crisis was when Jasmika at one point told me she had actually stopped the Effexor on her own the previous week. I urged her to call Dr. Daly and wondered if we all needed to meet again. When we did meet all together a few days later, Jasmika asked directly about Effexor and sexual dysfunction. We gently inquired deeper. She admitted that some problems were occurring "in that area" (technically called, *anorgasmia*). Dr. Daly answered a multitude of questions and discussed possible courses of action. We reviewed and made revisions to our previous cost-benefit analysis. I was trying to be very sure that Jasmika didn't feel like I was personally invested in her taking her medication, that my relationship or caring was somehow contingent upon her "compliance." Rather, I was invested in helping her decide and come to a good place about the decision. Our work was specifically about her having the information and support she needed to make the best decision for herself at that moment. She ended up having a good bit to say that day about being a woman, being with Rutherford, and the implications of this unfortunate (and relatively uncommon) side effect on her view of herself. With a lowered dose, Jasmika said she'd resume. They agreed to discuss discontinuation in 4 months. We continued separately for a few more sessions with our cognitive restructuring exercises and the problem-solving work we had been doing on expanding her social networks.

In our very last meeting, Jasmika's improvement in mood was notable, especially when she talked about Rutherford. He was a slightly older gentleman she had met through church, which she had started attending regularly again. He was handsome and funny and kind and made good money as a computer support person for a company that outsourced such services to corporations. He was into stock car racing just like Jasmika and had an old and dilapidated RV that he loved to take to the local track and camp out the day before the races. His 19-year-old daughter was a sculpture major at Virginia Commonwealth University. That didn't stop him from loving Derrick, and he didn't seem to care that the boy came with his own set of unique challenges.

We talked a lot about "what's next?" for everyone. Derrick was doing pretty well. He was getting Bs in school and had met a new friend in bowling league. In fact, Dr. Hawes had mentioned something to both of us about the possibility of a drug holiday this summer for him. In addition to the new relationship with Rutherford, Jasmika had been to lunch numerous times with her newfound second cousin and had attended the CHADD support group for parents four times. She felt hopeful again and quite active. She was doing well in understanding the connection between her cognition and her feelings, and in reframing and revising irrational overgeneralizations. She could write her own goals with little help now and understood how to design and plan the tasks and activities needed to reach those goals. Work at the furniture store (where she was a fiscal assistant) was continuing to go well. She was proficient in Microsoft Excel, Quickbooks Pro, and Sage 50, and the store had even offered to pay for her to receive additional accounting training. We reviewed our work together from beginning to end. I printed out a copy of the graphed data from the depression inventories she had been filling out. She laughed and said she'd put it on her refrigerator at home. Our goodbye hug lasted a long time.

CONCLUSIONS

There is a lot to feel good about in this case (which is one of the reasons I told you about it). I think the partnership approach worked really well with Jasmika. The practice philosophy of partnership truly formed the foundation for all of the treatment techniques and strategies we utilized. We built the relationship first. Knowing and caring about the details of Jasmika's life made it easy to love and appreciate her uniqueness and humanity, and to deeply empathize with her challenges. This was where we began. I ended up being a key resource for information and support around psychiatric medication. I did not shy away from this role but actually enjoyed the opportunity to go beyond the rhetoric of a "biopsychosocial perspective" to the reality of one. Thus, the intervention package was truly integrative and collaborative, just like they teach you in school. We pulled from lots of theories, frameworks, and perspectives, yet for the most part relied on interventions that have good effectiveness data to support their use. Jasmika set the pace and direction of change, and I helped to guide the process. There was an intentional emphasis on strengths. We kept our sense of humor.

Amazingly, there were no major conflicts with the doctors (this time), no second-guessing their decisions. In fact, I think I learned a lot from the doctors. There was true collaboration and mutual understanding and respect among the providers. How refreshing. The result was visible and meaningful improvement in the quality of a family's life. And we did it all, believe it or not, in 18 meetings total over the course of just under 11 months. Do I have doubts about anything? Sure. For one thing, in terms of medication, I wonder if she'll stop too soon (I'd be lying if I didn't say I was a little worried). Why am I telling you all this now? Jasmika called yesterday with two questions. First, did I know anything about a drug for schizophrenia called Risperdal. Turns out Rutherford's 62-year-old father who lives on disability in a group home near Carytown has just been put on this antipsychotic, and she wanted to know what I knew about it. I shared some research data with her and agreed to send some pamphlets and articles. I said I would ask Dr. Daly what she'd read or heard about this drug recently. I also told her about Central Virginia's Alliance for the Mentally Ill group, which meets on third Thursdays at the Jewish Community Center. She laughed and said she was "support grouped out" but would tell Rutherford.

She also had good news: There would be a wedding invitation in the mail soon, and she asked if I would come. I was thrilled and said I'd be there. I told her I'd be *here* for her too at James River Community Mental Health Center if she ever needs me again. Now, I know the "ever" part might be stretching it a bit. We all know people move up or move on or move away. But perhaps if I can't be there for her, or for Derrick, in the future, maybe you will be.

Case Study 5-4

Beyond Just Words: Multisensory Interventions Can Heighten Therapy's Impact

Danie Beaulieu[2]

I hear and I forget. I see and I remember. I do and I understand.

–Confucius

Practitioners search for new approaches to conducting individual treatment. This case study presents an innovative approach based on the use of multisensory interventions.

Questions

1. What is the underlying theory and logic of using a multisensory approach to treatment?
2. How did the worker modify their approach to treatment to address different multisensory applications?

[2]   "Beyond Just Words: Multisensory Interventions Can Heighten Therapy's Impact," by D. Beaulieu, 2003, *Psychotherapy Networker, 27*(4), 69–77. Reprinted with permission.

3. What techniques do you believe are most helpful in this approach?
4. Would you incorporate these strategies in your work, why or why not?

A client sits hunched in his therapist's office, his eyes fixed on the floor, unable to meet the therapist's gaze. He murmurs one-syllable replies to direct questions. Elsewhere, another client circles around and around the crux of her problems with an endless flow of talk, resisting all of her therapist's attempts to nudge her back toward the main issue. Most therapists spend the majority of every day talking and listening, often to clients such as these, trying to find the right words to make therapeutic progress. We're trained to use words to explore the client's problems, and we're trained to use words to find the solutions. No matter which therapeutic approach we favor, the challenge often comes down to communication and arousing enough interest to engage the client in a more-focused, problem-solving discussion by channeling the flow of words.

When the right words do come together in a breakthrough flash—an "aha!" moment of clarity for the client—we think, "Finally, I was able to help my client see where the problem lies! Now we can make some real progress!" In that thought lies the key to breaking through inertia and capturing the client's attention and energy. The key is to get beyond words and enlist more of the client's senses—seeing, touching, smelling, and even tasting. When we talk with our clients, we're engaging only a fraction of the sensory recourses of the mind, involving the auditory sense, but neglecting the other senses. There are simple ways to recruit those neglected sensory modalities in every therapy session, increasing our effectiveness every day.

The developmental pattern of the brain gives us clues as to why it's so important for therapists to engage more of the senses. A baby's feeling of comfort and security is cued sensorially, not verbally. The verbal centers of the brain are among the last to develop, long after myriad sensory impressions have been linked to emotional states, making words the last layer of information added during development. Babies know that feeling of vulnerability and isolation whenever they're separated from mommy for a long time before they're able to name that feeling "sadness."

In recent years, the intrinsic power of our sensory relationship with the world has been extensively applied in education. We now recognize that children explore and learn about their world more efficiently if they use more than one sense, even in the schoolroom setting. A math problem involving fractions suddenly becomes clear when a child is offered a real apple (or even a symbolic round piece of red construction paper) to cut into pieces. Seeing, touching, and manipulating objects helps ground the abstractions of arithmetic. The same principles of sensory involvement can be effectively applied to psychotherapy. When words fail, recruitment of other senses can help break through to another level of involvement, so that the therapist can have real impact on the client.

Convinced of the potential such an approach would offer, Ed Jacobs of West Virginia University developed Impact Therapy, a set of techniques that recruit all of the senses to the therapeutic process. These techniques add needed impetus when the interaction gets bogged down in words, allowing the therapist to rapidly translate the issues into concrete terms. The following case demonstrates how quickly visual and tactile metaphors helped a severely depressed young woman not only to see and touch her problems, but also to see and touch the solutions.

LEARNING THE HARD WAY

Louise, a 28-year-old veterinarian, was referred to me after a psychiatrist diagnosed her with severe depression with suicidal ideation, recommending medication or hospitalization. Louise categorically refused both, but she was willing to try psychotherapy. When I first met her, I was struck by her quiet voice, her simplicity of dress, and her straightforward but self-effacing manner of talking about—and taking responsibility for—her situation.

She had reached what seemed to her the end of her career. After graduation from veterinary school in Quebec, she had moved, with her boyfriend, to the United States, where they had been living for 2 years while he pursued a PhD. Because licensing procedures prohibited her from working in the United States, she took a job as a veterinary technician. Dissatisfied with this role, she returned to Quebec to work as a veterinarian before her boyfriend had received his degree. She found work in a clinical setting with a staff of about 15 people.

Louise was impressed with her new boss, an extremely competent and ambitious veterinarian who was also sharply critical and demanding of all the employees. Louise, who had always succeeded in her endeavors and rarely faced criticism, found it especially difficult to face criticism from someone she admired. As the negative comments mounted, she began to doubt her abilities. When she made a surgical error that could have led to serious consequences for an animal in her case, she held herself responsible—not only for what happened, but also for what *could* have happened. With her boss's ongoing criticisms providing reinforcement, Louise began to question her skills and judgment. She referred all but the simplest cases and feared meeting new clients. Her confidence plummeted. She became indecisive, couldn't function at work, and stopped sleeping. After less than 2 years, she quit her job and moved in with an aunt, falling into a pattern of passivity in which she spent most of her time talking about her problems and crying.

We devoted our first session to investigating Louise's history and current problems. Her father died when she was 3 years old, leaving her mother with three young children, including Louise's older sister, who has epilepsy. By the time Louise was 8 years old, her mother was going out several times a week, leaving Louise responsible for disciplining her younger brother and dealing with her sister's seizures. Over time, Louise became entirely responsible for the family, and her younger brother became progressively delinquent. Louise's mother spent most of her time and money on dressing up and going out, delegating adult responsibilities—cooking, cleaning, managing finances—to her daughter. Louise managed to fulfill those responsibilities, be an excellent student, and run the household on the little money that was left. In fact, it was only now, at 28 years old, that she felt for the first time that she was incapable of handling a difficult situation.

Clearly, Louise's history of always being the good child and the good student in the face of adversity had left her ill equipped to face the recent wave of criticism. Having never previously needed the skills for responding to negative comments, she was vulnerable to a situation that assaulted her view of herself in fundamental ways. Her susceptibility to criticism had led her to the erroneous conclusion that she wasn't competent to practice. Louise left me no doubt about her suicidal thoughts, so my first priority was to give her hope and the motivation to go on for another week. I wanted to offer her a few tangible experiences, to leave her with more than just words to hold onto after the session. As French neurophysiologist Guillemette Isnard said, "Information is integrated when all the senses have had their say."

Aware of Louise's scientific training, I guessed that an orderly, almost mathematical, analysis of the situation might connect with her personal logic. I wanted to give her a visual representation of how others perceived her, to counterbalance the inner vision that she'd developed. Presenting her with a blank piece of paper, I asked her to write down the names of 10 people who could evaluate her professional abilities. She listed her ex-boss, her boyfriend, two colleagues from the clinic, and six professors from her veterinary school. Next I asked her to tell me what rating, on a scale of 0 to 10, each person on the list would give her. With the exception of her ex-boss, she thought every person would rate her as a 7, 8, or 9. Her boss, she decided, would give her a 3 or a 4.

I then asked Louise to rate each of her evaluators in terms of their social or emotional health. Did they function well in personal and professional relationships? Were they happy, healthy individuals? Once again, most of the names on the list got 8s and 9s, with an occasional 7. Her ex-boss received a 3.

"So, how do we evaluate your worth as a veterinarian, Louise?" I asked. Louise looked at the list and was confronted by data that undeniably indicated that she was actually well above average in the view of others. Her training as a medical scientist and her reliance on statistics forced her to set aside her belief that she was a bad veterinarian and accept the possibility of a different view. This realization had a major impact on her. There was suddenly room for hope again.

I gave her the page to take with her, as her first anchor for the week. Anchors are reminders of the new ideas and new learning acquired during a session. Learning takes place most effectively (a) by repetition, (b) by association of something new with previous knowledge, or (c) by the effects of strong emotion on memory (as is the case in posttraumatic stress disorder). By giving Louise the sheet of paper, I provided an anchor to assure repetition of the learning process during the following week. Every time she looked at the chart depicting her evaluations, the idea that she was a competent veterinarian would sink in a little more. Words alone—which she may or may not remember to think about—couldn't have accomplished what that take-home form was able to do.

Louise needed to learn about healthy management of her thoughts and about accepting or rejecting the judgments of others. So I went on to the second method of strengthening new learning—attaching a new idea to a concept Louise already understood quite well: the life-sustaining nature of clean water. Most clients respond well to this intervention, because it touches on such a common concept of what's healthy and what isn't.

I picked up a glass and explained to Louise that it represented her mind. The mind is a reservoir for all sorts of experiences, good and bad, that influence the way we perceive the world and our place in it, I explained. When Louise nodded her understanding, I poured fresh water in the glass and said that good experiences (e.g., healthy interactions with good-willed, healthy people) were like clean water: beneficial and necessary to our normal functioning. I then emptied a plastic bag full of ashes and cigarette butts (reserved for this purpose) into the glass, along with a used tissue and other disgusting little things that I keep on hand for this intervention. Swirling the revolting cocktail, I extended the glass toward Louise, offering her a sip. She recoiled in distaste and stated: "I couldn't possibly drink that!"

I asked, "But isn't that precisely what you've been doing? Do you think that your boss has been adding clean water or garbage to your glass?" Now I picked up another glass and coffee filter. I poured the contents of the first glass through the filter into the second, letting the filter trap the nasty stuff.

"What you need, Louise, is a way of filtering out some of the garbage. Garbage is the stuff thrown at you by people who have problems of their own—maybe they're just tired or angry, or they might even have some emotional problems. In any case, it makes their interactions with others unhealthy and damaging." I showed her the filter, saying, "When you're living or working in a polluted environment, you need a filter that will keep some of the bad stuff from lodging in your mind."

Next, I handed her a clean filter, saying, "Keep this with you, this week, to remind you to filter out some of the bad influences or bad thoughts that might come up before our next session. Your own thoughts have become pretty polluted by what you've experienced, so some of the garbage thoughts are coming from inside. You don't have to accept them though—the filter works just as well on them."

Once again, just talking to Louise about garbage would have been addressing her brain's temporal lobe, where the verbal centers are, but with the concrete representation of the filtering process, I was connecting with the occipital visual centers, as well as eliciting limbic responses that dictated her physical recoil from the noxious mixture. She was much more likely to remember to try to filter out negative comments and self-talk when so much more of her brain was involved in the learning process.

My office is well stocked with a wide variety of props. I frequent the dollar store and seek inspiration in the knickknacks that I find there. The simplest objects often have the greatest power as metaphors, mainly because they're so recognizable and readily accepted. Your office is already full of useful props, if you look around with an inventive eye. Adding to your collection will become an addiction when you see how well such multisensory techniques work with your clients.

MENTAL GYMNASTICS

When Louise came to the second session, she told me that she didn't think she'd ever needed a filter before. "I can't get used to filtering comments; I'm not good at it. All my life I've mostly heard people say good things about me. I was the good girl in my family, who got good grades and behaved well, and I did well at the university too."

Resorting to one of my favorite exercises, I asked her to fold her hands together, interlacing her fingers. "Look at your hands and notice which thumb is on top. Now unfold and refold your hands, so the other thumb is on top. How does that feel?"

When Louise said it felt awkward and uncomfortable, I explained that she'd probably been folding her hands together in the same way all of her life—just like she'd been a sponge soaking up all comments about her. Now she needed to learn to use a filter, and it was bound to feel awkward and uncomfortable for a while, as she broke one habit and established a new one. Each time she folded her hands now, she should remember that she was learning some new life skills. By translating the discomfort caused by the new mental effort into a physical metaphor, the resistance to learning a new life skill was diminished to something quite easy to understand and overcome.

It seemed probable to me that Louise's childhood experience had made self-criticism and self-blame routine, as she tried to be a perfect child under stressful conditions. She'd told me that she felt responsible for every seizure her sister had, for every delinquent act her brother committed, and for every mistake she made in her efforts to be a dependable daughter. As an adult, it was difficult for her to recognize that part of herself was still trying to play the role of the perfect little girl and that another part was carping and criticizing her for it. I wanted her to see that more concretely, so I pulled out a plastic child's chair from the corner of the office.

"The chair is like you as a little girl. When you were a child, who was there to help the little Louise learn how to build a healthy life?" To introduce the concept of an adult figure, I placed a normal, adult-size chair next to the child's chair. "Was there anyone in the adult seat to guide that little girl?" I asked, referring first to the adult chair and then to the small chair. This tableau of her childhood situation struck home. Instantly, Louise saw that the adult chair had always been empty. As I explained to Louise, with no one there to guide her, part of herself had become her own "critical parent."

At this point in her life, Louise was in need of an alternative inner voice, one that would be more mature and supportive. I took out a third chair. "If that little girl had had a guiding adult or a nurturing parent, what would that person have told her? Would he or she have said that little Louise was responsible for everything that happened to her sister and brother?" Louise shook her head.

With the help of the chairs, it became clear to Louise that she was regarding her boss from the perspective of the child's chair—helpless, hopeless, and powerless. She needed to work on a presence to fill the third chair, developing within herself the heretofore absent nurturing parent. By "trying on" the two positions—the vulnerability of the child's chair and the protective authority of the third chair—Louise began to understand the conflict stirring inside her. Her lifelong "good girl" strategy was failing to meet her own needs and gave her insufficient resources to meet the challenges of adult life, in which pleasing others wasn't always possible. With no counterbalancing nurturing voice, her tendencies for self-criticism had been given free rein.

POWER STRUGGLE

Our third session began with a declaration of frustration. "I keep finding myself sitting in the little chair," Louise said. "I can't seem to get onto the big one."

"It's not easy, is it?" I said. "Imagine training just one arm, conscientiously, year after year, never working on the other arm. You've been training to sit in that little chair all your life. It's like a really strong muscle, and it's going to win hands down when you try to use the big chair instead. But every time you try, the big chair is getting stronger and gaining importance, and eventually it'll win." That metaphor provided considerable relief from the frustration that had been accumulating within her.

Louise was still depressed, and she complained that the fog of depression wasn't lifting fast enough. To adjust expectations to a more realistic level, I decided to use the metaphor of the internal accountant—a mathematical analogy that suited Louise's manner of logic. I handed her a page of figures—a long list of additions and subtractions concerning many rows—with a large equals sign at the bottom. "What's the total?" I asked. Louise was amused at the impossibility of the task. I explained, "Each of us has an accountant in our head that can add up all of our impressions from all of our experiences with anything in a split second. Do you like dogs?"

"Sure, I love dogs. I have two," she answered instantly.

"You see? Your internal accountant just did an instant calculation, adding up all the good times you've had with dogs, all the wonderful animals you've known, subtracting out the one or two times when something unpleasant might have happened to you with a dog, and came up with a grand total of 10,000 or so, in the dog section of your mental bank account!"

When Louise smiled her agreement, I went on. "Your ex-boss gave you an experience worth a minus 500 every day for 2 years in the veterinary category of your mental bank account. You're going to need some good experiences to get that total back up into the positive zone. And you're on the right path to do just that."

This metaphor became the basis for a secret code between us. In subsequent sessions, she'd mention that she'd made a lot of additions, or at least fewer subtractions, in the last weeks. During therapy, when her comments or her body language showed that she'd just reacted negatively to a thought, I'd say, "Uh-oh, we just made a subtraction, didn't we?" Gradually, Louise began to recognize her own reflex to strong self-criticism and negative perceptions, permitting her to interrupt her damaging thought patterns. Now she had concrete tasks to accomplish: getting used to sitting in the "big chair" and looking for ways to "make deposits in her mental bank account."

MAMA'S LITTLE GIRL GROWS UP

Two weeks later, Louise came in with an air of renewed energy. For the first time, she expressed appropriate anger toward her ex-boss. As the nurturing parent role became more familiar to her, she was leaving behind the timid, approval-seeking child.

All wasn't entirely well, however. Louise was anticipating an extended visit from her mother. These visits always left Louise feeling smothered by unwelcome affection and attention. When her mother hugged and kissed her repeatedly, Louise submitted passively, waiting for the uncomfortable moment to pass. Although she was gaining proficiency in assuming the adult role in the rest of her life, when it came to her family situations, the old pattern was harder to break. If Louise were to continue along her remarkable journey of rapid personal growth, the old script of behaviors and exchanges with her mother wasn't going to work anymore. I wanted to show her that she had a choice and that she wasn't restricted to following the same script for the rest of her life.

Picking up a blank piece of paper, I folded it in two. "We all have scripts for our lives. This is yours." I wrote *Louise's script: 1974–2002* on the cover. "On a scale of 0 to 10, what was the result of the script of your life when you first came to see me?" Louise said she'd been suicidal at that time, so it could be only a 1. I marked this prominently on the cover.

Opening the script, I began to read an imaginary text: "I must always please others, especially my mother. Even if I don't want to, I must always do what others expect of me." Louise winced and recognized herself immediately. "Are you going to continue with this script, or do you want to write a new one? Are you going to pick your mother up at the airport with this script?"

"No," Louise responded, recoiling slightly, "I don't want to do that anymore. That script's the little chair. I don't want to be in that chair anymore!" This instinctive combining of metaphors illustrates the power of psychical and visible representation to connect at the emotional level.

The third way that we learn new things is when they're linked to strong emotions. Louise has clearly indicated that she didn't want the script, offering me the opportunity to create surprise—even a shock—to help give the next message greater impact. Holding the script high between us, I tore the paper to pieces. Louise gasped and laughed nervously. She said she felt stripped of her protective covering, naked before the world. I'd succeeded in provoking the elemental emotional connection that's needed for instantaneous learning. Now was the time to offer new, healthy information.

I took out a new paper, folding it like the other, and wrote on the cover: *Louise's Script: 2002–*. "How about if we put a 9 on the cover, instead of a 1?" I asked and wrote a 9. "What would you like the theme of the new script to be?" I asked, writing her name with a flourish.

"I want it to be about respecting myself and what I feel and what I want."

"Now, what might you do differently at the airport with this script?" I handed her the paper.

"I can stand up for myself and tell my mother I don't want to be kissed and hugged like a little girl," Louise proposed, uncertainty etched on her face.

"That would be pretty tough, wouldn't it? Like the hand-folding exercise, that would be really difficult and uncomfortable the first time." I proposed to her that we do some role-playing, with myself in the role of her mother, to allow her to try out the new script for that relationship before meeting her mother. And with that exercise, we ended the session.

WALKING TALL

Our last session together took place 3 weeks later. Louise had made remarkable progress. She and her boyfriend had made plans to buy a house in Quebec as soon as he'd finished his studies. Louise realized that she was going to have to find a job. She'd decided to approach potential employers by simply stating the truth about her last job, concluding with how much she'd grown from the experience. She'd obtained a glowing letter of recommendation from a veterinary school professor. These decisions and concrete plans were clear evidence that Louise was well on her way to building a healthier life.

Her mother's visit had also taken place in the interim between our sessions. Although the relationship with her mother remained tense, Louise didn't feel that it warranted a large investment of energy. This was a reasonable decision, and we let the question rest. Louise also felt that she would need to continue to work on filtering bad influences from her life, as well as her tendency to do too much for others, ultimately despising them for exploiting her.

With this progress, and the clear signs of restored energy and hope, I suggested that she give me a call for a follow-up chat in about a month. During that follow-up call, Louise reported that she'd found a new job. Although her negative soliloquy had a tendency to raise its voice occasionally, she assured me that she was still careful to avoid minus signs on her mental account. She was thrilled with the idea of moving in with her boyfriend in a few months, and the young couple obtained a loan from her boyfriend's parents to buy their first house. Equipped with powerful new guiding metaphors and tangible anchors to serve as reminders, Louise was clearly on her way to building a better, stronger life for herself.

MAKING IT HAPPEN

Learning how best to choose and apply concrete metaphors is a gradual but simple process. Start by mastering a few that are nearly universal in their utility: the hand-folding task for learning new skills, the use of chairs to represent inner voices and authority figures, the balance sheet or arithmetic problems for the "emotional bank account." Build a collection of props in your office, as I've done, by visiting the dollar store and browsing for inspiration. Listen carefully to your clients for clues in their word choices for metaphors or language systems that are central to their way of thinking. A client who tells her therapist, "All my efforts amount to (or add up to) nothing," is clearly indicating that the accounting metaphor would make sense to her. When clients say that they can't seem to "get past" (or "see around") a particular event or problem in their lives, they're likely to respond well to a concrete representation of something—as simple as a piece of paper or a wall, perhaps—blocking their view when close up, then being less obstructive when one steps away from it or looks in a different direction.

The rewards of these techniques—the fast and lasting results for your clients—comes quickly. Almost every time you try a new visual or tangible metaphor with a client, you'll get an "aha!" breakthrough moment that you may have spent hours seeking with words. It still thrills me to see clients respond to such natural and intuitive representations of their difficulties and the solutions to them. Adding creativity, metaphors, and props to your practice are sure to add more efficacy, more fun, and more impact.

Case Study 5-5

Treatment of Depression and Coping With Chronic Pain Through Mindfulness-Oriented Recovery Enhancement

AMBER KELLY AND ERIC GARLAND

This case involved working with a client who had both depression and chronic pain. Through the application of mindfulness therapy, the client learned new skills and a new perspective that helped him improve his quality of life.

Questions
1. Why was mindfulness considered the treatment of choice for this case study?
2. How does mindfulness work as a therapeutic process?
3. Why was a mindfulness-based recovery plan suggested to the client?
4. In what ways can an intervention like mindfulness be used in addition to other treatment methods?

Charles was a 60-year-old, married, unemployed, African American man who entered into therapy for help with depression and anxiety related to his physical limitations and debilitating pain. Charles was a veteran of the Vietnam War and had been injured in battle. Although they were decades old, these injuries continued to adversely affect his quality of life. He was wheelchair-bound and complained of experiencing near-constant debilitating pain in his joints and extremities. Charles reported experiencing little relief from strong opioid analgesics unless he took so much that he became sedated. He also reported being hospitalized on a monthly basis to manage severe episodes of pain.

Charles grew up in a two-parent household with three sisters. He reported doing well in school, and he ultimately earned a Master's degree in the healthcare field following his deployment to Vietnam. He married his wife later in life, and the two of them had two children, both boys. At the time of the assessment, Charles lived with his wife and two children, ages 10 and 14. He reported feeling as though his relationships with family members were greatly affected by chronic pain and the depression and anxiety he experienced in relation to his pain. He reported feeling irritable much of the time, and feeling as though he had "missed out" on time with his family because of his injuries and pain. Charles was not able to work, despite being educated with a Master's degree in nursing, because of his uncontrolled pain and chronically disabling injuries. As a result of the extreme pain he experienced periodically, Charles reported being uncertain about whether he could get out of bed in the morning each day, and thus was not able to plan to attend events far in advance. This uncertainty fueled his sense of anxiety and shame.

At the time of intake, the clinician assessed Charles and learned the extent of his daily suffering resulting from his injuries and pain. Charles described feeling very overwhelmed by his pain, stating, "I just can't keep on like this" and that "I can't do this for another 10 years." Charles initially voiced being skeptical of the process of therapy, but he was willing to begin the practice of mindfulness after the clinician informed him about research indicating that such practices have been helpful for people dealing with both depression and chronic pain.

SUMMARY OF ASSESSMENT

Presenting Issue

Charles experienced difficulty coping with his chronic pain and struggled with symptoms of depression and anxiety. He also experienced strain on his family relationships, as well as a decreased quality of life.

DSM-IV Diagnosis

   I.   311 Depressive Disorder, NOS
  II.   No diagnosis
 III.   Degenerative disorder related to cartilage, acute pain
 IV.   Chronic pain, difficulty with mobility, financial strain due to limited income
  V.   Global Assessment of Functioning: 55

INTRODUCTION TO MINDFULNESS-BASED INTERVENTIONS AND MINDFULNESS-ORIENTED RECOVERY ENHANCEMENT

Clients generally come to the therapeutic setting because of some kind of suffering, often in the form of depression, anxiety, pain, trauma, or some other "diagnosable" condition. Whatever the presenting issue, a key aim of the therapeutic process is to assist clients in changing their relationship to their suffering (Germer, Siegel, & Fulton, 2005). Many people attempt to resist or deny their suffering, which is an exercise in futility that may result in exhaustion, hopelessness, and resentment. Rather than attempting to resist or deny the existence of suffering, clients may learn to first accept suffering and then transcend it by taking a broader perspective of their lives. Mindfulness is a potent means of changing one's relationship to suffering by broadening perspective.

Mindfulness-based interventions provide clients with training in mindfulness practices. Although these practices vary widely, they all typically involve focusing attention on a chosen object (e.g., the sensation of the breath moving into the nostrils, or the sensation of the feet against the ground while walking). When one notices that his or her attention has wandered from the object, he or she is instructed to take careful notice of where the mind has wandered, and to investigate that mental reaction with an attitude of curiosity and acceptance. After doing so, one is taught to let go of the distracting thought, feeling, or body sensation, and then return the focus of attention back to the object. Through such practices, one cultivates the state of mindfulness—a nonreactive, nonjudgmental awareness of present-moment experience. In so doing, mindfulness can be used to transform one's relationship to the vicissitudes of life. All humans face adversity in the course of a lifetime. The therapeutic process is often about finding ways to decrease the distress that can come from the difficult moments in life. Through the cultivation of mindfulness, clients learn to notice and savor the pleasant aspects of life, even in the midst of adverse conditions. At the same time, they learn to tease apart their emotional reactions to difficult life events, and in doing so, ease the suffering of themselves and others.

How Does It Work?

Mindfulness-based interventions have been shown to be effective for a wide variety of conditions, including depression (Teasdale et al., 2000, 2002), anxiety (Hayes, Wilson, Gifford, Follette, & Strosahl, 1996), eating disorders (Kristeller, Baer, & Quillian-Wolever, 2006), borderline personality disorder (Linehan, 1993), chronic pain (Bruckstein, 1999; Kabat-Zin, 1982), stress (Garland, Gaylord, & Fredrickson, 2011; Murphy, 1995; Perkins, 1999), posttraumatic stress disorder (Dutton, Bermudez, Matas, Majid, & Myers, 2013; Gordon, Staples, Blyta, Bytyqi, & Wilson, 2008; Orsillo & Batten, 2005), and substance abuse (Garland, Gaylord, & Boettiger, 2010; Zgierska et al., 2009). Research indicates that mindfulness-based therapies produce therapeutic effects by strengthening attentional control, improving one's ability to regulate difficult emotions, changing one's perspective on the self, and accepting difficult experiences (Holzel et al., 2011).

Mindfulness has also been shown to be associated with an increase in use of positive reappraisal (the process of reframing stressful events as beneficial, meaningful, or growth-promoting) (Garland et al., 2011). When clients try to avoid stressful thoughts, feelings, or physical sensations, this can ironically cause a rebound of unwanted symptoms and increase suffering (Follette, Palm, & Rasmussen Hall, 2004). Mindfulness-based interventions target clients' avoidance of difficult experiences by encouraging them to engage with the very difficult things they are trying to avoid, establishing a new understanding of and relationship with the difficult experience (Hayes et al., 1996). A sense of safety or well-being, possibly even relief, can be experienced as unpleasant emotions dissipate when they are acknowledged and honored instead of avoided (Holzel et al., 2011). Psychoeducation about the origin of emotional reactions and the adverse consequences of experiential avoidance can also encourage contact with difficult experiences. Ultimately, mindfulness may alleviate symptoms through the process of decentering (i.e., a cognitive "stepping back" in which one observes thoughts, feelings, and body sensations from the perspective of a dispassionate observer).

Some examples of manualized mindfulness-based interventions include Mindfulness-Based Stress Reduction (Kabat-Zin, 1982), Mindfulness-Based Cognitive Therapy (Teasdale et al., 2000), Dialectical Behavioral Therapy (Linehan, 1993), and Acceptance and Commitment-Based Therapy (Hayes, Strosahl, & Wilson, 1999). Additionally, psychotherapists across disciplines (psychodynamic, cognitive-behavioral, narrative, etc.) have also found ways to integrate mindfulness into their practices as an adjunct to the therapeutic modality in which they were originally trained. In the present case, Charles was treated with Mindfulness-Oriented Recovery Enhancement (Garland, 2013), a manualized therapy that integrates mindfulness training with techniques drawn from cognitive-behavioral therapy and positive psychology. Mindfulness-Oriented Recovery Enhancement combines traditional mindfulness meditation practices with instruction in positive reappraisal and savoring as a means of promoting positive emotion and a sense of meaningfulness in life.

COURSE OF TREATMENT WITH CHARLES

Charles was seen for eight sessions over the course of 2 months. Sessions involved building rapport; empathic responding to Charles's personal disclosures; psychoeducation about the relationship between emotional and physical pain; and mindfulness-based experiential activities. Charles left each session with assignments for the week to come. Each session began with a short, guided mindfulness meditation, and then led into discussion of the assignments for the past week.

After the first session, Charles was encouraged to practice 15 minutes of mindfulness meditation each day by following instructions delivered on an audio CD containing a recorded guided meditation. Charles was asked to continue this mindfulness practice over the 8-week course of therapy, as well as participate in other mindfulness-based activities. For example, Charles was asked to become mindful of stress triggers that led to an increase in his pain. He was also asked to cultivate mindfulness toward his experiences of pain in general. For instance, instead of trying to ignore his pain, Charles was encouraged to attend to his pain sensations with an attitude of curiosity and nonjudgment. He was asked to notice the quality of the sensations (e.g., sensations of heat, pressure, tingling, or tightness), the location and boundaries of the sensations (i.e., where they began and ended in the body), and how these sensations changed over time (e.g., waxing and waning in intensity). Charles was also encouraged to begin to notice any thoughts that might accompany his pain (e.g., "Oh no, it's going to get worse. I know it! I'm probably going to have to go to the hospital again!") and the emotions accompanying those thoughts (e.g., overwhelmed, sad, angry, defeated).

In the next several sessions, Charles reported becoming aware that when he engaged in catastrophic thinking about his pain, this led to more stress, which in turn increased his pain. After coming to this realization, he began a process of using meditation to shift his focus from his worried thoughts to the sensation of his breath or another neutral object of focus. As he refocused his attention on something more neutral, he noticed that his worried thoughts would dissipate and his emotions would be calmed. By focusing on his breath, he noticed that his breathing and heart rate slowed. He could take deeper breaths and begin to feel his muscles relax. By the fourth session, Charles reported that there were times when he was able to manage his pain without a visit to the hospital. He also found that through mindfulness practice, the opioid medication he was taking was often more effective; he could take a lower dose of medicine to achieve the same degree of pain relief.

In addition to becoming mindful of the body sensations, thoughts, and emotions associated with the experience of pain, Charles was encouraged to begin a regular practice of savoring by maintaining mindfulness of the pleasant sensory qualities of one of his daily activities. In the first week of this exercise, Charles chose to savor the experience of drinking his morning coffee on his porch. At the next session, Charles reported that the whole experience of drinking coffee became more enjoyable. Charles shared his appreciation of the warmth of the mug in his hand as he sat on his porch enjoying the cool fall air. He discussed noticing the singing of the birds as they moved about the tree branches above him. He noted the smell of the coffee and how his mood lifted as he smelled the delicious aroma. He also reported noticing the warmth of the liquid as it entered his mouth, and being able to follow that warm feeling down his throat and into his belly. Charles reported that this was the first time he had ever experienced a deep sense of joyfulness from this simple activity. He was especially amazed at how he could experience joy despite the painful sensations in his body that typically compelled his attention.

During the following week's session, Charles discussed attending a baseball game with his older son. He reported enjoying watching the sunlight on his son's face, as well as savoring his own positive emotions as he appreciated his son's smile and laughter during the game. Charles reported appreciating positive thoughts and sentiments that he had not previously noticed because of being fixated on the pain sensations in his body and the negative thoughts and emotions associated with those sensations. He reported noticing less pain during these moments of joy, and he was surprised by this discovery. Charles expressed feeling happy and grateful for the momentary relief from pain. The clinician pointed out that there were likely many other moments in Charles's life where his pain was lessened, yet he had likely not noticed them because of the cognitive habit of focusing on pain and distress. By savoring positive events, Charles was retraining his attention and was becoming better able to notice and appreciate other pleasant aspects of his life. During the session, Charles described moments with his family that he'd enjoyed and the positive effect he felt like this was having on his relationships with his wife and children. "They all say I just seem happier. They joke that I should be meditating every day!"

Charles's last session was focused on creating a mindfulness-based recovery plan to prevent him from slipping back into negative pain coping habits. Charles was also encouraged to list his stress and pain triggers, and to identify ways of coping with these triggering situations using mindfulness skills and strategies he had learned. During this session, Charles's experiences of therapy were reviewed. He reported feeling hopeful about his ability to recover from his physical injuries for the first time since he'd gotten hurt. He also reported feeling "happier and more positive" throughout daily life. He was able to describe several difficult experiences (such as an incident where he fell in the driveway while transferring from his wheelchair to his car), in which he was able to use mindfulness to deal with the pain and catastrophic thoughts associated with the event. He discussed feeling relieved to finally have some tools to deal with such moments, and expressed a greater sense of contentment about his relationships.

SUMMARY

Mindfulness Techniques Used

- Mindful breathing
- Mindful body scan
- Savoring of pleasant experiences
- Mindfulness of experience of physical pain and associated thoughts/emotions
- Acceptance of difficult experiences

Results

- Decreased pain intensity
- Reduced functional impairment caused by pain
- Increased effectiveness of pain medication
- Enhanced family cohesion
- Increased positive emotions
- Reduced stress
- Increased resilience
- Decreased hospitalizations
- Enhanced quality of life

CONCLUSION

When clients seek out social work services to help manage their suffering, they can be effectively empowered through the principles and practices of mindfulness. As clients build their repertoire of effective coping responses through mindfulness training, they are able to experiment with these newly learned skills and attitudes in the context of a safe and trusting relationship with the therapist. Through this experiential learning opportunity, clients may discover their innate capacity for cultivating well-being. No amount of convincing or lecturing would have led a client like Charles to "believe" that mindfulness would help alleviate his pain, increase his quality of life, and strengthen his relationships. Instead, Charles was asked to put aside his prejudices, experiment with new ways of being, and "just see what happens." In so doing, he was able to experience these benefits firsthand. By adopting a mindful awareness and acceptance of difficult thoughts, emotions, and sensations, Charles transformed his relationship with suffering: He realized that, even in the face of adversity, he was ultimately free to focus on the beautiful, pleasurable, and meaningful aspects of his life.

REFERENCES

Bruckstein, D. C. (1999). *Effects of acceptance-based and cognitive behavioral interventions on chronic pain management* (Unpublished doctoral dissertation). Hofstra University, Hempstead, New York.

Dutton, M. A., Bermudez, D., Matas, A., Majid, H., & Myers, N. (2013). Mindfulness-based stress reduction for low-income, predominantly African American women with PTSD and a history of intimate partner violence. *Cognitive and Behavioral Practice, 20*(1), 23–32.

Follette, V. M., Palm, K. M., & Rasmussen Hall, M. L. (2004). Acceptance, mindfulness, and trauma. In S. C. Hayes, V. M. Follette, & M. M. Linehan, *Mindfulness and acceptance: Expanding the cognitive-behavioral tradition* (pp. 192–208). New York, NY: Guilford Press.

Garland, E. L. (2013). *Mindfulness-oriented recovery enhancement for addiction, stress, and pain.* Washington, DC: NASW Press.

Garland, E., Gaylord, S. A., & Boettiger, C. A. (2010). Mindfulness training modifies cognitive, affective, and physiological mechanisms implicated in alcohol dependence: Results of a randomized controlled pilot trial. *Journal of Psychoactive Drugs, 42,* 177–192.

Garland, E. L., Gaylord, S. A., & Fredrickson, B. L. (2011). Positive reappraisal mediates the stress-reductive effects of mindfulness: An upward spiral process. *Mindfulness,* 59–67.

Germer, C. K., Siegel, R. D., & Fulton, P. R. (2005). *Mindfulness and psychotherapy.* New York, NY: Guilford Press.

Gordon, J. S., Staples, J. K., Blyta, A., Bytyqi, M., & Wilson, A. T. (2008). Treatment of posttraumatic stress disorder in postwar Kosovar adolescents using mind-body skills groups: A randomized control trial. *Journal of Clinical Psychiatry, 69,* 1469–1476.

Hayes, S. C., Strosahl, K., & Wilson, K. G. (1999). *Acceptance and comitment therapy: An experiential approach to behavior change.* New York, NY: Guilford Press.

Hayes, S. C., Wilson, K. G., Gifford, E. V., Follette, V. M., & Strosahl, K. (1996). Experiental avoidance and behavioral disorders: A functional dimensional approach to diagnosis and treatment. *Journal of Consulting and Clinical Psychology, 64,* 1152–1168.

Holzel, B. K., Lazar, S. W., Gard, T., Schuman-Olivier, Z., Vago, D. R., & Ott, U. (2011). How does mindfulness meditation work? Proposing mechanisms of action from a conceptual and neural perspective. *Perspectives on Psychological Science, 6,* 537–559.

Kabat-Zin, J. (1982). An outpatient program in behavioral medicine for chronic pain based on the practices of mindfulness meditation. *General Hospital Psychiatry, 4,* 33–47.

Kristeller, J. L., Baer, R. A., & Quillian-Wolever, R. (2006). Mindfulness-based approaches to eating disorders. In R. A. Baer (Ed.), *Mindfulness-based treatment approaches: Clinician's guide to evidence based applications* (pp. 75–91). San Diego, CA: Elsevier Academic Press.

Linehan, M. M. (1993). *Cognitive-behavioral treatment of borderline personality disorder.* New York, NY: Guilford Press.

Murphy, R. (1995). The effects of mindfulness meditation verses progressive relaxation training on stress egocentrism anger and impulsiveness among inmates. *Dissertation Abstracts International: The Sciences and Engineering, 55.*

Orsillo, S. M., & Batten, S. V. (2005). Acceptance and commitment therapy in the treatment of posttruamatic stress disorder. *Behavior Modification, 29,* 95–129.

Perkins, R. (1999). The efficacy of mindfulness-based techniques in the reduction of stress in a sample of incarcerated women. *Dissertation Abstracts International: Section B: The Sciences and Engineering, 59,* 9.

Teasdale, J. D., Moore, R. D., Hayhurst, H., Pope, M., Williams, S., & Segal, Z. V. (2002). Megacognitive awareness and prevention of relapse into depression: Empirical evidence. *Journal of Consulting and Clinical Psychology, 70,* 275–287.

Teasdale, J. D., Segal, Z. V., Williams, J. M., Rodgeway, V. A., Soulsby, J. M., & Lau, M. A. (2000). Prevention of relapse/recurrence in major depression by mindfulness-based cognitive therapy. *Journal of Consulting and Clinical Psychology, 68,* 615–623.

Zgierska, A., Rabagto, D., Chawla, N., Kushner, K., Koehler, R., & Marlatt, A. (2009). Mindfulness meditation for substance use disorders: A systematic review. *Substance Abuse, 30,* 266–294.

PART VI

Case Studies in Preventing Problems and Developing Resourcefulness

Traditionally, social workers have waited until clients presented themselves for help, usually after their difficulties became quite serious. However, another option is for social workers to intervene at an earlier point in time and help clients learn the skills they need to cope with future difficulties. Preventive approaches to social work are needed in order to reach out to clients before their problems become serious. This is what is meant by "primary prevention"—reducing the likelihood of new clients needing help in a population.

Because there are so many social problems and so many people needing help, it is important to have services that reach people quickly. Methods for preventing problems and developing resources can respond to this need. There are several characteristics of successful prevention programs:

1. *These programs are designed to benefit people who have not specifically asked for help*. Many people could benefit from social work services who have not specifically asked for help or

who cannot ask for help. For example, teaching parents positive parenting skills is likely to have long-range benefits for children, although they have not asked for help. Other people may not be aware that they are at risk for developing mental health problems or becoming too stressed or that they are in need of some social service.

2. *Such programs are designed to reach large numbers of people.* Much of direct practice is focused on individual casework, counseling, or case management. Programs for preventing problems and developing resourcefulness are designed to benefit groups of individuals, such as families, classes, schools, and communities.

3. *Such programs many have indirect effects.* Because of the broad focus of these programs, their effects are often indirect and influence individuals other than those specifically targeted. For example, a program designed to provide support to caregivers would be expected to benefit both the caregivers and the individuals being cared for. Likewise, a stress management program should reduce stress for the participants but also have a positive impact on all those who come in contact with the less-stressed participants.

4. *Many of these programs become self-perpetuating.* Numerous preventive interventions are designed in such a way that they can continue once they have been established. For example, in some prevention programs, each new set of leaders will train the next set of leaders. The result is that the preventive intervention can have continued impact.

Social workers play a critical role in the development of preventive interventions (McCave & Rishel, 2011). A focus on prevention is consistent with social work's purpose of alleviating distress and helping people realize their aspirations. Social workers often need to design programs that encompasses both treatment and prevention goals. As you read the case studies in this chapter, consider how the social workers intervened to prevent clients from needing additional help.

The section begins with the case study by Magen, who presents a detailed description of how a stress management group is conducted. Stress management is a logical preventive intervention for addressing the complexities of postmodern life. The case by Parnell presents the use of mediation, showing how it can be used in a variety of settings. Her work exemplifies mediation's unique combination of law, social work, and counseling. The case by Sammons presents the innovative housing first model for addressing homelessness. Although this would not typically be considered a prevention program, it is nonetheless designed to develop resourcefulness among people who are often depleted and demoralized. Gustavson tackles a complex issue—addressing both depression of older persons and the stress of caregiving. In her case study, she effectively demonstrates the use of problem-solving therapy and case management—both essential ingredients in a successful outcome of her case. The final chapter by LeCroy addresses a contemporary issue—the socialization of young girls. The case study presents a universal prevention program designed to address some of the unique challenges facing early adolescent girls and describes a program to promote the successful transition to adulthood.

REFERENCE

McCave, E. L., & Rishel, C. W. (2011). Prevention as an explicit part of the social work profession: A systematic investigation. *Advances in Social Work, 12*, 226–240.

Case Study 6-1

A Group-Based Approach
to Stress Management

RANDY MAGEN[1]

Multiple methods are used in a group format to reduce stress. This case study presents a highly structured model of group treatment that emphasizes systematic collection of data, use of empirically based techniques, and a group format for teaching stress management.

Questions

1. What group leader skills were demonstrated in the case study?
2. How were group members involved in the treatment process?
3. How did the group leader gather feedback from the group members and incorporate it into the group process?
4. What key techniques were used to reduce stress among the group members?

In this chapter we present a case study of a group designed to assist members in managing stress. The foci are on the tasks of the group leader, the group interventions,

---

[1]   Previous editions of this chapter were coauthored with Sheldon D. Rose, PhD. Professor Rose passed away in 2010.

the data collection procedures, and the generalization strategies used over the 10 sessions. Brief excerpts are provided from the pregroup assessments, all 10 group sessions, and from the postgroup interviews.

Social workers in a multiservice agency noticed an upsurge in clients whose presenting problems appeared to be stress related. Trained and interested group leaders, as well as a treatment manual, were available, so a decision was made to offer a group-based stress management intervention. Public service announcements and flyers sent to social service agencies helped to recruit additional members for the group.

If a client or applicant expressed interest in the stress management group, an appointment was made for a 1-hour individual pregroup interview. The pregroup interview had several purposes. First, the applicant was given a brief description of the group program and its schedule (2 hours once per week for 10 weeks). Costs were also clarified. The applicant was informed that the group had four major components: relaxation training, social skills training, cognitive restructuring, and group exercises. Members would be provided selected readings and would have the opportunity to examine and work on specific stress problems of concern to them. Second, the client's stress levels and triggers were assessed. Third, the interviewer explored situations that the client wanted to work on in the group.

The following applicants participated in the pregroup interview and were accepted into the stress management group:

Ellen M. noticed a poster recruiting members for a stress management group on the bulletin board in her social worker's waiting room. Ellen reported that she has been managing a clothing store for the past 12 years. Until recently, she had lived alone, a situation with which she was content. Last month, Ellen's 15-year-old grandchild came to live with her. Ellen's peaceful life has been shattered by loud music, phone calls, and the responsibilities of caring for a teenage girl. Ellen told the interviewer that she feels a great deal of stress from having to deal with her grandchild.

Susan B.'s friend, noting her inability to handle the transition from college to the working world, told her about the stress management group. Susan had graduated from college two years earlier. Since graduation, she had been working as a secretary for an insurance company. Many of Susan's college friends moved away or got married. Susan feels alone in the world and wonders if she will ever fall in love. She doesn't like her job and doesn't know what to do about it.

Jim W.'s social worker at Catholic Social Services referred him to the stress management group. Jim works on the line at a factory. His wife of 14 years recently moved out and is divorcing him. Jim feels depressed and nervous. The effect of the divorce seems to have resulted in constant stomachaches and feelings of uneasiness. He has little idea of what to do with his life.

Rosemary M., who read about the group in the newspaper, is a homemaker. She has a husband and two daughters. Now that her children are older and need her less, she feels bored with life. The stress of this period in her life has left Rosemary without purpose and with a sense of hopelessness. She also complains of increasing insomnia.

Janet A. noticed a poster in her dormitory advertising a stress management group. Janet is an undergraduate student at the university. Every semester, she feels so much anxiety that she fails to complete most of her assignments. She has dropped more classes than she has completed. Her advisor has told Janet that if she does not complete her work, she will not be permitted to finish college. This threat adds to her inability to function.

Frank C. read about the stress management group while waiting for his online game to start. Frank has had several different jobs over the past two years—working in a grocery store, at a car rental agency, and waiting tables at a restaurant—but each time there was a cutback, Frank was the first person to be laid off. Frank wonders whether he just has bad luck or if something is wrong with him that prevents him from hanging on to a job.

ASSESSMENT

Because all of the assessment interviews were structured similarly, we focus on Frank's pregroup interview. On arrival, Frank met with Lydia, one of the agency social workers who agreed to co-lead the stress management group. Frank asked several questions about the group, and after his questions were answered, he was given three paper-and-pencil assessment instruments—the Brief Stress and Coping Inventory (BSCI; Rahe & Tolles, 2002); the Brief Symptom Inventory (BSI; Derogatis, 1993); and the Hassles Scale (Kanner, Coyne, Schaefer, & Lazarus, 1981)—to estimate his level of stress and coping skills. Frank took about 25 minutes to complete the three tests.

After Frank completed the Hassles Scale, the social worker, Lydia, discussed those items that were scored "3" (i.e., occurred often). Some of Frank's "often occurring" hassles included having too many responsibilities, having trouble relaxing, having problems getting along with his fellow workers, not liking his fellow workers, being dissatisfied with his job, worrying about the decision to change jobs, and being concerned about getting ahead. The discussion of these hassles revealed that Frank was feeling pressured by work and by his partner. Frank readily identified these as two issues he would like to deal with in the group. (The reader should note that the tests were used not only to obtain a score, which was later used to evaluate outcomes for Frank and the group, but as a point of departure for determining specific situations on which to focus interventions in the ensuing weeks.)

To assess Frank's ability to use the group effectively, Lydia asked him about his previous experiences as a member of groups. Lydia inquired how Frank felt about talking and sharing his problems with six to eight strangers. Frank stated that he had participated in several discussion groups at his church. He added that he had attended a weekend church retreat that he did not like, although he did feel it opened him up a little. He remarked that he might be hesitant at first in talking with strangers, but once others began to talk, he thought that he would have little trouble participating. (On the basis of Frank's successes in past groups and his avowed willingness to participate, Lydia concluded that Frank could effectively use the group but would have to be eased in slowly at the beginning.)

Finally, Lydia reviewed with Frank the treatment contract, which covered extra-group tasks (i.e., homework), types of interventions, attendance, promptness, and other issues. Frank asked how much time the extra-group tasks would take. Lydia responded that because they were negotiated, it would be up to him. Both Frank and Lydia signed the contract.

Prior to the first session, the group leader examined the assessments of all clients. She redesigned the format of the 10-session group based on the common need to improve social skills and the expressed need for relaxation training. Although these two elements were to be given proportionately greater emphasis, no interventions from the treatment manual were dropped.

GROUP SESSIONS

The 10 group sessions, as designed, could be roughly divided into three phases. The early phase continued the orientation and assessment begun in the pregroup interview. In addition, group cohesion was built up, and basic training in dealing with stress was initiated. Provision of information and skill training were continued in the second or middle phase. In this phase, clients began to identify and work on their own unique problems. In the final phase, clients focused on more complex stress situations and began to prepare to transfer what they had learned in the group to the real world.

The Initial Phase: Sessions One Through Three

In the first session, the leader's goals were for group members to learn about each other, to increase their attraction to one another (group cohesion), and to continue to identify and further clarify their target problems. For the first exercise, members broke into pairs and took turns interviewing each other for 2 minutes each. Suggested interview questions were put on the whiteboard as a means of reducing anxiety. When members returned to the large group, they introduced their partners. Their partners reminded them when they forgot anything. Some joking and laughter accompanied these introductions. (Introducing one's partner rather than oneself is likely to reduce initial anxiety. Moreover, this exercise elicited the active participation of all members within a few minutes in the first session. Broad participation, as well as a snack in the midgroup break, is likely to increase group cohesion.)

After a mini-lecture on the nature of stress and stressors, the members completed an individual checklist to identify their specific physical cues of stress. First Lydia, as a model, and then the group members, one at a time, summarized their unique physical stress responses in front of the group. After the break, in which decaffeinated coffee and soft drinks were served, members described a stressful situation they had recently encountered and their response to it. (During both exercises, Lydia noted that Rosemary and Ellen chatted with each other but did not participate in the general group discussion, except when called on.)

To prepare for the next week, Lydia suggested two extra group tasks. In the first, members would monitor their daily stress levels on a 10-point scale. The second task was to record their physical cues when they were feeling high levels of stress. When the members agreed to these suggestions, Lydia asked them to report on their monitoring at the beginning of the next session. Lydia mentioned that because self-monitoring was probably not a common experience for them, they might require a system to remind them. Frank, who stated that he never forgot anything, was the only one who did not develop such a system. (It should be noted that to increase the likelihood of compliance, extra-group tasks were negotiated rather than assigned, and use of a self-monitoring system was encouraged.)

At the end of the first session, Lydia distributed and explained the postsession questionnaire, which is used to collect the members' perceptions of the session. Three of the questions asked were (1) How useful was this session? (2) How supportive were the other members? and (3) How close do you feel to other members? Although these questions were open-ended, Lydia noted how hard the members had worked and looked forward to the next session. (The leader in the early sessions attempts to find every opportunity to reinforce the real achievements of individuals and the group.) Ellen said she would bring cookies next week to enliven the break. Lydia chatted informally with the members as they slowly departed.

As members arrived for the second session, Lydia purposely sat between Rosemary and Ellen to encourage them to talk to others in the group. She chatted with both of them while the others arrived. Lydia praised those who were present for their punctuality and started the session on time to establish promptness as a norm, even though Frank and Janet had not yet arrived. As they trickled in, Lydia smiled and indicated the free seats to them, and said "we've just started." (Apparently, by reinforcing those who were on time and not commenting on the tardiness of the latecomers, the norm was established. For the remaining sessions, all but one person arrived on time.)

In session two, after Rosemary read the agenda, Lydia briefly summarized the postsession evaluations from the first group meeting. Lydia remarked that group members had given the group a 3.8 on a 6-point scale for usefulness. A few of the members' written responses to the open-ended questions were read aloud. Lydia stated that one member remarked that he had found learning about other people in the group helpful. Another member wrote that Lydia had used some technical words that she did not understand. In response, Lydia asked the group if there were any specific terms she had used the previous week that could be clarified. No one responded. Lydia stated that she would attempt to use clearer language in the future. She also encouraged members to stop her when something was unclear. (Several principles should be noted here: (1) if evaluations are to be used, they must be commented and acted on; (2) by using feedback, the leader provides opportunities for the members to assume increasing responsibility for structuring the group; and (3) by having the members read the agenda and encouraging them to ask questions, the leader decreases her activity and increases participation by the members.)

The next agenda item, as in all sessions, was review of the tasks performed between sessions. Lydia asked members to state what parts of the extra-group tasks they had completed. Three members responded that they had written down physical stress cues in their diary, and five members remarked that they had monitored their stress levels, although not every day. Frank said he was too busy to do any of it. As each person mentioned an achievement, Lydia offered praise, giving little attention to those who did not complete tasks.

Next, Lydia noted that most people did some part of the task. She then remarked that homework is not something one does on a regular basis when no longer in school.

Members expressed a variety of other reasons for not doing the homework completely: "having a busy week," "not remembering," and "not understanding what I was supposed to do." Frank, in particular, noted that he should have developed a reminder system for himself, as he was more forgetful than he thought. Once the obstacles were identified, Lydia asked for suggestions about what members could do to overcome them. Many ideas were generated. One was that each member could call another group member between sessions to remind him or her to do the homework. In line with another idea, Lydia would spend the last 10 minutes of every session explaining the task and responding to questions. All of the suggestions were evaluated, and the two mentioned here were selected by the group to be implemented. (Note that, as in most groups, homework completion rates were low at the second session and required attention; in this case, the leader used group problem solving rather than attempting to solve the problem herself.)

One additional theme of session two was introduction to relaxation training. After a brief review of the use of relaxation to cope with stress, Lydia cautioned members about muscle spasms, medications, and other factors that in combination with relaxation might result in negative side effects. Lydia then led the group through progressive muscle relaxation, in which she had them alternately tense and relax muscle groups. The group members were asked to rate their tension before and after the exercise. After the relaxation practice, members discussed their response to the exercise, and several agreed to try relaxation at home. At the end of the session, other homework assignments were negotiated in pairs and then read to the group. Finally, the members completed the postsession questionnaire. As they drifted out of the room, they talked informally with each other.

The third session was similar in many respects to the second. As Lydia reviewed the experience with the extra-group tasks, she noted enthusiastically that almost everyone had completed the tasks. Lydia also informed the members that their evaluations of the group had gone up dramatically this week. Several members noted that they could better understand what happens in this kind of group and how it might help them. Two people expressed their enthusiasm for relaxation in particular. Lydia concluded the evaluation by saying that she was pleased that each person was finding his or her own way of making the group useful.

Lydia then introduced a new group exercise designed to help members identify and change those thoughts that seemed to increase stress, such as putting oneself down or making a catastrophe of an insignificant event (self-defeating thoughts). Because this exercise involved assimilation of a great deal of information, Lydia supplemented the instructions with a handout explaining the exercise and wrote down the important points on a whiteboard. Lydia began the exercise by providing a rationale to show the link between self-defeating thoughts and stress. This rationale also demonstrated how a person can replace self-defeating with self-enhancing thoughts. (In the dissemination of information, the leader used several didactic strategies, including audiovisual aids and demonstrations, brief lectures with ample opportunity for questions, and handouts to supplement the lecture. This discussion, like all lectures, was held to a maximum of 5 minutes to maintain members' attention.)

Lydia modeled different types of self-defeating thoughts, which were identified and discussed by the members. For example, one type of self-defeating thought is *absolutizing*. Lydia said, "One of the things I have often said to myself just before a meeting is, 'I'll never be able to explain that concept understandably.'" After the group discussed why this statement might be self-defeating, Lydia demonstrated how she would stop it. She would yell "Stop!" to herself. She then immediately replaced her earlier statement with "Clear explanations are sometimes difficult for me, but if I take my time and check to see whether people understand, I can do a better job of explaining concepts."

Next, the members discussed how the latter statement was more effective and honest than the first. (To increase self-disclosure, the leader modeled self-disclosure. In addition, she involved the members by having them discuss her self-statements, which was less threatening than discussing their own.) The members were asked to read a list of 10 different self-statements, after which they took turns identifying the self-defeating or self-enhancing statements and changing the self-defeating ones to self-enhancing statements. After the 10 statements had been reviewed and modified, each member was asked to contribute a personal self-defeating statement.

> **Rosemary:** When I start to worry at night, I say to myself, "I'll never be able to sleep. There's nothing I can do about it."
> **Janet:** Sometimes when I'm studying, I think I'm just too dumb to do this kind of work. I should drop out of college.
> **Jim:** I keep thinking, "I failed with my wife; I'll probably fail with every other woman I come into contact with." Sometimes I add, "My life is finished."
> **Susan:** Today I just met a new guy at the office, and I said, as usual, "No sense talking to him. He won't like me, anyway."
> **Frank:** I can't think of one at all. While the others were talking, I kept worrying about it. I don't know why it is, but when anyone asks me to do something, I always freeze.
> **Group Leader:** Can anyone find a self-defeating statement in what Frank just said? (Occasionally, members are not able to come up with a self-disclosing response during an exercise. Usually, the leader acknowledges the difficulty and goes on. In this case, the self-defeating statement was obviously implied, so the leader involved the group in helping Frank find it.)

After each of these statements, the other members pointed out why the given statement was self-defeating and brainstormed about how to replace it. For example, Rosemary replaced her "I'll never be able to sleep" with "It may be difficult for me to sleep, but if I relax it sometimes helps a lot." (Throughout this and most exercises, the leader praised members on their work; for example, for successfully identifying and changing self-statements, or for giving feedback to each other.)

Session three ended, as did the earlier sessions, with additional relaxation practice, extra-group task planning, and a postsession questionnaire. For the extra-group task, all of the members agreed to record specific stressful situations in which they were dissatisfied with the way they coped. Lydia handed out the criteria for selecting a stressful situation and provided the members with examples of situations that met these criteria.

At this meeting, Lydia noticed that Rosemary and Ellen were addressing most of their comments to the group at large even though they sat together. During the session, Frank was somewhat reluctant to talk about himself, although he had comments for the others. (Unless the lack of self-disclosure is persistent by one person or characterized by several group members, the leader would not act on such observations; however, if it persisted or included more than one person, the leader might deal with it as a group problem.)

The Intermediate Phase: Sessions Four Through Seven

In the fourth session, after review of the previous week's data, the monitoring of extra-group tasks, and the rate of completion (which continued to be high), Lydia provided a feedback exercise. After breaking into pairs, each member wrote down one specific thing that his or her partner had done well in the group and one specific thing the partner might do differently. Using a handout specifying criteria for useful feedback as a guide, each group member provided his or her partner first with positive feedback, then with constructive negative feedback. Each member was evaluated with respect to how well the feedback criteria had been met.

After this exercise, Lydia talked briefly about the relationship between stress and unsatisfactory performance in interpersonal situations. She provided the group with some examples, and some members came up with some of their own examples. Then Lydia described how one can learn concrete skills in handling difficult situations by getting ideas from others, by demonstration, by practice, and by feedback. She noted that the group would be doing a lot of role-playing demonstrations and practice from now on. Lydia then suggested that they look at the stressful situations they had observed during the week.

Each member had the opportunity to present and to deal systematically with his or her own problematic situations. Frank brought up a situation even though he had not agreed to the previous week. (Some clients function better if they feel free to do what they want.) The problem-solving and modeling process is exemplified by Rosemary's situation.

> *Rosemary:* I was speaking with my mother the other day and was upset with what she said. You should know that we don't see eye to eye on many things, particularly childrearing. I wonder if you could tell me what I could do to get my mother to stop telling me how to raise my children?
>
> *Group Leader:* Does anyone have any questions that might help us see the situation more clearly?
>
> *Frank:* What did your mother say exactly?
>
> *Rosemary:* We were talking on the telephone, and out of the clear blue sky (can you imagine?), she said it was wrong that I allowed the children to eat their meals while they watched television.
>
> *Ellen:* What did you say to your mother after her advice?
>
> *Rosemary:* I told her that things have changed since she raised me and that she doesn't understand. That always seems to stop her advice, but then she sounds angry and I end up feeling guilty. (Several other questions were asked: "How often do you talk to your mother?" "Is this a common exchange?" "Do others in your family have the same difficulty?" Rosemary's answers to these questions resulted in greater specification of the problem.)

Susan: Rosemary, I wonder if you could tell us when the "critical moment" occurred.

Group Leader (noting that Rosemary looks confused): Why doesn't someone explain what the critical moment is? Some people may have forgotten.

Susan: Isn't it the point in time when you are faced with a situation and have a choice of how to respond?

Janet: Yeah, the point at which you wished you had done something different.

Rosemary: I remember now. I guess my critical moment was after she said, "You shouldn't allow your children to eat their meals while watching television. I never did."

The Multimethod Approach in Action

Now that Rosemary, with the help of the group, had identified the concrete situation, the response, and the critical moment, the next step was goal setting.

Susan: Rosemary, could you tell us what you would like to have achieved in this situation?

Rosemary: I want to get my mother to stop telling me what to do about my kids.

Group Leader: Group, who is this a goal for, I wonder?

Ellen: I think it's a goal for Rosemary's mother. I do that all the time. I want everyone else to change when it's me that has to do the work.

Rosemary: You're right. I guess my goal for myself is to let my mother know how I feel on this issue. Can you believe it, I've never told her?

Note that in the preceding dialogue, the group leader guided the discussion while maximizing member participation by asking questions rather than providing answers. Once the goal had been established and accepted by Rosemary, she was then encouraged to state specifically what she could do or say differently to achieve that goal.

Susan: Rosemary, what do you want to tell your mother? Use that phrase we were told to use, "State a feeling and make a request." (Note that Susan is beginning to assume a leadership role. The group leader usually encourages this unless the given member discourages active participation among others; however, if possible, the leader encourages more than one person to assume a variety of leadership functions.)

Rosemary: I want to tell my mother I am angry and ask her to not give me advice. . . . That is, unless I ask for it. (laughing)

The next step in the behavioral rehearsal process was for Rosemary to evaluate the risks involved in stating her feelings and making this request. The members then brainstormed alternative responses that Rosemary could make to her mother.

Frank: Maybe you could tell her that her advice pissed you off and that you really don't need it.

Rosemary: Oh, I could never say that to my mother.

Group Leader: Remember, group, we don't evaluate brainstorming ideas—any suggestion is valuable. Who hasn't given an alternative? How about you, Ellen? What would you say?

Ellen: I might tell her that she was a good mother and did a fine job raising me and that I had to do what worked for me.

After 2 minutes of brainstorming, Susan asked Rosemary to pick out something she could say to her mother that met her goal.

Rosemary: I think I could say, "Mom, sometimes I feel incompetent when you give me advice, especially since I usually have ideas of my own. It's important to me to stand on my own two feet and find my own way of doing things. I know this will be difficult for you, Mom, but I really don't want you to give me advice unless I ask for it, okay?"

Practicing the alternative response was the next step in the modeling sequence. Ellen volunteered to role-play Rosemary's role, and Rosemary played her mother. When they finished, Lydia asked Rosemary if she wanted to repeat the statement in the way Ellen had said it. Rosemary responded that she liked it a lot and would be willing to try it out herself, with Ellen playing the role of the mother.

After Rosemary practiced the response in a role-play, the group provided her with feedback on the performance.

Susan: What did you like about what you did in that role-play?
Rosemary: Not much . . . well, I guess I told her how I felt. That would be an improvement over how I usually handle it.
Group Leader: It's important that you see improvement, Rosemary, and I do, too. What did others like about Rosemary's role-play?
Jim: Well, Rosemary looked directly into Ellen's, I mean her mother's, eyes.
Janet: She made a request for change.
Group Leader: Tell Rosemary what she specifically said that was a request. (The leader shapes more specific feedback while helping people give their feedback directly to the person involved.)
Janet: Rosemary, you told your mother to wait until you asked her to give advice, and I think you did it gently.

When the members had finished giving both positive and negative feedback, Lydia asked Rosemary to rehearse one more time. Lydia complimented Rosemary on the quality of the role-play and commented on Susan's and Ellen's active participation in the role-playing. She also said that she was "impressed by the excellent comments" of the other members and noted how well they adhered to the feedback criteria. At the same meeting, Jim's and Janet's situations were problem-solved and role-played. Because the time needed to get through all of their situations was not available, Lydia asked if they could continue next week.

Lydia reviewed the problem-solving steps, in particular the modeling sequence. (The leader continues to teach the general principles after the group has had experience with the sequence, to enhance the generalization of change. The frequent use of review is an important leadership function.) She then ended session five in the same manner as the four previous sessions, with relaxation practice, extra group task negotiations, and completion of the postsession questionnaire. As their extra-group task, most members decided to see how many other stress situations they could come up with in addition to the one they were working on. Everyone committed to practicing relaxation at least

10 minutes per day. Ellen, in addition, decided to role-play her situation several times into a tape recorder to get it down perfectly.

After the meeting, because she had noted that Janet's evaluation of the group had gone down dramatically, Lydia called Janet. Janet said that she was thinking of not returning to the group. Lydia listened to her concerns. She wondered aloud whether Janet may have felt too much pressure after last week's role-play. Janet admitted that the group was going too fast for her, and it was making her anxious; she had had the same trouble in another group she had been in. (The leader may have made a mistake in not using warm-ups before role-playing to accustom members to role-playing. Examples of warm-ups are role-playing neutral situations, playing a game of charades, and so forth.)

Lydia noted that perhaps others were feeling the same way and suggested that this problem could be talked about in general in the group. Janet thought this was a good idea and said she felt better about coming back to the group next week. She was glad Lydia had called. (The preferred procedure when identifying group problems is to present the problem to the entire group. In this case, the leader was concerned that Janet would drop out before the problem could be brought up in the group. However, after talking to Janet, the leader still had the option of bringing the problem to the group in the event that the concern was shared by more than one member.)

In the sixth session, after review of the extra-group tasks and evaluations, which had dropped slightly, Lydia stated that a few people were concerned that the group was going too fast or putting too much pressure on them to change. In the discussion several members agreed, although Jim noted that he needed pressure to change. Frank laughed as he agreed with Jim, "I'm finally ready to talk about myself." After further discussion, the members agreed that everyone should go at his or her own pace without pressure from anyone. They also suggested that members could back off on any exercise that was too difficult for them to handle. Jim reminded the group that if they took too much pressure off themselves, "they probably wouldn't get much from the group." Janet listened intently to the discussion, occasionally nodding agreement but saying nothing. The rest of the session dealt with the stressful situations that were not discussed and rehearsed the previous week. Jim and Ellen had time to deal with a second situation. The evaluations were extremely high at the end of this session, and all comments were positive. (It is not uncommon for mere discussion of a group problem to result in an increase in group cohesion.)

During the seventh and eighth sessions, members continued to handle stressful situations but added cognitive elements to the behavioral role-plays. For example, Janet told of a situation in class where the instructor called on her and she panicked, telling herself, "I'm too dumb to answer any question." The members suggested that because she usually knows the answers to questions in class and in this group, when called on, she might instruct herself to take a deep breath and relax and to repeat the question in her mind. Before class, she would prepare herself to say, "I know the answers to almost all questions asked, and it's not so terrible to make a mistake." Jim then cognitively modeled what she had to say. This was followed by her own cognitive rehearsal (in a stage whisper), combined with an answer to the question aloud in a behavioral rehearsal. In the final practice, everyone in the group asked her one question as if she were in class. (Janet had provided the members with the questions.) She stood up and answered them while silently reassuring herself of her ability to answer. Her success was met with wild applause from the group.

These sessions also ended with extra-group task planning and session evaluations. In these extra-group tasks, the members actually tried out in the real world many of the behaviors and cognitions learned in earlier groups. In addition, most members continued to practice relaxation and to note their successes and failures in handling stress.

The Final Phase: Sessions 9 and 10

During the final phase, the emphasis was placed on reviewing the skills that had been taught and planning for dealing with stress after the group ended. In session nine, Lydia suggested some extra-group tasks that would help members think of how they could maintain the skills they had learned during the previous 8 weeks. Lydia prepared them for the task of maintenance and generalization with a 5-minute mini-lecture.

Lydia began by emphasizing that there are limits to how much people can change after 20 hours of stress management training. Although the extra-group tasks extend the power of the group during its 10-week course, without planning for the maintenance of skills after the group ends, any benefits of stress management training would greatly diminish over time. The members discussed, one at a time, the principles of transfer and maintenance of change. Lydia suggested, as an extra-group task, that they use the principles to develop a personal maintenance plan that would be the focus of the last session. Everyone agreed to try it out.

At the beginning of the 10th session, the members reviewed each other's plans. There were a variety of ideas. Jim planned to read several books on assertiveness and stress management; he had even purchased two the previous week. Ellen was going to maintain contact with Susan as well as keep a diary of stressful situations and how she handled them. She was going to continue her new regimen of walking two miles per day, and Susan would accompany her. Group members questioned Ellen how she would continue this exercise plan in inclement weather. Ellen replied that she had purchased a gym membership so that the walking could be completed on a treadmill. Susan had already joined a church group in which she planned to try out the assertiveness techniques she learned in the group. She was considering joining an assertiveness training group to bolster her newly learned skills. Rosemary decided together with her husband to enter marital counseling, something the members had suggested earlier. Janet was going to join a yoga class to improve her relaxation. Jim felt he should join another stress group. "I passed this one, but just barely," he joked.

Frank asked whether any of the others might be interested in a booster session in three months. They could discuss how they had used their stress management skills, refresh any skills that had been forgotten, and do problem solving. Most of the members were willing to attend, and Lydia noted that she and the agency would be happy to cooperate with such a plan. Frank and Ellen agreed to help organize it. The most important purpose of the booster session, they agreed, would be to see how well they were carrying out their maintenance plans (a focus on development of a maintenance plan, public commitment to the maintenance plan, and monitoring of the plan in a booster session contribute to implementation of the plan).

Lydia commended the members for their hard work in developing these plans. She organized the following closing exercise. Each member distributed to every other member a note on which was written one positive comment. The members were not to read the notes until they went home. Thus, the group ended with the exchange of positive feedback.

At the end of the 10th session, the members were asked to retake the three assessment tests from the pregroup interview in order to assess individual gains in stress management skills. Lydia arranged to meet with the members individually during the week following the last session to inform them of the assessment results. At that postgroup meeting, members would be able to provide Lydia with feedback about the program.

CONCLUSIONS

In this 10-session group, the leader used a wide variety of assessment and intervention procedures, including the modeling sequence, reinforcement, cognitive restructuring, self-instructional training, and relaxation training. The leader dealt with group problems before they interfered with the group's functioning (e.g., the negative subgrouping by Rosemary and Ellen, a drop in group cohesion, and low productivity). She encouraged broad participation through the formation of positive subgroups and the use of exercises. Lydia was also purposefully involved members wherever possible in leadership functions and decision making. The leader brought her warmth, her interviewing skills, and her humor to the group. She encouraged self-disclosure but protected clients from revealing too much too soon. She opened herself up to criticism and accepted it without becoming defensive. She acknowledged her mistakes. At the same time, she kept the group moving and provided a flexible structure while the focus on improving coping skills was maintained. She recorded data and used them for evaluation and to improve practice.

This group is typical of the many multimethod groups we have dealt with through the years. No two groups are exactly the same, even when they have the same general purpose. They vary with respect to specific purpose, composition, primary means of intervention, assessment strategies, and in every other aspect. They hold in common a focus on problem solving, goal orientation, cognitive-behavioral interventions, coping skills training, and varying approaches for the different phases of group development. Of equal importance is the use of the group as a major tool of assessment, intervention, and generalization in the treatment process.

REFERENCES

Derogatis, L. R. (1993). *Brief Symptom Inventory (BSI): Administration, scoring, and procedures manual.* Minneapolis, MN: National Computer Systems.

Kanner, A. D., Coyne, J. C., Schaefer, C., & Lazarus, R. S. (1981). Comparison of two modes of stress measurement: Daily hassles and uplifts versus major life events. *Journal of Behavioral Medicine, 4,* 1–39.

Rahe, R. H., & Tolles, R. L. (2002). The Brief Stress and Coping Inventory: A useful stress management instrument. *International Journal of Stress Management, 9*(2), 61–70.

Case Study 6-2

Mediation and Facilitation: Alternatives to the Adversarial Process of Conflict Resolution in Child Welfare Cases

SUSAN K. PARNELL[2]

Mediation is being increasingly used as an alternative to judicial intervention. The case study illustrates how the practice of mediation requires the blending of law, social work, and counseling.

Questions

1. What social work skills are used in conducting mediation between two parties?
2. How do you think mediators accomplish the essential task of uncovering underlying interests, and why is it so essential to do so?
3. Mediators strive to be neutral, impartial, and nonjudgmental third parties. What do you think are the ongoing challenges to this effort?
4. How do the interventions used in mediation reflect social work values?

---

[2] Due to the confidential nature of child welfare cases, the names of all parties and certain details have been changed to protect the confidentiality of the families served.

In 1997 I wrote the following:

> Every time I walk into the Juvenile Court Center I remember that I have once again forgotten my vow to carry with me a plant, a picture for the wall, and a box of tissue. I am put off by the starkness of the rooms we use there for conducting Child Welfare mediations. The rooms are not only more formal than I would choose for a mediation setting but, with their large, imposing conference tables, rather formidable.

At that time, I was a visiting volunteer mediator at the Juvenile Court. Now, more than 14 years later, I am pleased to report that mediation and facilitation have become an institutionalized element of the dependency system in Pima County, Arizona. Four full-time mediators have welcoming offices complete with round tables, art, plants, and tissues. Although the four of us have different styles and approach our cases from our own unique perspectives, we share our passion for self-determination and our belief that the best outcomes for children involve the participation and input of family members. Whether we are engaging a family early in the case, midway through the case, or as it nears its conclusion, our shared goal is to engage parents into the decision-making aspects of their child welfare case.

A CASE BEGINS: THE FACILITATED SETTLEMENT CONFERENCE OF JENNIFER K.

Within 7 working days after a dependency petition is filed, the Court must conduct its first hearing, the Preliminary Protective Hearing. This is the parents' and family members' first exposure to the court system, and it begins with a facilitated prehearing conference. At this conference, a trained facilitator leads a discussion that includes an introduction of the various parties to the case and the gathering of additional informa-tion on topics such as education, paternity, and Indian Child status. Also discussed are the current placement of the children, how the parents and children will have time together as the case proceeds, and the services, tasks, and behavioral changes that need to be completed in order for a reunification outcome to occur. What is not addressed at this point is whether a basis exists for the Court to find the children dependent (i.e., adjudicate them as dependent children). That issue will be addressed in approximately 30 days and is one of the topics addressed by one of the Court's mediators in a session called a Facilitated Settlement Conference (F-Set).

Preparation for an F-Set requires review of any available documents. The petition filed by the Department of Economic Security–Child Protective Services (CPS), the report prepared by the CPS investigator for the Preliminary Protective Hearing, and any minute entries that have been generated from previous hearings provide the foundation materials for my review. The challenge for me (the facilitator) is to read the various accounts and reports and yet maintain an open mind about the truth of any element contained therein. My task is not to be the finder of the truth, but to assist the various voices at the table in their exploration of a version of the events that all can agree upon. An agreement on the facts/truth/basis of the case may lead to the Department asking the Court to dismiss their petition, but that is a rarity. More often, such an agreement brings about an outcome in which the Department agrees to amending the language of its petition and the parent acknowledges the situation and admits that the children are dependent. When there is no agreement, the matter is set for trial and, following testimony and evidence, the Court determines if the children are dependent or not. Those involved in an F-Set include the investigating CPS worker, the ongoing CPS worker, the Assistant Attorney General representing CPS, the parents and their respective attorneys, and the children's attorney. The task at hand for the parties is to determine if the question of whether the children are dependent will be resolved by trial or by agreement of the parties. For the purposes of this case study, I will use a one-parent session, although both parents are often involved in the session.

Jennifer is the mother of four children. She resides in Florida and has one of her children in her care. (The father of that child is not the father of her Arizona-based children and is not involved in her life at this time.) Her three other children reside in Pima County, Arizona, and are the subjects of the dependency petition. They are the children of a common father. The oldest child, a 15-year-old girl, has been in the maternal grandparents' care since she was born. The other two children were in the father's custody until their removal by CPS as a result of allegations of physical abuse. They are now placed with a maternal aunt and her husband. Jennifer is completing parole for a human trafficking charge, for which she served time in federal prison.

Although telephonic participation is not ideal, we do not preclude parents from participating in alternative dispute resolution sessions because they are unable to be present in person. After gathering the required parties into my room seated around the table, I reach Jennifer using my conference phone. I begin the session by ensuring that Jennifer is aware of everyone in the room and that she remembers the various roles of those present from her earlier Prehearing Conference. I explain that my role will be unique and limited in that I am not a decision maker nor am I a reporter to the Court. I will not be making reports or recommendations to the judge nor will I be called to testify about what is discussed during the session. I explain that those who do this work routinely understand the confidential nature of the conversations held with a court mediator and they, too, are not allowed to disclose the content of these discussions unless all agree upon that disclosure. I go on to explain that even given that confidentiality, I am a mandated reporter for certain things, and if I have reason to suspect that a child or a vulnerable adult is being abused or neglected, or if someone threatens harm to self or others, I would need to report such information to the proper authorities. I say that my role is to assist the parties as they explore possibilities for resolving the case and to slow things down in a way that allows her to understand and actively participate in this settlement process.

With the required elements of my introduction complete, and the Department having stated that they are looking to proceed on their petition and are willing to negotiate amendments to the allegations in the petition, I ask Jennifer and her attorney if they are willing to engage in an exploration of settlement options. (Jennifer will encounter many situations during her case in which her participation is mandatory. However, when it comes to her involvement in this setting, her participation is voluntary. The session will be concluded at any point at which any participant says it is over, because voluntary participation is a hallmark of a mediated session.) Bailey Copeland, Jennifer's attorney, states that she has mailed the petition to Jennifer, and they have discussed settling the case. I confirm with Jennifer that she has the petition in front of her and can follow along with us. I explain to her that working over the phone puts us both at a disadvantage, and I encourage her to stop us whenever she has a question, needs clarification, or simply can't hear something. I silently remind myself that without her facial expressions and body language to assist me in listening to her, I will have to listen intently to all aspects of her spoken word (i.e., her tone, timbre, volume, etc.). The preliminaries being addressed and all parties agreeable to explore possibilities for a nontrial resolution, I begin my work of guiding them on that exploration.

A dependency petition is a thick legal pleading that can be daunting to someone who is unfamiliar with its contents. I ask Jennifer to turn to the page that lists the specific allegations that CPS has made about the parenting of her children and let her know that that is the only area that we'll be addressing. I explain to her that cases are often settled when the language of those allegations is revised to fit the needs of all parties at the table. I continue by describing that my role, as a neutral party, is to facilitate the negotiation of the language of those allegations. I explain that, for the Department, the allegations must set forth a factual basis in order for the Court to find the children dependent and adjudicate them as dependent children. For the Department, the allegations also need to create a legitimate reason for it to ask the Court to order a parent to participate in and benefit from a specific service (e.g., drug testing, parenting classes) or to accomplish a specific task (e.g., resolve any outstanding legal issues, secure a legal source of income and safe housing). For the children's attorney, the language has to set forth the account of the situation as the children have relayed it to their attorney.

For Jennifer, the statements must reflect the identified problem areas of her parenting of her children in wording that she can admit is true. If they are able to find language that is acceptable to all, then Jennifer will need to determine if she is willing to admit that the statements set forth create a situation in which her children have been abused and/or neglected and that they establish the foundation for a finding of dependency. These concepts are complicated and confusing and, when combined with the emotional component of having one's children's in out-of-home care, can be all the more challenging. The need for empowerment of the parent through understanding and active involvement in the process is one goal of my work.

As we begin, it is clear from Jennifer's comments that she is deeply distressed about the abuse the children have suffered. I have found over the years that the nonoffending parent, especially one who has been absent from the children's lives, carries a heavy load of guilt and/or shame. Those at the table listen patiently as I listen to and reflect back to Jennifer her myriad of feelings and thoughts about being far away, about having trusted the father to care for the children, and about feeling stuck in Florida while she completes parole. Having read in the report that she is on track to successfully complete parole and has a child in her care, I invite her to share the positives in her life and her goals for her Arizona-based children. Jennifer says she wants to work on a reunification case plan and plans to return to Arizona when Florida releases her in order to work toward regaining custody of the children. I lead the parties through the petition's allegations one line at a time. When either Jennifer or her attorney find issue with the wording of an allegation or the allegation itself, I use curious questioning, clarifying, and brainstorming to move the parties off the words as they exist on the paper and into the area of the lived experience of the event being recounted. I ask Jennifer to give her own account of an event as she experienced it and, having listened to her account, I reflect it back to all at the table, inviting them to see the event or situation experience from her perspective. I strive to make it apparent to those present that while this is a case for the professionals involved, it is the life of the parent or child that is being discussed.

Any narrative of the parent's experience or behavior, whether written or spoken, must resonate with the parent as accurate in order for the parent to make a genuine admission that the children are dependent. At a point where they get stuck, I ask the investigator to express the problem area in terms of the behavioral change that the Department is looking for as opposed to the problem statement as it appears in the petition. I then check with Jennifer to assess her understanding of the Department's concern and the required change that it is looking for to remedy the situation. In this back-and-forth way, both parties make their way through each allegation, working with the language and the meaning of each until they find language they all agree upon. Jennifer is able to say that every allegation as stated is true, and the Department is satisfied that they have the basis for a finding of dependency and for the services and tasks that they require. At this point, I almost routinely caucus with the parent and his or her attorney, and I decide to do so with Jennifer and Bailey.

With all other parties seated in the lobby, I explain the caucus process to Jennifer. I explain that I will not be reporting back to the larger group the content of this separate conversation. She or her attorney may choose to disclose what we discuss, but I will not do so unless they give me permission. I begin by reminding Jennifer that the next part of the session has to do with deciding if she wants to go to trial and have CPS prove that the children are dependent or if she wants to admit that they are dependent based on the agreed-upon revised allegations. Jennifer, like so many parents, fears the loss of her children forever, and I am careful to ensure that she understands that her admission to the dependency does not mean a termination of her parental rights. I hear the panic in her voice about the distance, and I join her attorney in explaining again that the goal of the case is reunification with a parent. I do my best to explain over the phone that the journey of a dependency case is from a problem situation to a safe, permanent home in which the children's needs on all dimensions are met in a consistent, stable, and predictable way. I make sure she understands that reunification with a parent is the preferred outcome.

Ms. Copeland explains that Jennifer is as much in the running for custody as the father, perhaps more so because he is facing criminal charges arising from the abuse and neglect. This elicits another emotional response from Jennifer, and I reflect back what I hear as her pain, her fear, and her sense of responsibility. I remind her of the positive things she said she has going for her and invite her to look forward with a focus on her strengths and solutions and not on the problems that got her here. After a final discussion with her attorney, Jennifer decides to admit to a dependency. I invite the others back into the room, and once Bailey and and the mother have conveyed the mother's decision as to the matter of the dependency, I initiate the discussion of case plan services.

Jennifer is clear that she intends to come to Tucson as soon as she completes her parole. The ongoing case manager and Ms. Copeland are in agreement that services for the mother must be set up in Florida and begun while the mother remains there, or too much time will have passed if she waits until she gets settled back in Tucson. I lead a discussion of the services and tasks being requested by the Department and hear in Jennifer's voice the resolve that is so often characteristic of a parent at this point in their case. I listen intently for any indication of a question, confusion, or misunderstanding on Jennifer's part. I intentionally ask questions that all the system players know the answers to in order to ensure that Jennifer has this information, too. When it appears that all are clear on who needs to do what by when in order to get things moving, I summarize what I hear to be their agreements and assist them in completing the documents that will move their agreements forward. Our work concluded, I wished Jennifer well and continued success as she moved forward.

ISSUES DURING THE PENDING OF THE CASE: REUNIFICATION AT RISK FOR JENNIFER K.

Many cases return to mediation at a later point in the legal process. Specific visitation issues can arise between a parent and the placement family. Placement issues arise when more than one household is vying for placement of the children. However, the return sessions that I personally find the most rewarding to conduct are what we call Reunification at Risk sessions. These sessions are set for cases in which at least one parent is working on his or her case plan tasks and services, but projections for a successful reunification with that parent appear to be at risk. The risk may be arising from minimal effort applied by the parent or from challenges within and without the system itself. These sessions have a twofold purpose. The first is to discover and make explicit the barriers to reunification and then to explore possibilities for overcoming those barriers. The second is to engage the parent or parents in active planning for an alternative to reunification. When the overriding paradigm is one of win-lose (i.e., win: you get your children back, and lose: you don't), it is nearly impossible to engage a parent in a meaningful exploration of an alternative plan. However, when approached from a paradigm of effective and responsible parenting, parents have repeatedly demonstrated to me that they can and will step up and become active participants in this effort. Jennifer K.'s case returns to me for such a session.

Preparation for any session involves a review of any CPS reports submitted to the court, the minute entries generated from the hearing held, as well as a review of my own case note if I have seen the case before. In reviewing my case note, I am reminded of the strengths and challenges I noted about Jennifer following our first encounter and, in doing so, hope to bring her uniqueness and individuality to mind so that she doesn't become just another parent in a long chain of parents. My review of the court reports and minute entries inform me about the current status of the case as seen by those who authored them. According to the CPS report, Jennifer has not relocated to Tucson as she had planned and has not engaged in the services set up for her in Florida. The younger two children, Jason, age 14, and Mark, age 12, remain in the care of their maternal aunt and uncle. Kayla, the oldest daughter, remains with the maternal grandparents.

According to the report, Kayla is terrified that this "reunification talk" means that someone is going to take her away from the only parents she has ever known. Her grades in school are slipping, and she is showing signs of depression. The boys continue to do well in their relative placement. Neither boy expresses a desire to reunify with the father, and only Mark expresses a desire to even have visits with him. The father settled his criminal matter with a plea bargain and got four years' probation. He refuses to participate in the case plan services because he believes CPS never had the right to remove the boys from him in the first place, yet he expects the boys to be returned to his care. He has been clear from the start that he has no desire to reunify with Kayla. With the statutory clock ticking and both parents in noncompliance with their case plans, reunification is clearly at risk.

On the day of the session, I go to the lobby and call the case. I am told that the father will not be attending this session because he does not believe he needs it. Once again, after seating the case manager, his attorney, the children's attorney, the mother's attorney, the maternal grandparents, and the maternal aunt around the table, we reach Jennifer by telephone from Florida. I have everyone identify himself or herself so that Jennifer knows who is in the room. I review my role as well as the confidential and voluntary nature of the session that we are about to begin. I explain the two topics that will be addressed—barriers to reunification and an alternative plan for the children. I inform the mother and her family members that I have reviewed the case reports and court record in order to get a sense of where the case has been. I then make a point of letting them know that my focus will be on helping them explore possibilities for the future of the case. Having obtained the commitment from those present to engage in a respectful but candid conversation on these two topics, we begin our work together.

I begin the work by asking the case manager, Don, to tell me a bit about what has gone right for Jennifer on her case plan. I'm thankful that Don picks up my plan to start with some positive aspect of Jennifer's case. He recounts how Jennifer has been faithful with her phone calls to the children and acknowledges that she has tried to put Kayla's concerns to rest by assuring her that she supports a plan of Kayla remaining with the maternal grandparents. I look to the maternal grandparents, and they acknowledge that Jennifer has consistently given them the same message. They express relief that the father didn't use this case as an opportunity to try and rout Kayla out of their home. Jennifer sounds strong when she announces that she would support an adoption of Kayla by the grandparents. I invite her to share with those present how she sees that decision as serving her daughter's best interests. Jennifer reminds me of what I had said during the first session about the goal being a safe, stable, permanent home where a child's ongoing needs are met predictably and consistently. "This decision," Jennifer says, "is me doing my best to meet that goal for Kayla." The Assistant Attorney General voices what is likely the thinking of all at the table when she tells Jennifer that her decision takes courage and demonstrates her love for Kayla. The attorneys take a minute or two to discuss the steps needed to move this plan forward. Given what is understood about the father's position at this point in time, it appears that they are in agreement to change the case plan goal for Kayla from reunification with a parent to adoption by the grandparents.

The warm moment ended when the topic was shifted to Jason and Mark. Don pointed out the obvious (i.e., that Jennifer did not make the expected relocation to Tucson following completion of her parole). I inquired as to the status of the ICPC (Interstate Compact on the Placement of Children) or if one had been initiated.[3] Don said that the ICPC process hadn't even been discussed, because the plan had been for Jennifer to relocate to Tucson. She hadn't indicated to him that she had changed her mind. A change in Jennifer's voice was apparent once the discussion began on what would need to happen in order for reunification to occur with her in Florida. I reminded her that working over the phone was challenging and, while I could be very off-base, I wondered if I was hearing a mixture of frustration, anger, sadness, and perhaps even something more. Jennifer went with her anger first, at the father who was supposed to care for the boys appropriately while she was in prison, at the lack of services available to her where she was living, and how she didn't feel like Don had done anything to really support her chance at reunification. I reflected back what I heard in content and asked Jennifer if I also heard a sense of helplessness behind her words. She stated that she still hadn't forgiven herself for the physical abuse that the boys underwent at their father's hands because she wasn't there to protect them. She expressed disgust at the father's aloof stance and said she couldn't understand how he could just be bailing on the boys. I said it sounded like she very much wanted to make up for lost time and lost opportunities with them, and Jennifer readily agreed. I asked if it was time to address the barriers to reunification with Jennifer and explore for possible solutions to those barriers.

Once again looking to take a strengths-based approach to Jennifer's situation, I asked how things were progressing for her now that she had successfully completed her parole. She reported that she is enrolled in school and that she is enjoying the parenting class that was on her case plan. She said she is doing a good job with her youngest child and is trying everything she can to be a good mother to her. She stated how hard she is trying to create a safe home for her boys, too, by getting back on her feet, and how anxious she is to have them with her again. She expressed frustration at how difficult it was to find the services she needs to work on her case plan and how difficult it is to be going to school, caring for her little girl, and trying to get to her required

---

[3] This compact is entered into by all of the states in which they agree that a child in the State's custody is not to be sent from one state to another without the express written permission of the receiving state. Basically, it entails the local worker putting together a complete package of materials about the case and sending it to the home state's main ICPC office. That office sends it to the receiving state's main ICPC office, which in turns sends it to the CPS office in the locale of the proposed placement. A worker from that office then conducts an investigation of the proposed caregiver. Although the end result could be a refusal to accept the placement of the children, in many cases, the result is positive, and a worker in the receiving state is assigned to work the case though to eventual closure. From start to finish, the ICPC process can take from two to six months to complete.

services—when she can find them. I clarified with Jennifer that reunification with her children in Florida is her goal, and she responded with a clear and strong, "Absolutely." I confirmed with those present that the two topics on hand appeared to be revisiting the ICPC and services for Jennifer in Florida.

Don said he would get started on the ICPC, but he added (with an edge in his voice) that Jennifer would have to stop making excuses and start getting to work on her services if she wanted to get a positive ICPC home study. I suggested that we take the elements of her case plan one at a time. Don would identify a service and his attempts to arrange a provider in Jennifer's locale. Jennifer stopped him at every point. She couldn't afford anything larger than an efficiency apartment until she got a decent-paying job. She couldn't get a job until she finished her school program. She couldn't afford bus fare to get to the services that Don had set up for her. It seemed as if any attempts at problem solving the challenges facing Jennifer only seemed to further frustrate and upset her. I found myself wondering if Jennifer's frustration and anger were masking something very different—loss, resignation, something else? I wasn't sure, but I knew it was time for another caucus. I asked everyone but the family members to take a seat out in the lobby.

Once it was only the family members and me, I told Jennifer that I may be wrong—and please tell me if I am—but I thought I heard tremendous conflict in her voice and in her words. I said it seemed to me like she was struggling with more than accessing services. Her voice cracked, and then gentle sobbing could be heard. The maternal grandmother and aunt looked to each other and then at me. I let the silence rest with them for a moment and then said, "Jennifer, in your words, I hear that reunification with you in Florida is what you want for your boys, but at some level I think I'm hearing another message. It's as if I'm hearing two messages, one from your heart and one from your head. The message from your heart wishes all would be well and you would complete school and get a job and provide a stable home for them. However, the message from your head is saying that you have everything you can handle, and that perhaps the best outcome for your sons is the stability that your sister and her husband can provide them." There is silence again, and I ask if the three of them have discussed an alternative to reunification among themselves and offer them privacy to do so if they would like. Jennifer says she would like that, and I leave the room.

In the lobby, I tell those present that the maternal grandmother, aunt, and mother are taking a few minutes to discuss the situation. After several minutes, I tap on the door and ask if they are ready to bring the others back in. When they say they are, everyone returns to the mediation room, and I ask the family members if there is anything they would like to share with the others before I begin. Jennifer speaks up and tells Don that he does not need to start the ICPC process on her. Her children are rooted in Tucson, and she is unable to come back to Tucson. She repeated her plan for Kayla to be adopted by the maternal grandmother and says that she wants her sister to adopt the boys if their father is unable to successfully reunify with them. She wants assurances from Don and the children's attorney that he would only regain custody if he proved he could parent them safely.

NEAR THE ENDING OF A CASE

Not all of my work involves conflict. I am often called upon to assist counsel in determining if a parent has sufficient comprehension to admit to or agree upon a plan. My work with Heavenly provides an example of this sort of intervention.

Heavenly is developmentally delayed. Although she is 28 years old, she functions at a 9- to 11-year-old age level. When Heavenly was 14 years old, she was impregnated by her father. She became a dependent child as to her parents, and when her baby was born, a healthy baby girl named Cissy, she was also taken into CPS custody. Although Heavenly's case had long since closed, Cissy's case had remained open all these years. Cissy, now herself 14 years old, had remained all these years in the same loving foster home. Heavenly, who now lives in a sheltered home setting, had maintained a relationship with her daughter. According to the caseworker's most recent report, this great kid had started acting out. When they explored what was going on with her, Cissy said that she was tired of being a CPS kid and wanted to be adopted by her foster mother. She didn't want a case manager and an attorney and a judge anymore. However, she felt conflicted because she didn't want to hurt Heavenly's feelings either. According to the referral I had in my hand, no one wanted to see the case go to a severance trial, but they were not sure that Heavenly could consent to the relinquishment of her parental rights and the resulting adoption of Cissy by her current foster mother. The case was sent to me to explore the possibility of a consensual adoption.

Heavenly, Marjorie (the foster mother), Elise (Heavenly's house-mother), Emery (Heavenly's attorney), Greg (the caseworker), Shane (the Assistant Attorney General), and Chris (Cissy's attorney) arrive on time for their session. I begin by explaining the voluntary and confidential aspects of the session, using simple, concrete terms for Heavenly's benefit. Although I read the referral and know the main topic for discussion, I routinely begin by asking the parties to tell me about what brings them in. They may all see the situation exactly as it was reflected on the referral form (which was completed in the courtroom by the judge), or they may have a different agenda or simply define the situation differently and thereby still provide me with additional information. In this case, what I hear from them agrees with the information on the referral. No one wants a trial, but they need to be sure that Heavenly's consent to an adoption would be informed, freely made, and not coerced in any way.

I ask Heavenly to tell me about Cissy. Her eyes light up as she tells me that Cissy is a smart girl. She's smart in school and she can do lots of things. I then ask Heavenly to tell me about the times she spends with Cissy. Again, her face brightens as she tells me about the games they play and how they laugh together. Reflecting back her joy and pride in her daughter, I move forward and ask her to tell me what she knows about adoption. She thinks a bit and says, "It's when a kid gets a new mother." And then quickly adds, "I don't want Cissy to have a new mother. She can keep me and she can keep Marjorie. She doesn't need a new mother." Looking around at the faces around the table, I see concern in all of them. I call a caucus and ask to meet privately with Heavenly, Marjorie, Elise, and Emery.

Quite frequently I use my whiteboard to draw pictures or simple diagrams to assist parents and family members in comprehending complex legal concepts inherent to child welfare cases. I decide to do so with Heavenly. Having asked her to describe for me what mothers are and what they do, I graphically illustrate her responses, checking as I go for accuracy. For example, she tells me that Cissy was in her tummy and then came out. I draw a pregnant stick figure (drawing is not my forte) and then another with the baby on the outside. The others at the table join in the conversation of describing what mothers do, and the end result is several drawings describing mothering, including shopping, doing laundry, taking a child to the doctor, cooking, helping with schoolwork. I draw a strong red circle around the pregnant stick figure and the figure next to it with the baby and ask Heavenly how many of those mommies Cissy can have. She giggles as if I am the silliest person in the world and says, "Just one." I then circle the other figures with a green marker and ask her how many of those kinds of mommies we can have. Heavenly thought for a moment and then, as if thinking out loud, said, "I have my mom; I was in her tummy. And I have Elise. And Cissy has me and she has Marjorie. Two."

I take two appointment cards from the holder on the table and write on the back of one with the red marker "Birth Mother" and on the back of the other using the green marker "Legal Mother." I put one in each of Heavenly's hands and tell her that she has both of the mother cards. They both belong to her right now. I invite her to look at the board and tell us what each card means, and she is able to do so using the illustrated examples. I then ask her which one of the cards does she think she could give away to someone else. She looked at the cards, back and forth, from one to the other as we sat in silence. She looked up and made eye contact with me and said clearly, "I can only give the green one away." Emery, who has been Heavenly's attorney from the time she came into the system as a child herself, says gently, "Heavenly, Cissy is asking that you give the green card to Marjorie so she can be the legal mommy. Adoption would make Marjorie the legal mommy, and Cissy won't have to be a CPS child anymore." We sat in silence again as Heavenly looked back and forth at the cards and then at Marjorie. In a determined voice that indicated that she really meant business, she addressed Marjorie: "I know that you do the legal things for Cissy. I know that you love her and take good care of her. If I give you the green card, do you promise that you'll keep it?" Misty-eyed but smiling, Marjorie replied that she would treasure it forever. Once more looking at the two cards in her hands, Heavenly closed her hand tightly around the Birth Mother card and handed the Legal Mother card to Marjorie.

Following a brief discussion on how Cissy would continue to have her visits with Heavenly, the other parties were asked to rejoin us. I provided them with a brief summary of the meaning of the stick figures on the board. Heavenly then jumped in and told them about the green card and the red card and that she was going to keep the red card forever but was giving the green card to Marjorie so she could adopt Cissy. And Cissy would have two mommies and would be happy because she wouldn't have to be with CPS anymore, even though Greg was very nice. Emery then went over the questions that the judge would ask her about letting Cissy be adopted by Marjorie. It was apparent by the relieved expressions on the faces of those around the table that they believed that Heavenly could consent to an adoption. Just at that point, the bailiff tapped at the door and asked if the parties were ready to go before the judge. They looked at one another and then at Heavenly, who said, "Yes, I'm ready."

CONCLUSION

Contrary to what some of the judges and attorneys may think, I do not have magic dust in my mediation room. What I am able to offer is an environment within the courthouse that is more relaxed and informal. In this environment, parties to a case can engage in a confidential exploration of possibilities for resolution of whatever issues bring them through my door. I frequently say that I have the easiest job of them all: I do not have to come up with opinions and recommendations, I do not have to write court reports or go to court and testify, and I'm not shouldered with the decision-making responsibilities that fall to so many others who are involved in these cases. I only have to create the environment and guide a process that allows them to fully engage in their own roles, discover their strengths and capacities, and explore for possible resolutions. Perhaps there is magic dust in my room. Perhaps it is my hope and belief in the capacity of the participants, professionals and family members alike, to resolve differences and find mutually agreeable solutions to the difficult decisions faced in child welfare cases.

Case Study 6-3

Project Home Base: How Berto Came Indoors After 20 Years of Sidewalk Sleeping

Catherine Sammons

Homelessness is a serious social problem. This case reflects the difficulty of implementing interventions that can address this significant problem.

Questions

1. How does the housing first model depart from traditional shelter and supported living services for homeless persons?
2. What are some opportunities and challenges in adapting mental health services from the clinic setting to housing-based?
3. What fundamental social work principles did this case reinforce for the social worker?

When I first met Berto, I could not take my eyes off the neat creases in his T-shirt. I'd never seen a carefully ironed T-shirt, and especially not on a man who had been labeled "chronically homeless." From his closely trimmed beard to his sharply ironed khakis and pristine white nonbranded athletic shoes, his meticulous appearance gave no clue that he had just moved to a small single apartment after 21 years of eating, sleeping, and drinking beer on the downtown streets of this southern California metropolis. Well, that wasn't quite true: Sun overexposure had deeply lined and darkened his skin beyond its original Mexican American tone and also added at least 15 appearance years to his 48 chronological ones. His housing services coordinator, Elena, introduced me to my new client since I'd just arrived to fill the clinical social work position at the fledgling Project Home Base multiagency service program in this city's urban core neighborhood. Berto had a warm relationship with Elena and trusted her judgment, so when she advised him to get to know me, he felt obliged to follow her request. This is the story of how Berto regained his sobriety, his physical and mental health, and his dignity, and how our therapeutic relationship humbled and reinspired me as a social worker.

As a new team member, I had not witnessed Berto's initial entry into this housing first intensive services program. Our outreach worker Patrick had become a familiar presence at the parking lot where Berto slept under a cardboard lean-to attached with bungee cords to a chainlink fence. No one claimed there was any "befriending" or "trusting," just that the daily predawn visits made Patrick's short wiry figure, pale white face, and waist-length dreadlocks a predictable part of the landscape, along with scurrying rats and puddles of urine and vomit in the alley. Like most sidewalk sleepers in this skid row area, Berto described himself as "a loner" and "not a people person," so what got his attention was not Patrick's socializing attempts but his persistently repeated offer of *a sliding-scale rent, no strings attached, room of your own if you just come with me to check it out and sign some papers with the county housing department.* It had been a very cold, very wet winter with record-breaking El Niño storms. Every single piece of paper Berto had folded and stashed in his pockets and clung to over the years had recently disappeared or disintegrated during police enforcement of the no-sidewalk-sleeping-between-6am-and-6pm law, or the street cleaners' poorly aimed power hoses. Instead of rest, every night brought only brief naps caught between bouts of chaotic action, such as the time gang-bangers cruised by, jumped out of their low-riders, and stole his shoes while he slept. Then there were the stabbings, usually involving loan sharks or drug dealers, who Berto didn't mess with, but they were too close to ignore. And always the helicopters circling around, chop-chopping the dark sky and zapping down those bright search beams zigzagging over the sleeping bags, tents, and huddled bodies. He was tired. Tired of being hungry, tired of having to deal with these other unstable guys around him, and especially tired of being dirty; Berto was disgusted and repelled by the stench of his own body and raggedy clothes, though he was too suspicious and fearful to use the public showers. When Patrick caught him on a sober day, Berto agreed to get into the program van and visit the apartment building five blocks away. I can't say he never looked back.

No, like most of the other recently housed clients at Home Base, Berto's transition from sidewalk to apartment was bumpy. He slept on the floor for weeks because his bed felt like a coffin. He caused a fire in his kitchen because he tried lighting the stove with a match instead of the push-button (it had been many years since he'd lit a burner). He flooded the laundry room with suds by using a full cup of detergent concentrate instead of the one tablespoon specified on the label; his vision just wasn't up to that fine print. These were the challenges he overcame in the first three months, thanks to Elena's supportive coaching and the program's unique model of care. Traditional services for chronically homeless persons revolve around emergency shelters, typically private nonprofit programs, often religiously based, occupying massive neighborhood structures and aiming for outcomes such as number of meals served and number of beds filled each month. But to get from a shelter to an apartment, a homeless person has to navigate a system requiring social and community skills far beyond their current repertoire. Very few addicted, mentally ill, aged, or physically fragile persons could obtain the documents, complete the application, and—most of all—keep appointments, stand in lines, and otherwise demonstrate that they were ready to become apartment dwellers. Ready usually included clean and sober, taking psychiatric medications, and completing parole. Consequently, the homeless population continued to grow and increasingly fill jails, hospital emergency rooms, and even the morgue. Lessons learned in New York City's cleanup of Times Square (Fessler, 2011), as well as fieldwork by a Boston homeless healthcare specialist (Bornstein, 2010), suggested that the shelter-based service system may be helpful for recently evicted or other transiently homeless populations, but it bypasses the chronically homeless. It also costs taxpayers more than providing permanent housing with on-site, intensive, coordinated services.

Project Home Base was a demonstration project based on housing first principles (National Alliance to End Homelessness, 2006). I called it the come-as-you-are approach. Instead of requiring homeless people to produce an original social security card, proof of a negative TB test, three months of bank statements, proof of income, proof of disability, and weekly check-in meetings with a housing representative during the 6- to 9-month waitlist period, our program directly approached and engaged the sidewalk residents whose special needs were already well known to neighborhood residents and police. *First* come indoors, and *then* we will help you get documents and cope with housing-related challenges. You need not prove you are ready or medically compliant or even abstaining from addictive drugs. Just agree to pay one-third of your income (be that $250 from general relief or $850 from Supplemental Security Income, or a military pension or even an income of zero) and follow some basic housing rules. Along the way, homeless people gradually become service utilizers, responding to the personalized approach of the resident nurse practitioner, psychiatrist, housing coordinator, addiction counselor, and clinical social worker. Reduction in mental illness distress and dysfunction, as well as addiction recovery, are explicit program goals but not individual client requirements for secure, permanent housing.

As Berto settled into housing, his multiple special needs came into more specific focus. He demonstrated symptoms of severe and recurrent major depression, at times with psychotic features. His lifelong socially phobic behavior patterns suggested avoidant or possibly paranoid personality disorder. But the greatest threat to his housing stability was his alcohol dependence. Berto shared his psychosocial history over a series of interviews that began as just 10-minute check-ins that he maintained primarily because our team was his only social network, and his Mexican American upbringing meant that face-to-face greetings were an important daily ritual for him. I learned of his growing up in the desert town of El Centro, California, dropping out of school in the seventh grade, working for his brother's plumbing business, having a brief marriage, and fathering two daughters. He didn't like to talk about his past, and he really didn't see the point or purpose in meeting with me, but our relationship grew despite his doubts. Instead of focusing on psychiatric symptoms right away, as most mental health clinical social workers are required by their agencies to do, I could turn my attention to whatever mattered most to him in his daily life. Initially, Berto was most troubled by health matters such as stomach pains and poor vision. Our team took a very fluid approach to client contacts, meaning that I could ask the nurse practitioner to join my session, and she could ask me to join her visits, and soon Berto understood that we were all on his side and working together.

He was initially more comfortable providing health history, so we readily identified and assisted him with concerns such as hypertension, hepatitis C, a history of tuberculosis (treated), and age-related vision impairment. He also had accumulated three police citations, which caused him to sweat with terror whenever he went outdoors, thinking that the police would stop and arrest him. This was a rational fear, because our local law enforcement had begun a highly publicized campaign to "clean up the streets" of skid row by implementing what came to be known as the "broken window policing model" (Kelling, 2013). In this model, no crime is considered too small for attention, based on the theory that a broken window, graffiti, jaywalking, drinking from open containers, loitering, and many other minor offenses require swift attention and consequences in order to turn around a high-crime neighborhood and reinstate public safety and order. In our city, however, many of the police citations were characterized by community observers as homeless crimes; that is, the person's primary status as homeless led inexorably to their transgressions of multiple other laws. After accumulating three citations (without paying the fine or making the court appearance), the homeless persons then accrued a warrant for arrest, so that homeless persons were being incarcerated at high rates (and without improvement in their homeless status and multiple special needs).

Berto wanted help with his citations, so that was my entry into more therapeutic topics. While focusing on this problem, I used generic social work skills in terms of linking him with a legal aid program that advocated on behalf of homeless persons to prevent their incarceration. He also had a desire to eat food that was gentler on his digestion, food that reminded him of his childhood. I had learned through Project Home Base that, especially as homeless people age, their years of poor nutrition weigh heavily on their psyches (as well as their bodies). He had been eating Cup-a-Noodle with pork rinds, candy bars, chips, and grimy coffee from the corner store, but now Berto was thinking more about arroz con pollo, frijoles, warm tortillas, and freshly brewed coffee. With his own kitchen, he could now mobilize his energies to shop for and cook his own meals.

In the context of *his* goals (not getting arrested, eating better, not having stomach pain, sleeping better, getting glasses to read the newspaper, watching movies on his own TV), Berto allowed me into his life and into his emotional world. These goals provided the joint task focus for our meetings. Berto responded to my genuine compassion, the concrete information and guidance, and most of all, my consistency. He learned through experience, rather than intellectually or vicariously, many basic principles of standard therapeutic process, such as:

- We established a mutual trust that we would each follow through on our word.
- His time with me was protected, just for him, and details of our discussions were confidential.
- This was a no-fail relationship, without criticism or punishment.
- Our work was client-centered rather than agency-driven.

But in other ways, our psychotherapy process was atypical within the public outpatient mental health service system context, for example:

- Sessions varied in length and in location, including his apartment, the optometrist's office, the legal aid office, and other neighborhood venues; the 50-minute hour routine eventually developed after several months of as-needed, variable-length sessions; and if he did not show up, I would go knock on his door.
- Psychosocial, psychiatric, and substance abuse history was gathered gradually, as it seemed relevant in the process of problem solving the more concrete issues of daily living.
- His addiction issues were integrated into therapy and addressed as they manifested in daily life.

It did not take long for deeper clinical issues to arise. Through formal history gathering and behavioral observations in a variety of settings, the team psychiatrist and I were able to identify significant mood and cognitive dysfunction and to conceptualize them diagnostically. His pattern of distress and dysfunction met criteria for major depressive disorder, recurrent, with paranoid psychotic features, within a context of lifelong social phobia. He was well known in this skid row neighborhood as an alcoholic, with the street name of "Señor." But less known was the fact that his current binge drinking represented significant progress in a lifelong pattern of polysubstance abuse that began with his father urging him (at age 4) to have sips of beer, and at age 7 sneaking whiskey from his father's hidden bottle. By 11, he was following older male peers down to the convenience store to steal glue and spray paint to inhale. His father's involvement at home had always been minimal and sporadic, but after his mother's death following a brief illness (possibly cancer) when Berto was 14, the family disintegrated. His four older siblings shared responsibility for his care, which meant that he moved several times across three states, finally settling into work as a plumbing assistant in his brother's business. This brief period of work was his happiest life chapter, and he spoke with pride about his earnings, his marriage, and the birth of two daughters.

There was never a time when he didn't drink, though, and alcohol-related problems caused him to lose his job as well as his marriage. He spent all of his time drinking and sleeping in the city park, until finally the local police became particularly aggravated, and they drove him over 50 miles away to this major city's skid row. They opened the car door and said, "Get out, and don't you ever show your butt in El Centro again, or it's all over for you." This was his introduction to skid row lifestyle and to other drugs (with which he experimented) and a crack cocaine addiction. He described how profoundly ashamed he felt about his drug use, differentiating it from his alcohol use. Through a solitary process of will and hope, he eventually stopped using cocaine, but the alcoholism continued.

In working with Berto and our other clients, we did not require sobriety or even recovery activities as a condition of services. Although most clients dealing with addiction responded well to the outreach efforts of our substance abuse counselors, Berto did not. Despite the shared ethnic/linguistic background between Berto and the male substance abuse counselor, the closest he would get to a 12-step group was to greet the counselor in Spanish while walking by him, and this took many months to achieve. Berto had remarkably little knowledge about alcohol addiction; he did not know the term *binge* and had never been exposed to any of the basic recovery concepts that proliferate in contemporary popular culture. Having been trained in the Matrix Model (NREPP, 2013) of dual diagnosis treatment at my previous agency, I relied heavily on motivational interviewing techniques and stages of change theory (DiClemente, 2003). Berto was amenable to psychotropic medication early in the clinical evaluation process, which brought him significant reduction in anxiety, anhedonia, and insomnia. I learned through trial and error that his executive functioning skills were quite impaired, and this exacerbated his social fears and paranoia. For example, his concentration, auditory processing, short-term recall, sequencing, problem-solving skills, and other cognitive functions were very poor, even after his mood improved. The Repeatable Battery for the Assessment of Neuropsychological Status instrument (2013) helped me assess these areas of functioning. This information was critical in coaching him toward enhanced daily coping, as well as for his gradual education about alcoholism.

In keeping with our harm reduction model, I suggested that Berto set a goal of increasing the periods between drinking binges. One very powerful technique we used was a "sobriety calendar," which involved a common monthly wall calendar (chosen by him) that was kept in my locked file drawer and brought out at each office session. In reviewing his week, he would put a green sticker on every day that he was sober. We used this visual aid in exploring the detailed nuances of his daily experiences, such as when cravings occurred, what was happening just before, sources of stress, his thought processes, his coping strategies, and so on. We observed patterns, such as his habit of starting a binge on the Friday before I was to go on a vacation. We explored these patterns from the role of "compassionate detective," in that we had a definite goal in mind (less drinking), but we met relapse with curiosity and renewed commitment, rather than with shame or punishment.

Another successful strategy in Berto's treatment was to incorporate his friend Juan. Although Berto insisted that he did not have friends, that he never had friends, and that he didn't want to make friends, he did frequently describe experiences on the streets with Juan. He would relate that Juan "had his back" and vice versa. He had urged Juan to come into Project Home Base, and Juan had an apartment in the same building as Berto. He told many warm anecdotes about Juan, and yet, he would not knock on Juan's door in their new building. Juan was actively involved in treatment and had been clean and sober for more than a year, so he was a good role model for Berto. Both men were my clients. Both obviously knew that the other was a client, and I frequently suggested between-session home practice work that required the men to talk to each other. Eventually, and very gradually, they started to initiate contact on their own and even to provide mutual support. One particular episode became famous within the apartment building. Juan had saved his money and was ready to purchase a big-screen television, but he wasn't familiar with the bus system and asked Berto to go with him. Unbeknownst to Juan, Berto had been studying TV ads for some time and very much wanted to buy one but was overwhelmed at the prospect of the social encounter with a salesperson. Berto "did a favor for Juan" by accompanying him on the bus to the electronics discount store, where Juan handled the interpersonal part of the task, and Berto surprised him by saying, "I'll take one, too." Imagine these two middle-aged men, in their ironed T-shirts and jeans, pristine baseball caps, and white athletic shoes, each with a large, heavy box that they lugged onto a crowded bus and rode for several miles to their own homes. The dignity of this risk, the pride in having helped the other, the self-efficacy at having saved and sacrificed so long for this treasure—our unique program was a catalyst for many therapeutic experiences like this one in our clients' daily lives.

Over an 18-month period, Berto's binges were spaced further apart and shorter in duration. He had recently celebrated his third year of sobriety, his chronic health conditions were in good control, and his overall functioning was probably better than at any other time in his adult life. The housing first, harm reduction, integrated, on-site service model certainly provided what he needed, and I was deeply moved by his fortitude, persistence, warmth, and sense of humor. What I had a hard time accepting, however, was his disinterest—or rather, the very slow pace of his interest—in searching for his daughters and attempting to reconnect with them. My work with other Home Base clients had shown me that locating grown children can have a profound, usually positive effect on older men's sobriety and mental health treatment, as well as their quality of life after having lost contact because of homelessness. My previous career work in child and adolescent mental health had also shown me the deep and persistent wounds caused by parent loss and the potential for healing some of those grown children's wounds, or at least introducing some new and positive experiences with the estranged parent. A few of our clients had died of medical conditions or drug overdoses, and the city coroner in each case swiftly contacted their next of kin. I sat with some of those families and witnessed the pain of siblings and grown children who had given up hope years ago that their missing loved one was even alive. I wanted this potential healing for Berto, and for his daughters, but he was not prepared to address it. It was not on his emotional agenda, at least not yet, and I needed to accept this and understand it within the dynamics of his lifetime experience. Thankfully, peer consultation with the psychiatrist and nurse practitioner were key in helping me to examine my own priorities as distinct from the client's priorities and to deeply accept and support him on the path he chose. Clinically astute colleagues helped me to maintain self-awareness and appropriate management of my own responses to Berto, as well as to other clients, and I in turn supported them in the emotional issues raised in their professional roles.

REFERENCES

Bornstein, D. (2010). A plan to make homelessness history. The Opinion Pages, *New York Times*. Retrieved from http://opinionator.blogs.nytimes.com/2010/12/20/a-plan-to-make-homelessness-history/

DiClemente, C. C. (2003). *Addiction and change: How addictions develop and addicted people recover*. New York, NY: Guilford Press.

Fessler, P. (2011). *Ending homelessness: A model that just might work. Social Entrepreneurs: Taking on world problems*. Retrieved from www.npr.org/2011/03/07/134002013/ending-homelessness-a-model-that-just-might-work

Kelling, G. L. (2013). How New York became safe: The full story. *City Journal*. Retrieved from www.city-journal.org/2009/nytom_ny-crime-decline.html

National Alliance to End Homelessness. (2006). *What is housing first?* Washington, DC: Author.

NREPP, SAMHSA's National Registry of Evidence-Based Programs and Practices. (2013, April). Retrieved from www.nrepp.samhsa.gov/ViewIntervention.aspx?id=87

Repeatable Battery for the Assessment of Neuropsychological Status (RBANS) Instrument. (2013, April). Retrieved from www.pearsonassessments.com/HAIWEB/Cultures/enus/Productdetail.htm?Pid=RBANS_UPDATE&Mode=summary

Case Study 6-4

Treating Geriatric Depression in the Context of Caregiving

KRISTEN GUSTAVSON

This case tackles two related issues for the elderly: depression and caregiving. It is a timely case study as social workers address the issues of the aging population.

Questions:

1. How does the social worker integrate the strategies of both case management and problem solving therapy in this case?
2. How did this approach to treatment fit with the social worker's personal preferences?
3. How did the social worker organize her approach in working on this case?
4. What were the key ingredients of success in this case study?

BACKGROUND

Roberta was a 69-year-old, never-married woman who sought therapy for her depression. She reported "being in a funk all the time," having trouble sleeping, and being overwhelmed by the demands of caring for her 62-year-old brother, Jonathan, who had long been disabled by bipolar disorder. Roberta's mother, Edna, had been Jonathan's caregiver his whole life, but when she died one year ago after a long battle with

Parkinson's disease, his care fell primarily to Roberta and secondarily to her sister, Geraldine, who lives further away from Jonathan than Roberta and has children of her own for whom she is primary caregiver. Because Roberta has never been married and has no children, the family assumed she would take over Jonathan's care, but this was never discussed. Roberta had been employed for many years as a clerk in a local bookstore, but she was severely injured by an uninsured driver in a car accident 13 years ago and was forced to retire early on disability. As a result, Roberta has very limited financial resources.

Roberta resides in a one-bedroom apartment and has just received notice that her rent is being increased. She lives in an expensive community and, while the rent used to be affordable, the complex changed owners five years ago and her rent, which had been stable for 20 years, has been increased incrementally every year over the past five years to the point that she now feels she cannot afford to remain there and "feels overwhelmed" by the thought of leaving her home and community of more than 25 years.

Jonathan recently moved into Roberta's apartment and is sleeping on her couch. The move was necessitated by the need to get their mother's home ready to sell. The home needs a significant amount of work, but their mother owned it outright, and it is in a desirable neighborhood. The proceeds will be split between the three kids, which will help, but there is concern that Johnny will lose all of the medical and disability benefits, which he is used to and on which he depends, if he suddenly inherits some money from the sale of his mother's house.

Roberta states that, "we don't really get along." She sees her brother as very rigid in both his personality and expectations. Their mother "did everything for him," according to Roberta, and she feels that he expects Roberta to do the same. Roberta states, "I know Johnny has problems, but he has never worked and never lifted a finger. It's no wonder things never get better for him." In the past month, Roberta and Jonathan have argued frequently about "everything," and Roberta tearfully states, "I'm not sure how much longer I can take all this." Jonathan is relatively healthy but is easily distracted and "doesn't do anything for himself" according to Roberta. "He didn't clean up after himself, cook, or do anything when he lived with mom, and now he thinks I'm just going to take over," Roberta states through gritted teeth. Roberta reports that her brother's care was "just sort of thrust upon me" and that there is no short-term or long-term plan for his ongoing care needs beyond sleeping on her couch until her mother's house sells.

Roberta has several strengths and resources that have helped her through this difficult time since the loss of her mother. She is on the Board of Directors of the City Library where she lives, and she finds great pleasure in still being involved in "the world of books," as she calls it. She has recovered significantly from her car accident of 13 years ago and is able to walk and take care of herself independently, but she now gets periodic migraine headaches, which she says, "totally derail my whole day. I have to take medication that basically knocks me out, and I have to stay in the dark for many hours until the headache passes." She didn't get these headaches prior to the car accident, but since then gets them as frequently as twice a week, but usually once per week on average. The headaches prevented her from getting a job, as did the long road of recovery from her other injuries, which required years of physical therapy and three surgeries. Even so, Roberta feels optimistic about her recovery from the accident and often talks about "how far I've come." She says, "I can live with the migraines because they aren't every day. I can still have a life."

Furthermore, Roberta has lived and been involved in her community for almost three decades, so she has several close friends and many acquaintances, from the Library Board, for example, who have been a good source of support for her since her mother's death. She used to go out to eat with friends a couple times per week, but with her increased rent she has felt the need to cut back on that. She has further limited her time with friends over the past month since her brother moved in, because "he makes me feel guilty when I leave him to go out, but he's rude to my friends when they come over." For example, she was a part of a regular bridge circle for which hosting rotated, but she was so embarrassed when she hosted this week and her brother interrupted their game with this long rant about "oversexualized old ladies causing trouble" that she ended the game early and didn't attend the next meeting. So overall, Roberta reports that her social support has been significantly reduced because of finances and her brother. Roberta says, "Lately, I feel so alone, even though Johnny is here all the time."

Roberta stated that she thinks about dying, "mostly because I miss mom so much," but she denies suicidal ideation or intent. However, she did emphasize that "I can't continue to live like this—something has got to change."

When discussing therapeutic options with the client, we selected case management in conjunction with Problem-Solving Treatment (PST) as the most salient interventions at this time. The client has several unmet needs that may be addressed by case management. Furthermore, the client was adamant about "I need help, but I'm not crazy," and so refused any kind of talk therapy, stating, "I need practical help, not mumbo-jumbo." The structured behavioral nature of PST may be a good fit for this client. It is not unusual for older adults to seek social or behavioral approaches to treat their depression as they tend to embrace social and behavioral causes as the reason for their symptoms in the first place (Barg et al., 2006; Givens et al., 2006). It is known that a precipitating event is often the stressor for the onset of most mental health issues and disorders, with a significant loss being a common triggering event for those who suffer from depression. However, research also supports that taking on a stressful caregiving role also commonly contributes to the development and continuation of depression, with older adults being at particular risk given the caregiving needs of this population (Smith, Williamson, Miller, & Schulz, 2011). Although Roberta, the client in this case, reported moderately severe symptoms of depression, she was highly motivated and open to "practical" help for her issues.

OVERVIEW OF THE INTERVENTIONS: CLINICAL CASE MANAGEMENT AND PROBLEM-SOLVING TREATMENT

Clinical Case Management

Clinical case management has been in existence since the 1960s and thus is not a new model of care. Although several approaches to clinical case management exist, they all share in common the goal of improving quality of life through linkage and advocacy. Surber (1994) describes case management as a process of care that occurs in three stages: (1) comprehensive assessment and action planning; (2) linkage and monitoring of service use and advocacy; and (3) care coordination. Case managers—in Roberta's case a clinical social worker—collect information about unmet needs from a variety of sources, such as clients, family members, and existing providers. From this information, case managers, in collaboration with clients, create an action plan to overcome barriers that interfere with meeting needs. Once the plan is created, the case manager uses it to create a link between clients and the services they need. The case manager then monitors the clients' use of services, encouraging them to attend programs, complete needed forms, or any task that would help overcome their problems. Case managers often set up calls or appointments as part of their collaboration on the case management care plan. Case managers continue to advocate for clients and coordinate services to address their needs until case management assistance is no longer needed.

Problem-Solving Treatment

Problem-solving treatment (PST) is a brief form of evidence-based behavioral psychotherapy. PST has been used since the 1970s as a standalone intervention. It has been studied extensively in a wide range of settings and with a variety of providers and patient populations, and more than 80 peer-reviewed articles on its use have been published (Areán, 2012; Bell & D'Zurilla, 2009). Several of these studies have specifically shown the efficacy of this intervention with depressed older adults (Alexopoulos et al., 2011; Areán, Raue, & Julian, 2003; Areán et al., 2010).

Although there are many different types of PST, they are all based on the same principle of resolving depression by reengaging clients in active problem solving and activities. However, most types of PST involve the following specific stages:

1. Selecting and defining the problem
2. Establishing realistic and achievable goals
3. Generating alternative solutions
4. Implementing decision-making guidelines
5. Evaluating and choosing solutions
6. Implementing the preferred solution
7. Evaluating the outcome

An important underlying assumption of PST is that everyone has problems; problems are a part of life and not something to be avoided. In fact, PST can help improve clients' coping and problem-solving skills, give them a sense of accomplishment, help them begin to think more positively, and ultimately climb out of the depths of depression. Successful PST reinforces the rationale that our mood can be improved as a result of problem-solving efforts. PST can help reverse the downward spiral of depression and foster skills that clients can use to address ongoing and future problems that are sure to arise.

Roberta was seen on 13 occasions for about four months. The framework of her sessions was such that she received an initial in-depth assessment of about two hours, and subsequent sessions were shorter (average 45 minutes), with about 30 minutes of that time spent on PST activities and about 15 minutes on case management activities. This structure remained in place for the first 6 weeks, at which time most case management needs were resolved. The remaining sessions were therefore shorter in length (average 30 minutes) and were spent primarily on PST-related activities. The last session was spent debriefing the therapeutic work and establishing a relapse-prevention plan with the client.

Sessions were typically structured in the following format:

1. Set session agenda (1–2 minutes)
2. Check-in: client updates, symptom check, new events (5–7 minutes)
3. PST activities (evaluate action plan, work on new problem: 25–30 minutes)
4. Case management activities (5–10 minutes)
5. Feedback and wrap-up (2 minutes)

Roberta completed the PHQ-9 (Pfizer, 2005) before each session to provide a check-in on symptoms and a marker of progress. The social worker discussed the PHQ-9 with the client and kept track of weekly scores.

THE COURSE OF THERAPY

The first session involved an in-depth assessment from which much of the client information was obtained. Rather than using myriad intake forms, the structure of this initial assessment was more free-form and allowed for fluid discussion across a variety of directed topics (e.g., health, family, work, spirituality). Roberta's initial PHQ-9 was a 16, indicating moderately severe depression. The client endorsed the following symptoms: (a) feeling down, depressed or hopeless, (b) trouble falling or staying asleep, or sleeping too much, (c) feeling tired or having little energy, (d) feeling bad about yourself—or that you are a failure or have let yourself or your family down, (e) trouble concentrating on things such as reading the newspaper or watching television, and (f) little interest or pleasure in doing things. Roberta also said that her symptoms made it very difficult for her to take care of things at home and get along with other people. Roberta reported having had these symptoms for about 3 to 4 weeks, since around the time her brother moved into her apartment, though she did state, "I had already been feeling poorly before that, so maybe really since Mom died a year ago."

Following the in-depth assessment, the social worker spent significant time toward the end of the first session orienting the client to PST and specifically to a problem-solving orientation of depression (the idea that solving problems improves mood). The social worker explained the work of PST, including homework and weekly action plans, which Roberta found practical and was willing to do. From the initial assessment, the client and social worker formulated a one-page Problem List, from which they would choose one problem to work on each week as a part of PST activities. Furthermore, they also made a list of Unmet Case Management Needs, which the client ranked in terms of importance and included such items as: (1) finding low-income or subsidized senior housing in Roberta's community, (2) finding group housing options for Jonathan, and (3) finding utility-bill subsidies for low-income seniors.

In the second session, the client's PHQ-9 score remained a 16 with no change in the client's symptoms. However, the client was motivated for change and wanted to discuss how she might feel better. In order to help Roberta learn the PST model—and also with the hope that she would experience some initial success in solving her own problems—Roberta was encourage to choose an easy problem off the Problem List. Roberta decided that she would work on the problem of her recent social isolation. She defined the problem as "not getting out of the house and seeing people as often as I used to" and set a goal of doing something fun with a friend for the next week. As the social worker and Roberta discussed the problem, it became clear that Roberta wasn't ready to go back to her bridge group, because she was still so embarrassed by her brother's behavior with them and wasn't sure how to handle it. She also needed to make sure the social activity was free or low cost and brainstormed options with the social worker surrounding that requirement. After reviewing the pros and cons of possible solutions, the client decided that she would attend a free community concert and that she would bring a small picnic to share and invite a friend, not giving up until she found someone who was willing and able to join her. She made a list of several friends whom she could invite and planned to call them one by one as soon as the session was completed.

One thing researchers and clinicians know about implementing PST action plans is that they tend to be more successful the sooner they are implemented following the crafting of the plan. Furthermore, such plans also tend to be more successful if potential obstacles have been thoroughly addressed and planned around (Nezu, 1986). Roberta knew she couldn't simply invite a friend to dinner because of her financial limitations, and she was also accounting for a friend or two being unavailable or uninterested in the community concert by having a list of potential attendees ready when she began phoning them. The social worker also brought up Roberta's earlier comment that she felt guilty about leaving her brother, and they worked out a plan for discussing her leaving her brother alone while she attended the concert. The social worker also committed to exploring the low-income and subsidized senior housing options in Roberta's community and compiling a list for their next session. In terms of addressing Roberta's case management needs, the social worker promised to compile a similar list of group/supportive housing options for Roberta's brother.

In evaluating Roberta's progress and symptoms the following week (an important step of PST), Roberta's PHQ-9 score had dropped substantially (from 16 to 11), with Roberta reporting less severe or fewer symptoms in all areas except sleep. Roberta reported successfully completing her action plan to attend the community concert with a friend. She reported that she first called Joan, who had other plans, but who invited her to a church organ recital the following week. She next called Teresa, who came to the concert with Roberta, and they had a great time. Furthermore, Roberta reported that she told her brother about her plan to attend the concert, and that when he said, "You just hate spending time with me," she calmly replied, "If you feel that way, then perhaps it's time for you to find another place to stay." This response "stopped Jonathan in his tracks, because he's so used to getting a rise out of me. I think it made him scared that I might kick him out. He actually put his plates in the dishwasher all week without me having to nag him. I think he's on his best behavior."

Roberta was clearly empowered by this small step with Jonathan and felt relieved that her friends had missed her. She articulated that she had been secretly feeling that everyone had forgotten about her, but after calling Joan and Teresa, she realized they had been thinking about her, but that "people just get busy with their lives and forget to call." Roberta told Teresa about her struggles with her brother, and Teresa, who has long been a supportive friend, offered to pray for Roberta, which deepened their interaction and friendship. Roberta stated, "It just felt good to get out of the house."

In addressing the client's case management needs, the social worker brought a list of subsidized or low-income senior apartments. The social worker and Roberta discussed these housing options for Roberta in detail, and Roberta decided that "finding housing" was the problem she wanted to address during this session now that she had more information on what her options were. She was encouraged in looking at the list provided by her social worker that there were three low-income senior housing complexes within her town and five more in nearby suburbs. She had been convinced she would have to move out of her "nice neighborhood and into someplace shoddy" and was pleased to learn that there were affordable options nearby. Roberta defined her problem as "having housing that was too expensive," and her goal was to begin to take steps to secure less expensive housing. After brainstorming possible solutions, she decided that she could go see the three nearest low-income senior housing complexes within the next week and add her name to waiting lists and obtain applications if possible. She didn't think she could make it easily in just 1 week to the other five complexes that were farther away, but felt this would be a good place to start, especially in light of her social worker reminding her that her PST action plan should be realistic and achievable within the week. In terms of ongoing case management needs, the social worker agreed to obtain information for Roberta on establishing a Special Needs Trust for her brother so that he wouldn't lose his disability and medical benefits as a result of inheritance from the upcoming sale of their mother's house. In addition, the social worker committed to exploring attorney recommendations for Roberta regarding her brother's needs and care.

Case management needs that the social worker addressed over the next few sessions included:

- Connected the client's family with an attorney to oversee their mother's estate and the establishment of the Special Needs Trust for Jonathan. The attorney also agreed to delay invoicing the family for services until the money from the sale of the family home was in receipt.
- Received permission to work with Jonathan's case manager on a permanent housing plan. Jonathan's case manager found a supportive living environment for Jonathan, and the Special Needs Trust enables him to have a private room.
- Connected the client to benefits for low-income seniors with three local utility providers. The electric company also provided the client's landlord with a rebate to replace the old and inefficient refrigerator, which helped further reduce the client's utility bills.

232 CASE STUDIES IN PREVENTING PROBLEMS

A significant unmet case management need remained when the client's sessions ended: She still needed stable low-income housing and remained on waiting lists for such units. However, the sale of her mother's house was pending at the time of termination, and Roberta had hope that the income from that sale would relieve some more of her financial burden. Furthermore, she had felt some relief with the reduction of utility bills via senior subsidies, her brother gave her $200 for "room and board" from his meager disability benefits, and so she was making ends meet despite continued financial limitations.

Some of the problems and goals that the client successfully worked to address with PST in her sessions with the social workers included: (a) planning Jonathan's short- and long-term care in partnership with Jonathan and Geraldine; (b) finding and joining a support group for family members who have lost loved ones to Parkinson's disease; (c) reengaging in social relationships outside of the home; (d) obtaining a neurological consult regarding treatment for the migraine headaches; (e) reengaging in once-pleasurable activities outside of the home; and (f) participating in a sleep-hygiene clinic in order to improve sleep habits. Over the course of Roberta's treatment, her PHQ-9 score continued to drop until week 9 when it was a 4, where it held for the final three sessions, with sleep problems and lack of energy being the only reported symptoms.

One problem that Roberta was able to address, albeit with resistance, was her goal of getting her brother into a supportive living environment. Jonathan was vocally resistant to this idea and waffled between attempting to make Roberta feel guilty and being angry over his perception that she was abandoning him. A family conference with Roberta, Jonathan, their sister Geraldine, and Jonathan's case manager helped ease Jonathan's resistance and anxiety. Roberta's social worker connected her with a weekend of caregiver respite benefits through a local caregiver support agency. These benefits allowed Roberta to go on a women's retreat with her friend Teresa's church while Jonathan spent the weekend in a supportive group care setting. Surprisingly, Jonathan liked the facility, especially the cooking and the big-screen television. Upon Roberta's return, Jonathan agreed to live in the group home if Roberta could make sure that he could have his own room. Geraldine agreed to cover the extra cost of Jonathan having his own room until their mother's house sold. The Special Needs Trust set up by the family attorney and Jonathan's case manager worked together to secure Jonathan a place in the group home, where he permanently moved to during Roberta's 10th week of treatment.

Although Jonathan transitioned well, Roberta expressed guilt over not being able to have him live with her, stating, "I wish I loved him enough." In that session, she chose to work on the problem of being less connected to her brother after he moves out. She decided she needed to identify ways to continue to spend time with her brother. Roberta chose to talk to Jonathan about choosing one caring thing she could do for him each week and one fun thing they could do together. Jonathan asked Roberta to continue to manage his finances for him and asked her to have a meal with him at least once a week. Roberta was able to agree to these requests, maintaining her role as a caregiver for Jonathan and spending quality time with him as his sister.

SOCIAL WORKER REFLECTIONS

Working with Roberta was very satisfying for me, as I am someone who is results rather than process oriented. If you are someone who enjoys more high-process therapies, then the structure of PST may be frustrating. However, in keeping with the social work value of starting where the client is, PST was an appropriate choice for Roberta and just happened to also fit well with my own personality as a social worker and therapist. In this case, as with others, I have found the timing of case management linkages to at times be frustrating (lots of waiting for resources to connect), so it was helpful to be able to address other client concerns simultaneously. One challenge for me as a therapist is that PST is not particularly cognitively inclined. Specifically, I mean that this therapy is brief and not designed to spend time exploring the history and insights into problems that may be patterns for clients. For example, it was clear to me that some of the problems surrounding Roberta and her brother were a result of lifelong family patterns that we did not have the opportunity to explore in our brief and limited PST sessions. However, it was important to remind myself that the goal was to see improvement in Roberta's depression, which was achieved even without the focus on the deeper history or insights into individual problems or patterns. Besides, Roberta was clear that she wanted "practical help," not "mumbo-jumbo." So, while I recognize the limits of the combined case management PST approach, I feel positively about our work together. I have also heard other social workers express common stereotypes about working with older adults, such as, "Old people are just so set in their ways." Roberta's case and my larger experience as a geriatric social worker contradict this common misconception. Older adults, as all humans, are able to make meaningful changes and improvements in their lives.

CONCLUSIONS

This account illustrates the combined use of clinical case management and problem-solving treatment in addressing late-life depression. Roberta's symptoms began with the loss of her mother to Parkinson's disease and got progressively worse when her mentally ill adult brother moved in with her and she became his primary caregiver. Through careful clinical assessment in collaboration with the client, the intervention strategies were selected to maximize client engagement and therapeutic alliance.

Ample research supports the combination of case management and PST as treatment for late-life depression (Gum, Areán, & Bostrom, 2007; Unützer et al., 2007). Roberta thrived under this therapeutic combination of interventions, given her preference for behavioral or "practical" interventions. Behavioral changes are often enough to improve the symptoms of depression. Furthermore, with PST the client strengthens existing and develops new problem-solving skills that are particularly useful, especially in light of ongoing caregiving needs and stressors. Relapse prevention is an important part of any depression treatment, and clients need to be reminded that they will continue to have problems because problems are a normal part of life. It is also likely that clients will end treatment with one or more problems unresolved. However, they are now better equipped to solve their problems and improve their depression on their own.

It is also important to remind clients to periodically check their symptoms (perhaps by sending them home with several blank PHQ-9 forms) in order to make sure they are maintaining their depression-free progress.

REFERENCES

Alexopoulos, G. S., Raue, P. J., Kiosses, D. N., Mackin, R. S., Kanellopoulos, D., McCulloch, C., & Areán, P. A. (2011). Problem-solving therapy and supportive therapy in older adults with major depression and executive dysfunction: Effect on disability. *Archives of General Psychiatry, 68*(1), 33–41.

Areán, P. A. (2012, December 20). *National Network of PST Clinicians, Trainers & Researchers: Publications.* Retrieved from National Network of PST Clinicians, Trainers & Researchers: http://pstnetwork.ucsf.edu/publications

Areán, P. A., Raue, P. J., & Julian, L. J. (2003). *Social problem-solving therapy for depression and executive dysfunction.* San Francisco: University of California, San Francisco.

Areán, P. A., Raue, P., Mackin, R. S., Kanellopoulos, D., McCulloch, C., & Alexopoulos, G. S. (2010). Problem-solving therapy and supportive therapy in older adults with major depression and executive dysfunction. *American Journal of Psychiatry, 167*(11), 1391–1398.

Barg, F. K., Huss-Ashmore, R., Wittink, M. N., Murray, G. F., Bogner, H. R., & Gallo, J. J. (2006). A mixed-methods approach to understanding loneliness and depression in older adults. *Journal of Gerontology, 61B*(6), S329–S339.

Bell, A. C., & D'Zurilla, T. J. (2009). Problem-solving therapy for depression: A meta-analysis. *Clinical Psychology Review, 29,* 348–353. doi:10.1016/j.cpr.2009.02.003

Givens, J. L., Datto, C. J., Ruckdeschel, K., Knott, K., Zubritsky, C., Oslin, D. W., . . . Barg, F. K. (2006). Older patients' aversion to antidepressants: A qualitative study. *Journal of General Internal Medicine, 21,* 146–151.

Gum, A.M., Areán, P.A., & Bostrom, A. (2007). A. Low-income depressed older adults with psychiatric Comorbidity. Secondary analyses of response to psychotherapy and case management. *International Journal of Geriatric Psychiatry, 22,* 124–130. DOI: 10.1002/gps.1702

Nezu, A. M. (1986). Efficacy of a social problem-solving approach for unipolar depression. *Consulting and Clinical Psychology, 54*(2), 196–202.

Pfizer. (2005). Patient Health Questionnaire (PHQ-9). PRIME-MD.

Smith, G. R., Williamson, G. M., Miller, L. S., & Schulz, R. (2011). Depression and quality of informal care: A longitudinal investigation of caregiving. *Psychology and Aging, 26*(3), 584–591. doi:10.1037/a0022263+

Unützer J., Patrick D. L., Simon G., Grembowski, D., Walker, E., Rutter, C., & Katon, W. (2007). Depressive symptoms and the cost of health services in HMO patients aged 65 years and older. *Journal of the American Medical Association, 277,* 1618–1623.

Surber, R. (1994). *Clinical case management: A guide to comprehensive treatment of serious mental illness.* Thousand Oaks, CA: Sage.

Case Study 6-5

The Go Grrrls Program: Universal Prevention for Early Adolescent Girls

CRAIG WINSTON LECROY

Adolescent girls face unique challenges as they grow up in today's society. This case describes the development of a group program specifically designed to address these unique challenges.

Questions
1. What developmental issues confront early adolescent girls?
2. What biopsychosocial interactions impact early adolescent girls?
3. How was the program designed to address developmental concerns?
4. How could you implement this type of program in your community?

The decibel level rises as the last bell rings. Junior high students flood the hallways, their voices loud, and their laughter echoing off the walls. The participants in our new after-school program find their way to the alcove by the school entrance, where we wait to meet and greet them. Slowly they trickle in, girls of a remarkable variety of shapes, sizes, skin tones, and levels of development. I think to myself that, during the course of this program, I hope my co-leader and I can help all of them to appreciate their unique-ness and natural vitality.

In recent months, several popular authors have captured the attention of parents, teachers, administrators, and mental health professionals by outlining the challenges adolescent girls face in today's society. Through exposure to media stereotypes of women, girls feel cultural pressure to adhere to an absurd "ideal" of thinness. They watch television programs in which women are frequently given roles as passive, sexual beings. As they begin to mature, girls may find that their families and school environments offer less encouragement for them to participate in the classroom, in sports programs, or in other extracurricular activities. All of these elements affect girls during a time of rapid and sometimes perplexing physiological change. Potential manifestations of these combined cultural and developmental factors include increasing incidences among adolescent girls of eating disorders, substance abuse, teen pregnancy, depression, lowered self-esteem, and decreasing levels of confidence and assertiveness.

Early adolescence appears to be a particularly harrowing time for many girls. Pipher (1995), author of the popular work *Reviving Ophelia*, has stated that "American culture has always smacked girls on the head in early adolescence" (p. 23) and that for girls, "junior high (seems) like a crucible" (p. 11). Her contention is supported by research showing that, at all grade levels, boys have significantly higher self-esteem than girls (LeCroy, 2008a).

In addition to differences in self-esteem, adolescent girls' assessment of their body image satisfaction ranks lower than boys' satisfaction at all age levels (LeCroy & Daley, 2001). When young girls develop the belief that they are unhappy with their bodies and that there is little they can do about it, they can develop feelings of helplessness and hopelessness. Dissatisfaction with one's body image has been found to be associated with higher levels of depression (Kerr, 2010). Furthermore, girls who feel negatively about their bodies during early adolescence appear to be more likely to develop eating problems (Shroff & Thompson, 2006). The cultural ideal of female thinness has even greater effect on early-maturing girls, who tend to display the most dissatisfaction with their weight (Graber, Petersen, & Brooks-Gunn, 1996; LeCroy, 2008a).

There appear to be gender differences in the friendship networks of adolescents, with girls placing greater expectations on their friends and rating friendships as more intimate than boys rate their friendships (Besag, 2006). Close friendships offer girls an important sense of connectedness that may be critical to their development (LeCroy, 2008a). However, as girls experience society's lack of respect for such intimacy, they begin to struggle with competing choices between independence and responsiveness or connectedness. This, according to Gilligan, leads them to "silence" their "different voices" (Gilligan, Rogers, & Brown, 1990). Helping young girls bring to their relationships a strong, assertive, and authentic self while valuing their ability for intimate relationships is critical to healthy development. Close friendships enhance a girl's sense of self-worth and help facilitate more accurate understanding of others.

This research suggests that a need exists for programs designed specifically for adolescent girls. The *Go Grrrls* program seeks to address the unique challenges that early adolescent girls encounter by providing them with practical instruction and skill-building exercises. We have chosen seventh graders as our target population in the hope that we can provide a sort of inoculation of knowledge and skill early enough that girls may resist some of the common hazards of growing up in a culture that seems, in many respects, to be toxic to females.

AN OVERVIEW OF THE PROGRAM

We have chosen a social skills training/psychoeducational program to be administered in a group format. Social skills training has been found to be effective in programs that are designed to prevent as well as remediate problems in living for adolescents (LeCroy, 2008b). A group format is both practical for reaching large numbers of girls and developmentally appropriate, as adolescents tend to strongly value social interaction with their peers.

As the girls settle into the meeting room on the first day, they are greeted by a large posterboard sign (see Figure 6.1). The sign is decorated like a jigsaw puzzle, and each of the six major topic areas of the project are delineated on its pieces: *being a girl; establishing a positive self-image; establishing independence; making and keeping friends; when it all seems like too much;* and *planning for the future.* Some of the group sessions (such as the session on problem solving) will emphasize skill building in areas that are equally pertinent to boys and girls, but the examples and role-plays used to illustrate the skills will emphasize girls as the major actors. Other sessions (such as the session on being a girl in today's society) are designed to address areas of special concern to adolescent girls. An outline of the 12 sessions is presented as follows, with a more in-depth description of each session (see LeCroy & Daley, 2001).

The 12 Sessions

    Week 1: Being a girl in today's society
        Session 1: Introductory session/pretest
        Session 2: Being a girl in today's society

    Week 2: Establishing a positive self-image
        Session 3: Rethinking self-statements
        Session 4: Body image

    Week 3: Establishing independence
        Session 5: Problem-solving strategies
        Session 6: Assertiveness skills

    Week 4: Making and keeping friends
        Session 7: Qualities of a friend
        Session 8: Making and keeping friends

    Week 5: When it all seems like too much
        Session 9: Straight talk about drugs
        Session 10: Where to go to get more help

    Week 6: Planning for the future
        Session 11: Visions for a strong future
        Session 12: Closure/review/posttest

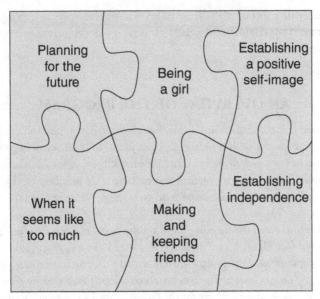

Figure 6.1 Content for the Go Grrrls Program

WEEK 1: BEING A GIRL IN TODAY'S SOCIETY

Session 1: Introductory Session/Pretest

The goals for the initial session are: (a) to create a supportive atmosphere and begin building cohesiveness within the group; (b) to collect baseline data for program evaluation; (c) to introduce participants to group standards such as confidentiality and respect for others; and (d) to introduce the program content. The girls fill out a questionnaire designed to assess their self-concept. Joan, a freckle-faced 12-year-old, looks up at me from her questionnaire and says, "Hey, this stuff is *personal*!" She's right, and her comment reminds me of the feminist stance that the personal is political.

We then play a "name game" to loosen everyone up and to help with introductions. Following the game, we help the girls to establish group standards by asking them to suggest their own rules for the group. If the group-generated rules do not include important areas (such as confidentiality), then the group leaders bring up these subjects. Finally, we introduce the program content by displaying a large poster with the "Go Grrrls" puzzle and encouraging each member to read one of the topics aloud. Finally, we distribute journals, which the girls are instructed to use to complete brief assignments for the group and to express themselves in any way they wish. The journals are a tool for helping the girls incorporate what they learn into their personal lives and provide a mechanism for encouraging them to continue their self-growth and discovery after the group ends.

Session 2: Being a Girl in Today's Society

This group is intended to promote awareness of the profusion of negative images of women and girls that abound in popular media, and to equip girls with the ability and confidence to critically challenge these cultural stereotypes. Group activities for this session include creating a collage culled from teen magazines and evaluating lyrics from hit songs. Activities from this session will be delineated in depth later in this chapter.

WEEK 2: ESTABLISHING A POSITIVE SELF-IMAGE
Session 3: Rethinking Self-Statements

An important part of our program is teaching girls about the relationship between self-esteem, self-criticism, and depression. As previously mentioned, girls entering the seventh grade show a significant decline in their overall self-esteem. This session is designed to teach girls how they can avoid setting unrealistic standards for themselves and can instead give themselves positive messages to facilitate realistic goal achievement.

Participants complete fill-in-the-blank handouts listing their unrealistic "I should" messages (see Figure 6.2). We then help them to change these messages to "I want" statements that are more constructive. Finally, we describe how negative thoughts tend to generate even more negative thoughts in a sort of downward spiral, whereas positive self-messages tend to lead to increased confidence, in an upward spiral. An example follows:

"I should" statement: I should be liked by everyone.

"I want" statement: I want to have good friends.

Session 4: Body Image

As described in the introduction, adolescent girls are likely to develop a negative body image, and negative body image tends to relate to low self-esteem and depression. The goals of this session are (a) to help girls accept their bodies as they are and develop a

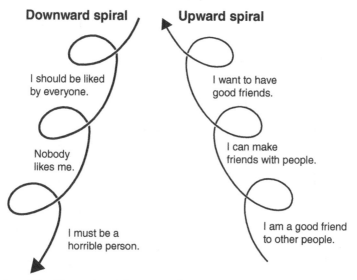

Figure 6.2   The Upward and Downward Spiral

positive body image; (b) to teach them that attractiveness is based on factors other than physical traits; and (c) to encourage girls to appreciate their unique qualities, talents, and skills.

We begin the group by asking participants to discuss the reasons that developing a positive body image is important for girls. We then embark on a series of image-boosting activities. In one such activity, girls are asked to make a list of five things they like about themselves and then share these things aloud in the group. Group leaders construct a chart of their responses as they are offered. The chart includes categories for physical aspects, social/personality traits, special skills and abilities, and cognitive abilities. Discussion then centers around the fact that each girl has a unique set of strengths in these different categories.

WEEK 3: ESTABLISHING INDEPENDENCE

Session 5: Problem-Solving Strategies

Adolescents often make decisions impulsively without considering the impact of their choices. Their decisions represent experimental attempts to acquire skills for dealing with new situations, but unfortunately these attempts may lead to serious consequences. Session five is truly a skill-building session, as we teach group members a method for solving problems and then ask them to practice this method.

Group leaders encourage members to discuss some unproductive ways that they have used to try to solve problems in the past (e.g., ignoring problems in the hope that they will just go away, or blaming someone else for the problem). Leaders then describe a five-step strategy for problem solving. Each girl receives a handout (see p. 241) delineating this process. The group divides into two smaller groups, each of which is given a hypothetical problem to solve. One such example follows:

> Your best, oldest friend asked you to sleep over at her house on Friday night, and you told her you could. On Thursday, though, a really popular girl at school invites you (and not your friend) to her party on Friday night. What do you do?

Session 6: Assertiveness Skills

Girls are often socialized to be accommodating to others. One positive result of this socialization is that girls may acquire sensitivity to others' emotions and may develop insight into the intricacies of relationships. One potentially negative result of this socialization is that they may overlook or disregard their own thoughts and feelings in an effort to "keep the peace," or conversely, they may become frustrated when authority figures or peers do not demonstrate understanding of their needs.

Session six attempts to teach girls about three different options for responding to situations: assertive, passive, and aggressive. Group leaders define these terms for members, and then participants are provided with scripts depicting assertive, passive, and aggressive responses to provocative remarks or situations. They role-play these scenes for the group, and all members are asked to identify which responses are assertive, passive, or aggressive. Scripts are designed with an introduction that sets up the dialogue, and all are tailored to reflect situations that early adolescent girls are likely to face. One example follows:

Introduction to Situation 1:
One thing that really helps girls to be successful is being involved in outside activities like sports, dancing, exercise, and community work. Sometimes when girls reach Junior High, they feel pressure to stop doing activities that they've enjoyed for many years. Many girls stop doing these things, not because they don't enjoy them anymore, but because they are afraid that their friends will think they're not cool if they keep doing them. Let's see what happens in this situation and how being assertive can help.

Situation 1:
Your ballet teacher invites you to perform at the annual dance recital. You are very excited about it, so you tell your best friend.

1: Hey, Linda, my ballet teacher just asked me to perform at the recital!
2: You aren't really gonna do it, are you? Recitals are for geeks.
Response 1: No, I guess not.
Response 2: Yeah, I am, and you're just jealous because you're a total klutz.
Response 3: I've worked really hard to get this chance and I'm excited about doing it.

Handout: Making Decisions and Solving Problems

Here are the steps you can use for problem solving:

1. Define the problem. (What is it?)
2. Brainstorm choices. (Think of every possible solution . . . even silly ones! Don't criticize any of them yet.)
3. Evaluate the choices. (What are the pros and cons of each choice?)
4. Make your decision. (Select the best idea.)
5. If your decision doesn't work out, start over again at #1!

After reviewing these steps, complete the following:

1. Define the problem.
   My problem is: _____
2. Brainstorm choices.
   I could: _____
3. Evaluate the choices. (Put a + or – beside each idea above.)
4. Make your decision.
   I decided to _____
   because _____
5. If your decision doesn't work out, start back at #1, and try another idea!

WEEK 4: MAKING AND KEEPING FRIENDS

Session 7: Qualities of a Friend

As mentioned in the introduction, adolescents are social beings. Adolescent girls in particular seem to value close friendships. Friendship provides a social support system that helps to bolster self-esteem, lessen depression, and ameliorate hard times. The goal of this session is to teach girls to focus less on popularity and more on developing intimate, satisfying friendships.

Participants are asked to brainstorm a list of qualities that a good friend might have. Each group member then fills out a "friendship want ad." A sample follows:

> Seeking a new friend: I am looking for someone to talk with and go rollerblading with. I would like someone who is friendly, outgoing, and funny. I think a friend is someone who you can tell secrets to, so I have to trust you.

Group leaders collect these ads, then randomly redistribute them. Each girl must then write a response to the friendship ad they receive. A sample response to the ad above might read:

> I am a very active person and would enjoy rollerblading. I agree with you about wanting a friend you can trust. In the past I have had friends who I trusted, but they told my other friends things I did not want shared. I promise to be a person you can trust. I like to talk about boys! And right now I am having a lot of trouble with my Mom. Let's meet and we can see what happens.

Session 8: Making and Keeping Friends

Making and keeping friends requires a high level of social skill. This session is designed to teach friendship skills and provide group members with an arena in which they can practice these skills. Group leaders help girls to identify and practice using tools to start conversations (e.g., making eye contact, asking someone a question, and saying something positive about the other person). We also discuss and practice how to communicate positive feelings and how to deal with friendship friction when it arises. In addition to role-plays, the girls brainstorm different ways to build, maintain, and mend friendships. They write these ideas down on strips of paper, then place them in a "friendship toolbox," which they decorate and keep.

WEEK 5: WHEN IT ALL SEEMS LIKE TOO MUCH

Session 9: Straight Talk About Drugs

In early adolescence, girls, but not boys, are attracted to tobacco and alcohol advertisements that promote the product with an attractive social image (Covell, Dion, &

Dion, 1994). Girls are beginning to smoke and drink at younger ages. In this session, we attempt to counter these pro-drug messages by asking the girls to create their own anti–substance abuse advertising campaigns. We also facilitate a brainstorming session in which the girls generate possible reasons that kids use drugs, as well as reasons not to use drugs. An important goal of the session is to help girls develop a healthy lifestyle.

Session 10: Where to Go to Get More Help

In this session we acknowledge that some problems (e.g., depression, domestic violence, drug abuse) require more rigorous attention than a five-step problem-solving strategy can provide. We teach the group members about how to seek help when "it all seems like too much." The girls create a personal phone directory, in which each participant lists the names and numbers of friends, relatives, school counselors, and local social service agencies. We present the group with a series of hypothetical situations such as the following:

> Kaitlin's mom and dad have been fighting a lot lately. Kaitlin's mom has even been to the hospital once. Kaitlin doesn't want to be in the house anymore. She has stayed with friends for a week at a time, but she is embarrassed about not going home. She is thinking of running away.

We ask the group members to identify as many resources as they can to secure help for each scenario.

WEEK 6: PLANNING FOR THE FUTURE

Session 11: Visions for a Strong Future

During this session, group leaders encourage each girl to develop a positive vision of what her future might look like. We ask girls to list three goals they would like to achieve, then we help them to write down tasks they could accomplish in the next 5 days, 5 months, and 5 years to help themselves reach those goals. For example, one participant listed the following goal and attendant tasks:

Goal 1: I would like to become a veterinarian.

Five-day task: I can call my uncle (who is a vet) and talk to him about volunteer work.

Five-month task: I can read books about animals and take biology.

Five-year task: I can try to get good grades so I can get into a good college.

Finally, we play a "Planning for the Future" game, in which each girl stands in front of the group and takes a turn at drawing herself performing one of her goals while the other group members guess what goal she is drawing.

Session 12: Review and Closure

Our goals for the final session are (a) to review and summarize topics covered during the course of the group; (b) to collect final data for program evaluation; and (c) to provide participants with a sense of closure and accomplishment at the end of the program. We give each girl a copy of the *Go Grrrls* jigsaw puzzle with all of the topics listed on it and briefly discuss what we learned in each session. Group leaders join in a party that includes pizza, music, and prizes. Finally, group leaders say goodbye to each member of their group, and provide an opportunity for group members to say goodbye to each other.

CONDUCTING A SESSION: A CLOSER LOOK

By the second session, the six girls in our group already seem to feel fairly comfortable with each other and with us. At this point, it is still important to build a sense of group cohesiveness, so we begin the session by asking if anyone can remember the name game we played in the opening session. "Sharp Shannon," a smart 13-year-old, declares that she can, and she proceeds to reel off everyone's name along with the positive adjective they chose to describe themselves. This serves as a good icebreaker activity, and the girls relax into the session.

It is important to note that this program has been designed for all junior high girls, not just at-risk students. Lily, a bright and confident track star, has already emerged as one of the group's natural leaders. We encourage her, as the other girls are more likely to accept information that comes from a respected peer than from us. After we review each other's names, Lily volunteers to read today's topic from the large puzzle. We begin each session by referring to the puzzle. This little ritual serves two purposes: (1) it reminds the group members of topics that we've covered previously; and (2) it ties the day's topic into the larger program. She reads "being a girl in today's society" aloud, and I explain that today we will be discussing some of the messages and stereotypes about women that abound in the media and popular culture.

We divide the girls into groups by having them count off by twos. We specifically decide to split the group using this method so that group members may get to know everyone better, and not just one close friend whom they choose to sit beside at the start of the group. Each group will engage in a separate activity, and then we will bring the groups together to share what they have learned.

My co-leader instructs half of the girls to forage through a stack of popular magazines and construct a collage depicting media images of the "ideal woman." My half of the group huddles around a boom box listening to the lyrics of two songs: one rap and one country. I instruct them to listen for messages about what women "should" be like, and to write these messages down, graffiti-style, on a large poster. The songs are familiar to them, and they begin to dance around the room to the tunes. I spread some magic markers around the table and let them dance through the first half of the song, then I pass out the lyrics, which we have printed in advance.

They like these songs, and that's okay. We are not trying to stop them from listening to any single song or genre of music. We are, however, trying to help them listen to messages they are exposed to with a more critical ear. The songs end, and while I rewind to play them over again, I ask the girls what kinds of messages they heard about women. I'm glad that I just "let go" while they danced around, because now they are ready to work.

"You're supposed to be sexy," offers Eileen, a girl who has been very quiet so far. I tell her to pick a marker and write it down on the graffiti poster. We play the tunes over again, and this time the girls huddle around the poster, freely scribbling media messages. They've gotten the spirit of the exercise now, and they are writing upside-down and sideways and using all different colors. Words like "easy" and "hoochie mama" (!) appear beside phrases like "be a perfect mom" and "good cook." We did, after all, choose two very different songs to reflect these messages.

When the two groups have finished their tasks, we bring them together to share their findings. Each group can point to and be proud of a tangible product. Claire, a forthright student, volunteers to speak for the collage group. She points to several images of supermodels and notes that they are all tall and skinny. Anne, a girl with East Indian ancestry, adds, "Yeah, and most of them are white, too." "That's right," Claire responds, "and nobody has zits, and their teeth are all perfectly straight and real white." From these responses, I understand that they are comparing *themselves* to the airbrushed images on the page. (When women my age look at these images, we tend to notice that no one appears old enough to drive, and certainly no one has wrinkles.) I don't point out this self-comparison yet, as I want to let both groups share their information before we begin coming to any conclusions.

The whole group giggles as Claire points out an ad they have included in their collage. "You can even buy rubber boobs to make yourself look bigger, or a rubber butt to make yours look firmer!" There is a collective shriek in the room in response to these revelations.

Not surprisingly, Lily volunteers to speak for the music group. I am glad that we split the group in two to give Claire a chance to show her leadership abilities. Lily reads from the graffiti the girls have scribbled while listening to the familiar songs:

> Some stuff that we thought they are saying is, like, you've gotta be sexy . . . and you're supposed to be easy, but then you're bad, like a "hoochie mama," if you do stuff. Then you're supposed to take care of your house and your husband and kids . . . but you're supposed to wear make-up while you do.

They all nod and laugh. Now it is time to discuss the implications of the girls' findings. Although it would be easier to simply point out the fact that no one really matches the absurd media ideal, we want the girls themselves to come up with this idea. We lead them to the point with some open-ended questions. "What do the magazines and music lyrics have in common?" my co-leader asks. They review the traits and stereo-typed behaviors and roles that they uncovered, and, as leaders, we ensure that the word *stereotype* arises and is defined. (It is important to remember that our participants have a wide range of vocabulary levels.)

Then we ask the million-dollar question: "What happens when we compare our-selves to these stereotypes?" Until now, no one in the room has actually stated that she *does* compare herself to the stereotypes. We are reaching for a deeper understanding now, and the girls become more quiet and serious.

"Well, you feel bad. And there's stuff you can't do anything about. I mean, I know I'm never gonna be tall. Everybody in my family is short," Eileen offers. Her comments open the door, and other group members begin to reveal more personal comparisons. One already slender girl admits that she is on a diet right now. The others tell her that she looks great the way she is. We have reached a true work stage for the first time in this program.

We let these revelations unfold for as long as we can, but it is important that we don't close the group on this note, so we help summarize the discussion. We note that many girls and women strive to look or act like the media stereotypes, and when they cannot, they end up feeling frustrated, disappointed in themselves, and sometimes depressed. We ask them how many women they know in their real lives who look or act like the so-called ideal woman from the magazines and music. No one knows any such person.

We wrap up the group with a discussion of what the girls admire about the real women in their lives—teachers, parents, aunts, or others. We discuss the fact that the media stereotypes of women are not only unattainable, but also undesirable in many ways. We close the group by discussing the fact that it's okay to want to look and feel good, but that it's important to learn to accept who we are and what we look like.

CONCLUSIONS

Adolescent girls face an environment that often ends up being toxic to their healthy development. Our culture continues to portray successful and happy women as thin, long-legged, and beautiful. Body image problems become significant in early adolescence and can last a lifetime. Many girls begin to become obsessed with their bodies and develop serious eating disorders. Others simply become unhappy and develop feelings of depression. Adolescent girls present unique challenges, and the *Go Grrrls* program is designed to help confront those challenges and prepare girls for a healthier and happier lifestyle (LeCroy & Daley, 2001).

Using empirical studies that identify the developmental issues that impact early adolescent girls the most, a psychoeducational skills training program was designed. Further testing of the program (LeCroy, 2004a, 2004b) found evidence of program effectiveness, and the program was identified as a promising and effective program by the RAND Corporation. Based on practical instruction and skill building, our program provides an inoculation of knowledge and skills to help girls cope with the pressures of growing up in today's culture. It promotes the positive assets of adolescent girls and addresses relevant developmental issues. In a group format designed to build social support, the program builds skills in six critical areas: being a girl in today's society, establishing a positive self-image, establishing independence, making and keeping friends, when it all seems like too much, and planning for the future—critical pieces that compose the whole puzzle of *Go Grrrls: Building strengths for the future.*

REFERENCES

Besag, V. (2006). *Understanding girls' friendships, fights and feuds: A practical approach to girls' bullying.* New York, NY: Open University Press.

Covell, K., Dion, K. L., & Dion, K. K. (1994). Gender differences in evaluations of tobacco and alcohol advertisements. *Canadian Journal of Behavioral Sciences, 26,* 404–420.

Gilligan, C., Rogers, A., & Brown, L. M. (1990). Soundings into development. In C. Gilligan, N. P. Lyons, & T. J. Hanmer (Eds.), *Making connections: The relational worlds of adolescent girls at the Emma Willard School.* Cambridge, MA: Harvard University Press.

Graber, J. A., Petersen, A. C., & Brooks-Gunn, J. (1996). Pubertal processes: Methods, measures and models. In J. A. Graber, J. Brooks-Gunn, & A. C. Petersen (Eds.), *Transitions through adolescence: Interpersonal domains and context.* Mahwah, NJ: Lawrence Erlbaum.

Kerr, K. L. (2010). Sociocultural influences on body image and depression in adolescent girls. *Priscilla Papers, 24,* 8–16.

LeCroy, C. W. (2004a). Evaluation of a empowerment program for early adolescent girls. *Adolescence, 39,* 427–441.

LeCroy, C. W. (2004b). Experimental evaluation of the 'Go Grrrls' preventive intervention for early adolescent girls. *Journal of Primary Prevention, 25,* 457–473.

LeCroy, C. W. (2008a). Evidence-based treatment manuals: Some practical considerations. In C. W. LeCroy (Ed.), *Handbook of evidence-based child and adolescent treatment manuals.* New York, NY: Oxford University Press.

LeCroy, C. W. (2008b). Social skills training: A treatment manual. In C. W. LeCroy (Ed.), *Handbook of evidence-based child and adolescent treatment manuals.* New York, NY: Oxford University Press.

LeCroy, C. W., & Daley, J. (2001). *Empowering adolescent girls: Examining the present and building skills for the future with the Go Grrrls program.* New York, NY: W. W. Norton.

Pipher, M. (1995). *Reviving Ophelia: Saving the selves of adolescent girls.* New York, NY: Ballantine Books.

Shroff, H., & Thompson, J. K. (2006). Peer influences, body-image dissatisfaction, eating dysfunction, and self-esteem in adolescent girls. *Journal of Health Psychology, 11,* 533–551.

PART VII
Case Studies in Group Work

Group work has been a valued part of social work practice since the development of the profession. Mary Richmond, an early leader in the field of social work, recognized the need for social workers to understand small-group behavior.

Groups are designed to meet either socialization or resocialization objectives (Garvin, Gutierrez, & Galinsky, 2006). Socialization groups are used to help people who are unable to perform appropriate social roles. Clients join these groups on a voluntary basis to receive assistance from social workers with various life transitions. Examples of socialization groups include a group to help chronically mentally ill adults cope with the demands of having a job, a group for parents of children with cancer, and a group for patients coping with dialysis. Resocialization groups respond to people with inadequate socialization skills and are often formed in response to a need for social control. Examples of resocialization groups include groups for men who batter, groups for children who have conduct disorders, and groups for parents who have abused their children.

Gitterman and Schulman (2005) discuss the essential elements of the mutual-aid process in social work groups. The first element is for the group to become a system of mutual aid. This means the group must develop the capacity to help its members both individually and collectively. The second element is to help group members use the group process. In order to achieve this group, workers must be skilled at facilitating the group members to share experiences, respond to each other empathically, confront appropriately, and achieve an atmosphere of working together toward goal-oriented change. The third essential element is to enable the group to function more autonomously—to become a mutual support group. This helps facilitate successful termination and generalization of learning experiences. A related element to discuss is helping members to recognize how the group experience can help them as they leave the group.

What is unique about group work is that more interpersonal interactions take place than in individual casework (Toseland & Rivas, 2011). Furthermore, many of the relevant and helpful interactions that take place occur between group members, not between the group members and the social worker. As a consequence, many group workers stress the concept of the group as a mutual-aid system (Gitterman & Shulman, 2005). In the mutual-aid group, the group members are mobilized to help each other. The group leader has a mediating function to help the group members support and identify with each other, confront each other, and solve problems together. This results in a process whereby they help themselves as they help each other. Group leaders must be skilled in providing for this mutual aid as they work with the group to harness the healing power present in the group process. To do this, leaders facilitate the group to effectively share data about their experiences, experience the "all-in-the-same-boat" phenomenon, and explore mutual support and mutual demand, to name a few of the skills the group leader must possess (Gitterman & Shulman, 2005).

In addition to facilitating mutual aid, the group worker must also help group members achieve optimal social functioning (Toseland & Rivas, 2011). This refers to helping individuals adapt and cope with their social situations by making changes within themselves, their environment, or both. In order to achieve effective social functioning, group workers may assist members to change their behavior, thoughts, or feelings as they respond to various environmental demands. Groups have been successful in helping clients with various social-functioning problems, such as seeking employment, getting along with peers, preventing pregnancy, and reducing social isolation. The group context may be the most effective format for helping clients change their social functioning (LeCroy, 2009).

Two case studies in this section are excellent examples that demonstrate the mutual-aid process: First, Shulman's group example focuses on a support group for persons with AIDS who are in substance abuse recovery and emphasizes the process of developing support for persons struggling with these issues. Next, Berman-Rossi and Gitterman present a case example of a group for relatives and friends of institutionalized elderly clients. It is a splendid example of how a social worker might go about planning for and establishing a group that fills a service gap.

The case study by LeCroy depicts a specific type of group, a social skills group for children. The contribution here is in a clear and detailed description of the process of teaching social skills in a group format. He presents how to lead a structured group with clear goals for the group members. Tolman and Bennett describe a group for working with men who batter. This is a superb example of a resocialization group. The goal is to eliminate battering by men who are court ordered to receive treatment.

REFERENCES

Garvin, C., Gutierrez, L. M., & Galinsky, M. J. (2006). *Handbook of social work with groups*. New York, NY: Guilford Press.

Gitterman, A., & Shulman, L. (2005). *Mutual aid groups, vulnerable and resilient populations, and the life cycle*. New York, NY: Columbia University Press.

LeCroy, C. W. (2009). Child therapy and social skills. In A. R. Roberts (Ed.), *Social workers' desk reference* (2nd ed., pp. 652–658). New York, NY: Oxford University Press.

Toseland, R. W., & Rivas, R. F. (2011). *An introduction to group work practice*. New York, NY: Pearson.

Case Study 7-1

A Mutual-Aid Support Group for Persons With AIDS in Early Substance Abuse Recovery

LAWRENCE SHULMAN

Persons with AIDS who are in substance abuse recovery struggling with similar concerns can gain support and resources through mutual-aid groups. This case study illustrates the social worker's methods in enhancing mutual aid among participants in an intensive, 8-month, weekly group held in a residence sponsored by an AIDS Action Committee.

Questions

1. What skills are evident in the group leader's approach to working with the group and the individuals in the group?
2. What types of follow-up and supplementary services would be appropriate for clients during the life of the group and after completing the group?
3. How did the group leader address the issue of the group member–group leader dynamics referred to as the *authority theme* early in the first sessions?
4. What did the group leader do to create a "demand for work" in the group during the fourth session when he recognized the illusion of work?

5. In what ways did the group leader help move the group from the beginning through ending and transition phases of group work?

This is a case illustration of social work practice with a small group of five clients, all facing the dual struggle of coping with AIDS and early substance abuse recovery.[1] This group was held in the early days of the AIDS epidemic, with the triple drug therapy just undergoing testing. Three members were using the therapy and showing progress in lowering their viral counts and raising their white blood cell counts. They were hopeful for a cure. One member, Theresa, was waiting for her blood work levels to make her eligible for the treatment. The fifth member, Tina, was transgendered and, because of the use of hormone drugs for her transition from being a man to a woman, she would not be eligible for treatment. As she pointed out: "I know I'm going to die from the virus, but at least I would like to die with dignity and not be standing on street corners sucking old men's dicks for drug money."

For each client, an additional and related issue was dealing with the impact of serious early physical, emotional, and sexual abuse in their childhood and adolescence. Maladaptive efforts to cope during their teenage and early adult years, including serious substance abuse, also had a devastating impact on group members. For each client, there were added layers of complexity caused by poly substance abuse, criminal behavior, prostitution, homelessness, prison time, and destructive interpersonal relationships. The group members' ability to trust and to develop true intimacy after so many years of being exploited, as well as having exploited others to meet their emotional and drug needs, was severely diminished. Despite these obstacles, this is also a story of magnificent courage in the face of adversity and the wonderful ability of mutual aid to uncover and nurture the essential impetus toward social connection and caring.

The approach used in this case example focused on the development of a mutual-aid process in the group (Schwartz, 1961; Shulman, 2011, 2012). The underlying assumption was that these clients, who were struggling with similar concerns, could be helpful to each other. The task of the social worker was seen as helping the group members to help each other. In addition, as an example of longer term group work (8 months), the impact of time on the process is evident. The clients, my coleader, and I were conscious of the need to work directly and quickly in order to make the best use of the time available. As will be seen repeatedly in the case example, the clients are simply waiting for the signal from the group leaders that they are ready and willing to work on tough issues.

THE FIRST SESSION: THE BEGINNING PHASE

Our goals in the first session were to establish a clear sense of group purpose reflecting the common ground between the needs of the members and the service offered by the agency. We wanted the group members to get a sense of our roles not as experts on life

---

[1] For a more complete discussion of this group and the mutual-aid process, see Shulman, 2005, 2011.

but rather as group leaders (one social worker and one substance abuse counselor), who were there to help them to be sources of support for each other.

In addition, we hoped to set out the ground rules and to develop a beginning sense of trust in us as the leaders (leader–member alliance), as well as in other group members (member–member alliance). Also important was the need to convey what I call "the demand for work." We wanted the clients to get a sense that we meant business and that, in this group, we were prepared to deal with tough and painful issues and emotions just as soon as they felt ready. Our signal to them came in my direct opening statement as well as my effort to reach for painful feelings.

To fashion an appropriate opening statement, I had consulted with staff and other clients in similar situations and then decided on the following:

> Everyone in this group is struggling with AIDS and early recovery from some form of substance abuse. Most of you currently are or may have in the past attended 12-step groups such as AA or NA, at which you are able to share your experiences coping with addiction and recovery. In addition, you are currently or may have in the past attended groups at AIDS Action that address the particular struggles you face dealing with whatever phase of the disease you are experiencing. You can talk about recovery at your AA and NA groups, but most likely you don't feel comfortable discussing your AIDS. In turn, AIDS is on the agenda for your AIDS groups, but it may be more difficult to discuss addiction and recovery. This group is a place where you can discuss both—AIDS and substance abuse recovery—as well as how the two interact and affect each other.

Heads were shaking affirmatively as I spoke, so I continued to describe our roles and clarify the issue of confidentiality as follows:

> John and I will be the co-leaders of this group. We don't see ourselves as experts, here to give you advice. Our job is essentially to help each of you help each other. We think you are the experts on your own lives and that you have a lot you can give to each other, having experienced similar problems and challenges, so we will try to help you do that.

I pointed out that the discussion in the group would be kept confidential and that we would only be required to share information if they disclosed there was a danger to themselves, a danger to others, or criminal activity taking place in the residence. John and I could assure them of confidentiality as the coleaders, and I hoped they would agree to respect confidentiality as well. Heads were once again shaking affirmatively.

My next effort was to encourage more specifics in this problem-swapping process. I wanted to help them develop an agenda, one with which they could all connect. Also, it is only in the specifics that real help can be given. I asked them if they could take some time to share some of the specific issues they faced and that we could talk about in the group. I pointed out we did not need to solve all of these problems in one night, but it might help to identify issues for group discussion.

The issues they shared were mainly related to the problems they faced in early substance abuse recovery. Since the group started just before Thanksgiving, many members, including Tina, described the temptations they experienced going to parties where drugs were plentiful or attending family events (Jake) with significant consumption of liquor or drugs. One member, John, described the problem of wanting to see his friends at the local pool hall, but that was the place where drugs were sold. In an example of the members drawing on their AA and NA experiences, one member said to John: "If you hang around a barbershop long enough," and as he hesitated, the other group members said in chorus: "You are going to get a haircut." We all laughed at this AA saying. Another member, Theresa, told group members that she was living in a nearby single-occupancy building and was hoping to be accepted into this residence. She said: "There is drug dealing in that building, and I know I have to get out or I'm going to relapse."

The barbershop analogy was one example of their drawing on their 12-step group experiences. One member, Jake, had a problem understanding that this mutual-aid group was different from the 12-step groups since we actually encouraged them to respond to each other, which was not encouraged as participants told their "drug stories" or "drugalogues" at meetings. I noticed at the next few meetings that he brought handouts for me from the other programs. When I asked why he was doing this, he replied: "Well, it's obvious you need help in running a recovery group." I laughed and said I could use all the help I could get. I used this as an opportunity to address with the group members what they all perceived as a different kind of group. Even with a clear statement of purpose and our roles in the first meeting, it is wrong to think they all heard, understood, and even remembered what we said. As the meetings proceed, re-contracting is needed to help them really understand.

At the end of the first session, we asked them to comment on the group—both what they liked and also what they didn't like about this session. One member, Tania, commented on the tough time they faced dealing with early recovery and then pointed to me and my co-leader and said: "Well, you both understand." I took that as an indirect cue that she was raising the authority theme. I responded directly to what I perceived as an indirect cue and said:

> Tania, I think what you really are asking is have we been in recovery and would we understand what you are going through. I can speak for myself, and the answer is that I have not. I teach at the School of Social Work, and each year I lead a group to help me to stay close to the realities of practice, and this group is the one I decided to work with this year. If I'm to be helpful, I'm going to have to understand, and you are going to have to help me.

She smiled and said: "So, you're not a narc" (narcotics cop). I laughed and said I wasn't and pulled up my sweater and said, "See, no wire." A noticeable relaxing of the group members followed my response. I said, "Trust does not come easily, so you have to give us a chance, and I hope we can earn your trust over time." My co-leader, who was in recovery, responded by saying: "I am in recovery; however, recovery is different for each of us, so we will need to understand what it is like for you."

Who you are and what kind of group leaders you will be are the primary questions in a first meeting (the authority theme). These questions are often raised indirectly, as in this example, so the group leader has to be ready to hear them and to respond. In their theory of group development, Bennis and Shepard (1956) suggested that the group has to first deal with the leader and then members can turn to dealing with each other. It really didn't matter, in the long run, whether my co-leader and I had been in recovery.

As in this example, both I and my co-leader had to make clear we were there to learn from them as the experts in their own lives.

The meeting was ending at this point, and I noted that one member, Kerry, who had told us at the start that he could only stay for the first of the 2 hours, had stayed for the full session. I pointed this out and asked him his views on the session. He said he had been reluctant to come, but it looked okay as long as we meant what we said about keeping the discussion confidential. It's interesting to note that each member directly or indirectly raised an important issue for their work in the first session. The member, John, who was concerned about the pool hall, did relapse but then returned to the group after a week at a detox center. Both members who raised the authority theme, Tina and Kerry, were mandated to attend this group or some other form of service by the residence staff because they had broken the rules and used drugs in the residence. Kerry left the residence and moved to New York City and was the only dropout in the group. Tina stayed and participated fully in the remaining group sessions.

THE FOURTH SESSION: THE TRANSITION TO THE MIDDLE (WORK) PHASE

In a group such as this one, meeting 2 hours per week over 8 months, at some point the group must make the transition to the middle or work phase. If the contracting work has been clear and the group leaders have defined their roles and addressed the authority theme, then the group is now poised to move to the next phase. Note that I said *addressed* the authority theme, not *resolved* it. The authority theme will reemerge during the life of the group and return with some force as the group prepares to end.

The signal to the group leader that the group is prepared to shift to deepen the work often emerges as what I call "the illusion of work." That is, conversation is taking place and it looks like real work, sounds like real work, but somehow it's missing the emotions or content that may be experienced by group members as taboo. In other words, the group members have to address the culture of the group—the norms, taboos, stated and unstated rules, roles, and so forth—that make up what I call "the-group-as-a-whole." This organism is more than the sum of its parts. It is the culture that is created beginning with the first session—usually reflecting the general culture in our society—or in this case, the culture of addiction. It is not possible to physically see this group and its culture; however, the leader will see the group acting as if it is there. For example, a shared but unstated taboo subject may be AIDS. Their past experience in 12-step groups encourages a norm to maintain the AIDS discussion-free zone in this group.

The signal to me that this norm was blocking the group from moving into the work phase was the concentration in the first three sessions on substance abuse recovery, with almost no discussion of their struggle with AIDS. I decided to challenge this illusion of work, to make what I call the "demand for work," and to explore the possible reasons for the evasion of work in the following way:

> When we started the group, we said this was a place to discuss both your struggle with recovery and dealing with AIDS and how they impact each other. For the first

three meetings, all you have discussed is recovery, and you have avoided talking about AIDS. How come? Is it too hard, too painful, too scary, or maybe too embarrassing to talk about?

In most cases, this would result in a group discussion of what made it hard and what, if anything, would make it easier. As the members talk about what made it hard or easier, they were also talking about AIDS. For example, if they mentioned the issue of stigma as a barrier, they would actually be talking about what it was like to have AIDS, how others saw them and they saw themselves. There are many false dichotomies in our practice, where we think two ideas are diametrically opposed and we fail to see the connection. Talking about *process* in the group is often posed as a choice the leader makes instead of dealing with *content*. I argue that this is a false dichotomy, and as the members talk about what makes it hard to discuss AIDS (the process), they are really well into deepening the discussion of the content.

In this case, in response to my gentle confrontation, Theresa, who emerged as an internal leader in the group (the group leaders are the external leaders), began to talk with great emotion. Theresa started to talk about her concerns. She said she was 18 months clean and sober, and so she was in the middle of the second year, which was a "feelings year." She went on to describe that this was the period when she and, she thought, everyone in recovery, started to face all those feelings they had been running from. She said it was a complex and difficult time, and that it was hard to sort things out. She went on to say that her boyfriend had trouble sharing his feelings with her. When she wanted to talk to her boyfriend about issues, such as her AIDS, he pulled back and told her it was too painful. As a result, she backed off. She knows he's experienced a lot of losses, including the death of his wife from illness fairly recently, and she realizes he is still early in recovery, but she has things she wants to talk to him about. She has a closeness she wanted to achieve. She has some commitments she wants from him, and she is afraid that he can't make commitments at this point. He's holding back. I asked the others in the group if they had any advice for Theresa on this issue.

Theresa had spoken with great emotion, and I was determined not to do casework in the group, and instead, to wait for members to respond. Kerry, who usually sits quietly at the meetings, and who had indicated that he was going to have to leave early that night, jumped right in. Kerry said he thought that her boyfriend was having trouble dealing with his losses, and it wasn't easy. He described a very close relationship with his partner, Billy, that ended 2 years ago, when his partner died of AIDS on Christmas Day. He said he still didn't think he'd come to grips with all of the feelings that he had and the loss that he'd experienced. I said that must make each Christmas even more difficult for him, and he agreed. He went on to talk about how he had been raised by an extremely physically abusive mother and that his grandmother was the only person who provided him with any support and love. He said he didn't think he had gotten over her dying either. He told Theresa that she had to realize that the process takes a long time and that it might not be easy for her boyfriend to discuss it with her, because he knew it wasn't easy for him to discuss his loss with other people.

As Kerry talked, I saw a sensitive and caring side of him that he keeps covered up with his abrasive, grandiose, angry front, with his consistently telling us he doesn't need anybody and, if they don't care about him, "the hell with them." Theresa acknowledged his comments and thanked Kerry for sharing that with her, as did the other group members. Tania came in at that point and reinforced what Kerry had been saying. Jake was shaking his head as if he understood that difficulty as well.

In this next excerpt, we see the group members accepting our invitation to help Theresa and, by doing so, really also helping themselves. This is an example of another false dichotomy: "Do we deal with the individual problem or do we deal with the group?" By helping the group address each individual's specific concern, they are also addressing their own versions of the same issues. You do not have to choose between the individual and the group, just as you don't have to choose between content and process. You do have to recognize the connections between these supposedly alternative choices.

Whenever a group member raises a general problem, there is usually a specific, recent example that is creating a sense of urgency. I attempted to help Theresa elaborate on her "first offering" by using a skill I call "reaching from the general to the specific" (Shulman, 2011, 2012). I asked Theresa if anything had happened recently to make her feel so strongly about this issue. Theresa described an incident that led to a major fight with her boyfriend. They were in a car together, and she was in the back seat. There was another woman in the front seat whom she experienced as coming on to her boyfriend. The woman was asking him when they could get together and telling him how much she'd like to "bump and grind" with him on the dance floor. Every time Theresa described this woman's comments, she did an imitation of her, making it sound flirtatious and seductive. Theresa went on with a great deal of anger, saying that her boyfriend didn't even acknowledge that she was in the back seat and that she was his woman. Therefore, this woman, a friend of his, was going on right in front of her, which she felt was "disrespecting" her. She thought her boyfriend was "disrespecting" her by not stopping the woman and not being aware of her feelings.

I asked if she had talked to her boyfriend about this, and she said she had, but he had just told her that she was "insecure." Theresa said, "Look, I don't know how to deal with this. I try to use a prayer I know from the 12-step program. Maybe I can pray that he will change. But I don't think he's going to change because, even though he is in a 12-step program, I don't think he's really committed to it. I think he can talk the talk, but he doesn't walk the walk. He's got all the words, but he doesn't practice any of it. I'm not sure he's going to change at all." Theresa continued: "I realize for both of us this is our first recovery relationship, and I know I have to be patient because he's not where I am in recovery, but still it's very hard to sit in the car and have him disrespect me in that way." She said that she was absolutely furious at this woman and that maybe she ought to go have a talk with the lady. She had a great deal of anger as she described the fact that she was just recently released from the penitentiary, and there she learned how to fight (pointing to her two missing lower teeth). She said, "I can ask this lady nicely first, but, if I don't get anywhere, then it's my boot up her ass."

As Theresa's anger grew, I was aware of her pattern, one mirrored by most group members, of using what Bion (1959) described as "fight or flight" to deal with pain. Substance abuse itself is a form of flight and violence is a form of fight. These maladaptive approaches to coping with underlying feelings and cognitions have proved to be devastating to these group members. Most have been employing these techniques to cope with the deep pain and emotional damage of persistent exploitation and oppression related to gender, sexual orientation, race, and class. My goal was to help the members to become aware of their maladaptive defensive maneuvers. I used the idea from 12-step programs of the primacy of maintaining control over your recovery. Theresa had been in prison on prostitution and assault charges and had her 3-year-old daughter sent to live with her mother in the South. Her goal was to get child welfare to return her child once she showed she could maintain her recovery and be a good mother. I had Theresa's previous conviction for violence in mind when I confronted her solution to the problem.

I asked Theresa if confronting the woman would solve the problem, since it might get rid of this woman, but if she doesn't resolve the issues with her boyfriend, wouldn't there just be another problem? She agreed and seemed a bit deflated. I said that it seemed to me she had to talk to her boyfriend. Also, her anger was so strong that if she did take physical action against this other woman, she might be risking her own recovery and even her own freedom, and the last thing she wanted to do was to end up back in prison on an assault charge. She nodded her head and said, "I know it would mean I'd be losing control of my recovery and giving it to someone else, but I don't know if I could talk to him or if he'll listen to me without just putting me off."

Tania then spoke with great feeling about what an important and wonderful person Theresa was, and that she deserved respect and that, if she respected herself, which Tania thought she did, then she should stand up for herself and not let this guy get away with this behavior. She had to tell him directly that she wanted him to make a commitment to her, to recognize her as his woman. Also, if there were these kinds of issues, she had to deal with them out in the open and couldn't let them just fester, where she would get angrier and angrier. She said, "If you continue to get this angry, you're just going to hurt yourself, you're going to get sick, and eventually you're going to threaten your recovery." Theresa agreed that this was going to be a problem for her.

While Theresa presented a very real and painful problem, she had still not focused on her AIDS, even though she said at the start of the session that she wanted to. I was conscious of this as I tried to explore why she had accepted the current situation with her boyfriend. I was making what Schwartz (1961) had described as a "demand for work" and what I have called a *facilitative confrontation* (Shulman, 2011, 2012). It was a gentle demand in which I asked Theresa to examine her reasons for not pursuing the issues.

I asked Theresa why she let her boyfriend back off when she asked him to talk about his losses and her AIDS. She said, "Well, he told me it was hard to talk about." I responded, "Well, you could have asked him what made it hard. Why do you give up when he resists conversations with you?" There was a long silence, and then Theresa's face softened and she said, "I guess I really don't want to hear." Everyone in the room nodded their head in agreement. I said, "Good for you, Theresa. Now you're taking some responsibility. What are you afraid you're going to hear?" She went on and said, "I'm afraid I'm going to be rejected."

Jake jumped in at that point, with a lot of emotion, and said, "That's the problem when you've got the virus. People reject you." He went on and talked about his own family and how he'd gotten in trouble with the law over a fight, and he was in court and nobody knew him in that court. He said he was about to get released without having to do jail time because of the fight. He said, "My own mother was in the court and she hurt me deeply—she really pained me—when she stood up and told the judge that I was HIV positive. Well, that changed everything. These people got real angry at me, and they didn't want a guy getting into fights who was HIV positive, who had the AIDS bug, and they said: 'Go to jail.'" He said, "'I couldn't believe the rejection I felt from my mother. I tried to explain it to her later, and she didn't understand that I didn't want her telling people I had HIV, not in those circumstances." He then turned to Theresa and said, "So, I can understand why you're afraid of that rejection." He said, "I think we're all afraid of what people will do once they know we've got the virus." (At a later meeting, Jake told us the fight was with a drug dealer who had murdered his sister and had successfully avoided arrest.)

Tania had been very quiet, although I could tell she wanted to speak. At one point, I said, "I think Tania wants to get in here, and she's been well-behaved this session, so we have to give her a chance." Tania had at times been a monopolist and often had jumped in to speak, interrupting others. I had spoken to her about this, and she had been making real efforts to contain herself. After my invitation, she smiled and jumped in, telling Theresa how much she admired her and how much strength she had, and that she hoped that she could handle her own recovery in the way that Theresa was handling hers. She told Theresa that she just deserved a lot more.

Theresa asked Tania whether she thought she was an attractive person. There was a silence and Tania said, "I think you're a beautiful young woman and you could have any man you want." Theresa went on at some length about how men come on to her and, if she wanted to, she could "bump and grind" with them as well. But she didn't want that. She wanted one relationship. She wanted a serious relationship. She said she was getting older now and she wanted a commitment from someone, and this was just not enough, and that was what the issue was all about.

Jake, our often quiet yet very thoughtful member, had changed the norm and broken the taboo by raising the fear of rejection associated with AIDS. Theresa's question to Tania about her looks was an indirect way of getting at the issue of fear of rejection. I tried in the next excerpt to facilitate her expression by articulating her feelings. I said to Theresa, "Is the question really that you're afraid that he might not stay with you, that, if you actually confront him on this issue of the other women, that he might leave you?" She agreed that was her concern. At this point, I wondered if it might help Theresa to figure out what she might say to her boyfriend. Theresa said that would be helpful, because she didn't know when and how to say it. Then she laughed and said, "Maybe I should say it in bed." Tania said, "'Oh no. Don't say it before sex and don't say it after sex." And I added, "And don't say it during sex." Everyone laughed, and Tania did a hilarious imitation of having a conversation with Theresa's boyfriend, while pumping up and down as if she were in bed having sex with him.

After the laughter died down, Tania said, "You have to find a quiet time, not a time when you're in the middle of a fight, and you have to just put out your feelings." I asked Tania if she could show Theresa how she could do that. She started to speak as if she were talking to Theresa's boyfriend. I role-played the boyfriend, and said, "Oh, but Theresa you're just insecure, aren't you?" Tania did a very good job of not letting me put her off and, instead, putting the issue right where it was: whether he was prepared to make a commitment or too insecure.

Theresa listened carefully and then said, "I know I have to talk to him, but, you know, he told me that he's not sure he wants to be tied down, that he likes to have his freedom." Jake nodded his head and said, "Yeah, that's the problem, they want their freedom and they don't want to make a commitment, and you're afraid, if you push him, he'll leave you because you've got the virus." Theresa said she realized she had to sit down and talk to him because it couldn't keep going the same way. She would just get too angry and do something crazy and screw up her recovery. She felt she had to find another way to get through to him and talk to him. Otherwise, this thing was just going to continue and it was going to tear her up inside.

In Tania's moving response to Theresa, we can see the dynamic of "resonance" as described by Fidele (1994) in her discussion of women's groups and "relational theory" as a resounding or echoing and a capacity for empathy.

The session was approaching the ending phase, and I wanted to bring the maintenance of recovery issue front and center. This would normally have been a focus of John, my missing coleader. I said to Theresa, if she did confront him, it was going to be very rough for her, especially with the holiday, and I wondered whom she'd have for support, especially if he said he didn't want to continue the relationship. She said she had her sponsor, and Tania said, "You also have me. You can call me anytime you want." Tania said, "I didn't realize when I started this group there were people who have lived lives just like me, who had feelings just like me, who had struggles just like me. You—you're a woman—you've really helped me see that I'm just not the only one going through this. I'd do anything I could to help you."

Once again, Theresa asked Tania how she looked, saying, "You're a woman. I know, as a woman, you will be honest with me and just tell me what you think. Do you think I look okay?" Tania seemed confused and said, "Well, sure, you look wonderful." I said, "I wonder if Theresa is really asking, 'Am I pretty enough? Am I attractive enough? If my boyfriend leaves me, can I find someone else who could love me even though I have AIDS?'" Theresa said, "That's it," and started to cry. She said, "I'm so afraid if I lose him, I won't find anyone else." She said, "I know I could have guys, and I know I could have sex, and I like the sex. I sure missed it during the time I was in prison, but can another guy love me?" Several group members tried to reassure Theresa, with Tania summarizing by saying, "Theresa, it's not what you look like on the outside, it's what you're like on the inside, and you, honey, you've really got it where it counts."

THE FINAL SESSIONS: THE ENDING AND TRANSITION PHASE

The ending phase offers the greatest potential for powerful and important work. Group members feel a sense of urgency as they realize there is little time left, and this can lead to the introduction of some of the most difficult and important themes of concern. The emotional dynamics between group leader and member are also heightened in this phase as they prepare to move away from the other. Termination of the relationship can evoke powerful feelings in both members and the group leader, and the group leader can often connect discussion of these feelings to the members' general concerns and tasks. The ending phase holds tremendous potential for work, yet ironically this phase is often the least effective and can be characterized by missed meetings, lateness, apathy, acting out, and regressions to earlier, less mature patterns of behavior. Moreover, the group leader—as well as the members—shows these behaviors at times.

In many ways, the ending sessions are the most difficult ones for both the group leader and the members. The source of the strain stems from the general difficulty we have in dealing with the end of important relationships. Our society has done little to train us how to handle a separation; in fact, the general norm is to deny feelings associated with it. For example, when a valued colleague leaves an agency, the farewell party is often an attempt, usually unsuccessful, to cover the sadness with fun. The laughter at such parties is often a bit forced.

Schwartz (1961) has outlined the stages of the ending process in group work as follows:

- Denial
- Indirect and direct expressions of anger
- Mourning
- Trying it on for size
- The farewell-party syndrome

The reader who is familiar with the classic work by Kübler-Ross (1969) on the stages of death and dying will note similarities. Even though there is some question about the Kübler-Ross model, the discrete aspect of the stages as described previously, and the fact that they rarely proceed in a linear manner, nevertheless practice experience tells us the model is useful for understanding group dynamics in this phase of work. Every ending represents a loss, which is usually not as powerful as death, but still evoking strong emotions.

Denial was evident in another group I led for married couples: When I told the members that we were ending in 4 weeks (the end of May), they insisted I had given a later date in the first session (the end of June). That group was videotaped, and when I showed the members an excerpt of the first session when I said the end of May, one member jumped in and said: "See, you said the end of June!" It was the next session, when I entered the room and commented that everyone was quiet and looking down, not having their usual pre-meeting conversations, and that it felt like a wake, the same member said: "It is a wake. We are mourning the end of the group."

The next week after our reminder that the married couples group was coming to an end, the same sense of sadness dominated the session. I asked the members to think about our work together, and at the next session I would ask them four questions: What did they learn from the group? What work do they still have ahead of them? What were the positives about how we and they handled the group? What were some of the negatives?

In the long-term AIDS and Recovery group, it was important to start the ending process early. We did this by pointing out we only had five meetings left. When one of the members protested that she thought we were going longer, I reminded her that we had given this ending date at the first session. It was clear that most members experienced a form of denial.

The next session was dominated by feelings of sadness and loss. It was interesting to note that the ending in the group evoked discussion by the four remaining members of losses in their lives, as well as the loss of Kerry, who left the city and moved to New York after 4 months. A few members also made some barely disguised joking comments about the leaders that were actually expressions of anger. When we pointed this out, they admitted they were angry that the group was ending. At the next session, the "trying-it-on-for-size" phenomenon was evident when a member raised a problem with his partner and the group members immediately began to offer support and help, even ignoring comments made by me and my coleader. I settled back and let myself feel the pride I had for the group and the admiration of their strengths in the face of an uncertain future. I commented on this at the end of the session.

The farewell-party syndrome emerged as members suggested that instead of meeting at the residence, we might meet at a corner coffee shop and celebrate the ending of the group. We pointed out that the last session was an important one and that we might want to meet as usual and then go out for coffee after the session. They reluctantly agreed, and it was at this final wrap-up session where we talked about what they had found helpful and where, if they wished, they could continue to get this help. Jake pointed out he had retreated into his apartment and had failed to reach out and make connections with others, but that he had learned in the group that he can't deal with these issues alone and that he needed to find friends to help him. All of the members agreed that they had helped each other in the group and that they had learned it was okay to risk and to ask for and give support to each other.

The last part of the session, in a striking example of doorknob therapy, addressed the issue of their mortality and the fact that even if the new triple-drug therapy seemed to be working, there was no guarantee of a real cure. Many of their friends had died of AIDS, and they had to face the fact that this could be their fate as well. Tina, who showed up to the meeting in pajamas and a bathrobe, had not been able to be treated by the drugs. Her viral count had soared recently and her white blood cell count had sharply decreased. She said: "I know I don't have long to live, so I think I have to make the best of the life I have left." The other members reached out to her verbally and emotionally, even leaning forward in their seats in her direction. Theresa, who was seated next to her on the couch, said that she felt she was a real friend and that Tina could call on her for any kind of help she needed. (Tina died just 1 month after the end of the group.)

My coleader and I told them how much we had admired their courage and their willingness to fight, their willingness to be honest with themselves, and their willingness to care for each other. I said: "I will miss this group and I will stay in touch with John (my coleader) to see how you all are doing." I wished them luck in their battle with the disease and their recovery, and the group came to an end. While we stayed for a while in the lobby of the residence, we decided it was not necessary to go out for coffee.

REFERENCES

Bennis, W. G., & Shepard, H. A. (1956). A theory of group development. *Human Relations, 9*(4).

Bion, W. R. (1959). Experience in groups. In W. R. Bion, *Experience in groups and other papers*. London, UK: Tavistock.

Fidele, N. (1994). *Relationship in groups: Connections, resonance and paradox*. Wellesley, MA: Stone Center Papers.

Kübler-Ross, E. (1969). *On death and dying*. New York, NY: Macmillan.

Schwartz, W. (1961). The social worker in the group. In *New perspectives in services to groups*. (pp. 7–34) New York, NY: National Association of Social Workers.

Shulman, L. (2005). Persons with AIDS in substance-abusing recovery: Managing the interaction between the two. In A. Gitterman & L. Shulman (Eds.), *Mutual aid groups, vulnerable and resilient populations and the life cycle* (pp. 266–289). New York, NY: Columbia University Press.

Shulman, L. (2011). *The dynamics and skills of group counseling*. Monterey, CA: Cengage.

Shulman, L. (2012). *The skills of helping individuals, family, groups and communities* (7th ed.). Monterey, CA: Brooks/Cole, Cengage.

Case Study 7-2

A Group for Relatives and Friends of the Institutionalized Aged

Toby Berman-Rossi[2] and Alex Gitterman

It is often necessary to develop new services when none exist and there is a need for them. In this case study, the social worker discovered the need for a mutual-aid or support group. The worker describes the process involved in developing and working with the group.

Questions

1. How did the structure of the group reflect the specific needs of the participants?
2. What barriers and obstacles need to be anticipated when attempting to develop a new service?
3. What factors do you think contributed to the group's success?
4. In what ways did the group leader influence the outcomes achieved in each of the group sessions?

Metro Home and Hospital for Aged (MHHA) is a 520-bed, nonprofit, long-term care facility with a 130-year history of serving older persons within the community and institution. Originally, MHHA served the healthier aged who needed a residential

---
[2]   Professor Toby Berman-Rossi, a close friend and collaborator, died in October 2004.

facility. Over the years, as community services for older persons increased, and as funding priorities shifted, it has increasingly cared for the frail elderly. The average age of the MHHA resident is 86 years. As a facility, it has two central functions: (1) to provide a home for those for whom Metro is their last home, and (2) to attend to the healthcare needs of residents. Conceiving of inhabitants as residents, rather than as patients, speaks to the home's belief that a sense of home and community, rather than hospital, should prevail. As a home, it is organized to be responsive to the normative, recreational, educational, and social needs of older people, as well as the additional needs engendered by institutionalization. As a medical facility, it provides 24-hour medical care through a wide range of interdisciplinary departments. Balancing the competing pulls of "home and hospital" provides a challenge for residents, relatives, friends, and staff.

Social workers have been employed at MHHA for the last 40 years. Originally, workers were assigned to individual residents on 15 floors. This arrangement was later changed, whereby workers were assigned by floors and consequently to all residents, relatives, and friends on these floors. This structural shift was based on the belief that each floor constituted a small community within a larger community. Each floor was thought of as a block within a neighborhood and created an interdependence of need and resources, demands and opportunities. The development of the floor as a responsive community was thought of as a step toward counteracting the deleterious effects of institutionalization. Isolation, alienation, inequities in power, and passivity—all negative features of institutional life—were to be minimized. A strong floor community would support residents' natural inclination toward mutual aid and communion with each other. Weekly floor group meetings with the social worker facilitated connections and provided a structured means for dialogue among floor members, between floor members and floor staff, and between floor members and the larger institution.

FORMING A GROUP FOR RELATIVES AND FRIENDS

Although weekly floor group meetings became an established part of offered social work services, similar services on a floor-by-floor basis had not been established for friends and relatives. Social work services to this population were provided through a monthly friends and relatives group and on an as-needed individual basis by the floor social worker. Through individual discussions, the floor social worker, Ms. Cara-Bruno, learned that many relatives and friends felt isolated from others and locked into their own individual experiences. Although some had been able to establish cordial or friendly relationships with others, many knew no one besides their resident. A casual nod on seeing a familiar face was often the extent of contact. These visitors subtly indicated that they would welcome contact with others. Some thought that a little friendliness could go a long way in decreasing tension for them when they visited; others stressed their interest in learning the various ways families and friends coped with the impact of institutionalizing a loved one; and still others wanted additional "muscle" in making service demands on MHHA. At the same time, some seemed not to want greater connections. They expressed that theirs was a private experience and not one about which they could tell strangers. They wanted to visit and leave.

As Ms. Cara-Bruno thought about her contact with families and friends, she became increasingly concerned about the sense of isolation many felt in their experience with MHHA. She noticed that her services more often concentrated on crises, and there were fewer contacts around less-emergent situations. Although she felt good about her ability to respond to critical situations, she felt less confident about providing services in relation to ongoing needs.

Ms. Cara-Bruno wondered whether a floor group for relatives and friends could serve the same purpose as the floor group served for residents (Berman-Rossi, 2001). Similar concerns and a shared need to cope with an institutionalized loved one could represent a common ground from which to start (Gitterman & Shulman, 2005). Relatives and friends could potentially help each other with the various issues and dilemmas they faced related to having an elderly loved one living in an institution. By sharing and helping each other with their common concerns, their sense of isolation could be lessened and replaced with a sense of greater strength and mastery. At the same time, a floor group for relatives and friends could also be taxing and induce further stress. For some, it wouldn't be easy to speak about how it felt to bring a relative to a nursing home or how it felt to be visiting an aging friend. Relatives and friends were totally dependent on, and at the mercy of, the institution; hence, some might be hesitant to make public complaints about the quality of its services. If individual concerns were raised at all, they usually were presented through a well-thought-out and carefully crafted approach. They feared reprisals and minimized risk. They, therefore, might be somewhat cautious and concerned about joining a group. With these anticipatory ideas, the floor social worker decided to discuss with prospective members the possibility of a relatives and friends group. She envisioned a series of four meetings to explore the possibility of such a group. At the end of the meetings, she and the group would determine whether it should be developed. She thought that a short-term commitment would be less threatening and more inviting to prospective members.

Before discussing the proposed group with members, the worker realized that she had to gain organizational supports and sanctions (Gitterman, 2005). She knew her department head would have confidence in her idea. To be successful, however, she would need tacit approval from others as well. Active rather than passive sanction would provide a strong base for the action to come. Strong vertical support from administration would be necessary to garner resources for the group (e.g., worker time, space to hold the meetings, secretarial assistance, and money for refreshments). In addition, horizontal support from members of the floor team and their administrators would be essential, or the service might be undermined or sabotaged. Marshaling initial administrative and interdisciplinary support would pay off further along when and if group members brought matters to their attention.

To develop institutional sanctions and supports, the worker began by thinking through how the various organizational representatives might experience the service. She tried to imagine what institutional forces would support and constrain the creation of the service. The worker's belief that those most affected by the group service would have a greater vested interest in, as well as be most threatened by, its creation prompted her to think about how it would be experienced by her team, and nursing staff in particular. She hoped that members would experience the relatives and friends floor group as a team effort, though she alone would be staffing it. Strengthened by her strong relationship with Ms. Wilson, the head nurse, the worker discussed the idea of the group with her and Ms. Schwartz, the nursing supervisor. Both were supportive. They said they knew they would get complaints from relatives, but they saw these complaints as opportunities to improve service or to clarify why things were done the way they were (e.g., encouraging residents to push their own chairs). In addition, they immediately saw opportunities for their own self-interest. They thought about all the times they had said they wished they had an opportunity to raise certain issues with relatives and friends. They imagined that from time to time, they could attend the group both to answer complaints and to raise their own matters (e.g., when relatives give medication or alcohol without informing nursing staff). With this support behind her, the support of the rest of the team was easy to secure. In fact, team members began to imagine a range of things they could do together (e.g., coffee hours, informational programs, and seasonal parties). A potential common ground between the team and the relatives and friends emerged.

The group's purpose determined its composition. After the four sessions, the group might develop into an open-ended floor group designed to be responsive to the ongoing needs of relatives and friends (all relatives and friends would have to be eligible). This broad designation would most likely result in four subgroups: children, siblings, more distant relatives, and friends. In some instances, children, siblings, and friends were around the same age. Cultural, religious, and social class attributes of relatives and friends would reflect the character of the floor itself, where only 14 percent of residents were minority. Although the worker was concerned with difference, she believed that the common bond of shared concern about residents would provide the basis for a core stability of interest, energy, and affection (Gitterman, 2005).

The eventual time boundary would need to be thought about with group members, but the time structure of the initial meeting had to be determined by the worker. A 90-minute session would be offered as a starting point, with the worker open to members' ideas. It was anticipated that members would have a good deal to discuss and would have the energy, capacity, and skill to do so in a sustained manner. For the remaining three sessions, the worker preferred weekly sessions. This time arrangement would provide continuity, intensity, and a time-limited framework in which to arrive at a decision. The time of 5:30 p.m. was chosen to allow members to come after work but also to allow others to get home before dark. The worker understood that a middle ground would be necessary to attend to the diverse environmental needs of members. An ideal time in the winter months would be more difficult to determine, as it would get dark earlier in the day.

Group size was very difficult to anticipate. Potentially 50 to 75 people could attend, though the probability of this occurrence was low. For space, a meeting room off the unit and near the cafeteria was chosen to ensure privacy of discussion and attendance. Some relatives might not initially want to be seen either by staff or by their residents. Comfortable chairs were arranged in a circle designed to facilitate member-to-member interaction and mutual aid. Beverages, cookies, and fruit were provided.

Ms. Cara-Bruno was originally overwhelmed by the need to recruit and invite members to the meeting. Although it would have been easy enough to write a letter to all relatives and friends, she believed that personal contact would be more likely to ensure attendance. The expected hesitancy of members about involvement would best be responded to personally. Phone contact would allow her to deal with negative and ambivalent responses. Reassurance and discussion of issues could diminish uncertainty and lessen the buildup of additional fear. Two seemingly contradictory principles were established as criteria for recruitment: primary responsibility and inclusiveness. In each case situation, at the time of admission someone had been designated as the "next of kin," the person to be called in case of emergency. Most residents had either a family member or a friend. In a formal sense, this person was a primary person in the resident's life and therefore would be automatically invited. At the same time, the worker was concerned about limiting access to service and recognized that the residents' social supports were broader than the one person named as next of kin. Recruiting only these primary people would exclude others who had frequent interaction with the MHHA and residents. What if the next of kin designee was next of kin in name only (e.g., in making burial arrangements)? The worker decided that with each primary person, she would discuss for whom else the group might be helpful. Reviewing each case record and recalling past contacts would help her to think of others for whom the group might be helpful. The worker and the primary person would decide together whom each called (e.g., they might call siblings and she might call friends).

The worker made 37 calls within a 2-week period. About half of those called expressed interest. About one-third indicated they would attend a series of meetings to explore whether the group could be of help. Others lived too far away, felt too frail to attend in the evening, had other obligations, or simply didn't think the group was necessary for them. Through these calls, Ms. Cara-Bruno developed a better understanding of the nature of the residents' relationships with significant people in their lives.

PHASES OF WORK AND STRESSORS-IN-LIVING

Our presentation of the relatives and friends group is framed within a discussion of phases of work. Gittterman and Germain (2008) and Schwartz (1971) define four phases of work: (1) anticipatory empathy (tuning in), (2) beginnings (initial), (3) ongoing work, and (4) transitions and endings. These phases ebb and flow in response to the interplay of internal group processes as well as environmental forces. Although these phases are not always distinct in actual practice, they can be used to describe the work of a single group session as well as the work of a group of many sessions, over time. During each phase, worker and member tasks take on a distinctive character, which when considered together define the dominant nature and work demand of the phase. The manner in which these phases of work evolve is affected by the length of the group and by its open- or close-ended nature. In single-session and short-term groups, they are truncated. If work is to occur and if the group is to develop, it must do so quickly, so that time doesn't elapse without much having occurred. In addition to thinking about the processes of helping (i.e., how the worker helps), one also has to consider the types and content of the clients' problems (i.e., what the worker helps). Gitterman and Germain (2008) suggest that people experience stressors in three interrelated areas: life transitions (e.g., changes in life stages and situations), environmental pressures (e.g., organizations, social networks), and maladaptive interpersonal processes (e.g., scapegoating, testing worker's authority). We will further use the concepts of phases of work and stressors in living to organize and develop a practice illustration.

The anticipatory (tuning-in) phase concerns itself with the worker's initial preparation prior to each individual group session and prior to the group's first session. Through a process of understanding the ways in which members offer veiled communications (i.e., anticipatory empathy), the social worker develops a state of readiness to receive the group and its members. Individuals often find it difficult to confide directly to a group of strangers about important thoughts, events, and feelings. In addition, subtle aspects of experience are not necessarily clearly known or understood by members. The worker, therefore, thinks in advance about the ways in which members might express themselves in coded ways. Understanding these ways increases worker receptivity and can influence the development of increased responsiveness. As workers ready themselves, they actively use their knowledge about the particular client population before them, and the nature of the problems in living that bring individuals to the group. The development of preliminary empathy facilitates the work to come.

As Ms. Cara-Bruno prepared for her first group meeting, she tried to imagine what it would be like for relatives and friends to come together. About 18 people, representing 12 residents, said they would try to come. The overall response to the initial outreach phone calls was positive. Prospective members stated that it felt particularly good to have a social worker reach out to them rather than their reaching out at a point of crisis. Although the overall reaction was positive, the worker also heard hesitation and fear. Some felt embarrassed about talking in a group, because that was new to them. Others worried that if they were really honest, administration and floor staff wouldn't like that. And still others couldn't envision how a group could help. They imagined that collective efforts might decrease continuance of individual arrangements already in existence. The worker was also aware of her own apprehension and excitement. First meetings always made her a little nervous. So much depended on her. She worried that the open-ended nature of the group would detract from continuity of work and hoped that a core membership would develop that would provide continuity from session to session. The worker understood that although she and group members had discussed these issues and she had offered reassurances, these issues would take center stage in the first session. During this first session, she wanted to develop an agreement with the members as to whether they wanted to meet to discuss the possibility of establishing a relatives and friends group.

Beginnings, the second phase of work, points to the need for the worker and the group to arrive at a working agreement as to the nature of their work together, their respective role relationships, and the specific conditions related to their work. This contract is based on a marriage of members, perception of their needs, and the agency's perception of its service offering. This agreement, although still open to negotiation, sets the framework for the work to come. Boundaries, requirements, and demands for work between worker and members and among members receive their legitimacy from and are strengthened by this pact. A division of labor between members and worker can more readily be achieved when each is clear about their contribution to the joint venture. A structure for work is also required. In contrast, service and role ambiguity (or a "hidden agenda") leads to anxiety, frustration, and disappointment. During this phase of work, the group as a whole is too fragile to offer much supportive sustenance to the members. Members experience each other as potential sources of satisfaction but currently as stress inducing. Mutual anxiety over the unknown predominates. Anxiety is perpetuated by the lack of structure and lack of norms for work and conduct. Introducing service and role clarity provides essential structure to engage members' attention and increases the potential for positive engagement. We turn to the record of the group's first meeting.

INITIAL PHASE

By 5:45 p.m., seven members, representing six residents, had arrived. After casual introductions and some small talk around refreshments, the worker suggested the meeting begin.

The group began with another round of introductions, some initial talk of who each other's residents are, and how well they all knew each other. I then stated, "I asked you to this meeting to think with you about whether it would be helpful to establish a floor group. The social work department and the home itself are interested in knowing whether closer, more consistent, more ongoing social work services in the form of a group would be helpful to you in relation to the kinds of stress and concerns you experience as relatives and friends of residents." I added, "You all know the ways in which residents are helpful to each other in their floor group, and I thought that because many of you might be experiencing similar troubles and concerns, the group might enable you to be helpful to each other. For example, the group could help with any concerns you may have about the services your relatives and friends are receiving and with issues more personal in nature such as the impact on you of having a relative or friend at MHHA."

A lively discussion ensued. Most of the initial concerns expressed were *environmental* in nature. Members brought up problems with laundry, lack of individualized programs for residents, residents not being taken off the floor frequently enough, irregularity of physical therapy, and aides not being involved enough with residents in the afternoon. As the issues were raised, I asked how widespread a concern these were and how members presently were handling their worries. There was a high degree of consensus with regard to ongoing concerns. Most members said they did very little with their concerns beyond suppressing them or raising the issue only when it became pressing. I said, "It seems that you find it either difficult or not particularly useful to raise your concerns with staff." Mrs. Somers changed focus and voiced the first complaint about social workers. She said they simply praised the home or did very little with her complaints. I credited her strength in bringing forth her criticism and asked others for their experiences with social workers. The consensus was that social workers were helpful in crises but simply did not provide sufficient ongoing service. In addition, they did not feel they could bring problems to staff. They generally felt isolated from others and left to solve their problems alone.

Having heard the members define ongoing problems for which they felt there was no available help, I asked whether they thought they might want to meet to work collectively on those problems they seemed to have in common. My question was met with silence. I waited, not being sure what was in the silence. I broke the silence with a smile saying, "Boy, this is a change for me . . . usually relatives are busy chasing me, and here it seems like I'm chasing you." There was some laughter, and members spoke and said it felt too soon for them to commit themselves to the group. Several said they would like to have another meeting to think further about whether they wanted to continue. Several said they felt good that they shared similar concerns and that they felt less alone. They agreed to meet the following week to discuss whether meeting in some ongoing way might be of help to them. The members left the meeting talking to each other.

Although members had clearly not resolved their hesitation by the end of the meeting, the connection they felt with each other appeared strong enough to encourage them to attend a second meeting. The worker understood that such uncertainty was natural after initial sessions. Experience within the group, rather than further discussion about the group, was key to its resolution.

ONGOING PHASE

As the members move into the initial period of the ongoing work phase, they have, for the moment, resolved their ambivalence about the group and are readying themselves for the work ahead. To move forward, they are particularly concerned with (1) developing a mutual-aid system that will support their use of each other in the service of work, and (2) contending with the power and control of the worker (Bartolomeo, 2009; Schiller, 2009). The substantive work of the group is obscured by the members' preoccupation with "the authority theme." The group as a whole must solve its relationship with the worker sufficiently before it can move on to fully developing its peer relationships. Criticism of the worker is at its greatest. We present practice excerpts from the group's second meeting.

I felt good approaching this meeting. I had a positive sense from last week's meeting. I had met several relatives during the week, and they said they were looking forward to another meeting. A few others said they were coming. I recalled that I had prematurely asked whether they wanted to formalize as a group. This time I really wanted to listen rather than push for a premature decision. I was somewhat uncertain how new members would be received.

After introductions, I recalled last week's meeting and said that they had agreed to meet today to consider whether they would like to continue working as a group and, if so, in relation to what issues and what concerns. Mrs. Elgin began with a concern of hers. She said that she found the floor unattractive and wondered if they couldn't spruce up the bulletin boards and add some plants. Others nodded. In an effort to make the covert overt and to help determine the degree of consensus about the physical environment, I said, "I notice you seem to be nodding in agreement and wonder if you feel the floor is not a very attractive place." Everyone agreed.

Mrs. Gladstein said that the types of residents on the floor, in addition to how the floor looked, bothered her. Others said they too were disturbed. Miss Wallace and Mrs. Velez were particularly expressive. They said that they thought these "disruptive" residents didn't belong on the floor. I said, "I think you are identifying an important concern; let's discuss this." Miss Wallace and Mrs. Bailey shifted focus and began to talk about residents not being taken frequently enough to the bathroom. Though I noticed the shift away from the more difficult topic of residents with Alzheimer's, I followed their lead. I knew that two group members had relatives with Alzheimer's, and I thought this would be a very difficult discussion for them at this point. The consensus of relatives was that not only is toileting a problem, but alienation exists between residents and floor staff. Mrs. Sherman offered the first comment of personal pain. She said that she thought she could understand how the aides feel. Sometimes she also has to withdraw.

Others returned the discussion to environmental troubles, steering away from the pain of their life transitional experience. They said they thought it was a matter of caring; if the aides cared, they would do more. A very lively discussion ensued. I acted on my hunch that members were afraid to mention names and asked whether this was difficult to discuss. Silence. I continued, saying, "I wonder whether you are concerned about how I might use the information. Are you wondering about the issue of confidentiality and possible repercussions as a result of the meeting?" Members denied any concern about me and jumped immediately to an aide of whom they were critical.

Before I could return to the question of confidentiality, Mrs. Somers said she wanted to talk about what happened when someone died on the floor. She confided how awful she felt when she saw a body being wheeled off the floor. I felt the power of the experience and encouraged discussion of this painful *life transitional* concern. The members discussed this for a short period, and for the next 10 minutes continued to raise problems. As the end of the meeting was approaching, I asked them about their reactions to forming a group. They found it difficult to commit themselves. I said that they had now, for two meetings, touched on a wide range of concerns, from those involving the securing of concrete services to those involving the quality of life on the floor. Mrs. Somers thought the group could address both kinds of concerns if they wanted.

In a surprising shift, all but Mrs. Velez said they thought such a group could be helpful in the future and would like to continue to meet for a few more sessions. Mrs. Velez said that her sister felt she should be able to handle all issues by herself and didn't really want Mrs. Velez involved. She said she would talk with her sister. I asked if the group and I could help at all. She said no. They agreed to meet the following week.

As the members develop greater comfort and confidence in the worker, they can more assuredly move forward toward the issues for which the group was formed and to becoming more fully involved with each other. Themes, problems, and concerns, which were previously only identified, become fleshed out as members gain strength in working on their troubles. The knowledge that members must work for what they get propels involvement. There is a growing sense that the group is satisfying. Intimacy becomes greater. This is even more evident in the third meeting.

I thought the group had taken a step forward in declaring its interest in continuing. Although for most of the group there was little commitment, to my surprise at the end of the group, all but Mrs. Velez said they would want to continue. I noticed that the group had worked particularly hard in identifying environmental problems but had developed an approach-avoidance pattern on any criticisms of me (i.e., *interpersonal* concerns) and any themes that spoke to the pain of their experience (i.e., life transitional concerns). A core membership, however, was developing, which provided leadership from week to week.

At the beginning of the third meeting, only four members were present. Over refreshments, the members expressed disappointment and anger about low attendance. Two members challenged me and asked if I had really done enough to get members. This led to a discussion of shared perceptions about why people were not attending. I inquired whether there were aspects of the group that might have been experienced negatively. The members were steadfast in their praise. They said that they couldn't speak for those absent, but they felt positive and appreciated the chance to work on their problems with the home and with their family members. I then asked, "If you are pleased with the group, I am puzzled by what your disappointment is all about." There was consensus that six was a better number than four. At that exact moment, Mrs. Anderson and Mrs. Bailey walked in. The timing was perfect, and everyone began to laugh.

Mrs. Gladstein pursued the group's strongest challenge to me and asked me again to share my outreach efforts. I once again detailed my efforts. Mrs. Sherman stated that having more outreach wasn't so important to her, because she was getting a lot out of the group as it was, and she wanted to move on to their work for today. At this time, we filled in Mrs. Anderson, who was there for the first time, about the group's purpose. Mrs. Bailey and Miss Fields moved on to a sensitive environmental issue by raising how they believed that the head nurse didn't really like family members to help on the floor. They felt pushed away. I asked for examples and many came forth. Mrs. Gladstein said she had made peace with herself—she is now pleasant but not too demanding unless there is something seriously wrong. I asked what Mrs. Gladstein felt about our nudging—was she concerned that the group might disturb that peace?

With Mrs. Gladstein answering yes, the group members moved to a new level of honesty and authenticity. Many spoke about the toughness of the group, because in some ways they were no longer as complacent. Individual and group complacency seemed to dissolve in the face of the possibility of change. They said it meant a lot to them to have a place to talk, and yet they were also scared. I tried to sustain the discussion of the negatives of the group. The members went back to the discussion of wanting to help on the floor but feeling cut off. I asked them to elaborate on their feeling cut off. The members spoke about their fear of retaliation: physical harm and withdrawal of services and emotion. I asked for details and they came forth easily. They said that incidents where they thought their relatives and friends were mishandled physically were the hardest to take. No one wanted to pursue a complaint. The tone was somber.

The theme of discussion changed, and more environmental troubles were raised. Mrs. Gladstein said she thought a dying resident should not be kept on the floor, because that has a negative effect on everyone else. The pros and cons were discussed. And then, for the first time, the group asked me to actively help them negotiate their environment by passing on their desire for dying residents to be placed on another floor. I stated that I would be willing to act on their behalf but wanted to get a better understanding of their concerns. Mrs. Bailey said that, for her, the mentally incompetent residents proved to be even more distressing. She thought we didn't place residents well. The others energetically agreed. I precipitated discussion of ways they might become involved in these decisions, and there was an emotion-filled discussion of how they felt MHHA kept tight control over their lives.

The time watcher announced that they had been working for 2 hours. I asked about having another meeting, stating that I would be available for two more, or we could quickly sum up and then plan to meet again after the summer. Miss Wallace, feeling the emotional weight of the discussion, asked whether they hadn't discussed enough already. I invited elaboration, and Miss Wallace simply stated that she would come if others did. It was clear that the intimacy level that was comfortable for most members was uncomfortable for her. I suggested that they use the next 2 weeks to further discuss this last question of the emotional life on the floor and their relationships with the home and then evaluate the experience in the last meeting. They agreed.

It seemed clear that the group had moved fully into the middle of the work phase. Perhaps the members' challenge of the worker's competence at outreach had cleared the air, and members were more actively able to pursue issues of importance to them. Perhaps they were also more trusting of each other. The group had become important to the members. This is poignantly evident in the fourth meeting. We turn to the worker's recording:

In the next to the last session, the group had one last major chance to raise and work on matters of concern. They had agreed to pursue discussion of the emotional life of the floor and their relationships with the home. I wanted to monitor the intimacy issue in an effort to ensure, if possible, a workable comfort level for Miss Wallace. All members arrived early, and after refreshments and small talk, the group began. Mrs. Sherman started with an environmental problem. After everyone agreed about the problem, Mrs. Elgin shifted the discussion by saying that she was beginning to feel better when she went on the floor. This led to a discussion of how the group members felt a greater sense of communion with each other, and with each other's residents, when they went on the floor. Mrs. Elgin said that her mother felt that the floor was beginning to feel like a family to her. Members pursued discussion about what they had done with each other's relatives. Mrs. Somers spoke of the social support she received from the group and credited the group with lessening her sense of isolation. She felt an interest in her and her mother. I wondered what they actually found different. They offered examples and noted how beautifully the aides cared for Mrs. Velez's sister's roommate.

The news that this roommate had died stunned the group. The main conversation of the evening shifted to a discussion of death, illness, and dying (the members' shift from environmental to life transitional concerns was evident). Mrs. Somers began to cry. I touched her arm and said, "It's okay to cry here." She said she felt awful and was pleased that she could show how she felt. Others said the same. (Clearly, the norms of the group had changed, and they had achieved a high level of intimacy with each other.) Others cried and shared various experiences with death. Mrs. Elgin's pained story of her sister's death 20 years earlier was particularly poignant. Miss Wallace said she found this discussion hard to take. She was 83 and only had her sister; everyone else had someone. Others suggested that although that was true, the loss of a loved one was hard for all of them. Miss Wallace persisted and said she felt they were dwelling on the pain too much. She asked "Why is it necessary?" She said she thought the group should focus on topics where change was possible. They were all going to die, and no one could change that. The room was silent. Members looked at me.

I said that I was a little confused because Miss Wallace had said that she had no friends to help her when she felt blue, and I had thought that meant she welcomed the chance to talk. Miss Wallace went on to describe herself as a private person and that when she went home she was more upset than when she came. The support from the group came forth immediately. Mrs. Elgin said that if Miss Wallace wanted, she would drive her home, or they could go get something to eat together. (The mutual aid in the group was strong.) Mrs. Sherman expressed her sentiment by stating that part of the group was for them to help each other. She spoke of how she had things locked up in her and maybe in the future she could talk about these things (e.g., the guilt she felt for bringing her sister here). Others agreed and reaffirmed that they thought the group could help with that. I stated that the group was there to help them in this way, too. They were in charge of what they would talk about, how much they would talk about, and how they would use each other.

After some additional outreach to Miss Wallace, members changed focus and brought up environmental problems: laundry, dentures, getting information. They explored ways of going directly to nursing staff, as I would have to do just that to find out what they wanted. Mrs. Sherman said she felt our work was so important and wondered if there was a way to get it to the other families. "Could they write a newsletter?" They all agreed that this was a wonderful idea and strategized about the division of labor between them and me. It was agreed that they would think about it over the summer, and it would take more final form in the fall.

Our timekeeper signaled that it was time to end. I mentioned that we had decided to have one more meeting and that they had agreed to evaluate their experience and to discuss plans for the fall. They agreed to have this be our focus next week. The mood was quiet as they acknowledged the work for the last session.

The members worked very hard during this meeting, fulfilling the potential of the final work phase. Their shift to the *life transitional* issues of death, dying, and loss seemed fitting for this fourth meeting, when mutual aid and intimacy among members were at their strongest. The quiet manner in which they acknowledged the forthcoming final meeting suggested they were already dealing with the loss of the group.

TRANSITION AND ENDING PHASE

In the transition and ending phase, the impending end of the group and separation of group members from each other and the worker provides the final momentum for participants to work on remaining issues. All energy shifts toward disbanding the group, which members labored to create. As a general principle, we suggest that the stronger the connection, the more difficult the process of separation. The tasks of evaluating the group's work and defining and completing remaining work—if possible, while contending with feelings of loss—become the major work of the group.

In the fifth and final meeting, the members' ambivalence about the ending of the group was clear. On the one hand, they understood the need to evaluate the group and project to the future, but on the other hand, they used the meeting to attend to unmet needs. In an important way, they used this last session to develop coping strategies, for over the summer, in the absence of the worker and the group. They noted ways they could approach staff directly and how they could continue to use each other to think through problems. They were particularly excited by Mrs. Gladstein's suggestion that they occasionally approach staff together. Although as part of the evaluation process, the worker encouraged discussion of negatives as well as positives, primarily positives were forthcoming.

Members agreed that the decrease in isolation they felt with each other and the greater receptivity they experienced from floor staff far outweighed any negatives. Strong positive sentiment was expressed about meeting in the fall. Members agreed to talk to relatives and friends over the summer, thereby keeping the group alive. Much physical affection was expressed as members and the worker left the room.

CONCLUSION

Including relatives and friends in making the decision about whether group services would be helpful to them proved to be an important element in the creation of the group service. A partnership relationship between worker and members made it possible for participants to advance at their own pace. Because the members were allowed to make their own decisions, the development of the group as a whole was encouraged and strengthened. Phases of work were clearly apparent to the worker, despite the short-term nature of the group. Equally apparent and interesting was the manner in which the members moved from their initial preoccupation with environmental obstacles to their more painful life transitional struggles.

REFERENCES

Bartolomeo, F. (2009). Boston model. In A. Gitterman & R. Salmon (Eds.), *Encyclopedia of social work with groups* (pp. 103–106). New York, NY: Routledge.

Berman-Rossi, T. (2001). Older persons in need of long-term care. In A. Gitterman (Ed.), *Handbook of social work practice with vulnerable and resilient populations* (2nd ed., pp. 715–768). New York, NY: Columbia University Press.

Gitterman, A. (2005). Group formation: Tasks, methods and skills. In A. Gitterman & L. Shulman (Eds.), *Mutual aid groups, vulnerable and resilient populations, and the life cycle*, (3rd ed., pp. 73–110). New York, NY: Columbia University Press.

Gitterman, A., & Germain, C. B. (2008). *The life model of social work practice: Advances in theory and practice* (3rd ed.). New York, NY: Columbia University Press.

Gitterman, A., & Shulman, L. (2005). *Mutual aid groups, vulnerable and resilient populations, and the life cycle* (3rd ed.). New York, NY: Columbia University Press.

Schiller, L. Y. (2009). Relational model. In A. Gitterman & R. Salmon (Eds.), *Encyclopedia of social work with groups* (pp. 106–108). New York, NY: Routlege.

Schwartz, W. (1971). On the use of groups in social work practice. In W. Schwartz & S. R. Zalba (Eds.), *The practice of group work*. New York, NY: Columbia University Press.

Case Study 7-3

A Social Skills Group for Children

CRAIG WINSTON LECROY

Group approaches can be an efficient and effective way of working with children who have various social difficulties. This case describes a structured approach to teaching children specific skills to help them address various situational difficulties.

Questions

1. What types of difficulties would be best suited to this model of treatment?
2. How are group members involved in the teaching of social skills?
3. How was role-playing used to teach social skills?
4. How can the group leader evaluate whether the skills are learned?

Ms. Thompson called the social services office of the school district for the third time. Her student Kevin had caused so much disruption that she lost complete control of her class. It was the end of an exhausting day that was beginning to become too familiar.

I met with Ms. Thompson and other teachers about important concerns with their various students. "Kerry is so insecure and withdrawn—I'm concerned about how her brother teases her." Another teacher exclaimed, "Tom can't control his anger; when he gets mad, he lets the other kids have it!" Ms. Thompson spoke mainly of Kevin: "I can't keep him in his seat and under control."

I listened to the complaints, feeling, as I had in the past, disappointed that the children could not get the individual time and attention they needed. It became clear that the children had a less than promising year ahead if they weren't able to gain some control or comfort in the classroom and with their peers.

Teacher concerns such as these frequently lead to the beginning of groups designed to respond to the various needs of troubled children. Groups that focus on social skills do well in addressing the various difficulties such children face in their day-to-day lives. The purpose of social skills groups is to teach children new ways of responding to their problematic situations.

A skills-based approach has become increasingly popular as we learn more about the relationship between poor peer relationships and subsequent social difficulties. Child developmentalists stress the importance of children learning necessary peer relationship skills, because without such skills, children are more easily beset with friendship difficulties, inappropriately expressed emotion, inability to resist peer pressure, and so on. Within a social skills framework, problem behaviors, such as the child behavior problems presented by the teachers, are viewed as deficits in appropriate skills. This suggests the need to teach children prosocial responses or social skills as opposed to an exclusive focus on the elimination of problem behaviors.

TEACHING SOCIAL SKILLS

The logic behind teaching social skills is based primarily on social learning theory. Social situations are presented, and then children are taught to implement skills in responding to the various social situations. The process begins with the social situation and the social skill being taught. The group discusses the use of the social skill, the rationale for the skill, and the steps used to implement the skill. Next, the stage is set for learning the skill through role-playing. The leader or group member models the skill, which is followed by feedback from the group members as to whether the criteria for successful demonstration of the skill were achieved. The group members take turns rehearsing the social skill in various role-play enactments. Following the acquisition of the basic skill, the group then works on more complex skill situations. Successful use of the skill requires the use and practice of the skill in the natural environment. Many variations of this basic format are used.

STARTING THE GROUP

As I reviewed the theory and rationale underlying social skills groups, the concerned teachers began to identify skills they would like to see their students learn. I try to encourage teachers to think in terms of desired outcomes they would like to see students develop rather than focusing on problems they want eliminated. Having teachers focus on outcomes brings them one step closer to specifying what objectives they believe are important for the children to acquire. I find that asking, "What would the child need to do differently to be less of a problem?" is helpful in moving the discussion to desired outcomes that are more specific and positive. When I asked this of Ms. Thompson, she began to express hope for Kevin: "Well, Kevin's a natural leader, but he needs to learn to ask for things politely and resist peer pressure to disrupt the class."

Together, we identified six children, 9 to 11 years old, who would benefit from a social skills group. The tasks of recruiting and scheduling the children, notifying and informing parents about the group, and arranging logistical details were shared by Ms. Thompson and myself. We agreed that the group would run for 10 weeks, which would give me adequate time to teach the children some specific skills, encourage application of the new skills to classroom and home situations, and teach problem-solving skills for difficult and complex situations.

AN EXAMINATION OF THE TRAINING PROCESS

The skills training process proceeds in a fairly straightforward, structured way (LeCroy, 2008). The following sections describe the key leadership skills and procedures in a social skills group. A brief process recording from a group session follows.

Selecting Skills and Situations

When I decided to conduct the social skills group for the school, the first step was to decide what basic skills I was going to focus on. Given the identified needs of the children, I decided to focus on the skills of giving and receiving feedback, making friends, and resisting peer pressure. Other social skills programs might choose a variety of skills to teach, such as negotiating, making requests of others, being assertive, handling encounters with police, practicing pregnancy prevention skills (e.g., discussing birth control, asking for information), getting a job, using independent living skills (e.g., using community resources), and practicing anger control skills (LeCroy, 2013).

When broad social skills are selected, as in our example with resisting peer pressure, then the micro skills that constitute resisting peer pressure must be identified. For example, the micro skills of resisting peer pressure include speaking slowly and calmly, saying "no" clearly and as soon as possible, continuing to refuse pressure, and suggesting another activity or leaving the situation. One of the critical and valuable aspects of social skills training is the discrete level at which the social skills are taught and learned. Breaking the skill down into small components facilitates learning and provides for an increased sense of control for the group members. As the children learn small steps, they master new ways of responding to situations and gain greater self-confidence in their abilities.

Another consideration that is important in planning a social skills group is the type of problem situations that are used in the group. It is important in a social skills group to provide the group members with situational problems that demand the use of the skill. Problematic situations need to be devised that reflect a realistic situation where the social skills can be practiced. For example, with resisting peer pressure, situations could be constructed around pressure to steal, pressure to cheat, pressure to have sex, and pressure to take drugs.

Discussing the Social Skill

To begin the process of teaching a social skill, I start with a discussion about the use of the social skills. The purpose of the discussion is to provide reasons for learning the skills and to give examples of where the skill might be used. I asked the group, "Why is it important to learn how to resist peer pressure?" If children understand the reason behind why they should use the skill, then they are more motivated to learn the skill. Furthermore, if children are given examples of how the skill can be used, then they will be motivated by understanding how to apply the skill in their day-to-day life. I also ask, "What examples can you think of where you used or could have used the skill of resisting peer pressure?" In discussing the skill with the group, it is important to describe the skill steps needed to operationalize the skill. It is critical to break down the skill and provide the group members with a clear understanding of how the skill steps compose the overall application of the skill. I list the skill steps on the board, and I often tell the students that they must remember them. Together the group works out games or acronyms to facilitate retention of the steps. In teaching the children the skill of resisting peer pressure, I listed five skill steps I wanted them to learn:

1. Look the person in the eye; be serious.
2. Say "no," clearly and quickly.
3. Continue to say "no" if you get repeated pressure.
4. Suggest an alternative activity.
5. If pressure is continued, leave the situation.

These skill steps break down the skill of resisting peer pressure and give group members a clear idea of how to respond to peer pressure effectively. We spend some time discussing what each step means in the children's own words.

Set Up the Role-Play

Next I must set up the role-play for the group members. There are several critical decisions in composing the role-plays. For instance, I usually select a protagonist who I think can do a good job as a model for the other group members. I get the group involved in setting up a realistic role-play by asking the group, "What is the situation?" "Where is this taking place?" "Who would be there?"

It is important to prepare the group members to participate in and observe the role-play. I structure the group so that the group members are actively involved with and listening to the role-play rather than sitting back passively, uninvolved in what is going on. I encourage the group members to define some of the characters in the role-plays. For example, I ask, "What is this person like?" or "What kind of character should we give this person?" "What does this person sound or look like?" I ask the students who play the roles to pay attention to their nonverbal as well as verbal behavior in the role-play.

I also instruct the group members to be observers by giving them observer tasks. I have the observers choose a name like *Detectives* or *Watchers*, and I say, "Make sure the skill steps are followed" or "Someone watch the nonverbal behavior," or I ask a more general question like, "Do you think this is similar to situations you know about?" By assigning the group or specific members to observation tasks, they become more actively involved in the role-play and therefore acquire the skills more readily. At this time I also discuss with group members how to give and receive feedback. I always have the children practice giving feedback before starting role-plays.

Modeling of the Skill

For each new skill, I either model the skill or select a group member to model the skill. I model the skill so that I can carefully follow the skill steps. When a group member is used to model the skill, it is important to ensure good modeling. This can be facilitated by reviewing the skill steps with the protagonist immediately before the role-play. It is important to briefly go over the plan of what the role-players are going to say in the role-play enactment. I then review the skill steps for the group members who are responsible for giving the protagonist feedback on his or her performance.

Role-Play and Rehearsal of the Skill

The role-play is enacted, and the role-players do a live demonstration of the problem situation. Although the situation is contrived, the role-plays frequently become spontaneous, and each role-player must act accordingly. Following the role-play, the group members are ready to respond with their feedback. I take an active role in soliciting positive feedback first by asking the group what the protagonist did well. I encourage and often require the protagonist to also state his or her self-evaluation. This is followed by a careful critique of the skill steps. "Were the skill steps followed?" "Which steps could have been performed better?" and "How would you do it differently?" The leader must structure the feedback and keep the group focused on learning the discrete skill steps.

The feedback is then incorporated into another role-play. Here the protagonist must concentrate on changing his or her performance to meet the demands of the feedback. It is critical for me to help facilitate this by asking, "What are you going to do differently this time to use the group's feedback?" The process is continued until the protagonist has performed all of the skill steps. For every skill, I provide an opportunity for each member to be the protagonist so that each member learns the skills proficiently.

Practice Complex Situations

As the group members became skilled in the basic skills of giving and receiving feedback, making friends, and resisting peer pressure, I introduced increasingly complex situations. The use of more extended role-plays was one way I accomplished this goal. I also asked the group members to bring in their own social skill situations so that the group can help them work out new responses to problematic encounters. After the group had acquired many of the basic skills, I taught the group accessory skills in dealing with problematic situations. For example, we began to focus on using problem-solving skills in addition to practicing social skills. During one of the later sessions, Kevin brought up a situation where he had successfully resisted his friend's pressure to skip school, but his friend said he would no longer be his friend. We worked on generating different alternatives for solving Kevin's new dilemma. In addition, I encourage the development of role-taking by having the members play different roles in various social situations. In this way, I can encourage the members to experience the role. I often ask, "What does it feel like to be ___?" In Kevin's situation, I helped him develop some perspective-taking or empathy skills when I asked him to play the role of his friend. When he did this, he was able to discover some new ways to try talking with his friend.

As a leader, I try to think about what goal I am trying to achieve with the group. If the goal is skill training, then I focus the group on the acquisition of the skill. "What would you do in that situation?" If the goal is role-taking or empathy, I focus on feelings by helping the children experience different feelings and roles. "How does this person feel?" or "Why does he feel this way?" If the goal is to encourage problem solving, I focus on alternative ways of solving problematic situations and various consequences for different alternatives. "What are some other alternatives?" "What would happen if you choose that solution?"

GROUP PROCESS ILLUSTRATED

The transcript pages from the group's fourth session demonstrate the techniques and procedures used in leading a social skills group.

Group Process

Leader: Today we are going to practice our social skills. One skill that we have talked about is learning to resist peer pressure. What does it mean to resist peer pressure?

Beth: It's when your friends try to force you into things.

Mark: It's when other kids get you into trouble and it's not your fault.

Leader: That's right, Beth and Mark; resisting peer pressure means other people are trying to get you to do something you don't want to do. So when you are in a situation where you don't want to do something that your friends want you to do, you need to be able to say "no" and do it in a way that your friends will leave you alone. What reasons can you think of for learning how to resist peer pressure? I'll start. You resist peer pressure so that you'll feel better about yourself because you didn't get talked into doing something you might feel bad about later.

> *Explanation of group leader's behavior:*
>
> The leader begins by soliciting an explanation of the skill.
>
> Encouraging and reinforcing the group members to share.
>
> Summarizing the skill.
>
> The leader points out the influence of peers and stresses the need to learn the skill.
>
> Providing rationales for the skill. The leader begins by modeling the first response, and the group members follow in a similar fashion.

Kevin: So you don't get into trouble with your parents.

Leader: Good, Kevin.

Wendy: So you don't get talked into using drugs.

Tommy: Your friends will listen to you and know you're not just saying things.

Leader: Great, Wendy and Tommy. As some of you have pointed out, there are a lot of good reasons to resist peer pressure. I think you have also talked about how hard it is to do. That's why we need to practice the skill. Let's go over the steps in how to resist peer pressure. Remember, practice good nonverbal skills and start by saying "no" as soon as possible, stick to your "no," and if necessary, leave the situation or suggest something different. Here's a situation we can use: Two friends come up to you at recess and ask you to steal someone's homework as a joke. This person gets picked on a lot, and he will probably feel picked on if you do it. Wendy, pick two people to do a role-play of this situation. Okay, role-players, take a minute to think of what you want to say. Everyone else can watch to see if Wendy follows the skill steps. Kevin, will you also see if she uses good nonverbal behavior? Okay, let's start.

Provides reinforcement for group member participation.

Summarizes and emphasizes the difficulty in resisting peer pressure.

Reviews the skill steps that identify a sequence that the members should follow in learning how to resist peer pressure. The leader puts these on the board or provides students with a handout.

The leader provides a situation for the group. This is provided to ensure that the skills are understood and learned. Later, members can bring in their own situations to practice.

The leader chooses a member who can do a good job with the role-play (i.e., modeling the skill) since this is the first time through.

Preparing the group members to listen and observe so that they can observe the model and give feedback.

Tom: Hey, Wendy, go get Todd's homework; it's sitting right there (points to a chair).

Kerry: Yeah, he'll never know you did it.

Wendy: Uh . . . I . . . Uhmmm . . . I don't think I better.

Tom: Come on, Wendy, just do it.

Wendy: No, I can't. You do it if you want Todd's homework.

Leader: Okay, break. Let's give Wendy some feedback. Kevin, let's start with you. What nonverbal behavior did you observe?

Kevin: Well, she spoke up and looked Tom in the eye.

Leader: Okay, good. What do you think she could have done better?

Kevin: She tripped over her words at the beginning.

Beth: Yeah, she could have said "no" better at the beginning, but the second time was better.

Leader: Beth, what do you think would be a better response when Tom asked her to take the homework?

Beth: She could have said, "No, I don't think that is right."

Leader: Why isn't it right?

Beth: Because it would hurt his feelings.

Leader: Yes, I think it would. Okay, any other feedback for Wendy? Well, I have some. I think Wendy did a good job of being serious. I think the second time she spoke, she could have suggested another activity like we learned. Any ideas on what she could have suggested?

Tom: You mean she should have said, "Let's go play outside"?

Leader: Yeah, she could have suggested they go outside and forget about taking Todd's homework. Okay, we've got a good start. Let's redo the role-play, and Wendy, try to use the suggestions for improvements the group gave you. For example, how could you say "no" right away after Tom and Kerry put pressure on you?

Wendy: I could say, "No, I think that's mean and I don't want to do it."

Leader: Good. That's better. Let's go ahead and try it out again. Remember to say "no" early on, be forceful, and suggest an alternative activity.

> One member is singled out for a special task to help ensure he pays attention. The leader must be responsible for getting everyone in the group involved in the role-play.

> The leader begins the process of feedback by asking group members to comment on Wendy's performance. The group members have been taught to use positive feedback at first before being critical, although here they move to being critical too quickly.

> The leader encourages students to share observations and then asks for specific critical feedback.

> The leader gets other group members to model better responses to the situation.

> Encouraging the members to think about what it is like when someone hurts your feelings.

> The leader gives feedback, making sure that the role-play incorporates the skills needed to resist peer pressure.

> The leader summarizes the suggestions and then prepares the group to redo the role-play and incorporate the ideas suggested by the group. Here it is important to make sure the role-players understand how to incorporate the feedback for an improved performance.

> The remainder of the session is devoted to continued practice and feedback. The leader helps students to identify situations outside of the group where they can practice skills in the upcoming week and assigns homework practice using the "buddy system." The group closes with a brief fun game to increase social connections among the children and to keep the group interesting and fun.

PRACTICING SOCIAL SKILLS IN THE NATURAL ENVIRONMENT

A primary goal in teaching social skills is that the skills learned will be used in the child's natural environment. Throughout the 10-week sequence, I encouraged the children to practice the skills outside of the group. This was accomplished by giving and monitoring homework assignments. At times all group members were working on the same skill (e.g., after the session where we worked on resisting peer pressure). At other times during the 10 weeks, group members would work on different skills; for example, Wendy would focus on starting a conversation (a discrete friendship skill), while Kevin focused on generating alternatives to peer pressure situations. Group members were given assignments to use the skill and record the outcome in a journal. The journals were helpful and were used by half of the group members; the other three members typically forgot or lost their journals. For those that used them, I reviewed the journals in the group and used them to reinforce the members' practice outside of the group. I also encouraged the use of the skills outside of the group by having the group members practice the skills with their buddy as a homework assignment. Buddies were rotated to promote increased social interaction among all group members and to provide a variety of peer role models for each member. As much as possible, I consulted with teachers to monitor the group members' interpersonal interactions, so that examples of when and where to use the skills could be incorporated into the group procedures.

CONCLUSION

Promoting competence in children and adolescents is a fundamental strategy for helping young people confront stressful situations and avoid problem behaviors. It has been effectively used to help children develop new patterns of interpersonal relationships, confront new social situations, gain membership in new social groups, and learn new behavioral responses. Without adequate social skills, such experiences can become avenues to pregnancy, delinquency, drug use, and social isolation.

Social skills training is perhaps the most promising new treatment model that has been developed for working with young people. It approaches treatment by building on the positive aspects of functioning—building needed skills for youth. Children and adolescents must adapt and cope with an increasingly complex society. As a normal part of growing up, young people must confront the developmental task of dealing with such issues as drugs, sex, and alcohol. To be successful, we must teach our children social skills so that they can respond to difficult social circumstances and do so with self-confidence and competence.

REFERENCES

LeCroy, C. W. (2008). Social skills training. In C. W. LeCroy (Ed.), *Handbook of child and adolescent treatment manuals* (pp. 99–138). New York, NY: Oxford University Press.

LeCroy, C. W. (2013). Designing and facilitating groups with children. In C. Franklin, M. B. Harris, & P. Allen-Meares (Eds.), *The school services sourcebook: A guide for school-based professionals* (2nd ed., pp. 611–618). Greenwich, CT: JAI Press.

Case Study 7-4

Group Work With Men Who Batter

RICHARD M. TOLMAN AND LARRY BENNETT

Social workers often work with nonvoluntary clients. This case study describes a group model of working with such clients because of battering behavior.

Questions

1. How can social workers respond to denial when working with nonvoluntary clients?
2. How did the social worker use confrontation in working with the resistant client?
3. What interventions contributed to the changes described in the client?
4. How does group treatment address the special circumstances of men who batter?

Sam, a White 26-year-old laborer who lives in a working-class suburb, was referred by the court to a group program for men who batter. He is employed full-time, earning about $20,000 annually. Sam has been arrested three times. His most recent arrest was for the battery of his wife. He received 6 months' probation and was mandated to attend domestic violence counseling. He had two previous arrests, one for auto theft when he was a teenager and one 2 years ago for disorderly conduct.

At the initial intake interview, Sam was secretive, and it seemed that he did not want the worker to know much about him. His flat affect and deceptive manner made it appear that he thought the agency was out to get him rather than help him. This type of presentation was not unusual for a court-ordered client. For the most part, men who batter do not come to treatment voluntarily. They are generally either court-mandated or "wife-mandated"; that is, their partners left or threatened to leave the relationship unless they receive counseling. Our experience is that despite the men's nonvoluntary status, they may be helped, and a court order can actually facilitate progress when they might otherwise drop out. In fact, some evidence suggests that batterers' contact with the criminal justice system in itself is effective in reducing violence (Sherman & Berk, 1984). In a national study of 840 male batterers and their female partners, court-ordered participants were more likely to complete the batterer intervention program and were less likely to reoffend than were participants who were in the program voluntarily (Gondolf, 2002).

To enter the program, men must minimally be willing to admit that they have battered and to verbalize a willingness to take responsibility for change. Ongoing denial of battering and responsibility for it is common and expected and must be confronted throughout the treatment process.

An important step in the intake process is taking a history of past and current abuse. The history taking may be facilitated by using structured interview protocols and checklists. In this case, the use of such checklists revealed that Sam had a significant history of both psychological and physical maltreatment of his partner, including interrupting her eating and sleeping; refusing to let her see people; frequently insulting, swearing, and screaming at her; threatening to hit her; pushing, grabbing, and restraining her; slapping her; driving recklessly to frighten her; throwing objects at her; hitting her with his fists; and hitting her with an object.

Generally, men who batter will minimize or deny their violent behavior. In addition, they may attempt to use the treatment program manipulatively, perhaps to convince their partners not to leave them or to drop charges in the court system. Treatment for the men can be stressful and can inadvertently increase the risk of abuse. Therefore, contact with the men's partners is crucial in delivering safe services. When Debbie was interviewed, she corroborated Sam's account of the violence. The fact that Sam accurately described his violent behavior was a good sign that he could come to take responsibility for his behavior.

At intake, Sam was asked about his own alcohol and drug use, and his perception of the role of drugs in his violence. This information is important, because untreated substance problems make progress in treatment for violence unlikely. Many clients attribute their violent behavior to the effects of the substance. It is important to uncover and challenge such a defense in treatment. In this case, Sam attributed none of his violence to alcohol or drugs. He has been abstinent for 5 years. His family history (adult child of an alcoholic, brother with drinking problem) and his own history suggest that he is an alcoholic (he reports blackouts, drinking-related amnesia, friends and family expressing concern about his drinking, and trying to cut down unsuccessfully). He has, however, maintained his abstinence without involvement in any treatment program or attendance of Alcoholics Anonymous.

Sam grew up in an alcoholic, violent family. His father and stepmother are active alcoholics. Sam's brother is currently facing a prison sentence for a felony. Sam witnessed physical abuse of his mother, and he was physically abused. As Straus, Gelles, and Steinmetz (1980) report, both witnessing and being a victim of abuse in one's family of origin are predictors of subsequent abusive behavior.

Sam met his wife, Debbie, when he was 21, 5 years earlier. At that time she was 15 and working as a waitress. He was attracted to her because she was "cute." He had been dating her for 1 week when he was kicked out of his home. Debbie's mother invited him to move in with their family. He never moved out. The first year of their relationship was stormy because of "forced closeness." Sam felt he was underemployed. He blamed money for the arguments between him and Debbie. He described his in-laws' household as very stressful.

Following intake, Sam was placed in an ongoing group. The group approach is preferred over couples or individual treatment for several reasons. Despite obvious problems in Sam and Debbie's relationship that might warrant couples counseling, conjoint sessions are potentially dangerous if undertaken before a man successfully stops his violent behavior. The safety necessary to foster cooperation and adequate self-disclosure cannot be assured while men are actively violent toward their partners. Conjoint therapy may compromise the goal of changing violence because of its emphasis on strengthening or healing the existing relationship. Some men won't change until they are threatened with loss of their partners and, in the couples treatment context, a woman may not be able to safely explore her ambivalent wishes to leave the relationship.

Furthermore, counseling in a couples context may be implicitly victim-blaming. Men have frequently told their partners that the battering would stop if she only changed her behavior. Bograd (1984) points out that there is a subtle but crucial difference between suggesting that a man's partner modify her behavior to protect herself and suggesting that she initiate events so that she can control him. As a result, even couples counseling that explicitly focuses on a woman's safety may reinforce a man's projections of blame on his partner. Although conjoint work to deal with marital discord can be very useful, it should not occur until the primary problem of violence has been addressed successfully and the woman feels safe when participating in the sessions.

A group format offers the men a variety of models and sources of feedback for learning to self-observe, change cognitions, and interact differently. Although many men who batter express regret about their behavior, they are given mixed messages by those around them. The importance of having other men in the same situation saying "I don't like what I am doing and I want to stop" supports a commitment to nonviolent behavior. In a follow-up study of a program for men who batter, Gondolf (1984, 2002) found that men ranked the group support as the most important element in helping them to stop their violence.

Sam's group treatment had several goals. First, Sam had to take responsibility for his violent behavior. This required confronting his denial. Second, he needed to learn skills to help maintain nonviolence. The necessary skills include self-observation, time-out, cognitive restructuring, and interpersonal skills training. They will be described in more detail in the following sections. Third, Sam needed to examine and adjust his attitudes and expectations that encouraged his violence. Fourth, it was hoped that Sam would begin to explore his family of origin and other personal issues that may be related to his violence.

The main ingredients of the group experience are the support and confrontation of the men by other group members and the leaders, education practice in group, and homework assignments. Each group session is relatively structured and begins with a check-in. At check-in the men report if they have been violent or controlling in the past week and if they have used any of the techniques they have learned in group. Problematic situations are then discussed in group in detail, and various techniques are practiced further. This work with the problematic situations the men describe is followed by discussions of specific themes, such as men's control of women or sexually abusive behavior.

In the first sessions with Sam, the primary focus was on helping him take responsibility for his violent behavior, to begin to observe the behavioral chain that leads to violent behavior, and to practice time-outs. Initial training in self-observation begins at intake. The use of a contract for nonviolence encourages men to identify physical, cognitive, affective, and situational cues for violence. Once these cues are identified, a plan for using alternative coping behaviors can be formulated. The metaphor of an early-awareness system is used: Intervention is easier when the cues are identified at subtler, earlier points in the chain of events.

Time-out is a crisis intervention technique that a man can use to take a break from conflict when he feels himself becoming extremely tense in a conflict. Men can use time-out to short-circuit what might become an abusive act. Time-out may include leaving the house or closing oneself in a room alone. Time-outs give men the time to use relaxation techniques, to problem-solve solutions to the conflict, or to reach out for support from others. The skill is often taught quite early in treatment, at intake, and may be incorporated into a no-violence contract, in which a man identifies high-risk situations and agrees to use a time-out or other skill rather than become abusive. When men first join the group, the leaders assign practice time-outs to help the men learn the technique and to troubleshoot problems in the men's application of time-out. Noncompliance with the assignment often becomes a point of confrontation.

For Sam, one problem in using time-out was that Debbie at times tried to block his leaving the house. This problem actually occurs frequently. Partners may perceive time-outs as an attempt to avoid discussing an issue or an attempt to punish her by withdrawing. Many men do abuse time-out in these ways. For Sam, the group helped him problem-solve ways of getting out of the house or taking a time-out when he needed to without using physical aggression toward Debbie.

At first, Sam disclosed relatively little in group. He seemed to have very little ability to be introspective. As he began to discuss details of his life, it was clear that he saw the conflicts he faced with Debbie as totally her fault. Although the leaders and group members could empathize with Sam's pain in the relationship, these descriptions were not accepted at face value, and limits were set on Sam's use of the group to complain about Debbie. The importance of keeping men focused on themselves rather than on their partners cannot be emphasized enough. If unchecked, the group sessions could easily become exclusively focused on how badly treated the men are by their partners. It is critical for the group leader to listen empathically to the men's complaints and the pain that underlies them but to appropriately refocus the group discussion on the men's responsibility for change. When modeled appropriately in the group, the other members begin to take over the function of confrontation from the leader. Such peer confrontation is more powerful, because it is perceived as coming from someone else who knows what it is like to be in the group member's place.

At first Sam was not confronted very directly in the group. His denial was addressed, however, in several ways. First, as mentioned, limits were placed on his complaining about his wife. Second, other members modeled taking responsibility for their own behavior. Gradually, the confrontation became more direct.

In the 10th session, Sam discussed an argument he had with Debbie:

Sam: I work two jobs and she just lays around. She's lazy, she doesn't work, and she doesn't even keep the house clean—her mother does all that. She's like a teenager. And then she goes out and bangs up my car.

Co-leader: You're blaming your wife for everything that's wrong in your relationship. What can you do to improve the situation?

Member 1: Yeah, you need to take more responsibility for problems at home. You're just trying to make it seem like your abuse is her fault.

Member 2: You don't even face the real problems. You just give us your "magic fairy" report every week. You have a big blowup, and then the next day everything is fine. You don't talk over the issues with her; you don't tell her the feelings that were underneath your anger—a magic fairy just comes and takes the problem away.

Member 3: That's stuffing—just like it talks about in the manual.

Member 2: Yeah, you're "saving stamps," man. If you don't work on the real issues and tell her how you feel, you are just going to store up those resentments and blow up again. We don't want to see that happen to you. You've got to get your head out of your ass and start to take care of yourself.

A group discussion of how to deal with resentments followed. The group leader followed up and asked Sam to focus concretely on what he could do between sessions to improve the situation. The plan was for Sam to praise Debbie for doing the bills. By framing the general discussion of the group into a specific homework assignment for Sam, the worker extended the work of the group into the week. Behavioral change was promoted by giving a concrete task and holding Sam accountable for accomplishing it. This particular directive had several purposes. First, in asking Sam to praise Debbie for her help, Sam had to take responsibility for using positive reinforcement rather than coercion in dealing with the issues he has with his wife. Second, focusing on praising Debbie for her help got at the issue of entitlement that Sam felt in regard to her labor. Frequently, men assume that they deserve their partner's labor and that she simply must comply with his requests for what she must do in the home. In this case, Sam was getting the message that labor in a relationship is negotiated and that he is responsible for showing Debbie that he appreciates those things she does for him in the relationship. Thus, the group challenges a sexist attitude that contributes to violence against women, because that attitude diminishes the status and value of women.

This directive also illustrates an initial application of interpersonal skills training. Men who batter are often limited in their ability to resolve conflicts with others assertively rather than passively or aggressively (Rosenbaum & O'Leary, 1981). An important component of group treatment for men who batter therefore involves teaching the man new interpersonal skills for conflict resolution. Applying skills training procedures with men who batter requires that a specific set of skills be identified and then taught to men, using situations that are personally relevant to them. Training in nonviolent conflict resolution often focuses on the man's ability to identify and express his own feelings about what is happening, identify and state his partner's point of view, offer solutions from which both he and his partner will benefit, and negotiate a final compromise.

It should be noted that although completion of the assignment might have led to improvements in Sam's relationship, that was not the purpose per se. The function was to teach Sam noncoercive means for dealing with conflict and with his feelings. It is possible that Debbie will not fulfill Sam's expectations for her behavior, despite Sam's attempts to change himself in a positive manner. In such a case, Sam would be reminded that his responsibility is to act noncoercively, despite her actions. Abusive behavior is never justified, however uncooperative she may be.

At the next session, Sam reported that the arguments with Debbie had continued and that he did not complete his assignment. Interpersonal skills training continued. Training often begins, as it did with Sam, by identifying interpersonal situations in which the man has experienced difficulties. Various ways of achieving a more positive outcome are explored in the group. After sifting through the alternatives, the man chooses one that is most likely to increase the chances of a positive resolution. This alternative can be demonstrated by the leader or a group member. After observing the modeling, the man rehearses the new skill, with someone else playing the role of his partner. Group members then offer feedback on the man's performance, and he may optionally rehearse the new skills a second time to incorporate the feedback. The skills training usually culminates with an agreement to use the new skills in an upcoming situation and report back on the effect.

In this session, the leader spent 10 minutes of rehearsal with Sam on how to praise his wife. During this discussion, several men praised Sam's empathic presentation of his wife's chronic unemployment problem. The evidence for Sam's progress in this session is mixed. His empathy indicated a willingness to view Debbie as a person rather than as an object. This empathy reduces the probability of violence and suggests that Sam was internalizing the group content. However, his issues of control appeared to be surfacing around homework completion. In regard to the noncompletion of his previous assignment, the leader reinforced the importance of assignment completion by confronting his noncompliance and dealing with it in a concrete manner. He was reassigned the same homework.

The following session demonstrated Sam's progress vividly. His adoption of new prosocial behavior is mirrored in his group behavior as well as reports of behavior outside of the group. Sam collected the group members' fees, a shared group responsibility, for the first time. He reported that he completed his assignment, to tell his wife that he appreciated her doing the bills. She blushed and felt good. Sam also reported a surprising improvement in the home situation: Debbie got a job.

During the next group session, Sam was discussing his relationship with Debbie and frequently remarked, "I'm just stupid." The group leader pointed out how easily Sam slipped into such negative self-talk; this was an opportunity to apply some cognitive restructuring techniques with Sam. Cognitive-restructuring techniques teach individuals to analyze and modify maladaptive thinking patterns. A man's rigid beliefs about how he and his partner should behave in a relationship increase the probability that he will be violent. Several interlocking steps are involved in the application of cognitive restructuring in groups. In discussing situations the men have encountered during the week, the following steps may be used: (1) elicit internal dialogue; (2) identify underlying irrational beliefs and faulty assumptions; (3) challenge irrational or faulty beliefs; (4) replace irrational or faulty beliefs with more realistic appraisals; and (5) generate self-instructions for using nonviolent coping behavior.

Much of Sam's negative self-talk in this case was self-referent; that is, he was making unrealistically negative appraisals of himself and his abilities. He had difficulty generating positive self-appraisals, so the leader asked if Sam would listen while the group made positive statements about him. Sam said he would listen, because nobody ever made positive statements about him. The depth of his problems with self-esteem and the role of his family of origin in the genesis of those problems was then revealed in his apparent off-task comments about his brother's impending prison sentence and how his father's long drinking binge put his family deep in debt.

The leader refocused the group on giving Sam positive feedback and then asked the group to proceed. About half of the group was able to give him positive comments. Sam was pleased with the feedback from the group members. Following the feedback, Sam commented that he wanted his brother-in-law to come to the group: "I didn't realize the different types of abuse there are; my brother-in-law is emotionally abusive."

Sam's comment illustrated that progress had been made on several important treatment goals. His recognition of his brother-in-law's emotional abusiveness demonstrated that Sam had come to redefine abusive behavior more broadly. He no longer limited his definition of abuse to physical aggression. Of course, it is critical that Sam recognize his own use of such behaviors and not focus only on others' behavior.

This session also illustrates how the group becomes an instrument of social change. Frequently, group members begin to reach out to their own social networks—and the abusive men that they know—to bring them to group (Douglas, Bathrick, & Perry, 2008). Such action can be seen as a demonstration that an individual man has internalized the need for change—confronting another man about his abuse takes a degree of courage and self-disclosure. In doing so, the man has begun to exercise an influence on his environment. One of the most important maintaining causes of violence against women is the lack of negative social sanctions and the sometimes overt social support for abusive behavior that men receive from other men around them. When men begin to confront other men, they are removing some of that social support. Involvement of men in efforts as allies in working to prevent violence against women is growing worldwide, and these efforts within programs for men who batter are part of the continuum of change efforts (Tolman & Edleson, 2011).

The need for Sam to focus on his own controlling behavior was apparent at the next session. Sam did not come to the group. He had called the crisis line earlier, saying he had gone to Debbie's workplace and been told by her boss that it didn't matter if she came in or not because she was always late and a poor worker. This checking-up behavior was illustrative of his need to control and infantilize his partner.

At the next session, Sam demonstrated that he continued to redefine abuse for himself and was beginning to address his responsibility for behavior change. During the group, Sam described as abusive his breaking of a mirror while talking on the phone. He recognized this behavior as indicating that he was at risk of using direct aggression toward his partner and that breaking a mirror could imply a physical threat to Debbie. The group confronted him on his checking up on Debbie at work, and Sam was able to see how such behavior illustrated his need to control Debbie.

Some of the core cognitions that support Sam's abusive behavior were also identified and challenged in this session. Sam began to discuss his belief that he was worthless without his partner. Such beliefs may lead men to extreme behaviors to control their partners. A plan was developed for how Sam can directly enact behavior that further challenges this irrational belief. He was to attend groups for adult children of alcoholics, to spend some time by himself away from Debbie, and to monitor his feelings of worthwhile with these people.

This session also began a direct focus for Sam on his family of origin. He began to be in touch with his own victimization as a child. Focusing on family-of-origin issues can be a tricky process. On the one hand, it is helpful because it can help Sam begin to empathize with Debbie and what his victimization of her feels like. He can begin to understand the role of his early learning in a way that can lead to healthier coping behaviors—that is, caring for himself rather than coercing Debbie into fulfilling his needs. However, a focus on family-of-origin issues can be counterproductive if it deflects responsibility and defocuses Sam and the group off of the primary issue of his current abusive behavior.

In the next session, men's control of women was the theme. Sam was quiet during most of the group. In commenting on another member's attempt to control his wife, Sam compared the man to his own father: "I was scared of him all the time. . . . If I would have stood up to him we would be talking today, but we aren't." Sam revealed that he recently told his father that he was coming to the group and that he wanted to live his life differently. His father was scornful. Despite the unsupportive response of his father, his self-disclosure to his father illustrated that Sam was actively integrating the work of the group into his life.

As it turned out, this session was Sam's last mandated session. His court supervision ended the following week. Through the period of his mandated treatment, Sam progressed steadily. He moved from blaming his partner for his abusive behavior to a sense of responsibility for his own behavior. He expanded his definition of abuse beyond direct physical aggression and began to modify his other abusive behavior, actively applying the skills that were taught in the group. He made linkages between his current problems and the problems in his own family of origin. He applied this connection positively; that is, he began to challenge family members to accept his new definition of himself as someone who was attempting to live nonviolently. He had initiated linkages with other services. The challenge for Sam in participating in the group following his completion of the court mandate is to maintain these changes and to progress.

CONCLUSION

Although this case focused primarily on intervention with one man in a group setting, it is important to recognize that the intervention did not occur in isolation. Intervention for men who batter needs to be part of a comprehensive, multisystem approach to ending violence. At a minimum, intervention in any community should include (a) immediate protection, support, and advocacy for battered women and their children; (b) intervention for the abusive men; (c) ongoing support and education for battered women and their children; and (d) coordinated intervention in social institutional responses to battering (Brygger & Edleson, 1987). When services are provided for men, they must be coordinated with intervention with other family members. If these services do not occur within the same agency, practitioners working with men must work to establish and maintain good working relationships with shelters and other agencies working with battered women.

A final point to be made here is that Sam's treatment was facilitated by a court mandate. It is important for programs working with men who batter to coordinate closely with institutions that provide social sanctions for violent behavior. When working with criminal justice systems, social workers need to provide pressure for the courts to impose meaningful sanctions if the man is not successfully complying with program requirements (Pence & Shepard, 1999). A court-mandated client for whom no sanctions are delivered upon failure in treatment will soon learn that police, court, and social service actions are not credible. The resulting message will be that he can continue his behavior without serious consequences. The message to his partner will be that his abusive behavior is not to be taken seriously. Social workers must be proactive in working for change in larger systems so that they may provide effective direct service to men who batter.

REFERENCES

Bograd, M. (1984). Family systems approaches to wife battering: A feminist critique. *American Journal of Orthopsychiatry, 54*, 558–568.

Brygger, M. P., & Edleson, J. L. (1987). The Domestic Abuse Project: A multisystems intervention in woman battering. *Journal of Interpersonal Violence, 2*, 324–337.

Douglas, U., Bathrick, D., & Perry, P. A. (2008). Deconstructing male violence against women: The Men Stopping Violence community accountability model. *Violence Against Women, 14*, 247–261.

Gondolf, E. (1984, August). *Men who batter: How they stop their abuse.* Paper presented at the Second National Conference for Family Violence Researchers, Durham, NH.

Gondolf, E. (2002). *Batterer intervention systems: Issues, outcomes, and recommendations.* Thousand Oaks, CA: Sage.

Pence, E. L., & Shepard, M. F. (1999). An introduction: Developing a coordinated community response. In M. F. Shepard & E. L. Pence (Eds.), *Coordinating community responses to domestic violence: Lessons from Duluth and beyond* (pp. 3–23). Thousand Oaks, CA: Sage.

Rosenbaum, A., & O'Leary, K. D. (1981). Marital violence: Characteristics of abusive couples. *Journal of Clinical and Consulting Psychology, 49*, 63–71.

Sherman, L. W., & Berk, R. A. (1984). The specific deterrent effects of arrest for domestic assault. *American Sociological Review, 49*, 261–272.

Straus, M. A., Gelles, R. J., & Steinmetz, S. (1980). *Behind closed doors: Violence in the American family.* New York, NY: Doubleday & Co.

Tolman, R., & Edleson, J. (2011). Intervening with men for violence prevention. In *Sourcebook on violence against women* (2nd ed., pp. 351–371). Thousand Oaks, CA: Sage.

PART VIII
Case Studies in Diversity

Social workers have had a long-standing commitment in their work with socially and economically oppressed people. However, there is often a great deal of difference between the social work practitioner and the client. Such differences include gender, sexual orientation, and socioeconomic, cultural, and racial disparities. It is not surprising that these differences may become barriers to understanding and providing effective social work services. Social workers must continually attempt to reduce the barriers that interfere with their helping someone in the most effective manner possible.

Social workers must recognize that each individual comes from a group with a specific cultural background. Group members want social workers to be aware of their existence and to know something about their group—its characteristics, values, beliefs, attitudes, and goals. Although such group members want you to know about them as a group, you must not forget that each person is unique and should be viewed in light of their uniqueness. Knowing something about a group often helps you identify what is unique for each person. Practice procedures should be varied depending on the client's ethnicity, sex, and age group but need to be assessed for each individual.

It is important to note that one of the most important factors in successful cross-cultural work is your attitude. Social workers communicate a lot through their reactions to clients. If clients perceive the worker as not having a positive attitude, they will

not be encouraged to continue working. Shulman (2011) has recommended "prepara-
tory empathy," or having a helping frame of mind before meeting with a client, as a
needed skill.

Cross-cultural social work emphasizes the importance of the client's worldview—or
how the client perceives his or her relationship to the world. This culturally based variable has an important influence on the interaction between the social worker and the
client. This is particularly true when social workers have a different worldview from
that of their clients. This difference can sometimes lead to negative judgments about the
client's attitude, values, or behaviors.

This subject is often discussed within the context of a "dual perspective"
(Ashford & LeCroy, 2013). The dual perspective is understanding the values, attitudes,
and behaviors of the larger dominant society and those of the client's immediate family and community. Clients are seen as part of two systems: (1) the dominant system,
composed of power and economic resources, and (2) the nurturing system, composed
of the family and community.

A major goal for social work is to develop ethnic-sensitive practice principles. In
order to accomplish this goal, it is important that you understand the client's worldview
within an ethnic or cultural context. An ethnic group (race, religion, or national origin),
social class, rural-urban residence, and regional residence determine a particular subculture within society. In analyzing ethnic variables, Seabury, Seabury, and Garvin (2010)
suggest a framework that consists of six dimensions: communications, habitat, social
structure, socialization, economics, and beliefs and sentiments. This type of framework
helps the social worker understand the behavior of the members of various ethnic
groups, because this behavior is affected by group membership. Ibrahim (1985) would
add variables that represent more universal factors: the modality of human nature, the
modality of human relationships, the relation of people to nature, the temporal focus of
human life, and the modality of human activity.

Given these considerations, it is critical for the social worker to understand the
client's worldview, the relationship of the client's worldview to the client's primary
subculture, and how the majority or dominant culture affects the client's values and
behavior. For example, the social worker receives a referral to help a Native American
woman. First, the social worker must try to understand the client's subculture or group.
General knowledge about Native Americans is helpful. The worker can attempt to
understand the subculture by analyzing the various ethnic variables—socialization,
economics, modality of human relationships, and so on. This knowledge is helpful but
limited, because it does not take into consideration the client's subjective reality. How
does this client perceive her relationship to the world? What is the relationship between
the client's worldview and the client's subculture? These questions focus on an understanding of the context of the client's perceptions and behaviors.

Also, what is the relationship between the client's perceptions, the client's subculture, and the majority or dominant culture? It may be important to know the extent
to which the client is bicultural or experiencing cultural contradictions. Is the client in
conflict with either majority values or those of the client's culture of origin? Lum (2003)
believes that social work services must be offered in a manner that enhances the client's

sense of ethnic group participation and sense of power. In order to accomplish this, agencies need to be responsive to the client by understanding the client's cultural and community background, as well as the nature of the problem being presented. Social workers need to develop culturally responsive practice skills.

The client's experience is one of the most important sources of information. It is critical to discover how the client represents the world. The process of change begins in helping the client integrate various aspects of the client's worldview to maximize the client's effectiveness (Sue, 2011). Cross-cultural competence can be determined by how well the social worker is aware of and can understand and accept the client's worldview. A few ways that social workers can become ethnically competent are to (a) be aware of one's cultural limitations, (b) be open to cultural differences, (c) possess a client-oriented learning style, (d) use the client's cultural resources, and (e) acknowledge the client's cultural integrity.

This section begins with a case study by Morrow and Tack, who describe their work with a lesbian couple following a tragic accident. This is a very difficult case, where the worker is simultaneously addressing such factors as recovery from the accident, the couple's relationship, homophobia that impacts the work, and the challenges homosexuals face in the dominant heterosexual society.

Ho presents a case study focusing on the difficulties that an interracial couple experiences. He describes in a clear and straightforward manner how to engage the couple in counseling and then sets forth how to help them build a better relationship. A major part of the treatment focuses on helping the couple understand and resolve their cultural differences.

Parnell and VanderKloot present one of the most important case studies in this book: social work practice with the urban poor. Social work has a special commitment to serve the socially and economically oppressed. These authors present the special skills and knowledge needed to work in this important arena. Their case is complex, and they refer to their difficulties as working with chaos—taking into consideration the poverty, the drug use, and the community. Their case study suggests that a different perspective and a different approach to intervention is needed when working with the urban poor. The final case study by Cox, Sullivan, Reiman, and Vang provides an overview of cross-cultural social work practice and describes the case of a Hmong American family. The case study reveals faulty assumptions that were made about the family and shows how these issues were addressed with the help of a cross-cultural consultant.

REFERENCES

Ashford, J. B., & LeCroy, C. W. (2013). *Human behavior and the social environment: A multidimensional perspective*. Pacific Grove, CA: Cengage.

Ibrahim, F. A. (1985). Effective cross-cultural counseling and psychotherapy: A framework. *The Counseling Psychologist, 13*, 625–638.

Lum, D. (2003). *Social work practice and people of color: A process stage approach*. Pacific Grove, CA: Brooks/Cole.

Seabury, B. A., Seabury, B., & Garvin, C. (2010). *Foundations of interpersonal practice in social work: Promoting competence in generalist practice.* Thousand Oaks, CA: Sage.

Shulman, L. (2011). *The skills of helping individuals, families, groups and communities.* Pacific Grove, CA: Brooks/Cole.

Sue, D. W. (2011). *Counseling the culturally different.* Hoboken, NJ: Wiley.

Case Study 8-1

The Case of Ruth and Janice

DEANA F. MORROW AND FRANCES E. TACK

This case involves an older lesbian couple who encounter the challenge of a life-threatening accident and its aftermath. Issues pertaining to chronic and acute medical needs are addressed, including the financial crisis of managing long-term nursing care through Medicare and Medicaid. In addition, issues of internalized homophobia and institutional heterosexism are factors in this case.

Questions

1. What is internalized homophobia? Heterosexism? How have each impacted the lives of Ruth and Janice?

2. How do you think Ruth's background as an elementary school teacher and long-time member of her childhood church impacted her openness about her sexual orientation? The social worker had an initial impression about Ruth's internalized homophobia, but he did not immediately address his thoughts with Ruth and Janice. What are your thoughts about the worker's decision to defer on addressing these concerns until later in his work with Ruth and Janice?

3. The social worker used both a micro and macro systems perspective in responding to this case. Describe his actions that support intervention across different systems.

4. Go to the Medicare website at www.medicare.gov to determine available Medicare coverage for skilled nursing home care. Based on your findings, how useful is Medicare in funding skilled nursing home care? What are its benefits? Its limitations?

Janice (age 70) and Ruth (age 74) have been in a long-term intimate relationship for 42 years. They live in a small town in a Southern state where same-sex marriage is not yet legalized. Janice is a retired sales associate who worked for a large home improvement chain for 42 years. She developed chronic back pain after years of being on her feet and doing lots of bending and lifting in her job. She has had two back surgeries since retirement, yet she continues to live with chronic pain and uses a cane to steady herself when walking. Janice can walk only for short periods at a time, but she remains able to drive and do small household tasks that do not involve lifting or standing for long periods.

Ruth is a retired elementary school teacher who has remained in reasonably good health since retiring 6 years ago. Although she has Type 2 diabetes, she walks daily, manages her diet well, and thus far has successfully avoided the need for insulin treatment. Ruth attends to many of the household chores for Janice and herself, including light cleaning, grocery shopping, and meal preparation. The couple has hired a cleaning service to come in and do a more complete cleaning of the house once a month.

Ruth and Janice do not have children, and they have minimal extended-family interaction and support. Ruth was an only child from a small family and has no connections with distant cousins. Janice has a brother who lives in another state, but he is not accepting of her as a lesbian. They talk on the phone once or twice a year, and their relationship remains strained.

Janice and Ruth have always lived a quiet life together. They enjoy reading, movies, and going out to dinner. They also have a small circle of lesbian friends, most of whom are also retired. Ruth remains active in the church of her childhood, where she has sung in the choir for more than 50 years. Church involvement is the one activity that Janice and Ruth do not share together. Attending church and singing in the choir has always been an important part of Ruth's life. Janice, in contrast, does not adhere to any particular faith tradition and does not accompany Ruth to Sunday services. She enjoys quiet reading on most days when Ruth is away at church.

THE ACCIDENT AND HOSPITALIZATION

While driving home from choir practice on a dark, cold, and rainy Wednesday evening, Ruth briefly took her eyes off the road while changing the radio station. In an instant, her car jolted out of control, and she skidded off the road and sideways into a large oak tree. Ruth never even had time to hit the brakes. The impact was on the driver's side of the car. As a result of the accident, the femur in Ruth's left leg was shattered and her left hip was broken. Her left arm was also fractured and her left shoulder was injured. Doctors performed hip replacement surgery on Ruth's damaged hip. They also implanted a steel rod in her leg to repair her shattered femur. Ruth's broken left arm was set with a soft cast. Her shoulder damage would possibly require surgery as well, but doctors wanted to wait until Ruth was more recovered from her other injuries before making a final determination on the need for shoulder surgery.

After 10 days of hospitalization, the hospital's utilization review committee determined that Ruth's care needs no longer met acute care requirements for Medicare insurance coverage, and they recommended that Ruth continue her recovery with intensive physical therapy at a skilled nursing care facility. The hospital social worker met with Ruth to discuss placement options. There were two skilled nursing facilities in town, and beds were available at each one. With Ruth's consent, the hospital social worker arranged for Janice to visit both nursing homes to determine which of the two would be most appropriate for Ruth's needs. Because of the looming end of insurance coverage in the hospital setting, Janice had to quickly visit both facilities within 24 hours in order to have information for Ruth to consider before the hospital's discharge deadline the next day. With Janice's support, Ruth chose to be admitted to Jennings Center to continue her recovery and rehabilitation.

NURSING HOME PLACEMENT

Ruth was admitted to skilled nursing care at the Jennings Center the next day. The fees for her skilled nursing care would be covered in full by Medicare for up to 20 days only. If Ruth needed continued skilled care beyond 20 days, Medicare would cover only part of her bill, and she would have to pay an out-of-pocket copayment of approximately $150 per day. If Ruth were to need skilled nursing care beyond 100 days, Medicare would no longer provide coverage. The $275 per diem nursing home charges would be Ruth's full responsibility at that point. It became clear to Ruth and Janice that Medicare coverage was time-limited, and their goal was for Ruth to recover enough to manage at home as soon as possible.

In addition to adjusting to the emotional upheaval of Ruth's accident and injuries, Janice and Ruth now found themselves coping with unanticipated challenges on a variety of new fronts. They found that the medical systems they were encountering were not well-designed for same-sex couples, which is a common disparity for older lesbians (Goldberg, Sickler, & Dibble, 2005; Pugh, 2005). Medical forms to be completed did not account for their long-term relationship, and staff presumed Ruth was heterosexual, asking whether she was married, divorced, or single. Despite their 42 years as a couple, Janice had no legal basis in the healthcare system for being identified as Ruth's official next of kin.

Also, Ruth and Janice had to make quick decisions about how much to disclose about their relationship with medical caregiving strangers. Because of Ruth's career as an elementary school teacher, the couple had always lived a private, low-key public life. Ruth had worked for the public school system during an era when many in public education still believed that gay people should not be allowed to teach children. Thus, like many lesbians who came of age in the pre-Stonewall era (Bayliss, 2000; Parks & Hughes, 2007), Ruth and Janice kept their personal lives private except for with their small circle of lesbian friends. In addition, Ruth was not "out" at her religiously conservative church and rarely had to explain her relationship with Janice given that Janice did not attend church events with Ruth. In essence, Ruth and Janice had a strong relationship that had served their needs well over the years, yet they were invisible as a couple beyond their small circle of friends.

SOCIAL WORK ENGAGEMENT AND ASSESSMENT

Joseph Mendez (age 25) worked as the Director of Social Services at the Jennings Center. He had completed his MSW degree 2 years ago, focusing his studies in the areas of gerontology and medical social work. Joseph met Ruth and Janice at the time of Ruth's transfer from the hospital to Jennings Center. Janice had followed along in her car behind the ambulance as Ruth was transferred from the hospital to the nursing home. Upon arriving at Jennings Center, Janice walked slowly and stiffly, cane in hand, behind Ruth's gurney as she was unloaded from the ambulance and moved to her new room. Joseph greeted Ruth and Janice and told Ruth he would return to talk with her more after she was settled in and the initial nursing assessment was completed.

When Joseph returned an hour later, he found Janice still in the room with Ruth. She had brought along some of Ruth's clothes and personal items and was helping Ruth settle in. At Ruth's request, Janice remained in the room as Joseph began to complete Ruth's psychosocial history and assessment. Sensing that Ruth and Janice may be a couple, Joseph was careful to phrase his assessment questions using open and inclusive terms, yet he carefully followed Ruth's and Janice's lead without being overly presumptuous that they were a couple. Neither Ruth nor Janice indicated they were a couple, and Joseph respected their privacy. Janice visited Ruth daily, and Joseph made a point to have some form of supportive engagement with both women each day.

After 2 weeks of encountering Joseph on a daily basis and experiencing his genuineness and respect toward her and Janice, Ruth asked to meet with Joseph. At that meeting, Ruth disclosed to Joseph that she and Janice were a long-term couple but that they had always been discreet about their relationship given Ruth's career in public education. Joseph wondered if Ruth's life of involvement in her religiously conservative church may have also impacted her tendency toward concealing her private life. That factor, Joseph thought, is a sensitive topic for another day.

Ruth expressed to Joseph her concern that her recovery was a slow and painful process that may not result in her becoming well enough to be independent again. She expressed that she was not progressing in physical therapy as well as her therapists had hoped. Ruth also expressed concerns that Janice would not be physically able to assist with her (Ruth's) care needs, such as bathing, dressing, toileting, and transferring from the bed to a wheelchair if she returned home. Ruth was worried that Janice was not faring well at home—that Janice was not eating well and that she needed help with the daily activities Ruth used to do, such as grocery shopping, cooking, and light cleaning. She was concerned that, given their lack of extended family, Janice would not have the support she needs now that Ruth was not at home.

Ruth was also concerned about the financial impact of continuing skilled nursing care. She had already completed 14 of the 20 days of full coverage from Medicare. The daily co-payment of $150 would begin with her 21st day of care. She wasn't sure how she and Janice would manage this expense, let alone the full private-pay expense of $275 per day they would incur if Ruth needed more than 100 days of skilled nursing care. Furthermore, Ruth expressed her frustration that some of the care staff at Jennings Center seemed to convey a thinly veiled intolerance of Janice's daily presence in Ruth's room.

Ruth suspected the coldness she perceived among these few staff members was centered in their bias against lesbian and gay people.

SOCIAL WORK INTERVENTION

With Joseph's now-confirmed knowledge that Ruth and Janice were a couple, he met with them together to develop an intervention plan for addressing Ruth's concerns. Given the lack of legal protection of their relationship, Joseph referred Ruth and Janice to an estate planning attorney, who assisted them with establishing living wills and powers of attorney to legally protect their decision-making rights for each other in the event that either woman would become unable to act on her own behalf. The attorney also advised the couple to revise the deed to their home to include a joint right of survivorship clause, so that if either one died, the other could retain ownership of the home. Because Ruth and Janice could not legally marry in their state, they were not entitled to the inheritance rights that are commonly afforded to legally married couples; therefore, on the advice of the attorney, they also each completed a will naming the other as sole heir.

Joseph also explored with Ruth and Janice their financial situation in light of Ruth's skilled nursing care needs. In this instance, not being legally married was potentially beneficial. If Ruth's financial resources became exhausted because of the expense of long-term care, the state could not encumber Janice's resources toward the support of Ruth's care. In this sense, the couple's financial resources that were in Janice's name would be protected. The estate attorney who assisted Ruth and Janice with their medical documents also assisted them in protecting their overall estate assets to the greatest extent possible if Ruth needed to apply for Medicaid coverage for continued long-term care.

Joseph also explored with Janice and Ruth the continuing challenges for Janice in maintaining her independence at home. Janice acknowledged that, given her chronic back pain and limited capacity for walking, she was experiencing difficulty in attending to the light housekeeping and grocery shopping tasks that Ruth used to do. The monthly cleaning service was still in place and remained a great help to Janice. With Janice's consent, Joseph contacted the local Agency on Aging and obtained light housekeeping and errand support for Janice on a weekly basis. In addition, he placed Janice on a wait list for home meal delivery (an opening was not immediately available). Until the opening became available, Janice could purchase a low-cost lunch meal each day at Jennings Center. Both Janice and Ruth embraced the possibility of sharing a meal together each day again.

Joseph now had an intervention in place for providing for the immediate needs of establishing legal protections for Ruth's and Janice's care decisions and for protecting their estate to the extent possible if Ruth required long-term care at Jennings Center. He realized, however, that an additional intervention would be needed to assist Ruth and Janice in exploring their internal cognitions and feelings related to decades of being mostly closeted and now navigating their lives in a more public arena. That work, Joseph knew, would require discussions about evolving generational and scientific understandings of sexual orientation, internalized homophobia, and social bias in the form of heterosexism (Morrow & Messinger, 2006; Parks & Hughes, 2007; Phillips & Marks, 2008).

At the broader facility system level, Joseph recognized the presence of heterosexist bias among some staff. Heterosexism is the presumption that all people are heterosexual and that heterosexuality is the preferred norm. Joseph knew from his training that this mindset is discriminatory and fails to recognize the validity of other forms of sexual orientation (Hash & Netting, 2009; Morrow & Messinger, 2006; Phillips & Marks, 2008). Joseph worked with the facility's training director to include content on lesbian and gay people in diversity education trainings for all staff. Affirmative services to lesbian and gay residents and same-sex couples were identified as a service standard, and all staff were expected to serve lesbian and gay residents and their families with the same respect afforded to other residents and families. Staff who failed to uphold this standard of service were responded to on an individual basis through the facility's progressive discipline program.

POSTLUDE

Ruth's progress with rehabilitation proved to be limited over time. She was never able to fully regain her independence. Although her broken femur and broken left arm healed, nerve damage that occurred to her left foot during hip replacement surgery limited her continued recovery. This nerve damage, combined with restricted recovery of the hip joint itself, precluded Ruth from regaining independent ambulation. Her shoulder injury also never fully healed, and she continued to have limited use and mobility of her left arm. Ruth adapted to using a wheelchair for mobility and to having regular assistance with bathing, dressing, toileting, and transferring. She also developed complications with diabetes and had to begin insulin treatment. Her blood sugar levels varied significantly and required continued monitoring.

Ruth began the private copay period of Medicare funding after 20 days at Jennings Center, and she had to fully fund the expense of her nursing home care after 100 days at the end of Medicare coverage. Within months, Ruth spent all of her lifetime savings on paying privately for long-term nursing care. With Joseph's guidance, she applied for and received Medicaid support to finance her continued skilled nursing care at Jennings Center.

Janice continues to function at home with weekly housekeeping and errand assistance from the local Agency on Aging. She continues with the monthly cleaning service she and Ruth had used before Ruth's accident. Janice also now receives Monday through Friday lunch deliveries arranged through the Agency on Aging. She has her dinner most days with Ruth at Jennings Center. With the legal assistance arranged by Joseph, Janice was able to protect her portion of her and Ruth's financial resources. Given that all but $30 of Ruth's monthly retirement and social security income is applied toward her nursing home bill under Medicaid, Janice provides for Ruth's basic needs, such as clothing and personal items. Janice continues to visit Ruth on a daily basis, and they each are slowly coming to terms with the reality that Ruth will likely not return home to live.

Joseph has worked with Ruth and Janice over the months in helping them explore their many years of experiences as lesbians in a sociohistorical period that was largely homophobic. Joseph has helped them explore their internalized homophobia—their internalization of negative messages about gays and lesbians. He has helped them reframe their cognitions about their sexual orientation in relation to current-day human rights and scientific understandings of sexual orientation diversity. Ruth and Janice gradually became more open with the Jennings Center staff about their relationship and, for the most part, found a welcoming milieu.

Given her mobility challenges, Ruth no longer attends her home church. Several friends from church visit with her regularly, and she has disclosed her relationship with Janice to a few of her closest friends from church. Although their lives changed so suddenly because of Ruth's automobile accident on that cold and rainy Wednesday evening, Ruth and Janice have discovered that they have greater resilience and coping skills (Comerford, Henson-Stroud, Sionainn, & Wheeler, 2004; Hall & Fine, 2005) than they ever imagined. Uncertainty about the future remains, but they are gradually becoming increasingly empowered in navigating their continuing life journey. Joseph remains a central resource of support and acceptance in their lives.

REFERENCES

Bayliss, S. (2000). My life in a lesbian community: The joys and the pain. *Journal of Lesbian Studies, 9*(1/2), 45–54.

Comerford, S. A., Henson-Stroud, M. M., Sionainn, C., & Wheeler, E. (2004). Crone songs: Voices of lesbian elders on aging in a rural environment. *Affilia, 19*, 418–436.

Goldberg, S., Sickler, J., & Dibble, S. (2005). Lesbians over sixty: The consistency of findings from twenty years of survey data. *Journal of Lesbian Studies, 9*(1/2), 195–213.

Hall, R., & Fine, M. (2005). The stories we tell: The lives and friendship of two older Black lesbians. *Psychology of Women Quarterly, 29*, 177–187.

Hash, K. M., & Netting, F. E. (2009). It takes a community: Older lesbians meeting social and care needs. *Journal of Gay and Lesbian Social Services, 21*, 326–342.

Morrow, D. F., & Messinger, L. (Eds.). (2006). *Sexual orientation and gender expression in social work practice.* New York, NY: Columbia University Press.

Parks, C. A., & Hughes, T. L. (2007). Age differences in lesbian identity development and drinking. *Substance Use and Misuse, 42*, 361–380.

Phillips, J., & Marks, G. (2008). Ageing lesbians: Marginalising discourses and social exclusions in the aged care industry. *Journal of Gay and Lesbian Social Services, 20*, 31–49.

Pugh, S. (2005). Assessing the cultural needs of older lesbians and gay men: Implications for practice. *Practice, 17*, 207–218.

Case Study 8-2

Counseling an Interracial Couple

MAN-KEUNG HO*

This case study identifies critical issues facing interracial couples and highlights characteristics of one Asian culture that may influence the counseling relationship.

Questions

1. How was the social worker able to engage the husband in the counseling process?
2. What developmental changes were challenging the couple in this case?
3. What kinds of tasks could the social worker assign this couple to enhance intimacy in their relationship?
4. What can social workers do to help interracial couples recognize and value each person's culture and improve communication skills?

Mrs. I, a 45-year-old Filipino American, was referred to the Transcultural Family Institute by her family physician, who diagnosed the patient's affective disorder as "psychosomatic" and "neurotic." In addition to periodic depression, Mrs. I had a minor heart problem. Her depression and family-related problems caused her to occasionally "forget" to take her medication for high blood pressure. Mrs. I frequently complained that she had no desire to live anymore.

---

*Man-Keung Ho (deceased) was professor of social work at the University of Oklahoma.

In the initial interview, Mrs. I impressed me as a neat, well-dressed, and well-groomed individual who appeared outwardly friendly and sociable but inwardly withdrawn and suspicious. Although she seemed to be relieved when she noticed my Asian physical appearance, Mrs. I avoided direct eye contact with me when I first greeted her.

[Asian way of conveying respect and interest]

To ease her discomfort and curiosity about my nationality and occupation, I volunteered that I am a naturalized American citizen from Hong Kong and that I help individuals and families with their problems.

[To return respect and collect data]

Mrs. I responded immediately that she too is a naturalized Asian American from the Philippines. As I nodded my head to establish communication with her, she explained that she had immigrated to the United States 20 years ago with her Anglo-American husband. He had been in the military in the Philippines.

[Empathizing]

Mrs. I then asked me about my immediate and extended family. I thanked her for her interest. When I told her about my family, I noticed that she began to relax. I then took the opportunity to inquire about her family.

[Client self-determination]

Mrs. I sighed, slumped down, and appeared to be teary. I responded immediately that she must have thought a lot about her family and that if talking about her family upset her, she could choose to change the topic.

[Relationship building]

Mrs. I apologized for becoming a "crybaby" and said, "Getting emotional has always been my problem." I responded by granting her permission to cry if she felt like it. "Family is a vital part of one's life," I empathized.

Mrs. I continued that she and her husband have two grown daughters. The older daughter resides in California with her husband and two young children. Her younger daughter, whom Mrs. I called "Baby," married 5 months ago. She and her husband moved to a neighboring state after marriage. I complimented her on raising two responsible daughters.

[Show of respect and courtesy]

Mrs. I sighed again, saying, "It was not easy." Mrs. I continued that she missed her daughters very much.

[Adjustment in family lifestyle]

As a way to "fill up her lost feeling for her daughters" and to occupy her time, Mrs. I began babysitting in her own home. "I enjoy taking care of babies, but—they are not mine," Mrs. I said regretfully.

[Empty nest syndrome]

I took the opportunity to assess her relationship with her husband by asking her how her husband had adjusted to their second daughter's departure. Mrs. I shook her head and responded, "It didn't bother him; nothing bothers him." I detected some anger in Mrs. I's voice, and I provided her a general lead by commenting, "Your husband reacted differently than you did." Mrs. I explained that her husband is an "easy-go-lucky" type of person. "He works long hours as a maintenance person for two elementary schools. Between work and after work, he drinks with his buddies and visits with his mother who lives in the same town as we do," continued Mrs. I.

[Enmeshment and family-of-origin issues]

I then asked her how she felt about her husband's activities.

[Assessing the couple's relationship]

Mrs. I said angrily, "It doesn't bother me." I clarified by reflecting that her husband's working long hours, drinking with his friends, and spending time with his mother did not bother her. Mrs. I commented, "What is the use?!" "It seems to me that you must have let him know how you feel about this, but that nothing has changed," I empathized. Mrs. I then burst into tears saying, "My husband and I have had nothing to do with each other for quite some time."

[Dysfunctional couple relationship]

"When I had my daughters with me, I was able to cope with it. Now my daughters are gone; I guess I just go crazy." Mrs. I also volunteered that lately she really did not care about living or dying (which explained why she often "forgot" to take her blood pressure medicine).

[Emotionally cut off]

"If my parents were still alive, I would have packed up and gone back to the Philippines by myself a long time ago," said Mrs. I.

As a means to combat Mrs. I's depression and her low emotional, mental, and physical state, I requested to see her husband as a first step toward improving the marital relationship.

[Ecological approach for helping]

Mrs. I agreed to ask her husband to contact me. Three days after my first interview with Mrs. I, Mr. I telephoned me to request a counseling session for the couple. I offered him an individual session. Mr. I rejected the idea and said it was not needed. I interviewed the couple conjointly 3 days later. Mr. I appeared very anxious and eager for the interview to start. He is a physically big, tall man. He spoke loudly and seemed to intimidate his wife. After a few sociable exchanges, Mr. I commented that he was glad to see an Asian therapist, who he believed could potentially help his wife with her problem. I asked Mr. I how he felt about an Asian therapist, and he replied abruptly, "Okay."

[To clarify Mr. I's potential doubt and discomfort]

I then asked Mr. I his impression of his wife's situation.

[To clarify]

Mr. I's immediate response was, "It blows my mind." I asked him if he would elaborate on what he meant by "it." Mr. I said that he did not understand why his wife did not want to do anything, including taking medication to save her life. I inquired if Mr. I understood why his wife did not seem to enjoy living.

[To assess empathic ability]

Mr. I responded quickly with a low voice and head down: "I wish I knew." To minimize Mr. I's anxiety and potential feelings of threat and guilt, I nurtured him by stating that he must care about his wife, since he made an early appointment to see me.

[To strengthen marital bond]

Mr. I spoke with a low but calm voice, "How can you not care about a person you have spent more than 20 years with?"

To accentuate the couple's marital bonding, I encouraged them to reminisce about some memorable moments in their marriage.

[Accentuate the positive to counter present conflicts]

Mrs. I assumed a less active verbal part in reminiscing, but she smiled and nodded to show her approval of her husband's stories about their relationship. To focus on the presenting problem, I asked about the couple's present relationship.

[Refocusing on the problem]

Mr. I responded defensively, "What relationship?" I empathized by stating how much both of them were hurting. Mr. I commented on his understanding of his wife's present predicament and social isolation. "I understand," whispered Mr. I with his head down again, "but I do not know what to do."

I turned to Mrs. I for suggestions.

[To help the couple reconnect]

After a long pause, Mrs. I admitted that she had not been "much of a wife" to her husband. She then complained that she and her husband had nothing in common.

[Common in interracial marriages]

They had different interracial interests, and they never saw things the same. Because Mr. I is a Protestant, she had ceased to attend the Catholic church a long time ago. "Since I don't go to a Catholic church, I have no contact at all with my close Filipino friends who are Catholics," complained Mrs. I. "Just because I do not think the way you do and do not do the same things you and your American friends do, does not mean that my way is wrong. I hate it when you use stereotypes to put me down simply because of my Asian ancestry," continued Mrs. I.

[Characteristic of dysfunctional intermarriage]

Mr. I sat up straight and appeared to be startled. "This is exactly how I feel too. You think your Asian way is superior to the American way. I cannot stand it when you call me a big-mouthed American."

I explained to the couple the dynamics and inherent cultural value conflicts intermarried couples usually experience.

[To shift from the personal to the cultural]

In addition, I shared with them the potential richness in mutual sharing between interracial couples (Ho, 1988) who experience cultural transition. I challenged the couple to stop widening the cultural gap and emphasizing value differences but instead to find commonalities that could repair and solidify their marital bond.

[To narrow cultural and emotional differences]

Mrs. I responded by saying, "Since we have never established a solid marital bond, I really do not know where and how to repair it." Mr. I appeared to be offended by Mrs. I's statement, and he stated that as far as he was concerned, they got along fine when they were first married. Mrs. I responded that during the initial period of their marriage, they tried their best to minimize their differences. "Besides, I didn't want my parents and relatives to think that I had made a mistake by marrying an American instead of a Filipino," added Mrs. I.

[Characteristic of initial phase of intermarriage]

Before the session ended, I encouraged the couple to recapitulate the parts of our discussion that had special meaning for them. Both partners agreed that although they felt uncomfortable and apprehensive, they were pleased to have an opportunity to ventilate their feelings. Mrs. I expressed surprise to learn about her husband's emotional hurt and feelings of isolation. Mr. I indicated that this was the longest and most helpful talk they had had with each other for quite some time. He also expressed hope that his relationship with his wife would improve and that his wife's depression would be lifted. The couple agreed to return for four more sessions aiming to improve their marital relationship.

The next three sessions with this couple were devoted to engaging them in communicating effectively with each other. Essential communication styles and skills for conflict resolution were taught. Assignments were given so that the couple could practice these skills at home. Despite the couple's strong motivation to learn about new communication skills, occasionally their interaction ran into barricades. The couple's old hurt and resentment erupted when they focused on personality deficits instead of cultural differences. The couple's newly learned problem-solving skills gradually helped them to agree to disagree. As a result, they began to enjoy spending time together at home.

[Importance of social network to systematic change]

Mr. I also encouraged his wife to rejoin the Catholic church to resume her fellowship with several Filipino families and interracial families. As the couple began to reconcile and find companionship with each other, Mr. I drastically reduced the time he spent with his friends. Mr. I's mother was somewhat puzzled and upset with her son's infrequent visits, but she later learned to accept her daughter-in-law as a means to entice her son to visit her. Two months after the last counseling session, Mrs. I paid me a surprise visit. She brought me freshly cooked banana dumplings.

[Use of a ritual for termination]

She informed me that she felt much better and that her physician had decided that she no longer needed medication for high blood pressure.

REFERENCE

Ho, M. K. (1988). *Family therapy with ethnic minorities.* Newbury Park, CA: Sage.

Case Study 8-3

Working With the Urban Poor

Myrtle Parnell and Jo VanderKloot

The urban poor face serious difficulties in their day-to-day lives. This case describes the complexity of working in an environment characterized by poverty, drug abuse, poor parenting, child abuse, and general chaos.

Questions

1. How did the social worker engage the client to become involved in treatment?
2. What specific barriers were present in attempting to deliver services to the client?
3. How did drug use affect the progress made by the social worker and the client?
4. How can an ecological perspective help in understanding the complex set of factors affecting this case?

Anyone who has worked with the urban poor is aware of the chaos in their lives as well as in the communities in which they live. Social work journals describe these families as multiproblem, disorganized, underorganized, crisis prone, enmeshed, and disengaged.

In the process of the usual intake, procedures and forms are used to provide order, which enables the clinician to then fit the client into the traditional psychiatric categories. However, this process of creating order leaves out crucial information about the client's life. The piece that is omitted is, in fact, vital to the clinician's understanding of and ability to connect to the client's reality. What seems to the clinician to be chaotic is rather a different way of being in the world—a way of being that is largely determined by the decisions of the dominant culture, which are often at odds with the needs and realities of the poor.

Just as the urban poor do not understand or know how to function in the mainstream, so too most middle-class clinicians must acknowledge that they do not understand or know the world in which the poor client lives. The need to create a knowable order on the part of the clinician is understandable, but if it is not resisted, this approach will yield information that does not provide the framework in which change can take place.

We suggest that the clinician must recognize chaos and learn to see the patterns within it in the interests of helping the client. In order to recognize and use the chaos, one needs to put aside the usual traditional theoretical structures—the reductionistic, linear way of viewing the client, often in isolation from his or her context. We make little or no attempt to structure the client but rather observe the patterns as they unfold. This leads to an understanding of the patterns and how they repeat across the different levels in the client's life—individual, couple, family, community, and society. We can then choose a level in which to intervene that will trigger change across all systems.

The following statement is from the Family Networker Symposium (Parnell & VanderKloot, 1988):

> We knew the frame had to be drawn differently and on a much larger scale than was originally conceived. What existed as a body of knowledge for working with the poor appeared to be a caricature in relation to the realities encountered in the field. Poor people did not believe in the models which were provided to be helpful to them. These were the theoretical constructs from the dominant culture which we attempted to impose on a different reality. This often resulted inadvertently in a negation of the world that the poor person knew to be true. What often followed was a negative experience for client and clinician which often led to a clinical picture of lack of motivation, resistance, etc.

The following case illustrates a way of using the theory of chaos when working with a client who would normally be described as extremely "resistant" to treatment.

Dorothea is a 27-year-old Black, single parent of five children. She is a tall, wraith-like woman, attractive even though some of her front teeth are missing. For the first 2 years she presented sporadically at the clinic and appeared like a frightened little bird, sad and noncommunicative. She saw no need for therapy or counseling and did not even know what that meant. She was only sure that she would not be seen in a positive light.

The presenting problem was that the childcare agency responsible for her three children in placement had mandated psychotherapy as a prerequisite for return of the children. The oldest child had been given to Dorothea's sister at birth, because Dorothea's mother did not think she was mature enough to care for him. The sister refused to return the child. Three children were in placement for neglect and abandonment; a fifth child was born after the others were placed and remained in Dorothea's custody. A sixth child was stillborn, and two more, born during treatment, remained in her custody.

Dorothea and the children's father, Ken, were known drug abusers who frequently left the children alone. On one of these occasions, a neighbor reported Dorothea to the child protective agency. The daughter, age 4, had been staying with a woman friend and had been sexually abused by the babysitter's boyfriend. It took several days to locate the child, because Dorothea did not know where she had been taken.

Dorothea remained in a relationship with Ken, who was diagnosed as paranoid schizophrenic with a secondary diagnosis of polysubstance abuse. His initial psychotic episodes followed PCP abuse. Ken's most significant achievement and the one he spoke of proudly was that he had used the $12,000 he received at age 18 (from a childhood accident) for PCP. At age 22 he had had four psychiatric hospitalizations, and, according to him, every psychiatrist who had treated him had been amazed he could function at all considering the amount of drugs he used daily over an extended period. This led to Ken's belief that he is invulnerable.

Dorothea is the seventh of 11 children. Very little is known about her family except that her mother married or remarried when Dorothea was 5 years old. The family had been on welfare but now were supported by the stepfather, Henry, who worked steadily. He was very strict and acted as if he did not particularly care for children. Her mother was so pleased to be married and off welfare that she required that the children accommodate Henry's every need.

Dorothea's view was that her mother definitely put her husband ahead of the children. She had personal evidence to corroborate this belief. When Dorothea was around age 12, Henry had begun sexually abusing her, as he had an older sister before her. At age 14, she told her mother about the ongoing abuse. Her mother was furious, denied that this had happened to her, and demanded that Dorothea leave the house. She left and never returned. She first lived with acquaintances and then began prostituting. At 16 she married and had her first child. After the separation from her husband (late adolescence), she began using drugs and continued until the placement of her three children into foster care, at which point Dorothea stopped using all drugs.

Dorothea was a street person with many superficial friends whom she saw episodically and who could not be counted on in times of trouble. With the exception of one older woman in her building, Dorothea had no kin or friendship networks in the traditional as well as the ghetto sense. This extreme degree of social disconnectedness made it very difficult for her to function in a community where most rely on kin and friendship to survive economically and emotionally.

Dorothea lived in a "crack building" (cocaine dealing) in a neighborhood where drugs were the major business. Parents had to worry about drug pushers on the street, as well as the possibility that their child might be molested in one of the many abandoned buildings along the way to school. It is not uncommon in these areas for children to be escorted to school by parents until age 10, or for some even longer. Needless to say, this poses a hardship for the children's growing need for autonomy. Most of the preceding information was not known until 2 years had elapsed in the treatment process.

Once the building was taken over by drug pushers, the landlord ceased all services and repairs. By the time Dorothea managed to leave the building, she had no working stove, refrigerator, or toilet and no lock on her apartment door. The lock on the main door to the building had been removed several years earlier. The family used to take turns leaving the apartment so that someone would always be left behind to protect their belongings. However, prior to Dorothea's leaving, all of her furniture was stolen.

At this time in the South Bronx, finding a new place to live for someone on welfare was all but impossible. The shelters were full, and the homeless were increasing in numbers. This particular community consisted of those for whom the larger society had no place: They had no jobs, inadequate education, little or no recreation, and inadequate public services. The small churches that remained struggled to provide support with clothing and food for emergencies as well as spiritual comfort. The community needs were so great that the churches hardly made a dent.

Dorothea's strongest connection was her identity as a female and as a mother. She was so disconnected to everything else that she did not even appear to have a clear tie to her own racial group. Her only connections with the dominant culture were through its institutions. The two connections she did have were abusive ones: She abused her body, and she abused her children through neglect.

Clearly, with these kinds of cases, the ordinary rules and techniques of traditional modalities are inadequate in the face of the enormity of the problems. It is not surprising that most agencies would tend to document the "resistance" and close the case. We have found that if the client is not doing what we think he or she should be doing at a given time, it is usually not because the person is willfully defying the norms. It is because that person lives with a different reality, one in which the treating person possibly could not survive. Just as the urban poor do not know how to function in the mainstream, so too the middle-class clinician does not know the rules of the world in which the client lives (Parnell & VanderKloot, 1989).

When one is working with chaos (Parnell & VanderKloot, 1988), namely in a domestic war zone, one must learn to extrapolate the pattern that runs across all possible levels of intervention rather than get lost in the myriad of presenting fragments.

Any of Dorothea's problems, taken one by one, posed a formidable challenge. Without attention to the overriding pattern of disconnection, one would be unable to help with the smallest fragment—that is, that Dorothea was unable to keep appointments. By permitting this woman to show up at will, we hypothesized that a pattern would emerge. There was only one logical intervention to make, and that was on the level of the pattern of disconnection. Engagement would be a lengthy and difficult process without which there would be no treatment. To Dorothea, being a mother was a major value and the only thing that mattered to her. She lived from one visit with her children to the next. It was the only thing that organized her life and was the only therapeutic hook. If the clinicians could not help the client with parenting, then they could not help the client.

For the first year and a half, Dorothea dropped by sporadically—1 month she might drop in twice and then she would disappear for several months. The sessions lasted as long as she needed. She would sit with her head down, looking more frightened than depressed. It was obvious she was there because she was sent. She spoke as little as possible, but after a while she could be engaged on issues concerning the children. In addition, there was a steady flow of complaints about the foster care agency, which she felt treated her with contempt. The clinical intervention during this phase consisted of persistence without pressure with the hope of gaining the client's trust. Telephone contact with the foster care agency bore out the client's complaints. The caseworker's tone was one of contempt, with an openly stated determination that this woman would never get her children back.

Therapy has been extremely difficult because Dorothea cannot maintain regular, consistent contacts. Fortunately, each time she came to the clinic, she was able to see one of the authors, even though a long time had elapsed between visits. In most clinics, administrative rules would have required that the case be closed. It was important for Dorothea that she be accepted and worked with on her own terms. Her inability to connect emotionally prevented her from learning enough about people to assess who would and could be helpful and who was simply taking advantage of her. She came across as unbelievably naive and childlike for someone who had been in the streets since age 14. She was unable to deal with any large system because she projected all problems, concluding that her situation, whatever it was, would not work out because "they" were not doing their job.

Dorothea began to drop in more frequently without a sense of being "sent." She gradually began to talk more about what was going on in her life. Given her experience growing up and afterward, Dorothea's evasiveness was largely the result of her inability to cope with what she expected from others, which was severe and unrelenting criticism. She was not used to being accepted for herself, and she was tested at every juncture. When she finally began to talk, she gave the authors a chance to focus on her strengths and how she might harness them. At first we used her visits with her children, praising her for the amount of time and effort she spent planning every detail of the time she was to be with them. She would save her money to buy a special something for each one.

During this time, the childcare agency moved to sever her parental rights to the youngest child in placement. She immediately became pregnant again and became more involved in treatment. It was not possible to prevent the loss of that child to adoption, but from that time on, the focus of treatment was on helping Dorothea regain the custody of her other two children in placement. She brought them to the office on several occasions, and it appeared that there was enough positive feeling and competence on the mother's part to give the situation a chance. The children seemed to adore her and talked mostly about returning home.

In order to help Dorothea connect to her peers and build a social network, she was urged to join a mothers' group in the clinic. This was in addition to individual weekly sessions. She gradually felt comfortable, learned a lot about children and parenting, and did connect to several women in the group. Unfortunately, the group was disbanded after 2 years, and there was not another group available appropriate to her needs. The experience helped somewhat in her relationships with acquaintances and neighbors, but the damage of her early life could not be significantly ameliorated in 2 years.

At the time, a decision had to be made regarding discharge of the children. One of the authors went to court and testified on her behalf. The children were discharged in Dorothea's custody. This occurred at a time when services in general had been severely cut back, and finding decent housing required a miracle. She was unable to find a decent apartment for the amount of money allowed by welfare, so she, Ken, and by that time five children were crowded into a dark, very dreary three-room apartment. The children's discharge coincided with a flooding of crack (cocaine) into the area in which they lived. Within a year there was hardly a family in her 60-unit building that was not either using or dealing in drugs.

Numerous home visits were made throughout the treatment process. Because the neighborhoods the clinic served were often dangerous, we made visits accompanied by whomever we felt would be most helpful at a given time—sometimes a mental health assistant, sometimes a psychiatrist or other clinician. In this case a mental health assistant was closely involved in working with the concrete service problems and accompanied the author(s) on each visit.

The 10-year-old son, Donald, and 8-year-old daughter, Olga, were overjoyed to be home, and all went well for a short while. As soon as it was clear that Ken was making a commitment to Dorothea and the children, his mother stopped paying her rent, was evicted, and moved together with a younger son into the three-room apartment with Ken, Dorothea, and the children. Despite the overcrowded conditions and the tension between Dorothea and Ken's relatives, the children made a good adjustment to school and seemed to be doing well at home. The major problem seemed to be Dorothea's difficulty with disciplining the children in a consistent way. Her rules seemed arbitrary and therefore confusing. The children began making their own rules, and Donald was becoming the parental child. At age 10, he could not handle this, and it was certainly not good for the three preschool children.

In cases of child abuse and neglect, the children's well-being is monitored both directly in sessions and through school contacts and observations and informal involvement with the children. Parents are encouraged to bring their children to appointments whether the children are to be formally seen or not. Other staff in the waiting area also help by keeping us informed of any changes they observe in the children or the mother–child interaction. Parents who are overwhelmed with daily survival issues may not be aware of the early signs of a child getting into difficulty. Joint sessions with Dorothea and Ken helped somewhat, because Ken had the ability to be more consistent. The situation stabilized temporarily. We had six family sessions in which the parents practiced jointly taking charge of the children and setting up reasonable rules.

The situation just described highlights the complexity of working with one of the difficult cases of the urban poor. Interventions were made to connect to Dorothea and help her connect to her children and a meaningful social network. As these interventions took hold, new problems emerged in force: (a) her neighborhood was one of the early ones to be overrun by crack; (b) Ken's mother accelerated her hold on her son as she moved dangerously close to Dorothea and the children. Another complicating variable was Ken's Social Security Disability check, which he had previously shared with his mother and now committed to the care of his children.

Although we were clear that family intervention should include Ken's mother and brother, they were definitely unavailable, despite many efforts to engage them. Mother had been on welfare all of her life and was extremely distrustful of any agency contact. His brother, also a polysubstance abuser, functioned at a considerably lower level than Ken. A home visit was not made during this time because of the description of the brother's potential for violence toward any agency representative. The mother and son's distrust bordered on paranoia. The children were not affected directly by these attitudes. They seemed to have good interactions with their uncle and spoke fondly of him. The couple's situation began to deteriorate because of the tension in the home and community. For two people who found it hard to connect, the pull of drugs in the community and the mother's hold on Ken undermined their fragile connection.

Ken was able to get his family other housing, but by this time he had returned to drug abuse and stopped going to the clinic for his prolixin injections. He became abusive to Dorothea and no longer contributed to the children's support. Then came the violence, followed by his attempt to take her money for drugs. The police were called for these incidents but took no action, although Dorothea requested that he be removed. When it was clear that she could not, on her own, get a reasonable response from the police, we helped her contact a District Attorney who was known to be effective in helping women get a fair deal in cases of domestic violence. The District Attorney informed Dorothea of her rights and of the procedures to remove Ken from the home. Once it was clear that he could legally be removed, the authors accompanied Dorothea to the police precinct with the request that he be removed. The police did not understand why we would bother with this woman and her problems. Their attitude was very judgmental, and they conveyed the feeling that they considered us naive in our efforts to help her. We contacted the District Attorney, who advised the police to remove the man from the home so as to protect the rights of this woman and her children. Still they refused to act. Fortunately, one of the officers we know from the local delicatessen came into the office at this time. After a prolonged discussion, the detective explained the legal difficulty that this type of case presents for the police. The issue was resolved when the detective agreed that because the man in question was a psychiatric patient, known to have discontinued his neuroleptic medication, and also known to be on crack, they could, on that basis, remove him from the home. They accompanied Dorothea home and removed Ken.

By this time the children had been subjected to too much chaos, tension, and violence. Dorothea's pressures were also too great. The basic appliances in her apartment were no longer working, and we had been unsuccessful in getting the landlord to make repairs either by working with him directly or by working through the welfare system to bring pressure on him. Shortly after Ken began using drugs, Dorothea joined him after what had been a 6-year hiatus. The five children were placed in foster homes, and Dorothea went voluntarily to a detox program, followed by a long-term drug rehabilitation program.

In this case, despite all attempts to help Dorothea parent, the combination of her own deprivation in childhood and the present unending series of problems in her environment and family made growth and change very difficult. Dorothea has, however, made personal gains. She is more available to people in general. She is beginning to understand her participation in what is happening to her children and to her. There is less projection and more responsibility. However, it is probably too late to get her children back; termination of her parental rights was being considered as the authors were leaving the agency. When last seen, Dorothea had completed the drug rehabilitation program and was living in a shelter but was expecting to be relocated within the month. She proudly announced that she has a full-time job, which she likes, at a large department store in the area.

In retrospect we were bothered over the outcome of the children again being removed, and we questioned our decision and persistence in helping Dorothea get the children back initially. There were seven compelling reasons for this intervention:

1. Dorothea's only connection was to her children; without them, if she were unable to become pregnant, she was at risk for suicide.
2. The children's verbal and nonverbal behavior showed a strong desire to be with their mother.
3. Dorothea cooperated fully with all that she needed to do to retain custody.
4. We had a strong impression that the foster care agency was sabotaging the mother's efforts to regain custody. For example, at the very time that Dorothea was working the hardest and was most cooperative, the agency informed the children that they were to be adopted by the foster parent. When Dennis began running away from his foster home, the agency said it did not know where he was and could do nothing about it. They also did not file a "missing child" report with the police.
5. We were aware that Dorothea would continue to have more children with each threat of the loss of a child. At age 33 she had had 10 children.
6. Dorothea discontinued all drug use on her own when the children went into placement and remained drug free for 6 years. This seemed to indicate a very powerful motivation to be a mother.
7. Our own personal bias is "when in doubt, try the parent."

CONCLUSION

We have illustrated a model for working with the chaos in the life of the urban poor. Intervention in the pattern of disconnection did not magically cure Dorothea and her family, but it enabled her to connect and thereby opened up new possibilities for her. She would probably never become middle class economically or in terms of values. The purposes of the treatment of the urban poor in difficult cases such as this one are amelioration of the presenting conditions and development of new skills that will enhance the client's overall functioning.

Interventions with this client included an extensive engagement process followed by interventions with the individual and in the family system by the school, police, courts, drug programs, and medical system. The initial pattern of disconnection was disrupted, and the client had a different experience. She connected to the clinicians, the agency, her children, and, for a while, her husband. This was a new pattern of connection in which she could receive feedback from others that was useful to her. This shift made new inputs, skills, and values available to Dorothea which she could then build on. Although Dorothea's ability to remain connected to her husband and children was disrupted, her connection to herself was solidified.

REFERENCES

Parnell, M., & VanderKloot, J. (1988). Chaos theory. *Family networker symposium.*

Parnell, M., & VanderKloot, J. (1989). Ghetto children growing up in poverty. In L. Combrinck-Graham (Ed.), *Children in family contexts: Perspectives on treatment* (pp. 437–462). New York, NY: Guilford Press.

Case Study 8-4

Highlighting the Role of Cross-Cultural Competence in Ethically Sound Practice

KATHLEEN COX, NANCY SULLIVAN, JENNIFER REIMAN, AND CHER VANG[1]

Cultural competence is a critical aspect of social work practice. This case demonstrates the value of cross-cultural competence when working with diverse people.

Questions

1. Why is cross-cultural competence necessary in social work practice?
2. What assumptions were made about this case that needed to be reexamined for cross-cultural competence?
3. How did the social worker use consultation to become more culturally competent?
4. What principles of cross-cultural practice were demonstrated in this case?

The National Association of Social Workers's *Code of Ethics* (NASW, 2006) is replete with references to the importance of cultural competence on the part of practitioners

---

[1]   From "Highlighting the Role of Cross-Cultural Competence in Ethically Sound Practice," by K. Cox, N. Sullivan, J. Reiman, and C. Vang, 2009, *Journal of Social Work Values and Ethics, 6*(1). Reprinted with permission from White Hat Communications.

serving diverse client populations. Social workers are admonished to "treat each person in a caring and respectful fashion, mindful of individual differences and cultural and ethnic diversity" (p. 4). They are further advised to "understand culture and its function in human behavior" and to "demonstrate competence in the provision of services that are sensitive to clients' cultures and to differences among people and cultural groups" (p. 9). Moreover, the expectation is made clear that they obtain education in order to acquire a knowledge base relative to the particular culture of the individuals, families, and communities that they serve (Ethical Standard 1.05).

The social work literature also highlights the importance of cultural competency in the delivery of human services to diverse populations. More specifically, it draws attention to inadequacies in service provision to ethnic-minority populations. For instance, a disproportionately high rate of unmet mental health needs for racial and ethnic minorities relative to non-Hispanic White Americans is clearly documented (U.S. Department of Health and Human Services, 2001). Recommendations offered toward the elimination of such disparities include the provision of mental health services that are tailored to culturally diverse populations and delivered by practitioners who respect the beliefs, norms, and values of the minority clients that they serve (President's New Freedom Commission on Mental Health, 2003).

Another emphasis in the literature is on providing a conceptual understanding of cultural competency and general guidelines for its development. Stanley Sue suggests that in order to attain a high level of cultural competence, providers should avoid drawing premature conclusions about the status of their culturally different clients and instead develop creative ways to test their clinical hypotheses. Practitioners are encouraged to avoid stereotypes, appreciate the importance of culture, and acquire culture-specific expertise (Sue, 1998). Authors Lynch and Hanson (1993) define *cross-cultural competence* as "the ability to think, feel, and act in ways that acknowledge, respect, and build upon ethnic, socio-cultural, and linguistic diversity" (p. 50). Like Sue, they assert that the development of this capacity includes learning culture-specific information about clients from varying cultural groups (Lynch & Hanson, 2004).

One strategy designed to enhance the cross-cultural competence of social work practitioners, *cultural consultation,* has received recent attention by authors. It involves the use of an ethnospecific cultural expert who offers services that supplement those provided by the primary worker. The consultant (typically a psychiatrist, psychologist, or social worker) performs an assessment of the client system and follow-up consultation to the primary provider in an effort to assist the latter in understanding the cultural meaning of the client's symptoms and the social context of their distress. Such services have been found to be successful in unearthing cultural misunderstandings, incomplete assessments, incorrect diagnoses, and the use of treatments that are inappropriate to the client's belief system (Kirmayer, Groleau, Guzder, Blake, & Jarvis, 2003).

What follows is a case study that demonstrates the value in using cultural consultation as an adjunct to social work services provided to ethnically diverse clients and their families. More specifically, it portrays the process through which workers providing behaviorally oriented social work services to a Hmong American youth recognized the need for assistance in order to serve their client in a manner that was culturally competent and, thus, ethically sound. This case also reveals how practitioners changed course following the use of cultural consultation—a shift in strategy that resulted in dramatic improvement in the youth's behavior and her family's responsiveness to services. Based on this case review, recommendations are offered to social workers who aspire to meet the highest ethical standards of their profession by understanding and appreciating the cultural values of clients served.

THE CASE OF MAI

Mai Khang[2] was a 15-year-old Hmong American girl who presented with frequent and serious suicidal gestures and episodes of aggression. Upon referral to a social work team that provides intensive, in-home, behaviorally oriented services, it was reported that she drank small amounts of toxic chemicals (e.g., bleach, nail polish remover, laundry detergent) two to three times per day and assaulted her mother or father roughly one to two times per day. Mai frequently ran away from home and "hooked up with undesirable strangers." It was also noted that she had, on occasion, threatened to kill her parents with an axe. The mental health therapist who referred her for behavioral intervention had given her a diagnosis of major depressive disorder with psychotic features, largely as a result of her reported visual and auditory hallucinations and suicidal ideations.

The behavioral specialists began, with the assistance of a Hmong-speaking interpreter, to attempt engagement with Mai's monolingual Hmong-speaking mother and father. The initial focus of services was on specifying the girl's high-risk behaviors and on developing a preliminary safety plan. The workers subsequently conducted a functional behavior assessment that defined the frequency and nature of the child's target behaviors, as well as their antecedents and consequences. Through this process, it was observed that Mai's aggressive and self-injurious behaviors were usually triggered by rejection by a "boyfriend," limit setting by her parents (particularly with regard to phone use), or boredom (her access to age-appropriate activities was limited because of her parents' unwillingness to transport). The typical consequence of her acting-out behaviors was determined to be increased access to the people, places, and attention she desired. Thus, these dangerous behaviors were thought to express an underlying need for connection and belonging with others.

Consistent with this assessment, the behavior specialists initiated strategies aimed at increasing Mai's access to recreational and peer-based activities in the community (e.g., Boys' and Girls' Club programs, youth group at Hmong Community Center). A safety plan was also developed to decrease her access to toxic solutions and "undesirable" strangers. With the assistance of the Hmong interpreter, her parents were encouraged to closely monitor her whereabouts at times when she was likely to sneak out of the home (late at night), limit her access to the phone, and utilize a behavior chart for tracking nonaggressive behavior. In addition, a system of positive reinforcement was set up in which Mai's parents were asked to reward her with stickers and other tokens when she behaved in a safe and responsible manner.

---

[2]   The client's name was changed to protect her privacy.

None of these interventions proved successful. Mai refused to attend peer-related activities in the community. Her parents did not follow through with the behavior management systems recommended, despite their reported willingness to do so. They continued to assert that Mai was of an age to be married and cared for by a husband, who would deal with her need for structure. Eventually, the service providers concluded that they were stuck. Not having a full understanding of the values and practices of the Hmong culture, they were operating in the dark and making little headway toward managing the risk involved with Mai's behavior.

These workers sought out the assistance of a cultural consultant, who contracted with the County Department of Mental Health to provide input to mental health providers regarding culturally specific issues that can impact a Hmong client or family's progress in treatment. Upon referral by the County Department, the Hmong psychiatric consultant contacted the service providers on this case to gain basic information regarding the need for his services. Next, this consultant conducted several meetings at the provider's office, the first of which was held with the child recipient of services. He subsequently met with Mai's mother and sister-in-law and elicited information regarding their perspectives of her behavioral challenges. Finally, he debriefed with the primary providers, at which time he shared his findings and offered recommendations.

As a result of this experience with consultation, the primary social workers learned a great deal about faulty assumptions they had made that contributed to poor progress on the part of the child and family. Those incorrect assumptions were as follows:

- *Mai's language of choice was English.* It was apparent to the consultant that, although Mai is bilingual (Hmong and English), she much preferred speaking in Hmong. When communicating in English, she often had difficulty grasping certain concepts that were being relayed by the English speaker.
- *Mai's parents understood her target behaviors to be dysfunctional and wanted them to stop.* One of the most striking insights that emerged out of the cultural consultation process concerned the parents' interpretation of Mai's symptoms and behaviors. It was revealed that they understood her high-risk behavior to be an indication of her call into shamanism, a form of healing that originated more than 10,000 years ago. The primary providers learned that, according to Hmong tradition, the call to shamanism occurs through the visitation of spirits. Typically, a young person is summoned to this vocation during a psychic or spiritual crisis that accompanies a physical illness. By overcoming the disease, the youth reportedly acquires the ability to heal others with compassion. In the Hmong community, the shaman is revered and thought to serve as a bridge between the material and spiritual worlds (The Split Horn, n.d.).

  Mai's parents reported that an elder shaman had once confirmed that she had, in fact, been called into this profession. Because they respected her emerging role as a shaman, Mr. and Mrs. Khang did not wish to curtail her risky behaviors entirely; they merely wanted to keep her alive and free from serious harm. Mai, on the other hand, was not convinced that she was a shaman and appeared anxious when the topic was raised. Once the primary providers demonstrated their ability to discuss shamanism with her in a nonjudgmental manner, her discomfort with this subject began to dissipate.
- *It is always appropriate to enter Mai's house for a home visit if a family member answers the front door.* The cultural consultant clarified for the workers that when a cluster of green

leaves is found hanging on the front door, it is a signal that spiritual cleansing is taking place within the home. This ritual, referred to as *caiv*, is performed to protect the family from evil spirits. It was advised that when the team encountered this type of leafy display that they avoid entering the house; otherwise, they would disrupt the ritual, resulting in a need for the family to reinitiate the cleansing process.

Based on these new insights, the behavioral specialists reconceptualized the therapeutic needs of Mai and her family. They redefined the function of her aggressive and self-harmful behavior as expression of her need to resolve identity confusion and attain validation within her family and cultural community. Consequently, their interventions focused on the following:

- *The use of written narratives and scrapbooking.* These activities were done to assist Mai in ethnic identity formation and goal-setting. Through this process, she identified an interest in pursuing a career as a translator, teacher, or mortician (interestingly, all aspects of the role of shaman).
- *Joining with the family by recognizing their cultural beliefs and customs.* The workers made an increased effort to recognize the family's beliefs and traditions. They began noticing and asking about pictures in the home that depicted extended-family celebrations. In addition, they expressed an interest in learning more about shamanism from Mai and her parents. Consequently, family members welcomed visits by the providers and appeared more open to input and suggestions aimed at managing Mai's behavior.
- *Building skills in emotions regulation.* Mai was taught how to formulate and utilize coping statements (e.g., "I can find something positive to do when I am bored," "I can control myself when I am mad," and "I don't need a boyfriend to be happy"). Social skills were also taught and practiced to prepare her for connection to age-appropriate social activities.

Following this shift in strategy on the part of the behavior specialists, Mai made substantial progress. She learned how to access reading material at the public library and discovered a particularly strong interest in Hmong literature. Most importantly, she evidenced marked improvements in her behavior. Although Mai continued to leave the home at times without permission, incidents of self-harm diminished, and she displayed a newfound ability to control her aggression.

When the providers neared completion of services, a Hmong-speaking staff member from their agency interviewed Mai and her parents with the intent to explore the extent to which they observed a change in the nature of service delivery subsequent to the implementation of cultural consultation. The family reported that the cultural consultant encouraged them to use the therapeutic services available, thereby granting implicit permission for them to accept help from members outside of their cultural community. Mai and her parents all noted that following the meetings with the cultural consultant, the primary workers appeared more open to their culture and respectful of their customs. Mr. and Mrs. Khang also stated that, over time, the providers began encouraging them to use their cultural practices to help Mai decrease her dangerous behaviors. They recognized these workers for not giving up on them or their daughter and expressed their gratitude and appreciation for services rendered.

DISCUSSION

This case study sheds light on the benefits that can result from the use of cultural consultation as an adjunct to social work services provided to individuals and families. In order to attain such benefits, providers must first be willing to recognize their limitations with regard to understanding the role of culture as it impacts individual or family functioning. Sadly, practitioners are often reluctant to admit when they are making minimal progress with a client or client system and, thus, in need of assistance from a consultant. Moreover, when provider–client cultural and linguistic differences are at play, the provider may inaccurately assume that the use of an interpreter is adequate in terms of meeting the individual or family needs. The worker may fail to detect that his or her own assessment of problematic behaviors or clinical issues misses the mark when it comes to reflecting clients' perspectives of their own strengths and concerns.

As can be seen in the case example, cultural consultation involves much more than linguistic translation. It offers an explanation of the client's cultural beliefs, customs, and traditions that may have eluded the provider's understanding or awareness. In addition, it places individual and family challenges into a rich context that leads the practitioner to previously undiscovered strengths and resources. As was illustrated, cultural consultation holds potential for illuminating the function that a particular target behavior serves within a family or extended-family system.

Another positive impact of this intervention is seen when the consultant is able to legitimize the role of the primary provider in the eyes of the client. By validating services and verifying the provider's trustworthiness, the consultant can pave the way to an increased level of client involvement in the therapeutic process. In the case of Mai, this benefit is reflected in the comments made by her parents indicating that the consultant encouraged them to utilize the assistance of the behaviorally oriented social workers. An intervention of this kind on the part of the consultant is invaluable; it serves to advance the client's willingness to engage with workers of differing cultural backgrounds, particularly if these providers begin to recognize and appreciate the client's values and customs.

In conclusion, the authors encourage social workers to consider the potential benefits of cultural consultation when conducting cross-cultural practice. Furthermore, they recommend that systems of care serving culturally and linguistically diverse individuals and families assemble a wide array of cultural experts and make their cultural consultation services readily available to human service providers. Such an investment in the provision of cross-culturally competent services is a requisite of service delivery that upholds the core values and ideals of the social work profession.

REFERENCES

Kirmayer, L. J., Groleau, D., Guzder, J., Blake, D., & Jarvis, E. (2003). Cultural consultation: A model of mental health service for multicultural societies. *The Canadian Journal of Psychiatry, 48,* 145–153.

Lynch, E. W., & Hanson, M. J. (1993). Changing demographics: Implications for training in early intervention. *Infants and Young Children, 6,* 50–55.

Lynch, E. W., & Hanson, M. J. (2004). *Developing cross-cultural competence: A guide for working with children and their families* (3rd ed.). Baltimore, MD: Brookes.

National Association of Social Workers. (2006). *Code of Ethics of the National Association of Social Workers.* Washington, DC: Author.

President's New Freedom Commission on Mental Health. (2003). *Achieving the promise: Transforming mental health care in America.* Final report. DHHS Pub. No. SMA-03-3832. Rockville, MD: U.S. Department of Health and Human Services.

The Split Horn. (n.d.). Retrieved from http://www.pbs.org/splithorn/hmong.html

Sue, S. (1998). In search of cultural competence in psychotherapy and counseling. *American Psychologist, 42,* 440–448.

U.S. Department of Health and Human Services. (2001). *Mental health: Culture, race, and ethnicity. A supplement to mental health: A report of the surgeon general.* Rockville, MD: Author.

PART IX

Case Studies in Using Practice Evaluation

Although research and evaluation have been a part of social work since its inception, there has been increasing interest in the role of research and evaluation in contemporary social work practice. In fact, schools of social work are now required to present information on how social workers are to evaluate their own practice. This current emphasis on evidence-based practice and practice evaluation, often referred to as empirical clinical practice, has been advocated because of several recent changes.

Social work practice has been increasingly under pressure concerning its accountability. For example, funding sources want to know if social work makes a difference for the clients it serves. Social workers became increasingly concerned about effectiveness following Fischer's classic review of research (1973) that concluded that social work was not effective. Also influential in the empirical clinical practice movement were early efforts by social work researchers to specify their interventions and evaluate the effectiveness of the interventions.

The social work profession has moved beyond the early concerns regarding effectiveness and is now concerned with harnessing the technology, knowledge, and skills to promote effective practice (Rubin & Bellamy, 2012). Thus, the question is no longer: Is social work effective? Instead, the emphasis is on more specific questions, such as: What type of social work intervention is most effective with what type of client group or problem? In addition to this emphasis on knowledge building, social workers are encouraged to use single-system designs to evaluate their practice. The idea is to teach a scientific approach to practice so that it can be used to enhance the performance of social work practice.

The central idea in single-subject designs is the ongoing monitoring and evaluation of the client. These designs are simply methods to collect ongoing data about a client and use that information to examine whether the intervention being offered is helpful. Therefore, the key steps include defining the problem in measurable terms; measuring the problem in an ongoing manner; evaluating the result; and making decisions based on the information being received. Practice evaluation focuses on questions such as: What intervention should I use? How long should I continue the intervention? Is my intervention effective in helping the client? Should I try something different?

For example, if you were working with a depressed client, you could measure the client's depression prior to any intervention. To measure the depression, you choose the Beck Depression Inventory, a standardized measure. You administer this two times prior to beginning your intervention—once at intake and once prior to your first session. The intervention consists of cognitive therapy. Each week the client completes the Beck Depression Inventory. The weekly data give you an idea of whether your intervention is working. Has the cognitive therapy led to a lower depression score compared with the first two scores prior to the intervention? The answer to the question has important implications for what you plan to do to help this client. But what if you didn't have this information? The client could be getting worse, and you might not know it.

Social workers have always been interested in assessing whether they are helping their clients change. However, in the past, the focus was on social workers' qualitative judgment of whether they were helping clients. Such judgments are usually subjective and unreliable. The current emphasis on evidence-based practice has dramatically shifted the focus, and now it is expected that social work practitioners will apply the best evidence in addressing client problems. Students must learn research and assess the true evidence of the interventions they are offering clients. Evidence-based practice and practice evaluation are the tools that social workers can use to ensure they are practicing in an effective and ethical manner.

Four case studies are presented in this chapter. The first three focus on practice evaluation. Blythe presents an example of practice evaluation with a difficult case of sexual assault. She was successful in helping the client clearly define the problems that resulted from the assault—flashbacks and accompanying depression. Also, her case study shows how the practitioner must individualize the methods for collecting data. Corcoran and Beers's case study presents the evaluation of family therapy with an acting-out adolescent. This case study is an example of how to use multiple measures to evaluate progress, using several assessment checklists and a measure of school absenteeism. This case is also intriguing because initially the intervention in this case was not successful, and the data that were collected suggested a need to redirect the treatment. The case study by Nurius and Green demonstrates that with some creativity, practice evaluation can be useful across a variety of human service settings. They show how practice evaluation was helpful with a client in an inpatient hospital setting, with a limited-contact intervention, and in a health setting where the focus is on high-risk clients.

The final case study by Bellamy demonstrates the use of evidence-based practice at an agency level. She demonstrates the steps and process of using an evidence-based practice approach.

REFERENCES

Fischer, J. (1973). Is casework effective? *Social Work, 18,* 5–20.

Rubin, A., & Bellamy, J. (2012). *Practitioner's guide to using research for evidence-based practice.* Hoboken, NJ: Wiley.

Case Study 9-1

Evaluating the Treatment of a
Sexually Assaulted Child

BETTY J. BLYTHE

Sexual assault is a devastating experience. This case describes the impact of sexual assault on a young adolescent and how the social worker designed and evaluated her treatment efforts.

Questions

1. What problems developed as a result of the sexual assault?
2. How did the social worker get the client to collect data that would be useful in evaluating treatment progress in this case?
3. How was the plan for treatment influenced by the results of the data collected about the client's problem?
4. How did the worker reduce the self-blame that is common among victims of sexual assault?

This case study describes the treatment of a young boy who was sexually assaulted. Services were delivered by a social worker in a sexual assault treatment program. As with all of her cases, the worker used measurement and research tools to define the target problems, specify indicators of these problems, and routinely monitor the client's progress throughout and following treatment. This paper describes the treatment and evaluation of this case.

The client, a 12-year-old boy named Gary, was sexually molested by an adult man. The boy was returning from softball practice when the man, who was dressed as a utility meter reader, enticed him into a wooded area. The man performed oral sodomy on Gary and forced the boy to fellate him. Before allowing him to leave, the man threatened to harm Gary and his family if he told anyone about the episode.

On returning home, Gary immediately told his older brother about the attack, and his brother called their parents. Gary's parents took him to the local hospital emergency room, where he was examined. The hospital social worker referred Gary to the sexual abuse treatment program at the local community mental health center.

As is typical at this agency, the intake was conducted over the telephone by the social worker who would continue to see the client. At the time of the intake, Gary was still extremely upset by the incident. He was afraid to leave home and walk anywhere by himself. He refused to attend softball practice, even if his parents drove him there. Most upsetting to Gary were frequent flashbacks in which he recalled the attack. Like many victims of sexual assault, he felt both depressed and guilty. Gary indicated that he feared that his assailant might carry out his threats to hurt Gary or his family.

The social worker told Gary that his feelings and the flashbacks were common responses by people who have been sexually assaulted. She also said that, working together, they could try to reduce the frequency of the flashbacks and improve his mood so that he was less depressed. Gary said he was willing to come for counseling and that he wanted to work on these areas.

The worker next began to further specify the two target problems, flashbacks and depression. She asked Gary to describe the flashbacks. He said that a flashback was like seeing and feeling the experience again, as if he were back in it. The worker also learned that reliving the attack through the flashback was accompanied by a strong sense of fear, increased heartbeat, sweating, fear for his life, and feelings of helplessness and rage. There did not seem to be any pattern that might predict when the flashbacks would occur. They happened throughout the day and evening, regardless of whether he was alone or with someone, and in any setting. Gary reported that a flashback lasted 4 or 5 minutes and that they all were of equal severity. After a flashback episode, Gary typically anguished about how he might have avoided the attack. He experienced strong feelings of sadness and guilt. This information helped the worker better understand the nature of the flashbacks and determine what interventions would likely be helpful or not helpful.

The worker told Gary that she wanted him to record how often he had flashbacks each day. She explained that this information would help her determine if she was helping Gary reduce the frequency of the flashbacks. If they did not occur less frequently after a few sessions, she said she would change the treatment in some way. In addition, information collected about what Gary was doing at the time of a flashback would confirm or disconfirm their conclusion that there was not any pattern associated with the flashbacks. The worker asked him to get some 3-by-5-inch index cards and make two columns, with one labeled "day" and the other labeled "flashbacks." She also told him to fill in the days and dates in the first column. In the second column, Gary was to record what he was doing when the flashback occurred and any other information he wanted to provide about the flashback itself. At the end of the telephone intake, the worker went over the request to collect information about flashbacks with Gary's mother, explaining how the cards should be completed and the purpose for doing so. She asked his mother to help him prepare the cards immediately and to remind him to carry a card with him and to complete it.

To establish the level of the problem before Gary talked to her (the baseline), the worker questioned Gary carefully to determine how many flashbacks he had experienced over the past several days. She did this by having Gary describe his routine on the previous day and then indicate if he experienced any flashbacks. The worker was able to get Gary to go back over the day of the intake and the 2 days since the attack in this manner. If, at any point, the worker had felt that Gary was not able to provide accurate information about the frequency of the episodes, she would have abandoned the questioning. This type of baseline is called a reconstructed baseline.

The worker then explained to Gary that she wanted him to complete a questionnaire when he came to the office. She said that the questions did not have right or wrong answers and that they would help her better understand his feelings of sadness and depression. She also told him that she would go over the questionnaire with him, and that he would complete it occasionally to help them determine if he was getting less depressed. Gary agreed to complete the questionnaire. The questionnaire actually was a standardized measure, the Generalized Contentment Scale (Hudson, 1982, as cited in Fischer & Corcoran, 2007). It is relatively short (25 items) and uses simple, understandable language to assess the client's level of depression. As with the self-report measure of flashbacks, the worker also described this measure and its application in the treatment to Gary's mother and gave her an opportunity to ask any questions.

Gary came in for his first session 4 days later. Before he saw the worker, the receptionist gave him the standardized measure to complete in the waiting room. When the worker saw Gary, she asked how he was doing. Gary soon volunteered the information he had collected about flashbacks. The social worker added these data to a graph she had started with the reconstructed baseline. She told Gary that they would add his information to the graph each time he came to a session, and she repeated that the information would help them determine if she was helping him. The information about what Gary was doing at the time a flashback occurred validated their suspicions that there was no discernible pattern associated with the flashbacks. The flashbacks apparently occurred in numerous settings and when Gary was alone and with others. The worker and Gary agreed that there was no need to continue collecting additional information about the antecedents of each flashback. The worker asked if Gary had any difficulty in collecting the information, and he said that he was embarrassed to get the card out when he was around other people. The worker asked Gary if it would be easier to carry some small beads in his pocket and move a bead from one pocket to another each time he had a flashback. At the end of each day, Gary could count the beads and put this information on the index card. Gary responded that he would prefer to use that method, and the worker gave him 10 beads.

At this point, she also scored the Generalized Contentment Scale. Gary's score of 54 indicated that he was depressed. The scale has a clinical cutting score of 30, which means that clients scoring above this level have a "clinically significant problem." The worker relayed this information to Gary in a matter-of-fact fashion and tried not to alarm him or otherwise lead him to worry unnecessarily about being depressed.

INTERVENTION

Having achieved some understanding of the baseline level of the problem, the worker was ready to begin intervention. The intervention was actually a package of several different techniques.

Psychoeducation

The worker gave Gary information about sexual assault and how people typically respond after being assaulted or experiencing other crisis situations. She emphasized that these feelings would not last forever. She also underscored that Gary was not to blame for the attack, but rather that the assailant had committed a crime against Gary. The actual attack was always portrayed as a violent act rather than as a sexual act.

Environmental Manipulation

With the approval of Gary and his mother, the worker contacted Gary's school and arranged for Gary to ride a bus to and from school (previously he had walked). She also involved Gary's family in the intervention by having a family member stand at the bus stop with Gary in the morning and meet his returning bus in the afternoon. Gary's mother was responsible for organizing this schedule to ensure that a family member was available to help Gary.

Empathic Listening and Normalizing Feelings

Gary was encouraged to express his feelings about being attacked. As noted in the intake, these feelings included fear, anger, sadness, and guilt. Later, Gary began to express a desire to gain revenge. The worker helped Gary "name" and recognize these feelings, as he did not always have words to describe them. She also attempted to normalize the feelings so that Gary realized that these feelings were not unusual or inappropriate.

Relaxation and Calming Self-Talk

Gary was taught deep-breathing exercises to help him calm himself when he felt a flashback coming or when he began to feel uncomfortable or fearful. The worker and

Gary developed a set of self-statements that Gary could also use at these times. The worker stressed the importance of making accurate statements to help Gary regain a realistic sense of security. Examples of calming self-statements were "Nobody will attack me here in the classroom" and "Try to stay calm. I am in a safe place now." By recording the flashbacks, Gary had become aware of his early feelings when a flashback was developing. Thus, he was often able to use relaxation and calming self-talk to interrupt a flashback before it fully developed. Over time, as Gary ventured out alone, these statements were revised to include messages reminding Gary that he knew how to respond if he saw a suspicious person or if someone approached him.

Reframing Gary's Role During the Attack

The worker repeatedly pointed out that Gary had demonstrated courage, intelligence, and fast thinking when he was attacked. He had managed to get and remember a clear description of the assailant. When the assailant asked his name, Gary gave a phony name. Moreover, he had managed to tell his brother about the attack and to talk about it with hospital staff, the police, and the social worker, all of which were stressful and difficult interactions. The worker also emphasized that Gary was a survivor rather than a victim.

These interventions were delivered over the course of five weekly sessions in the worker's office. The environmental manipulations were instituted immediately, followed by the educational intervention. The relaxation and calming self-talk were introduced during the third week. The other interventions were used as needed in each session. Because it was so difficult to track exactly when some of these interventions were used or if they were used at "full strength" during each week of the intervention, no attempt was made to specify the intervention beyond calling it a package consisting of these five components.

RESULTS

Each week, Gary brought in his information on flashbacks. He completed the Generalized Contentment Scale before two additional office visits and when it was mailed to him 3 months after treatment was terminated.

As depicted in Figure 9.1, the baseline data indicate that Gary was having an average of 8.42 flashbacks per day. Although the actual daily number varied from 7 to 10 flashbacks, the range was not too great, and the worker felt that she had a good idea of the general level of the problem. Also, the number of flashbacks was increasing somewhat before intervention, so it does not appear that the problem was being resolved without intervention. Over the course of intervention, the frequency of the flashbacks generally decreased, with a striking exception on Day 16. When Gary brought in these data, the worker asked about that day in particular. Gary told her that he was requested to give the police additional information about the attack and to examine some photographs of suspects. Talking about the incident in this way made him quite uneasy and brought the

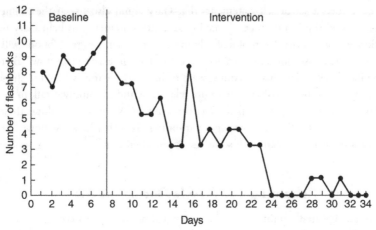

Figure 9.1 Number of flashbacks per day during baseline and intervention phases

whole incident back. Note that the trend did not continue to go downward for a few days after Day 16, as it had before that time. By the last week, however, the flashbacks had sufficiently reduced such that the worker felt she could terminate treatment.

At this last session, the social worker explained to Gary that she would contact him by telephone at a later date to see how he was doing. Accordingly, she called him 3 months after termination. The worker asked Gary if he would collect data on flashbacks for 1 week. He said he would do so but that he was no longer having any flashbacks. When the worker contacted Gary a week later, he indicated that he had not experienced any flashbacks.

Figure 9.2 depicts Gary's scores on the Generalized Contentment Scale. As can be seen, his scores dropped to just under 30, the clinical cutting score. Hudson (1982,

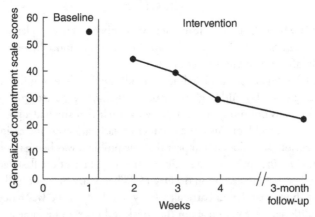

Figure 9.2 Generalized contentment scores during baseline and intervention phases

as cited in Fischer & Corcoran, 2007) indicates that such borderline scores must be interpreted cautiously. The worker observed, however, that Gary's mood seemed to have improved. He was involved in more activities again and generally showed more enthusiasm for whatever he was doing. His mother confirmed these observations. Thus, the worker decided it was safe to close the case.

At the 3-month follow-up, the social worker also sent a copy of the depression inventory to Gary and asked him to complete and return it. His score, also depicted in Figure 9.2, was 23 and suggests he was continuing to be less depressed. During the telephone call to set up the follow-up data collection, the worker also asked Gary some general questions about how he was doing. This anecdotal information confirmed the quantitative information, all of which suggested that Gary was continuing to improve.

DISCUSSION

The data Gary and the worker gathered portray continued improvement in terms of the frequency of flashbacks Gary experienced and the severity of his depression. Although in no way do they "prove" that the intervention led to Gary's improvement, the data provided ongoing, routine information about the two problems being dealt with in treatment: flashbacks and depression. Had the trends not been in the direction of improvement, the worker could have quickly revised the treatment plan.

Defining the exact nature of a flashback so that it could be measured through self-report by the client yielded information for practice, as well as evaluation. The worker learned that there were no apparent precipitants of the flashbacks, so the intervention package did not need to focus on particular events that might be leading Gary to experience the flashbacks. Information about the intensity and nature of the flashbacks suggested that certain components of the treatment package might be helpful, particularly using relaxation and coping self-statements, normalizing feelings, and reframing his role in the assault. Because the baseline could be reconstructed in part and then continued after the telephone intake, the worker was able to get an idea of the level of the target problems without withholding intervention. If the baseline had not been stable (i.e., had it fluctuated widely so that it was difficult to know what the average level of the problem was), the worker probably would have initiated intervention anyway, because her goal in collecting data was to measure client progress rather than to determine if her intervention was responsible for the progress.

The treatment plan was allowed to unfold in the manner the worker thought was best for Gary, without being modified in any way because the case was being evaluated. The intake process could have had certain treatment qualities, thereby affecting the baseline levels recorded by Gary, but the worker did not worry about this. In fact, the data suggest that the client experienced flashbacks with approximately the same frequency both before and after the telephone intake. Furthermore, the intervention did not have to be artificially carved up, with certain components being delivered in certain sessions, because the worker was not interested in determining what were the more or less effective ingredients of the intervention.

At the close of treatment, the termination date was set when the social worker thought that Gary had made sufficient progress, based on both the data and her clinical impressions, including interviews with Gary and his mother. Termination was not artificially delayed to allow more data to be collected. Moreover, the follow-up point provided an opportunity for the worker to determine if the client was maintaining his gains.

CONCLUSION

In short, the evaluation of this case did not needlessly consume the client's or worker's time. The information gathered through data collection was helpful to the client and to the worker. As the data began to suggest improvement, Gary felt both relief and increased motivation to continue practicing the relaxation exercises and calming self-talk. The data informed the worker as she made certain clinical decisions. Although it did not lead to tremendous clinical revelations, the monitoring helped the worker and client stay focused on the treatment goals, readily see that the client was making some improvement, and eventually realize that the case could be closed. Obviously, adjunct information collected in the sessions and through interactions with Gary's mother also were helpful in the clinical decision-making process.

REFERENCE

Fischer, J., & Corcoran, K. J. (Eds.). (2007). *Measures for clinical practice* (pp. 207–308). Oxford, UK: Oxford University Press.

Hudson, W. W. (1982). *The clinical measurement package: A field manual*. Homewood, IL: Dorsey Press.

Case Study 9-2

Doing Family Therapy With an Acting-Out Adolescent: Using Rapid Assessment Tools in Clinical Practice

KEVIN CORCORAN AND KRISTIN BEERS

Family problems are a typical concern for the clinical social worker. This case discusses the use of structural family therapy and homework assignments, and demonstrates the use of rapid assessment tools in monitoring treatment evaluation.

Questions
1. What major treatment strategies were used to help change family patterns?
2. How did the social worker respond to the lack of progress in treatment?
3. How did the measures chosen to evaluate this case reflect the problems being addressed in the treatment?
4. What are some other ways that the presenting problems in this case could be measured?
5. Are you able to develop structured homework assignments for any of your clients?

Few clients enter treatment with a single problem; most, in fact, present multiple clinical issues. This is especially true for casework with families where the number of people alone makes for more complexity. The following case study—fictitiously called the Olivetti family—demonstrates the complexity of family problems. The case also displays the importance of assessment in determining whether an intervention is a success or a failure by illustrating both failure and success. In other words, the case illustrates how the assessment initially led the clinician in the wrong direction and to a lack of effectiveness. Rapid assessment tools are shown as a "pulse beat" to inform and guide clinical practice. By using measurement tools to monitor the case, the clinician was able to see the need to change interventions in order to effectively help the Olivetti family.

THE FAMILY AND THE FAMILY'S PROBLEMS

Genny Olivetti was referred to treatment subsequent to her discharge from a psychiatric hospital after reaching the limits of her parents' insurance coverage. Genny's admitting and discharge diagnosis was dysthymic disorder, a mental disorder similar to "neurotic depression" (American Psychiatric Association, 2013). The essential feature of this condition requires more days than not where the patient is depressed and has been depressed for most of the day for the past 2 years—a considerable proportion of life for a 16-year-old. Genny's symptoms also included sleep disturbance, fatigue, and low self-esteem. The discharge summary recommended group and individual therapy. No mention was made of family problems or the need for family therapy. The psychosocial assessment was based on a 45-minute telephone conversation with Genny's mother, a 2-hour family interview and home visit, an individual interview with Genny, and her responses to the Multimodal Life History Questionnaire (Lazarus, 1981).

Genny is a 16-year-old White female who appears her stated age and is slightly overweight. She reports having few, if any, close friends. She is very intelligent and was refusing to attend school. Genny complained of "being depressed" for more than 2 years. She seemed overwhelmed by her emotions and unable to express them verbally; consequently, she acts them out. Her parents, Curtis and Lane, complained of family conflict with frequent—often daily—arguments, which twice included physical altercations between Lane and Genny; these fights resulted in Genny's hospitalization. All of the family members agreed with Lane, who stated, "We have problems in communication."

In summary, the identified client appeared depressed, with a flat affect and inability to understand and express her emotions. She seemed to have low self-esteem and lacked a sense of control over her life. Consequently, the client was perceived as acting out her feelings instead of verbally communicating them. The acting-out behavior was considered to be an effort to exert control over her life by forcing her parents to establish strict limits on her behavior. Essentially, the client seemed to be trying to have her parents provide the control she could not; for many adolescents, a controlled environment provides a sense of security and psychological safety. Curtis and Lane, on the other hand, seemed intimidated by Genny and allowed her to run the family. Finally, Genny's lack of intrapersonal emotional control and her parents' inability to set limits seemed to exacerbate her depression.

As a consequence of this assessment, two general goals were established: (1) to improve communication among the family members, and (2) to establish more appropriate family roles between Genny and her parents. Communication skills training and structural family therapy, respectively, were used. The clinician also used homework assignments to further the change that occurred during the therapy sessions.

OVERVIEW OF TREATMENT TECHNIQUES

Communication Skills Training

This behavior therapy is part of social skills training, which is designed to systematically train effective communication skills in human relations. Theoretically, social skill deficits are considered to be a cause of interpersonal dysfunctioning (Kazdin, 1978, 2011). The therapy is based on the clinician modeling effective behaviors, the client's behavioral rehearsal, and positive reinforcement in the form of feedback from family members and the clinician. The Olivetti family had several communication skills deficits, including the lack of expression of content and affect between Genny and her mother, "mind reading" (where one member would speak for another), and a lack of active listening.

Structural Family Therapy

Unlike many therapies, which begin with the middle and upper class, this therapy originated from work with the poor (Minuchin, Montalvo, Guerney, Rosman, & Schuner, 1967). It focuses on the functioning of families as determined by their structure, namely the social organization. Structure essentially refers to the relationships, codes, rules, and norms that regulate the way members relate to each other. The transactions are determined by the boundaries between family members, their alignment with each other, and each member's power (Aponte, 1981). Briefly, *boundaries* refer to the rules that define "who participates and how" (Minuchin, 1974) in terms of the degree of enmeshment and disengagement; *alignment* refers, in part, to the coalitions and alliance of family members; and *power* describes the amount of influence each family member has in determining the outcome of transactions. In general, the goal of structural family therapy is to reorganize the family. To these ends, the clinician assumes a very active role by creating, joining, or restructuring transactions.

Homework Assignments

The treatment also used homework assignments. This approach is designed to use the natural environment to initiate change and to generalize the change from clinical sessions to the natural environment. When possible, the homework assignments followed Reid's (1975) five-step format: (1) discussing the assignment's benefits in order to enhance compliance, (2) planning the task implementation, (3) evaluating obstacles to completing the task, (4) conducting a behavioral rehearsal, and (5) summarizing the homework task.

The use of homework in clinical practice has expanded considerably in recent years, includes a wide array of mental health conditions (e.g. Carroll, Nich, & Ball, 2005;

Corcoran, 2003; Edwards, 2011), and even has several videos on YouTube (2012; also search Kazdin on youtube.com). Homework is useful to engage children and adolescents in the treatment process and to master the skills and tasks learned in cognitive-behavioral therapy. It can also be beneficial in resolving imbalance in family systems (Kazantzis, Deane, Ronan, & L'Abate, 2005; Kazantzis & L'Abate, 2004) and is used about 75% of the time by therapists working with couples (Dattilio, 2002). The reason for this prevalence is indisputable: Homework assignments promote the use of skills outside of the therapy session, where the majority of individuals and families spend time interacting in the "original environment where the dysfunction" often occurs (p. 536).

THE TREATMENT PROCESS

The clinician approached the case from the empirical clinical practice model, which uses rapid assessment tools to monitor a client's progress and evaluate one's effectiveness (Corcoran & Fischer, 2013; Jayaratne & Levy, 1979). Genny was instructed to complete the Child's Attitude Toward Mother (CAM) scale, which assessed her discord with her mother; Lane completed the Index of Parental Attitudes (IPA), which assessed her discord with her daughter; and Curtis completed the Index of Family Relation (IFR), which was used as a measure of intrafamilial stress. These scales have excellent reliability and validity data and have cutting scores of 30 (plus or minus 5 points), where scores below the cutting score suggest the absence of a clinical problem (Hudson, 1982; all instruments are in Corcoran & Fischer, 2013). The assessments were taken weekly. One retrospective assessment was made of the problem "in general over the past year" during the home visit. Additionally, a pretreatment assessment was also taken during this interview. These two data points served as the baseline data. Additionally, the school registrar reported Genny's weekly absenteeism rate, which served as an unobtrusive measure of the child's progress.

These data were plotted on graphs on a weekly basis (see Figure 9.3). Curtis's IFR scores are plotted against the left axis of the upper portion of the figure, and school absenteeism is plotted against the right axis. Genny's and Lane's scores are in the lower portion of the figure.

Over weeks 2 through 4, the clinician systematically trained the family in communication skills. The sessions consisted of modeling, behavioral rehearsal between Genny and Lane, and positive reinforcement with feedback. Training included use of I-statements, where each would be responsible for their communication; having members "ask for what they wanted"; confrontation and correction on "mind reading"; and attentive listening, which included having members "check out" what another said and asking for clarification. During session three, Lane and Curtis reported feeling frustrated over Genny's single-sentence correspondence at home, where she would talk by only saying "yes," "no," or "I don't know." Consequently, they were taught to use open-ended questions in response to this passive-aggressive behavior. Between each weekly session, the clinician gave the family homework

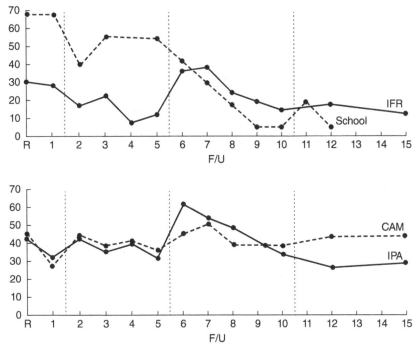

Figure 9.3 Index of family relations, number of school absences, child's attitude toward mother, and index of parental attitudes during the 15 weeks of treatment

assignments to further their communication skills. One assignment, for example, was for the family to review Genny's application to college and develop a contingency plan in case she did not get admitted.

During the fifth week, the parents said they thought "things were better around the house." However, little change was occurring on the rapid assessment instruments, and Genny's school absenteeism rate remained unacceptable. This troubled the clinician, who brought it up during the fifth session. Curtis and Lane acknowledged that they tried to have "good" conversations with Genny and not those that would be confrontational or disputatious, such as whether or not she was going to school. They admitted they felt manipulated by Genny.

The next day, Curtis telephoned to report that "all hell broke loose." The parents reportedly confronted Genny about "just playing games with us" and had "put our foot down about school." An argument ensued, and Genny assaulted her mother and then barricaded herself in her bedroom. For the next week, she refused to talk with her parents or to eat dinner with them. This discord is clearly reflected on all three rapid assessment scores for week 6 (Figure 9.3).

Because of the lack of noticeable progress on the rapid assessment tools and because of the current crisis, during the sixth session treatment moved immediately to the goal of restructuring the family. This was to be accomplished through a variety of subtle and direct techniques aimed at emphasizing the difference between Curtis and Lane's role as parent and Genny's role as child, as well as blocking inappropriate transactions when Genny attempted to be in control. To illustrate, the clinician's office had two large leather wing-backed chairs and a Chesterfield sofa. The chairs were rather massive and powerful, whereas the Chesterfield sat lower to the floor. The clinician had the parents sit in the chairs that directly faced Genny in the Chesterfield. Additionally, the clinician structured questions that empowered the parents, whereas those directed to Genny could be answered only in submissive ways. For example, during the crisis phone call, Curtis stated that he did not think Genny would come to the next session; thus, the clinician stated, "I see you got your child to come today. How did you make her do that?" Genny, on the other hand, was asked questions demanding more conciliatory answers, like "Do you understand what your mother is telling you?"

The structural family therapy used more direct techniques as well. For example, during session six Genny was dismissed from the office and told to wait in the car, while the parents discussed how to respond if she was to hit her mother again. They also discussed how to manage Genny's school absenteeism. Lane later told Genny that if she missed school once again during the next 2 weeks, they would sell her car. Part of the success of restructuring is a consequence of the power it bestowed on the parents. This, however, requires that the parents be sincere on their positions and carry through with threats if necessary. To the reassurance of the clinician and the dismay of Genny, some lucky soul purchased a used car in good condition during week 7. Genny was told she would be using the school bus for the rest of the year, and the money would be used to pay the family therapy bill.

The structural family therapy also included homework assignments. Many of these assignments focused on the symptoms by exaggerating, deemphasizing, or relabeling them. For example, during the seventh week, when Genny refused to eat with her parents and was eating in her bedroom, Curtis and Lane were instructed to move the entire dinner—table, chairs, dishes, and all the food—into the bedroom with her. From the next evening on, Genny joined her parents in the dining room.

Over the course of the next three sessions, additional efforts to reorganize the family structure occurred. Curtis and Lane reported that although Genny did not seem to like it and remained rather taciturn, she was participating in family responsibilities more. This progress was also reflected in the scores on Curtis and Lane's IFR and IPA scores for weeks 6 through 10. While Genny's CAM scores were not significantly improving, which isn't too surprising, her school absenteeism had.

Additional homework assignments were given to restructure the family. For example, before session 10, Lane and Genny were instructed to play an hour of miniature golf—a game they both hated. They were told that Genny had to pay for one-half of the game and Lane the other half; that one was to drive to the golf course and one was to drive home; and that they were to play to win. Most important, they were told they could not talk for the entire assignment. Reportedly, on the way home, one of them said "I beat you," and both broke into laughter.

TERMINATION AND FOLLOW-UP

Treatment—totaling 11 sessions—terminated after week 12 because the family was relocating. A follow-up visit was scheduled for the 15th week. As displayed in Figure 9.3, progress was noted during the structural family therapy sessions (weeks 6 through 10), with gradual decreases in scores on familial stress (IFR) and Lane's discord with Genny (IPA). Additionally, Genny was going to school, despite having to take the bus. The only time she skipped school was during week 11, which was Senior Skip Day. The clinician was not too troubled by this, because Genny was out with a group of newly formed friends; alternatively, the behavior simply may have been an effort by Genny to "test the limits" the week before the follow-up session.

Subsequent to the relocation, the clinician had a final telephone follow-up with the family. Curtis and Lane both reported the family was doing well. Genny had not graduated but was completing school over the summer and had enrolled in a local college for the Fall semester. Genny stated, "I still don't like my mom much, but I guess I'm not supposed to; I'm a teenager, you know."

REFERENCES

American Psychiatric Association. (2013). *Diagnostic and statistical manual of mental disorder* (5th ed.). Arlington, VA: American Psychiatric Press.

Aponte, J. J. (1981). Structural family therapy. In A. S. Gurman & D. P. Kniskern (Eds.), *Handbook of family therapy* (pp. 310–360). New York, NY: Brunner/Mazel.

Carroll, K. M., Nich, C., & Ball, S. A. (2005). Practice makes perfect? Homework assignments and outcome in treatment of cocaine dependency. *Journal of Clinical and Consulting Psychology, 73,* 749–755.

Corcoran, J. (2003). *Clinical applications of evidence-based family interventions.* New York, NY: Oxford University Press.

Corcoran, K., & Fischer, J. (2013). *Measures for clinical practice: A sourcebook. Vol. 1: Couples, families and children* (5th ed.). New York, NY: Oxford University Press.

Dattilio, F. M. (2002). Homework assignments in couple and family therapy. *Psychotherapy in Practice, 58*(5), 535–547.

Edwards, S. M. (2011). The relation between homework compliance and treatment outcome for individuals with social phobia. *Psychological Thesis,* paper 81. Georgia State University, Atlanta.

Hudson, W. W. (1982). *The clinical measurement package: A field manual.* Homewood, IL: Dorsey Press.

Jayaratne, S., & Levy, R. L. (1979). *Empirical clinical practice.* New York, NY: Columbia University Press.

Kazantzis, N., Deane, F. P., Ronan, K. R., & L'Abate, L. (2005). *Using homework assignments in cognitive behavior therapy.* New York, NY: Routledge.

Kazantzis, N., & L'Abate, L. (2004). *Handbook of homework assignments in psychotherapy: Research, practice and prevention.* New York, NY: Springer.

Kazdin, A. E. (1978). Sociopsychological factors in psychopathology. In A. S. Belleck & M. Hersen (Eds.), *Research and practice in social skills training.* New York, NY: Plenum Press.

Kazdin, A. E. (2011). Evidence-based treatment research: Advances, limitations and next steps. *American Psychologist, 66,* 685–698.

Lazarus, A. A. (1981). *The practice of multimodal therapy.* New York, NY: McGraw-Hill.

Minuchin, S. (1974). *Families and family therapy.* Cambridge, MA: Harvard Press.

Minuchin, S., Montalvo, B., Guerney, B., Rosman, B., & Schuner, F. (1967). *Families of the slums.* New York, NY: Basic Books,

Reid, W. J. (1975). A test of the task-centered approach. *Social Work, 22,* 3–9.

YouTube. (2012). Youtube.com/watch?v=FF_hrgR4q8.

Case Study 9-3

Practice Evaluation Methods: Practical Variations on a Theme

PAULA S. NURIUS AND SARA GREEN[1]

T hree case examples are provided to suggest the diversity and flexibility in which practice evaluation tools can be applied. The examples, which are purposefully not ideal, reflect the realities of integrating evaluation methods with practice.

Questions
1. What difficulties were evident in applying practice evaluation methods to each of the cases?
2. When is it necessary to devise your own measure rather than rely on a previously developed and standardized measure?
3. What conclusions can be drawn from the social work interventions in each of the examples?
4. What skills and knowledge were evident in the implementation of the practice evaluation techniques?

---

[1]   The authors would like to acknowledge the very useful input and stimulation from a host of students and practitioners over the years, including, but not limited to, Donna Linz, Murray McCord, Jani Semke, and Misty Cleman.

". . . there is a sense in which investigation continues as long as does treatment."
(Richmond, 1917, p. 363)

Practice evaluation is a constantly evolving area of direct service. Social service funding and billing requirements, the implementation of evidence-based and evidence-informed practices, the nature of client problems and the roles of the workers who see them, and the evolution of the social work field all impact the ways in which social workers conceptualize cases, assess clients, and evaluate their own practice. As the opening quote suggests, social work has a historic commitment to systematic inquiry as a fundamental component of its interpersonal practice. What changes with each passing decade are the tools with which to pursue this mission and the organizational context within which that mission must be pragmatically fashioned. It is toward this fitting of tools to setting that the present case studies will speak.

Specifically, this series of case studies advocates a creative and credible approach to employing various aspects of practice evaluation across the spectrum of human service settings. Three case examples of very different types of social work intervention are used to illustrate the diversity and utility of practice evaluation tools that are flexibly and practically employed. Each case example is followed by discussion of how features of this particular application could generalize to other interventions or services.

Because the focus of this chapter is on practice evaluation methods and because space is limited, information on the clients, treatments, and settings are necessarily abbreviated. Moreover, no attempt was made to locate textbook-perfect examples. Rather, the goal was to offer cases where compromises had to be struck, constraints balanced, and creative alternatives generated. This reflects both the blessing and the bane of social work—its enormous diversity of service and thus the need for diverse and flexible means of depicting, tracking, and evaluating that service. This chapter concludes with a reference list that provides a broadly applicable range of resources on the topic of practice assessment and evaluation tools, aimed to provide guidance at multiple points and when pragmatic adaptations may be needed.

SCENARIO 1: ONGOING TREATMENT AND CASE MANAGEMENT

A host of case examples are presently available in the literature of longitudinal single-system designs with individuals, families, and even groups. For this reason, emphasis is placed here on less conventional applications—those that do not lend themselves quite so readily to standard counseling models. The first example comes closest to this standard in that ongoing therapeutic client contact is involved. Features that complicate evaluation efforts include client limitations as a collaborator in monitoring, use of interdisciplinary team approaches that tend to cloud the social worker's unique input, and the rapidly growing emphasis on types of casework whose outcomes are difficult to measure (e.g., prevention, case management). The case example described here involves an inpatient psychiatric setting followed by case management and monitoring through an outpatient setting.

Case Example

The client is a 32-year-old Mexican American female, who was admitted to an inpatient psychiatric center following increasing disorientation, delusional ideation, depression, and sleep and appetite disturbance. The worker established target problem areas for this client to be psychosis—as evidenced by auditory hallucinations, confusion, and delusional thinking—and depression—as evidenced by agitation, an inability to concentrate, latency, tearfulness and depressed affect, and sleep and appetite disturbance.

For purposes of monitoring and evaluation, the worker selected three primary indicants—auditory hallucinations, confusion, and depressed affect. Rationale for selection of these indicants included: (a) They were viewed either by the worker as both observable and representative or by the client and her family as most debilitating; (b) they were reflective of the treatment goals (i.e., reducing or eliminating psychotic and depressive symptoms and enhancing the client's self-management abilities); and (c) they were able, with a reasonable degree of accuracy, to be operationalized and monitored by family members and, to a more limited extent, by the client and by human service workers.

The worker then devised a series of rating scales to tap key dimensions of target symptoms. A 1–5 rating was assigned to varying degrees of auditory hallucinations, confusion, and depressed affect, with each rating level operationalized for each indicant. For example, 1–5 ratings for confusion included:

1 = No confusion noted or reported, processing information well

2 = Mild confusion, some periods of clear cognitive functioning, minimal latency

3 = Moderate impairment, moderately confused, distracted about half the time, some latency

4 = Very confused but still attempting to function and process information, very marked latency

5 = Extremely confused, disorganized thinking, unable to function or process information

For auditory hallucinations, the worker drew on client self-report, whereas for confusion and depressed affect, direct observations by treatment team members were used.

The profiles of these indicators over the course of treatment are depicted in Figure 9.4. As is evident, stable positive change was not achieved with the first two treatment components—that of antidepressants (B1) followed by use of antidepressants and antipsychotic medications (B2). Rapid and sustained change was evident on the use of electroconvulsive therapy alone (C); no medications were given during this period. The final phase (D) represents outpatient case management. This phase of treatment included a maintenance dose of antidepressants, daily attendance at a day treatment program, and periodic follow-up contact with a staff psychiatrist and case manager.

As in most cases, compromises between research and service delivery agendas were necessary. Specifically, decisions based on clinical and organizational factors qualify and constrain data-based interpretations. For example, the course of treatment

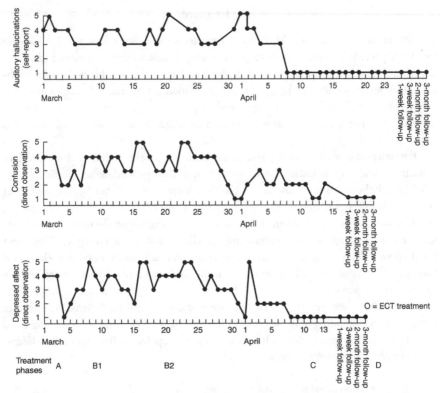

Figure 9.4 Degree of auditory hallucinations, confusion, and depressed affect during phases of the treatment

(i.e., "design") renders inferences of causality tentative because of lack of controls. On the other hand, (a) the immediate, consistent (across three measures), and stable change in indicators with the onset of electroconvulsive treatment, (b) the lack of prior consistent change, and (c) an existing empirical literature base supporting the efficacy of this treatment with patients who present with this diagnostic profile combine to suggest the likelihood of causality. Practical significance was achieved in that treatment outcome goals were met and the client's improved functioning areas stabilized, permitting her to return home.

The case manager who was assigned to the case continued to monitor maintenance as reflected by these indicators and added other indicators appropriate to her specific work with the client (not depicted here). Notably, the client and her family members were also able to monitor her functioning and adjust as needed as a result of learning the early indicators of slippage, the ways in which this could be distinguished from normal variations (e.g., mood, stress), and options for adjustment. The combination of observational monitoring (by workers, family members) and self-monitoring (often entailing client education) holds utility across a broad spectrum of case management and maintenance and prevention-oriented interventions.

SCENARIO 2: LIMITED-CONTACT INTERVENTION

In some settings, use of practice evaluation methods has been seen as untenable because of the nature of the services (e.g., discharge planning) or of the circumstances (e.g., very limited client contact). In addition, practice evaluation has tended to be portrayed in terms of ongoing care, thus involving longitudinal designs, individualized goals, and measures of incremental progress toward goals. Yet in an increasing proportion of human services, this evaluative model is not well suited to setting realities. One case in point is that of discharge planning.

The case example described here involves an injured adult in a hospital setting. The issues encountered are broadly generalized across a variety of populations (e.g., those in correctional settings, frail elderly, the acutely or chronically mentally ill, individuals with terminal illnesses) and across residential, long-term care, or transitional settings where discharge planning and preparation are needed. Despite its prevalence, guidelines for distilling and evaluating the relative *effectiveness* of discharge planning have thus far not been adequately addressed. The following scenario presents several creative applications of practice evaluation methods tailored to the needs and constraints of the case and setting. As noted earlier, the following illustrations are not intended as templates of "correct" evaluative approaches but rather of viable examples generated by busy practitioners on the job.

Case Example

The client is a 43-year-old African American male, who was referred to a spinal cord injury unit for treatment and rehabilitation of spinal cord lesions. The client's injuries, sustained through an accident, left him a complete paraplegic and a partial quadriplegic. The client has limited financial resources, has not worked for several years because of a prior injury, and lists only a sister living in another state as a family member with whom he has contact.

The client was referred to the hospital's social services department by the medical staff for discharge planning and assistance in obtaining community resources. The client's presenting problems were consistent with this referral agenda, with a clear preference to live by himself and be as independent as possible.

The worker used a two-pronged approach to outcome evaluation. First, a standardized inventory of criteria constituting an effective discharge plan was developed. In circumstances such as discharge planning involving high frequency, limited client contact, and similarity across cases, repeated use of standardized as opposed to individually developed instruments tends to be most viable. An attractive alternative is the ability to individually tailor, on a manageable scale, a standardized format.

Figure 9.5 details one such approach used here. The social service department staff had previously constructed a listing of various goals that practitioners typically consider or strive toward accomplishing in discharge planning. The extent to which each of these is attained, as applicable, is indicated on a 0–3 scale: 0 = not at all, 1 = a little, 2 = moderately, 3 = substantially or completely. In addition, spaces are available to write in

3	1. Planning process started early
2	2. Comprehensive assessment completed
3	3. Problem list established and prioritized
3	4. Problem-specific goals with action plans developed
2	5. Patient involved in planning process
NA	6. Family/significant others involved in planning process
3	7. Action plans adjusted as needed to fulfill goals (i.e., problems resolved)
2	8. Planning goals achieved (prior to discharge)
3	9. Follow-up arranged (care and/or contact)
3	10. Patient discharged by scheduled date
1	11. Patient satisfied
NA	12. Family/significant others satisfied
2	13. Initial evidence of discharge follow-through (e.g., patient received in new health care site)
2	14. Patient thriving in new setting
NA	15. Patient readmitted within 1 month of discharge
2	16. *Other: Knowledge of IL/housing options
2	17. *Other: Patient locus of control
1	18. *Other: Social support network
	19. *Other:
	20. *Other:

Key

0	Not at all
1	A little
2	Moderately
3	Substantially
NA	Not applicable

*Anchors for each rating level need to be specified on back of form.

Figure 9.5 Discharge planning criteria and outcome evaluation

individualized goals for each client and to rate their degree of attainment on the same 4-point scale.

In the present case, the worker used this latter option to detail specific factors related to this client obtaining and sustaining his independent living goals. These included his knowledge of independent living/housing options, the level of personal control (locus of control) the client assumed toward establishing and maintaining an independent life plan (ILP), and the extent to which the client had peer and professional supports in the community that would facilitate maintenance of his independent living.

To enhance its validity and reliability of use across cases and raters, it is optional that each level for each criterion be operationalized or "anchored." As an illustration, the locus-of-control ratings were operationalized as:

0 = client does not take any responsibility for establishing his ILP

1 = client is minimally involved in establishing his ILP

2 = client is moderately participating in establishing his ILP

3 = client is actively involved in establishing his ILP

This charting format has proven useful in a variety of ways. First, it provides a multi-dimensional approach to assessing client outcome vis-à-vis the discharge process with more interventionally relevant detail than is typically afforded. This detail is of value to the practitioner, the supervisor, and the manager alike. It can be an efficient communication aid among staff involved with a case, particularly in those circumstances where several caseworkers may be coordinating the discharge plan or sharing discharge duties for a given case, some of whom may be less familiar with the client. It also provides valuable data at the point of referral to community service agencies as to the status of the patient (e.g., relatively low level of social supports and moderate degree of engagement in independent plan maintenance).

A variety of other limited-contact situations may be aided in practice evaluation efforts by this type of pool. Among others, this could include a variety of crisis interventive circumstances, information and referral, and short-term education, mediation, and brokerage services.

SCENARIO 3: CASE ACUITY AND HIGH-RISK ASSESSMENT

Primary prevention, long a concern of the social work profession, has been growing as a service objective across a wide spectrum of client populations and problems in living. The following case example illustrates one healthcare center's efforts to identify and operationalize factors constituting high risk for a given client group and then to systematically assess, be guided by, and monitor these factors over the course of client contact. For purposes of brevity, only the assessment and risk classification steps are illustrated. Monitoring of stability or change in risk factors over time and outcome evaluation based on these trends can, however, readily be pursued by recording client status on these factors over time.

Case Example

The client population involves pregnant women receiving prenatal care at a county healthcare setting. High-risk factors with respect to pregnancy resulting in both a healthy full-term birth and satisfactory mother–infant bonding were targeted by the women's clinic staff.

The staff had been discussing and employing mental checklists regarding factors each had come to see associated with problematic pregnancies, births, or bonding. Over time, this informal and somewhat idiosyncratic method proved inadequate (e.g., clinic staffing became less stable, the proportion of complex cases began rising, hospital administration was considering cutting funding of the social work component in the clinic), motivating staff to develop more formal assessment instruments and monitoring procedures.

Figure 9.6 presents the high-risk profile of a sample of clinic patients. The 10 targeted factors by no means represent an exhaustive list. They were, however, viewed as adequate given the delimited goals and intervention options the clinic was in a position to pursue with respect to their clients. Note also that weights were assigned to each factor such that youth, lack of early prenatal care, and a history of drug or alcohol misuses carried greater risk relative to other factors.

Figure 9.7 presents the high-risk classifications of these women. This classification provides one indicator of the acuity of each case and thus the need for more immediate and/or intensive services. It does not suggest that the same interventions will be designated within each set. For example, clients D and E are both classified at the same level of risk, but their risk profiles are quite different and will require intervention plans tailored to those differences. This underscores the importance of using both sets of information in relation to each other. Also important in weighing the various factors and alternatives are the client's priorities and perceptions of need.

A third step taken was to develop clusters of interventions that generally correspond to level of risk and, thus, need. This treatment planning aid was necessarily viewed as

Weight	Risk Factors	A	B	C	D	E	F	G	H	I	J	K	L	M	N	O
1	1. History of sexual abuse			•												
3	2. History of drug and/or alcohol misuse				•			•	•				•	•		•
1	3. History of depression/ psychiatric					•	•	•				•		•	•	
1	4. History of runaway/street life	•	•					•	•							
1	5. History of physical abuse			•			•				•	•				
2	6. Under age 18	•	•	•				•	•	•		•				
1	7. No stable partner			•				•	•			•				
2	8. First prenatal visit > 20 weeks	•			•					•			•			
1	9. Education < 12th grade	•	•			•	•	•		•	•					
1	10. Low income (AFDC, WIC, etc.)	•	•			•			•		•		•	•		•

N=15

Figure 9.6 Sample patient profiles of pregnancy high-risk factors

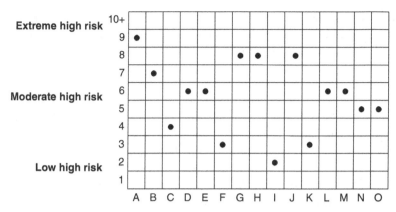

Figure 9.7   Service provision priorities based on high-risk profiles

suggestive rather than directive for many of the same reasons noted previously. For example, because of her history of drug/alcohol use, medical and counseling services targeting this factor would be provided to client E immediately.

The majority of clinic services are more brokerage related than therapeutic oriented. The overarching goal is to get the client through the pregnancy safely and to increase the likelihood of adequate mother–infant bonding and parenting ability. Therefore, specific goals and progress indicators established for individual clients tend to be operationalized vis-à-vis those outcomes. Broadly generalizable outcome indicators, which are useful for both clinical and quality assurance purposes, include the term delivery of a healthy infant, good health of the mother, and satisfactory indicators of preparedness to parent and to maintain the health of mother and infant.

CONCLUSION

As the opening quote from Mary Richmond illustrates, social work has historically sought and grappled with ways to keep one's finger on the pulse of progress toward achievement of client goals, as well as sensitive indicators of impediments to achievement. Client engagement to locate or create progress-monitoring tools that can transcend formal services, to support client insight and encouragement in longer term self-management, has also long been a priority. Questions regarding whether to employ practice evaluation methods, how, under what circumstances, and to what end are legitimate questions that can and need to be continually examined and flexibly dealt with. It is a joint mission for the social caseworker, administrator, and academician, and one in which an informed and active contribution by the direct practitioner plays a vital role.

As the case studies and reading list included in this chapter illustrate, the specific therapeutic evaluation strategies workers may use can span a considerable range across different clients, settings, and problem foci. In this reading list, we have included resources that provide depth on the topic of practice evaluation, including case conceptualization, assessment, progress monitoring, and use of data to inform service changes and termination across various populations. We conclude in noting that this dimension of practice continually undergoes scrutiny, with productive and meaningful critique and discourse. As many life problems derive from social conditions, including inequalities and injustices, legitimate questions are raised, for example, about the use of clinical tools that are directed more toward coping with rather than changing conditions. The professional literature is dynamic. As contexts, conceptualizations, priorities, and pragmatics of professional helping services evolve, so too must the progress and practice monitoring tools. We have been attentive in selecting resources that are useful to the social work direct service practitioner and practice student, while also being broadly applicable to practitioners in related helping professions.

REFERENCE

Richmond, M. W. (1917). *Social diagnosis.* New York, NY: Russell Sage Foundation.

READING LIST

Antony, M. M., & Barlow, D. H. (Eds.). (2010). *Handbook of assessment and treatment planning for psychological disorders* (2nd ed.). New York, NY: Guilford Press.

Berman, P. S. (2010). *Case conceptualization and treatment planning: Integrating theory with clinical practice* (2nd ed.). Thousand Oaks, CA: Sage.

Bloom, M., Fischer, J., & Orme, J. G. (2009). *Evaluating practice: Guidelines for the accountable professional* (6th ed.). Boston, MA: Pearson/Allyn & Bacon.

Boutin-Foster, C., Euster, S., Rolon, Y., Motal, A., Belue, R., Kline, R., & Charlson, M. E. (2005). Social Work Admission Assessment Tool for identifying patients in need of comprehensive social work evaluation. *Health & Social Work, 30*(2), 117–125.

Bufka, L. F., & Camp, N. (2010). Brief measures for screening and measuring mental health outcomes. In M. M. Antony & D. H. Barlow (Eds.), *Handbook of assessment and treatment planning for psychological disorders* (2nd ed., pp. 62–94). New York, NY: Guilford Press.

Comier, S., Nurius, P. S., & Osborn, C. J. (2013). *Interviewing and change strategies for helpers* (7th ed.). Belmont, CA: Brooks/Cole.

Drummon, R., & Jones, K. D. (2009). *Assessment procedures for counselors and helping professionals* (7th ed.). Upper Saddle River, NJ: Pearson.

Fischer, J., & Corcoran, K. (2007). *Measures for clinical practice and research: A sourcebook* (4th ed.; Vol. 1: Couples, Children, & Families; Vol. 2: Adults). New York, NY: Oxford University Press.

Goldfinger, K., & Pomerantz, A. (2010). *Psychological assessment and report writing*. Thousand Oaks, CA: Sage.

Groth-Marnat, G. (2009). *The handbook of psychological assessment* (5th ed.). Hoboken, NJ: Wiley.

Hays, P. A. (2008). *Addressing cultural complexities in practice: Assessment, diagnosis, and therapy* (2nd ed.). Washington, DC: American Psychological Association.

Hepworth, D. H., Rooney, R. H., Rooney, G. G., & Strom-Gottfried, K. (2013). *Direct social work practice: Theory and skills* (9th ed.). Belmont, CA: Brooks/Cole.

Hunsley, J., & Mash, E. J. (2010). The role of assessment in evidence-based practice. In M. M. Antony & D. H. Barlow (Eds.), *Handbook of assessment and treatment planning for psychological disorders* (2nd ed., pp. 3–22). New York, NY: Guilford Press.

Lambert, M. J. (2010a). *Prevention of treatment failure: The use of measuring, monitoring, and feedback in clinical practice*. Washington, DC: American Psychological Association.

Lambert, M. J. (2010b). Yes, it is time for clinicians to routinely monitor treatment outcome. In B. L. Duncan, S. D. Miller, B. E. Wampold, & M. A. Hubble (Eds.), *The heart and soul of change: Delivering what works in therapy* (2nd ed., pp. 239–266). Washington, DC: American Psychological Association.

Leibert, T. W. (2006). Making change visible: The possibilities in assessing mental health counseling outcomes. *Journal of Counseling & Development, 84*, 108–118.

Nezu, A. M., & Nezu, C. M. (2010). Cognitive-behavioral case formulation and treatment design. In R. A. DiTomasso, B. A. Golden, & H. J. Morris (Eds.), *Handbook of cognitive-behavioral approaches in primary care* (pp. 201–222). New York, NY: Springer.

Paniagua, F. A. (2005). *Assessing and treating culturally diverse clients: A practical guide* (3rd ed.). Thousand Oaks, CA: Sage.

Persons, J. B. (2008). *The case formulation approach to cognitive-behavior therapy*. New York, NY: Guilford Press.

Rubin, A., & Babbie, E. (2011). *Research methods for social work* (7th ed.). Belmont, CA: Brooks/Cole.

Stone, A. A., Shiffman, S., Atienza, A. A., & Nebeling, L. (2007). *The science of real-time data capture: Self-reports in health research*. New York, NY: Oxford University Press.

Whiston, S. C. (2009). *Principles and applications of assessment in counseling* (3rd ed.). Belmont, CA: Brooks/Cole.

Case Study 9-4

Becoming Evidence-Based: A Social Work Agency's Effort to Move Research Into Practice

JENNIFER L. BELLAMY

Evidence-based practice is increasingly being integrated into social work practice. This case describes one agency's effort to become more evidence-based and to change their approach to practice.

Questions

1. Why is evidence-based practice important to social work?
2. How did the social worker encourage the use of evidence-based practice in the agency setting?
3. What is the difference between the evidence-supported intervention approach and the evidence-based practice process model?
4. What did the agency learn about the process of using an evidence-based approach as an organization?

THE RESEARCH–PRACTICE GAP

Evidence-based practice (EBP) has become a prominent theme of social work research, writing, practice, and education. Social workers, as well as allied professions, have experienced increasing pressure to become evidence based through funders, licensing and accreditation organizations, professional organizations, and other entities. EBP reflects a deceptively simple idea: Use research knowledge in social work practice. However, despite growing pressure to use EBP and a mountain of research designed to identify effective interventions, the distance between research and practice has been so large and gaping that it has been described as a chasm (Institute of Medicine, 2006). So, why don't practitioners use more research-based knowledge to deliver services?

Much of the social work literature on EBP describes the potential barriers, but very little of this conclusion is based on efforts to actually implement EBP in practice (Addis, 2002; Bellamy, Bledsoe, & Traube, 2006; Gira, Kessler, & Poertner, 2004; Kirk & Reid, 2002). A colleague of mine once framed this as a seed versus soil problem: We have a lot of knowledge about some seeds (efficacious social work interventions) but little knowledge about the best way to prepare the soil (social service agencies and social work practitioners) so as to successfully find, plant, nurture, and sustain them. This case study is an exploration of the efforts of a team of social workers at a social work agency to integrate research evidence into social work practice, as well as some of the lessons learned in one effort to navigate the difficulties in the messy reality of social work practice.

Over the past 10 years or so, I've worked with many social work agencies as they have sought to learn about and use EBP. This case study is the story of one such partnership. In many ways, our work together typifies the experiences of other agencies and practitioners whom I have worked with as they grappled with these issues. This case study is specifically focused on moving mental health research knowledge into practice. Although EBP is by no means limited to mental health practice, social workers provide the majority of mental health services in the United States, and the pressures to provide evidence-based services are perhaps most prominent in the health and mental health service sectors.

The social service agency that is the focus of this case study is one that reached out to me as an expert in EBP. My work as a researcher has focused on the development of partnership models and training strategies to support the implementation of EBP in social work practice. On occasion I share this work at conferences, and this particular agency learned about my work from one of these presentations. For the rest of this case study I will refer to this agency as the Family Service Center (FSC). After my talk, the director of the FSC came to the front of the room to speak with me. He explained that the FSC had been trying to meet the demands of funders to become evidence-based. He had a vision for the FSC to become *the* leading provider of evidence-based child and family services in his city by not only providing gold standard services to clients but also serving as a model and training center for other social service agencies. He thought that this branding of his agency would give the FSC a competitive edge in a tough nonprofit market with limited resources. We thought that his agency could serve as a natural lab in which I could study the implementation of EBP while I helped the FSC to implement EBP.

GETTING ON THE SAME PAGE

As we began our partnership, I suggested to the director that I come to the FSC and give a presentation on EBP to front-line staff, program managers, and administrators. After several years of teaching social work classes about moving research into practice, doing surveys of practitioners and students about their perceptions of EBP, and talking to funders, government officials, and a whole lot of other stakeholders in the research and practice world, it has become very clear to me that there is a lot of confusion and disagreement as to what EBP actually means. So, getting us all on the same page seemed like a reasonable first step. This kick-off presentation was also a way to get everyone at the FSC thinking and talking together about moving research into practice, motivate the FSC staff to participate in the effort, and address some common concerns and misconceptions about EBP. The director had shared with me that some staff would likely interpret his efforts as just another burdensome project that would likely yield little if any benefit to them or their clients, so buy-in may be a challenge.

I began my presentation by asking everyone what they thought of when I said the phrase *evidence-based practice*. I encouraged people to be honest, because after all, I said, "I did not invent EBP." The words that I got back included *research, cookie-cutter, cost-cutting, what works, boring,* and *outcomes.* In this discussion we talked about the pressures to use EBP and concerns that EBP would be used to unfairly limit practice and undercut the quality of services. Others felt that EBP was just the buzzword of the day, and one day would be replaced with something else. One senior staff member said, "I figure that if I wait long enough, this too will pass." On the flipside, we also talked about a real desire to have a better handle on research that is relevant to social work and to find ways to make research more accessible and useful.

As we continued our conversation, some of the furrowed brows, crossed arms, and frowns that populated the back of the room seemed to loosen up—not all of them, but some of them. In earlier partnership efforts, I would often start off by trying to motivate people to become card-carrying members of the EBP club, but I have learned that it's generally a better approach to lay out the concerns and problems, and acknowledge the barriers and negative feelings from the beginning. Not everyone has to wholeheartedly buy in, but everyone needs to be heard. As it turned out, the director's concern about staff buy-in to the larger idea of EBP as a vision for the agency didn't turn out to be a significant barrier.

For the rest of this kick-off presentation, I focused on laying out the two dominant models of EBP. The first, and most popular, approach to EBP is something that I like to call the *bright shiny object* approach. A more scholarly name for this take on EBP is the evidence-supported intervention (ESI) approach. This is usually what people think of when they hear the term EBP and often what they are thinking about when they have a gut-level dislike for the concept. In this model of moving research into practice, social work practitioners are expected to pluck packaged interventions off the shelf and use them in practice with as much fidelity to the manual as possible. These packaged interventions are the bright shiny objects—or, using our analogy from earlier, they are the seeds meant to be planted in practice.

The ESI approach on its surface seems straightforward: Just find interventions that are shown through rigorous research studies to be efficacious, and use them in practice. *Et, voilà!* You have EBP. Upon closer inspection, this approach exemplifies the inherent difficulties in using research-based knowledge in practice. First, there are many social work problems and populations for which there are no bright shiny objects. And even the best interventions don't work for some people. Many of these interventions are expensive to implement and maintain because of training, materials, consultation, and other costs. Many are too burdensome to be used in often time-limited service contexts. And it can be difficult to imagine learning a different manual for every problem that walks in the door. In the end, the bright shiny objects often lose some of their luster.

Many of my colleagues at FSC expanded on these concerns as I laid them out. One of the staff members said that she thought this was just the newest effort by HMOs and other funders to get out of paying for expensive, but needed, long-term services for low-income and high-risk populations. Another person talked about getting sticker shock when she found out how much it would cost to implement a gold standard intervention. Others said that they didn't even know where to start to try to find training, or even basic information about the costs involved in using evidence-supported interventions.

Next, I outlined a second approach to EBP: the evidence-based practice process model. This EBP model is most often described as a series of steps whereby social workers pose a researchable question, seek out the best-available research to answer that question, evaluate the quality of that research evidence, apply an intervention using the research knowledge along with client assessments, clinical judgment, and other sources of information in accordance with client needs and preferences, and evaluate the outcome of this process. This is EBP as originally conceptualized in medicine and later translated to allied professions (Bellamy et al., 2013; Sacket, Rosenberg, Gray, Haynes, & Richardson, 1996).

The EBP process model has the benefit of placing practitioners and clients at the center of the practice decision-making process; however, it is terribly burdensome to slog through all of the research evidence. Practitioners often don't have the time, resources, or training to access databases and journal articles and make sense of it all. Research findings can be inconsistent, the statistics are intimidating to many social workers who would rather work with people than with numbers, and there is rarely any guidance as to how to actually implement the interventions that are identified in research. One FSC social worker said that the results and methods section of research studies made her eyes "glaze over," so she would often just skip to the end. Much of the difficulty involved in this process, I explained, relates to specialized skills, knowledge, and resources that are not readily available to social work practitioners—but are exactly the sort of things your friendly neighborhood researcher (in this case, me!) might offer to an agency partner.

After the presentation, we had a discussion about how we might work together moving forward. Nearly everyone felt more comfortable with the idea of working on becoming evidence-based through the evidence-based practice process, rather than just choosing evidence-supported interventions to implement. As a result, we initiated a series of meetings where we would form a team to take a close look at current services. This would give me a chance to get to know the FSC services better and help the agency locate where we might target our initial efforts to bring research to bear on the agency's work. That's when the trouble began.

IDENTIFYING CURRENT PRACTICES

Following my kick-off presentation at the FSC, the director decided to ask the five program managers to form the EBP team that would work with me to shepherd the agency's effort to become evidence-based. He felt that these midlevel managers were best positioned to both understand the needs of front-line staff and to supervise any activities related to the implementation of new practices. The five programs at the FSC included a teen parenting program, a home visiting program, a foster care program, a preschool for low-income families, and an individual counseling program that served mainly children and adolescents.

At the first EBP team meeting, I asked the program managers to tell me about their programs, including which interventions, programs, and curricula were currently in use. Each of them looked at the other, and no one initially volunteered a response. Gradually, individuals began to say things like, "We've brought in training for staff in a wide variety of interventions, but I'm not sure which one we're using now," and "I would have to ask my workers," and "We have the curriculum for a program that we use, in part, but that's not everything that we do." The one exception was the home visiting program, which was using a national model to guide services that they thought was evidence-based.

The other program managers felt that most of what the front-line workers were using was probably not evidence-based, but they weren't sure. As the discussion continued, it became clear that no one could confidently articulate what exactly they were delivering, why they were using what they were, and whether they were using any evidence-supported interventions. At this point we decided the next step would be to go to our respective corners, and the program managers would work to map out current services more precisely so that our team could think about what we might want to preserve in terms of current practices, which evidence-supported interventions workers or the agency had already invested in, and where the targets for improvement might lie.

What seemed initially to be a simple task of reviewing current practices became a complex and time-consuming endeavor. Ultimately, this effort to describe services and unearth the reasons why current curricula, interventions, and programs were being used became a 6-month-long project. For me, learning about the *what* and *why* of each program was fascinating. For example, the relatively recently hired manager of the teen parenting program inherited a curriculum from the former program manager. She asked staff who had a longer organizational memory where the curriculum had come from. One thought that the former program manager had attended a conference where she learned about the curriculum when the teen parenting program was first initiated, and that's where it had come from. We took a closer look at the materials that were being used. After some sleuthing, we thought it was a combination of at least three different curricula, one of which was actually an evidence-supported parent training intervention. Other materials came from a popular but generally untested intervention, and the third remained a mystery in terms of its source.

All told, the agency seemed to have absorbed the components of no less than 11 evidence-supported interventions into their programs. None of these interventions were being delivered in their entirety. Some were adapted to fit the constraints of practice, often by shortening the intervention or reducing the complexity. Others had been adapted to meet the needs of the service population. For example, the teen parenting program had translated materials meant for older parents to fit the needs of their younger clients. In other cases, program managers were unable to clearly determine why services were being delivered the way they were, other than to say, "That's the way we've done it for years." In yet other cases, we felt that the interventions used by workers were largely based on personal preference.

Our team reflected on what we had learned and what it meant in terms of the agency's quest to become evidence-based. Did this mean that everything that the agency delivered in terms of services had to be supported by research evidence? Was that idea even possible given the breadth and depth of services offered to clients? Which elements of current services were worth preserving or even evaluating within the agency rather than seeking research evidence produced in other contexts? What could the agency reasonably sustain in terms of evidence-supported interventions in light of the potential costs of training, curricula, and other materials? Would we spend the time and resources to train staff in chosen evidence-supported interventions only to risk losing them to other agencies?

STARTING SOMEWHERE

Our team chose one program to start with and focused on that area of service for the remainder of our partnership. Despite the director's vision for quickly implementing EBP throughout the FSC and our team of invested social workers with both clinical and research chops, it seemed too overwhelming to address the challenges and concerns that were being raised in each of the five programs at once. We chose to focus on the child and adolescent counseling program. This program seemed to be a good choice, because many of the workers in that program had Master's-level degrees in social work or other allied professions, and many of the currently available evidence-supported interventions are intended for use by professionals with clinical training. The teen parenting program by comparison was largely delivered by paraprofessionals, who may or may not have the clinical skills to easily implement evidence-supported interventions. The home visiting program model in use was required by the agency's current funder, so there was relatively less wiggle room there in terms of the clinical content of the program. The foster care program often referred families to other programs and services both within and outside of the agency. Research evidence certainly might be brought to bear on the way those services were delivered, but those workers also seemed the least inclined to take on yet more training and burden, given the current caseloads and other complexities involved in those services. The preschool was not therapeutic in nature, and the research in this area was mostly an unknown to me in terms of potential programs, interventions, and the like.

All of this work, discussion, and reflection preceded what is most often described in the literature as the first step in the EBP process: asking a researchable question. Drilling down to the child and adolescent counseling program was a good, if not essential, first step given that we clearly thought through the pros and cons of implementing the EBP process across each of the programs. The program managers said that it was a lot of work, but they enjoyed having the chance to reflect on the content and logic of their programs, which was something they didn't normally have the luxury of time to do. One of them said to me, "It was a slow and somewhat painful effort, but I feel like I have such a better handle on what's going on in my program and across the agency."

When we were finally in a position to ask a researchable question, we engaged the front-line workers in the counseling program in the process. They helped our team identify which outcomes or targets of intervention they most wanted to improve, which they felt less certain about or less successful with, or which they would otherwise nominate as an area of intervention that might benefit from research evidence. Children's behavioral problems quickly rose to the top of the list. Even the kids they worked with who came in with other presenting problems, such as trauma, anxiety, depression, or substance use, often had behavioral problems as well. So, our researchable question became, "Which interventions are most effective for treating children with externalizing behavior problems?" None of the workers was using a manual or curriculum to specifically treat behavior problems. Many were using elements of cognitive-behavioral therapy, play therapy, and solution-focused therapy, along with a variety of other clinical tools and techniques.

At this point, I was the one with a lot of homework. This is the part of the EBP process where my research skills and expertise really came into play as a key resource. After selecting a researchable question, the subsequent steps of the EBP process include identifying the best-available research to answer the question and evaluating the quality of that research. I first engaged in a comprehensive search of the published literature on interventions designed to treat children's behavior problems. As an affiliate of a university, I have ready access to almost any publication source that might describe the results of intervention studies. My agency partner, by comparison, could not afford to purchase access to full-text databases. The FSC had subscriptions to some journals and a small library that staff could access, but that was about it. Some of the staff supervised social work students at local universities, so they could access academic resources that way, but not one of them reported actually ever doing this. Others said that they occasionally used the resources of their local library, many of which increasingly provided electronic databases of academic sources, but that they had to do this on their own time.

Even if my FSC partners did have access to this research knowledge, making judgments about the quality of the research evidence was a tall order. Most of them had taken one or two research classes and felt that this training (what they remembered of it) ill-prepared them to understand the complex issues involved in intervention study design and analysis. At first I envisioned our working together to find the research and train my colleagues in the interpretation of these studies, so they could engage in a similar process without me. In the end, I largely did this work for them, and they pretty much trusted my search for and assessment of the research. This approach runs counter to the original idea of the EBP process, in which individual practitioners continuously engage in question formulation, search, and evaluation of research. In our case, it took a whole team, including a researcher, to work through this process just once.

EXAMINING THE EVIDENCE

I assembled the available research on interventions for children's behavior problems, including systematic reviews, meta-analyses, and individual effectiveness studies in the published literature. These sources are essential for examining the evidence base on the effectiveness of interventions, but they are limited in terms of information about implementation—including the training requirements and costs involved. To meet the need for both research and implementation information, I also collected information from other sources, such as the California Evidence-Based Clearinghouse for Child Welfare and the Substance Abuse and Mental Health Services Administration's National Registry of Evidence-Based Programs and Practices. Building on these raw materials, I assembled a matrix of interventions that our team might consider implementing with summary information, including (a) the number and type of studies available, (b) the outcomes achieved in each study, (c) the populations and contexts for which these interventions had been tested, (d) costs, and (e) training data. My aim was to attempt to present this information in a digestible yet detailed format, so that our team could debate the potential fit of the options before us using a balance of research-based and pragmatic implementation knowledge. Even with my years of training in research, this task was daunting. The spreadsheet I created with this information stretched across several worktables in the FSC training room.

When I presented this work to the FSC team, they shared several reactions and observations with me. First, despite my efforts to organize and summarize the information, it was still a case of data overload. It was difficult to keep all of the details of individual studies and interventions straight. We met no less than three times just to go over this information and talk it through. Second, they were shocked about how inconsistent the study results were, even for a single intervention. For example, one intervention that we examined sometimes demonstrated efficacy in reducing externalizing problems among children. However, the most methodologically rigorous study found that the program did not achieve statistically significant effects on externalizing behavior problems beyond treatment as usual, but did seem to improve other valued outcomes, including children's social skills and relationships with their parents. Moreover, none of the best studies included a long follow-up period, so we didn't know how long improvements might be maintained. Another study suggested that the intervention worked well for younger children but had less clinically impressive results for kids over age 10. Furthermore, many of the interventions that had the best research support for their efficacy were parent training programs, and the FSC services were organized around individual counseling sessions with kids, not their parents. Finally, few of the interventions had been tested with the diverse low-income, inner-city population served by the FSC. One of our team members said, "It's amazing how much of this stuff is for middle-class White people in Oregon."

IMPLEMENTATION

The next step of the EBP process is to implement an intervention based on the best-available research, while keeping in mind client needs and preferences, as well as the resources and constraints of the service context. We decided to thin out the field of intervention options based on what was feasible. We knocked out many possibilities because they were too expensive, too long, or required extraordinarily burdensome training and consultation to support their use. We discussed the possibility of adapting some of these more pragmatically challenging interventions, but felt that the process of responsibly adapting the intervention in and of itself would be too much to take on at this point. In addition, once we adapted an intervention, we couldn't really say we were using an evidence-supported intervention. We landed on an intervention that was not, in fact, a gold standard intervention in terms of the best-available research. However, preliminary studies suggested that it was promising in terms of impacting behavior problems, and we felt that it could be implemented as intended, in its entirety, at the FSC. This intervention had been tested with diverse low-income families, including those in contact with child welfare, which was another important consideration for the FSC, who received many referrals from that system.

Even though the intervention generally fit within the service context, the decision to adopt it had some immediate consequences for the program. First, we had to figure out how to get everyone trained in the new intervention while balancing the competing demands on staff time. The ideal approach to training staff would be to engage everyone in the intervention certification process, which included a 2-day off-site training, ongoing technical assistance, video or audiotaping of sessions to check for fidelity, and the completion of client evaluations for review by the intervention developers at every session for at least 12 clients. This process was not affordable for the FSC to support because of the expense of the training and the opportunity cost involved in pulling staff away from billable service hours. We settled on a plan to train one worker in the new intervention and support this person to first become a certified therapist in the intervention, and then also a trainer. Our idea was that this staff person would train both current and future therapists at the FSC, and also begin to offer training in the intervention to other therapists in the area. This way we felt we were more likely to retain and benefit from the training and resource investment.

Another complicating factor was that this intervention happened to require some service delivery to parents as well as children. This meant that the FSC would have to change its traditional model of practice for this population. Parents would no longer be able to simply drop off their kids at therapy, but would rather have to be motivated and engaged to actively participate in the treatment as well. Workers who were unaccustomed to interacting with families in this way were skeptical about their ability to do so successfully. Some felt that they were child therapists, not family therapists, and therefore were reluctant to buy in to this new approach. We tried to do a lot of cheerleading in an effort to rally the support of the less-enthusiastic therapists. Some of these workers ultimately left the agency, perhaps to seek opportunities to deliver services as they preferred.

LEARNING FROM THE EFFORT

The last step in the EBP process is usually described as evaluation, which can be understood in terms of both processes and outcomes. In terms of achieving better outcomes for the children and families who received services after the implementation of the evidence-supported intervention that was designed to address behavioral problems, it's difficult to say what was achieved. Outcomes at the program level were largely tracked in terms of numbers of clients served. The agency had just implemented a new management information system, which included some ability to track goals for clients, but this system was not in place before our implementation project, and I heard through the grapevine that it was so clunky and difficult to use that the quality of the data collected was likely suspect. I wasn't involved in the process of identifying or implementing this new system, although the agency did see this as part of their effort to become more evidence-based.

Upon reflection, we could have identified some sort of outcomes evaluation design to collect baseline data and compare program effectiveness for clients before and after implementation. However, I am doubtful that my agency partners would have been interested in layering on more complexity into the effort. After all, I imagine they might have said, wasn't that the point of implementing an evidence-supported intervention? That you could trust that the intervention would work? Of course, they don't always work, even in the best of circumstances. Ultimately, what matters on the front line is the client in front of you.

One of the things that our team learned from this process was that the organization had very little in place to monitor what was actually happening in practice or the achievement of desired goals for clients. Although we tossed around different ideas about how to do this on a regular basis agency-wide, perhaps using various fidelity tools or observations, nothing really came together. The intervention that we implemented in the child and adolescent counseling program had some fidelity measurement tools that were designed to support the intervention, and when I ended my work with the FSC, these tools were in use, but this was a fairly unique concept within the agency.

Unfortunately, there is little research to inform the field as to what it takes to implement high-quality interventions, let alone to continuously monitor and implement multiple interventions and sustain them over time. Models of implementation exist, but most of them are focused on bringing in a single evidence-supported intervention, not many different interventions at once. Research also exists on how to support an organization's ability to identify and uptake innovations in practice, such as interventions, assessment tools, and procedures, but most of this work comes out of business and healthcare. There is something to learn from these contexts, but there have been few studies of these processes in social service agencies. I didn't have much in the way of research to offer my partners in this project in order to inform our efforts to implement the EBP process beyond the one intervention we identified. We started off trying to implement the EBP process, but what we ultimately ended up doing looked a little bit more like the bright shiny approach the staff originally felt was unappealing.

That being said, we learned a great deal from our own struggles and explorations. For me, the partnership revealed the need for much more intensive supports to offer to practitioners and agencies if we hope to see widespread adoption of EBP. Agency staff constantly remarked on how they did not think that this effort would have been possible if they tried to go it alone without a researcher to help them identify and examine the research evidence. Since my time at the agency, the FSC has continued to partner with a variety of researchers, including doctoral students and university faculty. However, many social service agencies don't have directors who are so invested in the idea of EBP or friendly neighborhood researchers who are willing and able to support them along the way.

My FSC partners also taught me a lot about the need to improve the flow of communication—not just *from* the ivory tower to the trenches, but also back again. Many robust interventions are too burdensome for agencies and practitioners to absorb with fidelity, yet there is little opportunity or guidance for social workers to shape the adaptation of these interventions to address their needs. Adaptation of evidence-supported interventions at the ground level appears to be the rule rather than the exception—and for some very good reasons—but there is little guidance for practitioners as to how to do this well. Nor is there a clear conduit of communication for social workers to provide feedback to intervention developers to guide the development of more feasible interventions.

As far as I know, the FSC is still on its quest to become evidence based. And, in the spirit of the EBP process model, this really should be a continuous learning process. This agency has managed to survive and even grow in an extraordinarily harsh and limited funding environment of recent years. Many of their sister agencies have failed or diminished their services over the same period of time in the wake of the U.S. economic meltdown. I like to think that our EBP partnership effort had something to do with their relatively strong performance as the agency director hoped. But this partnership and the agency also benefited from the charismatic leadership of the director, a long history in the community, excellent staff, and other qualities that may be equally, if not more, deserving of the credit.

REFERENCES

Addis, M. E. (2002). Methods for disseminating research products and increasing evidence-based practice: Promises, obstacles, and future directions. *Clinical Psychology: Science and Practice, 9,* 367–378.

Bellamy, J. L., Bledsoe, S. E., & Traube, D. (2006). The current state of evidence-based practice in social work: A review of the literature and qualitative analysis of expert interviews. *Journal of Evidence-Based Social Work, 3*(1), 23–48.

Bellamy, J. L., Spring, B., Mullen, E. J., Satterfield, J. M., Newhouse, R. P., & Ferguson, M. (2013). Implementing evidence-based practice education in social work: A trans-disciplinary approach. *Research on Social Work Practice, 23*(4), 426–436.

Gira, E. C., Kessler, M. L., & Poertner, J. (2004). Influencing social workers to use research evidence in practice: Lessons from medicine and the allied health professions. *Research on Social Work Practice, 14*, 68–79.

Institute of Medicine Committee on Crossing the Quality Chasm: Adaptation to Mental Health and Addictive Disorders. (2006). *Improving the quality of health care for mental and substance-use conditions.* Washington, DC: National Academies Press.

Kirk, S. A., & Reid, W. J. (2002). *Science and social work: A critical appraisal.* New York, NY: Columbia University Press.

Sackett, D. L., Rosenberg, W. M. C., Gray, J. A. M., Haynes, R. B., & Richardson, W. S. (1996). Evidence-based medicine: What it is and what it isn't. *British Medical Journal, 312*(7023), 71–72.

Key Words

Part I: Case studies in generalist practice

Case 1-1: generalist practice, ecological theory, gerontology, case management

Case 1-2: case management, referral, generalist practice, medical social work, illness

Case 1-3: community development, community organization, strengths approach, organizational development

Part II: Case studies in integrating theory and practice

Case 2-1: ecological model, strengths approach, generalist practice

Case 2-2: cognitive behavior therapy, social learning theory, phobic disorders, therapy

Case 2-3: relational theory, therapy, interpersonal problems, integrating theory and practice

Case 2-4: family systems, family theory, special needs, adoption, strengths approach

Part III: Case studies in child and family welfare

Case 3-1: multidisciplinary teams, inpatient settings, hospitalization, case management, children's mental health

Case 3-2: drug court, child welfare, foster care, substance abuse

Case 3-3: supervision, child welfare, case management, generalist practice

Case 3-4: family systems, family violence, family therapy, strengths approach

Part IV: Case studies in family therapy

Case 4-1: homebuilders, family therapy, parent management training, child welfare

Case 4-2: family systems, strengths approach, generalist practice, case management, ecological theory

Case 4-3: family systems, family ritual, grief and loss, family strengths

Part V: Case studies in treating adult problems

Case 5-1: mental health, homelessness, case management, generalist practice, strengths approach

Case 5-2: cognitive behavior therapy, depression, therapy, mental health

Case 5-3: psychiatric medication, case management, mental health

Case 5-4: multisensory interventions, therapy, mental health

Case 5-5: mindfulness, coping, chronic pain, depression

Part VI: Case studies in preventing problems and developing resourcefulness

Case 6-1: group therapy, stress management, behavior therapy, group dynamics

Case 6-2: mediation, facilitation, conflict management, case management, child welfare

Case 6-3: homelessness, mental health, case management, PTSD, generalist practice

Case 6-4: caregiving, geriatric depression, behavior therapy, problem-solving therapy

Case 6-5: social skills, prevention, adolescents, gender-specific treatment

Part VII: Case studies in group work

Case 7-1: mutual aid, group work, generalist practice, AIDS, substance abuse

Case 7-2: group work, generalist practice, gerontology, strengths based practice

Case 7-3: social skills training, group therapy, children's mental health, behavior therapy

Case 7-4: group work, men, cognitive behavior therapy, group dynamics

Part VIII: Case studies in diversity

Case 8-1: gay and lesbian, diversity, lesbian couples, relational difficulties

Case 8-2: marital therapy, diversity, interracial couples

Case 8-3: family systems, poverty, urban poor

Case 8-4: diversity, cross cultural work, supervision, family systems

Part IX: Case studies in using practice evaluation

Case 9-1: practice evaluation, children's mental health, sexual abuse

Case 9-2: practice evaluation, family therapy, adolescents, assessment

Case 9-3: practice evaluation, medical social work, case management, generalist practice

Case 9-4: evidence-based practice, organizational change, community practice, integrating research

Index